# Names and Context

**Mind, Meaning and Metaphysics**

**Series Editors:**
*Christopher Gauker*, University of Salzburg, Austria
*Mark Textor*, King's College London, UK
*Johannes Brandl*, University of Salzburg, Austria
*Max Kölbel*, University of Vienna, Austria

The *Mind, Meaning and Metaphysics* series publishes cutting-edge research in philosophy of mind, philosophy of language, metaphysics and epistemology. The basic questions in this area are wide-ranging and complex: What is thinking and how does it manage to represent the world? How does language facilitate interpersonal cooperation and shape our thinking? What are the fundamental building blocks of reality, and how do we come to know what reality is?

These are long-standing philosophical questions but new and exciting answers continue to be invented, in part due to the input of the empirical sciences. Volumes in the series address such questions, with a view to both contemporary debates and the history of philosophy. Each volume reflects the state of the art in theoretical philosophy, but also makes a significant original contribution to it.

**Editorial Board:**
*Annalisa Coliva*, University of California, Irvine, USA
*Paul Egré*, Institut Jean-Nicod, France
*Olav Gjelsvik*, University of Oslo, Norway
*Thomas Grundmann*, University of Cologne, Germany
*Katherine Hawley*, University of St. Andrews, United Kingdom
*Øystein Linnebo*, University of Oslo, Norway
*Teresa Marques*, University of Barcelona, Spain
*Anna-Sophia Maurin*, University of Gothenburg, Sweden
*Bence Nanay*, University of Antwerp, Belgium
*Martine Nida-Rümelin*, University of Freiburg, Switzerland
*Jaroslav Peregrin*, Czech Academy of Sciences, Czech Republic
*Tobias Rosefeldt*, Humboldt University of Berlin, Germany
*Anders Schoubye*, University of Edinburgh, United Kingdom
*Camilla Serck-Hanssen*, University of Oslo, Norway
*Emily Thomas*, Durham University, United Kingdom
*Amie Lynn Thomasson*, Dartmouth College, USA
*Giuliano Torrengo*, University of Milan, Italy
*Barbara Vetter*, Humboldt University of Berlin, Germany
*Heinrich Wansing*, Ruhr University of Bochum, Germany

# Names and Context: A Use-Sensitive Philosophical Account

Dolf Rami

BLOOMSBURY ACADEMIC
LONDON • NEW YORK • OXFORD • NEW DELHI • SYDNEY

BLOOMSBURY ACADEMIC
Bloomsbury Publishing Plc
50 Bedford Square, London, WC1B 3DP, UK
1385 Broadway, New York, NY 10018, USA
29 Earlsfort Terrace, Dublin 2, Ireland

BLOOMSBURY, BLOOMSBURY ACADEMIC and the Diana logo are trademarks of
Bloomsbury Publishing Plc

First published in Great Britain 2022
This paperback edition published 2023

Copyright © Dolf Rami, 2022

Dolf Rami has asserted his right under the Copyright, Designs and Patents Act, 1988, to be identified as Author of this work.

For legal purposes the Acknowledgements on p. viii constitute an extension of this copyright page.

Series design by Louise Dugdale
Cover image © shuoshu / Getty Images

All rights reserved. No part of this publication may be reproduced or transmitted in any form or by any means, electronic or mechanical, including photocopying, recording, or any information storage or retrieval system, without prior permission in writing from the publishers.

Bloomsbury Publishing Plc does not have any control over, or responsibility for, any third-party websites referred to or in this book. All internet addresses given in this book were correct at the time of going to press. The author and publisher regret any inconvenience caused if addresses have changed or sites have ceased to exist, but can accept no responsibility for any such changes.

A catalogue record for this book is available from the British Library.

Library of Congress Cataloging-in-Publication Data
Names: Rami, Dolf, author.
Title: Names and context: a use-sensitive philosophical account / Dolf Rami.
Description: London; New York: Bloomsbury Academic, 2021. | Series: Mind, meaning and metaphysics | Includes bibliographical references and index.
Identifiers: LCCN 2021017374 (print) | LCCN 2021017375 (ebook) | ISBN 9781350180628 (hardback) | ISBN 9781350180635 (ebook) | ISBN 9781350180642 (epub)
Subjects: LCSH: Onomastics. | Names–Philosophy.
Classification: LCC P323 .R36 2021 (print) | LCC P323 (ebook) | DDC 412–dc23
LC record available at https://lccn.loc.gov/2021017374
LC ebook record available at https://lccn.loc.gov/2021017375

ISBN: HB: 978-1-3501-8062-8
PB: 978-1-3501-9722-0
ePDF: 978-1-3501-8063-5
eBook: 978-1-3501-8064-2

Series: Mind, Meaning and Metaphysics

Typeset by RefineCatch Limited, Bungay, Suffolk

To find out more about our authors and books visit www.bloomsbury.com and sign up for our newsletters.

'Everyday language is a part of the human organism
and is no less complicated than it'
*(Ludwig Wittgenstein)*


*For Cordula, Florian and Pauline*


*To the memory of Jonathan Lowe*

# Contents

Acknowledgements ix
Preface x

Prolegomenon: The Diversity of Uses of Names in Natural Languages 1

**1 Proper Names and Rigidity** 43
   Setting the stage: Kripke and his followers on different notions of rigidity 43
   Intuitive tests for the rigidity of proper names 48
   Possible reasons in favour of obstinate rigidity 52
   Actualized accounts of rigidity 55
   Two new additional actualized accounts of rigidity 58
   Four possible conceptions of rigidity and their application to names 61

**2 Proper Names and Reference Determination** 65
   Introduction: the development of Kripke's picture of reference into a theory 65
   On the individuation of proper names 68
   On the determination of reference of names 74
   On the nature and explanatory role of acts of naming 81
   On the implicit and unintentional constitution of name-using practices 88
   Summary: the main theses of my pluralist conception of reference determination 92

**3 Proper Names as Use-Sensitive Expressions** 95
   Setting the stage: proper names as context-sensitive expressions 95
   Four motivations for context-sensitive views on proper names 98
   Against the two most popular formal versions of a context-sensitive view on names 106
   Towards a new context-sensitive semantics for proper names 112
   My alternative context-sensitive semantics for proper names 119

**4 The Fictional Uses of Proper Names** **129**
   Setting the stage: key features of fictional names 129
   The meaningfulness of names without a semantic referent 131
   The semantic status of fictional names 135
   Different kinds of uses of fictional proper names in sentential contexts 137
   The semantic and pragmatic functions of fictional names 154

| | | |
|---|---|---|
| 5 | **Apparent Predicative Uses of Proper Names** | 159 |
| | Setting the stage: referential and predicative uses of proper names | 159 |
| | The linguistic mechanism of meaning transfer | 161 |
| | The derived nature of the meaning of the original examples | 168 |
| 6 | **Apparent Anaphoric Uses of Proper Names** | 173 |
| | Setting the stage: an overview of different apparently anaphoric or bound uses of names | 173 |
| | Three approaches of apparent bound or anaphoric uses of proper names | 178 |
| | Arguments against the three types of proposed accounts | 182 |
| | An alternative metalinguistic pragmatic explanation | 190 |
| | Summary | 196 |
| 7 | **Proper Names in Hyperintensional Contexts** | 197 |
| | Three semantic properties of names in the scope of attitude verbs | 197 |
| | The *de re*/*de dicto* distinction | 198 |
| | The nature of the *de re*/*de dicto* ambiguity | 199 |
| | A comparison of three different formal approaches to attitude verbs | 200 |
| | Attitude verbs as non-normal modal operators: the formal analysis | 206 |
| | A comparison with Priest's original version of the proposed semantics | 216 |
| | Internally represented *de re* readings relative to our semantic framework | 224 |
| Notes | | 229 |
| Bibliography | | 245 |
| Index | | 255 |

# Acknowledgements

The author and publisher gratefully acknowledge the permission granted to reproduce the copyright material in this book. Chapters 1, 3 and 5 are substantially revised and expanded versions of the following articles, with permission from Springer Nature:

Rami, D. (2019) 'Names and Their Kind of Rigidity', in: *Erkenntnis*, 84, 257–282.
Rami, D. (2014) 'The Use-Conditional Indexical Conception of Proper Names', in: *Philosophical Studies*, 168, 119–150.
Rami, D. (2015) 'The Multiple Uses of Proper Nouns', in: *Erkenntnis*, 80, 405–432.

Chapter 2 is a revised version of Rami, D. (2016) 'Names, Namings and Name-Using Practices', in: Stalmaszczyk, P. and Fernandez Moreno, L. (eds), *Philosophical Approaches to Proper Names*, Frankfurt am Main, 55–93, with permission from Peter Lang.

I would like to thank all those involved from Bloomsbury Academic for their great help, especially during the production stage of this book.

# Preface

This book contains the third and most detailed of my attempts so far to develop a semantics of proper names. I developed the so-called *use-sensitive* view on proper names defended in this book in three different phases.

The first phase was in 2007 where I made two different attempts to figure out my own view on names. Firstly, I held a view that could be seen as a compromise between a Fregean and a Millian view of names and that assumed that proper names have quite minimal senses from an explanatory point of view. Secondly, I also presented a very sketchy contextualist predecessor version of the use-sensitive view of names contained in this book at two conferences, one in Barcelona and one in Paris.

The second phase was between 2009 and 2014. In this phase, I visited King's College London for two years with a Feodor-Lynen-Fellowship of the Alexander-von-Humboldt Foundation. I had a lot of very good discussion partners during this phase, but the one person who probably had the most important influence on my work on names in this phase was Mark Textor. I would like to thank him for his advice and lots of fruitful and helpful discussions. In November 2014, I submitted a first version of this book as my *Habilitationsschrift* and it was accepted by the department of philosophy of the University of Göttingen in March 2015.

The third phase of my work on names was between 2015 and 2019. In this phase, I tried to improve and rewrite some of the chapters of my *Habilitationsschrift*. I also skipped some chapters that were mainly concerned with other topics than names, namely existence and quantification. Furthermore, I also added a new chapter on anaphoric uses of proper names. Hence, here we are with some new twists and fine-tuning in 2020.

The development of one's own philosophical views and thoughts essentially depends on the interaction with other philosophers who are interested in the same philosophical topics and problems. As far as I can remember, and certainly at present I cannot remember every discussion on names that I have had since 2007, I benefited significantly from discussions with Stephen Barker, Laura Delgado, Stacie Friend, Christopher Hughes, Hans Kamp, Tobias Klauk, Wilfried Keller, Ruth Kempson, Jan Köpping, Shalom Lappin, Jonathan Lowe, Genoveva Marti, Wilfried Meyer-Viol, Eliot Michaelson, Edgar Onea, David Papineau, Stefano Predelli, Graham Priest, Brian Rabern, Francois Recanati, Peter Ridley, Louis DeRosset, Mark Sainsbury, Wolfgang Spohn, Peter Sutton, Alberto Voltolini, Timothy Williamson, Elia Zardini, Thomas Ede Zimmermann and Sarah Zobel. I also would like to thank the following people, either for their support, help, corrections or discussions: Christian Beyer, Adrian Bruhns, James Conant, Anthony Everett, Giulia Felappi, Manuel García-Carpintero, Aidan Gray, Daniel Gutzmann, Volker Halbach, Bruno Haas, Robin Jeshion, Max Kölbel, Tilmann Köppe, Wolfgang Künne, Gail Leckie, Ora Matushansky, Felix Mühlhölzer,

Peter Pagin, Benjamin Schnieder, Julian Small, Markus Steinbach, Jan Stühring, Sarah Tropper, Lee Walters, Heinrich Wansing, and Jennifer Wright. I would like to thank them all for their interest in my work and their helpful comments or objections.

Special thanks go to my friends Sarah Zobel and Jan Köpping, who always had time to give me their feedback on my philosophical and linguistic views.

Finally, I would like to thank two anonymous reviewers for their comments and suggestions.

Göttingen, January 2021

# Prolegomenon: The Diversity of Uses of Names in Natural Languages

## A very brief history of the philosophical debate on names in the analytic tradition

Since the ground-breaking works of Frege and Russell on this subject,[1] *the semantic analysis of proper names* is one of the central and most discussed topics in analytic philosophy. Common wisdom holds that Frege and Russell defended similar versions of a so-called *description theory of names*. According to such a theory, ordinary proper names and ordinary definite descriptions have very similar semantic properties. Under the influence of Frege, Russell, Quine, Strawson, Searle and Wittgenstein,[2] description theories of names became the widely accepted orthodoxy until the latter part of the twentieth century.

In early 1970s, description theories of names were famously attacked by Donnellan and Kripke.[3] Their works significantly changed the philosophical debate on names. Firstly, they presented an array of arguments that aimed to show the fundamental incorrectness of description theories of names. Secondly, they aimed to purport an alternative view on names that can partially be traced back to the works of Mill on this topic and that is often referred to by the labels 'Millianism' or 'direct reference theory of names'. During the last few decades, this view on names became the *new orthodoxy*.

The engagement with Donnellan's and Kripke's arguments shaped the philosophical discussion on names for several decades and the debate since the 1970s has been *mainly* divided into two camps. The first camp consists of those philosophers that aim to defend some version of the description theory of names against Donnellan's and Kripke's arguments. The second camp aims to develop some version of Millianism that is able to deal with those familiar problems that Frege and Russell tried to overcome by means of their description theory of names. Hence, for purely descriptive purposes, it seems to be a useful idealization in respect of the recent history of the philosophical discussion on names to distinguish the following two main streams:

> One stream starts with J. S. Mill and consists of theories according to which a proper name's contribution to language is exhausted by its referent. Understanding a name consists in knowing what it refers to. The other stream, sometimes held to derive inspiration from Frege, is descriptivist: according to descriptivist theories,

the meaning of a name is given by or is equivalent to some body of associated information, and the referent of the name is whatever this information is true of, if anything. Understanding a name is linking this body of information with the name.[4]

However, such an idealization may lead to an incorrect view concerning the real nature of the *logical space* concerning the philosophical debate on names. Some philosophers at least seem to be tempted to assume that every possible and prima facie plausible view on names must either be a Millian or a description theory of names. Closer inspection clearly shows that the distinction between these two kinds of views on names is not exhaustive. This can be shown without going into the details of both distinguished views. The two views *assimilate* the semantics of names to the semantics of two significantly different kinds of singular terms: description theories assimilate the semantics of proper names to the semantics of definite descriptions; Millian theories typically assimilate the semantics of proper names to the semantics of individual constants in (modal) classical predicate logic. Alternative views are at least possible that assimilate the semantics of proper names to the semantics of other kinds of singular terms in natural *or* formal languages that have significantly different semantic properties than individual constants and definite descriptions. So, for example, the assimilation of proper names to complex demonstratives, third-person personal pronouns or individual variables at least has some prima facie plausibility and has also attracted the attention of some philosophers and linguists.[5] Against this background, Sainsbury is perfectly right if he complains: 'Much debate has consisted in unproductive oscillations between Millian and descriptivist theories[.]'[6] But not only would it be wrong to limit the philosophical debate on names to an 'oscillation between a Millian and a descriptive pole', more importantly, it also seems to be the case that neither of these two kinds of theories can account for the overall use of proper names in natural languages in an adequate way and, hence, satisfies all requirements that an adequate semantic analysis of names has to satisfy. Both theories only seem to be in the position to capture *some* important aspects that constitute our overall use of proper names in natural languages. But the advantages of one theory seem to pose problems for the other theory and the other way round. Or as Sainsbury correctly puts it: 'Both poles have attractions. [...] The very merits of each pole are closely associated with their defects. [...] Many of the arguments for one pole consist in nothing more than pointing out problems with the other.'[7] If this description is correct, then it is really necessary to find a more adequate alternative or intermediate position that avoids any of the typical weaknesses of both standard theories of names. The search for such an *alternative position* concerning the semantic analysis of names is one of the main goals of this book.

There is also another aspect of the philosophical discussion on names that is typically associated with the two standard theories of names, namely the infamous philosophical discussion between *internalist* and *externalist* conceptions concerning the determination of the referent of proper names. Description theories of names are typically considered to be paradigm examples of an internalist conception on this issue. According to such a view, the reference of a name on a given occasion exclusively depends on which definite description a speaker *cognitively associates* with a specific name. Millian theories, on the other hand, are conceived of as typical examples of an externalist conception on this issue, because according to them the determination of the referent of a specific use of a name typically depends on the prior history of uses of this very same name by other people. However, I also think that one important assumption of this discussion is incorrect, namely that we have to choose either between an *overall internalist* or an *overall externalist* conception of reference determination. In this book, I will argue for an intermediate position concerning this issue. That is, I will argue that there are uses of names where an externalist determination of reference is necessary, but I think that not all uses of names are of this kind and relative to certain background assumptions a purely internalist determination is also possible.

Against the background of the given description of the history and logical space of the philosophical discussion on names, the remaining five sections of this prolegomenon will be concerned with the following issues. Firstly, I will introduce in the next two sections the main assumptions of the old and new orthodoxies concerning the semantic analysis of proper names. After that, I will, secondly, show which kind of data an adequate semantic analysis of proper names has to satisfy in general and why the two orthodox views have problems in satisfying some of these requirements. Thirdly, I will give a brief outline of the view on proper names that I aim to defend in this book, which is an intermediate position between the two classical main rivals and a new version of a contextualist view on names. In the seven chapters of this book I will try to show that this account has the resources to meet some of the biggest challenges that every semantic account of names has to meet. Finally, I will briefly describe the methodology that is is used in this book and outline the main theses of my view on names.

## The old orthodoxy: descriptive theories of names

As we have already said, the key feature of the description theory of names is on the semantic side an assimilation of the semantics of proper names to the semantics of definite descriptions, and on the cognitive side an association of names with descriptive modes of presentations. Several different versions of the description theory of names have been proposed and the matter is also complicated by the fact that there are several different rival accounts concerning the semantic analysis of ordinary definite descriptions. However, the most important general distinction is the already anticipated distinction between *semantic* and *cognitive* versions of description theories of names.[8]

According to the semantic version of the description theory of names, names are semantically equivalent to specific definite descriptions. That is, proper names have the same meaning relative to a certain public natural language as definite descriptions of a specific kind that are expressible in this language. In this sense, names are only abbreviations for certain definite descriptions.

According to the cognitive version, competent speakers associate relative to their idiolect certain descriptive conditions with proper names that could be expressed by a specific definite description. That is, if we aim to capture and specify the content of the utterance of a sentence S that contains a proper name N used on a certain occasion O by a speaker A in a correct way, we have to substitute the name N in S by some definite description D that is associated with N relative to O.[9] This distinction shows that semantic versions of the description theory of names are attempts to specify the core semantic properties of proper names in natural languages, while the purpose of the cognitive version seems to be a more fundamental one: it aims to capture the nature of thoughts that speakers aim to express or convey by using ordinary proper names.

There are other important additional distinctions that one can draw with respect to the specific nature and content of those definite descriptions that are abbreviated by or associated with names. It is clear that a semantic description theory has to satisfy more strict and specific requirements concerning the nature and content of those definite descriptions that are abbreviated by a name than does a cognitive description theory. In the case of the cognitive version, any definite description that picks out the correct and desired single object can *in principle* be associated with a name by a speaker relative to an occasion of use.

Let us therefore focus in the remaining part of this section on the question: Which definite descriptions could be used in a prima facie plausible way by a semantic version of the description theory? An implausible version of the description theory of names that is sometimes mentioned for introductory purposes is the so-called *famous deeds descriptivism*.[10] According to this version, a name like 'Kurt Gödel' abbreviates a definite description that reports a famous deed of the bearer of this name that uniquely singles out this object. In the case of Gödel, we might use the definite description 'the man that proved the incompleteness of arithmetic'. However, it is clear that such a conception is a complete non-starter. Firstly, there is no good reason why a *semantically* competent user of a name should be able to associate a description with a proper name that specifies a famous deed of a specific bearer of this name. Secondly, there are quite obviously people that did not perform any famous deed and, furthermore, there are objects that bear names that cannot perform any actions. Thirdly, even considered as a variant of the cognitive version of the description theory, it is not clear why we should restrict the descriptive contents of certain names to uniquely satisfied descriptions that concern certain famous deeds of a bearer of such a name. However, this relatively dull example shows how difficult it is to formulate a prima facie plausible version of the semantic variety of the description theory of names.

There is a second, often cited variant of the semantic description theory of names, the so-called *cluster theory of names*, which was first proposed by Searle.[11] But this version also does not seem to be a very plausible variation of a semantic description theory of names. There are different possible sub-varieties of this variant. The most notable are the following two:

1. a name 'N' is semantically equivalent to a definite description of the following general form: 'The object that satisfies the majority of the following descriptions: $d_1, \ldots, d_n$';
2. a name 'N' is semantically equivalent to a definite description of the following general form: 'The object that satisfies a contextually sufficient number of the following descriptions: $d_1, \ldots, d_n$'.

These two versions could be seen as reactions to the second mentioned problem of the famous deeds variety, but they share with this version the first mentioned problem. Both versions seem to set much too high a standard in respect of the contents that a competent user of a meaningful name has to grasp. It is highly implausible that a competent user of an ordinary proper name must in general be able to grasp lots of different descriptions that are typically associated with the bearer of a specific name.

Are there any more plausible semantic versions of a description theory of names? In my opinion, the prima facie most plausible variants are the following two: the *nominal* and the *causal* description theories of names. According to the first variant, a name like 'Alfred' is semantically equivalent to the metalinguistic description 'The bearer of the name "Alfred"'.[12] According to the second variant, a name like 'Alfred' is semantically equivalent to a definite description such as 'The origin of the name-using practice connected with "Alfred"' or 'The individual dubbed at the origin of the name-using practice connected with "Alfred"'.[13] Both variants have their problems, and we will focus on some of them later; nevertheless, they seem to be by far the most plausible variants of the *semantic variety* of the description theory of names.

Notable variations of both accounts are so-called *rigidified versions*. According to the rigidified version of the nominal description theory, for example, the name 'Alfred' is considered as semantically equivalent to 'The *actual* bearer of the name "Alfred"'. This completes my very brief and general outline of description theories of names.

## The new orthodoxy: Millian theories of names

Mill famously holds the view that there is a significant semantic difference between *proper names* and *definite descriptions*. According to him, proper names only have denotation, but no connotation, while definite descriptions have both: 'Proper names are not connotative: they denote the individuals who are called by them, but they do not indicate or imply any attributes as belonging to those individuals'.[14] If we translate this original Millian thesis into more familiar current terminology, it can be, I think, formulated in the following way: *Proper names have semantic referents, but unlike definite descriptions they do not have a descriptive meaning that is linguistically expressed by a name and that describes and determines the semantic referent of a name*. Some current philosophers have interpreted Mill in an even more radical way such that he is committed to the thesis:

(SM)    For every proper name n: the meaning of n = the semantic referent of n.

That is, the meaning of a proper name *is exhausted by* its semantic referent. Such an interpretation of Mill is not implausible if one assumes that denotation and connotation are the only possible kinds of meanings of an expression according to Mill. Such a stronger interpretation is also backed up by the following additional remarks of Mill: 'A non-connotative term is one which signifies a subject only, or an attribute only. [...] Thus John, or London, or England, are names which signify a subject only.'[15]

(SM) is a relatively bold thesis and, together with the following prima facie plausible and natural addition about the understanding of names,

(KM)   For every speaker s: s understands n iff s knows what the meaning of n is,

it leads to the view that the understanding of a name requires a certain *de re* knowledge about a specific object, namely that this object is the semantic referent of a specific name. However, this is a very implausible and highly demanding view of the understanding of a name. We may call a version of a Millian theory of names that is committed to (SM) *Strong Millianism* or a *strong* version of a Millian theory of names.[16] A natural formal semantic variant of Strong Millianism assimilates the semantics of proper names either to individual constants in classical first-order logic or even classical modal first-order logic.

Strong Millianism is not very popular among current defenders of Millianism. Salmon and Soames, probably the two most famous defenders of Millianism, reject (SM). According to them, the real core of Millianism can be captured by one of the following two weaker theses:

(WMT)   For every proper name n: the contribution of n to the truth-conditions of a sentence that contains n = the semantic referent of n.
(WMP)   For every proper name n: the contribution of n to the propositional content expressed by a sentence that contains n = the semantic referent of n.

The commitment to (WMT) and (WMP) allows one to remain neutral on the issue as to whether or not the meaning of a name is exhausted by its semantic referent. For example, (WMT) and (WMP) are both compatible with the view that proper names have, like automatic indexical expressions (e.g.: 'I' and 'today'), a Kaplanian character as their conventional linguistic meaning that determines the semantic referent of a name relative to a context of use. The character of an expression determines the contributions of an expression to the truth-conditions and propositional content, but it is no constituent of the absolute truth-conditions of a sentence[17] nor the proposition expressed by a sentence relative to a context of use. Let us, therefore, call a variant of a Millian theory of names that is committed to (WMT) or (WMP) *Weak Millianism* or a *weak* version of a Millian theory of names.[18]

The acceptance of (WMT) commits one to the view that meaningful sentences that contain proper names have *object-dependent truth- and falsity-conditions*. A sentence has object-dependent truth- and falsity-conditions if the truth or falsity of this sentence depends on the existence or presence[19] of a specific object that such a sentence is about. The acceptance of (WMP) commits one to the view that meaningful sentences that contain proper names express *object-dependent* propositions. The existence or presence of an object-dependent proposition depends on the existence or presence of a specific object that is a constituent of this proposition.

The choice between (WMT) or (WMP) depends on which general semantic framework one favours. Kaplan's influence on this issue is quite important. He reintroduced *Russellian propositions* into the current philosophy of language – since they were rejected by Russell himself in 1905. Russellian propositions are structured propositions that contain individual objects, properties or relations as their constituents. A Russellian proposition is *singular* if it contains at least one individual object as a constituent; it is general if it contains no individual object as a constituent. Kaplan uses

Russellian proposition to characterize the *informal and metaphysical part* of his semantics concerning indexical expressions[20] and he makes use of the truth-conditional semantics of a specific two-dimensional classical modal logic to characterize the *formal part* of his semantics.[21] Defenders of Weak Millianism that accept the thesis that (declarative) sentences *express propositions* have at least a strong tendency to make use of a Russellian conception of propositions.

A moderate combination of Millianism and Russellian propositions draws a distinction between the linguistic meanings of a sentence and the propositions expressed by this sentence that are also the contents of assertions and other kinds of speech acts. This combination is quite popular among current defenders of Millianism.[22] A more radical combination identifies linguistic meanings of sentences with the propositions that are expressed by these sentences and can, hence, combine a Russellian conception of propositions with (SM).

There is also the purely *truth-conditional variety* of Weak Millianism. Defenders of this view either in general reject the idea that sentences express propositions or at least conceive of Russellian propositions as inadequate candidates to model propositional content. There is a large variety of different truth-conditional frameworks that are combinable with (WMT). One might use a more traditional Davidsonian truth-conditional framework for this purpose, or some one-dimensional or two-dimensional (possible) world framework.

The use of a truth-conditional semantic framework allows one in any case to draw a clear distinction between the *linguistic meaning* and the *semantic content* of a sentence. This distinction can be drawn on the basis of another purely truth-conditional distinction, namely the distinction between *generalized* and *absolute* truth- and falsity-conditions of a sentence.

Formal semantic frameworks typically make use of a *relativized truth-predicate* to characterize the truth- and falsity-conditions of closed formulas. In the simplest case, such a truth-predicate is relativized to an interpretation parameter. However, relative to a truth-conditional (possible) world framework it can additionally be relativized to a world parameter, a time parameter or a context-parameter. We get generalized truth- and falsity-conditions of a sentence if we universally quantify over these parameters of our truth-predicate. Hence, these kinds of truth-conditions have the following general form:

(GTC) For every interpretation I, world w, time t and context c: s is true relative to I, w, t, c iff ... I ... w ... t ... c ...

Such generalized truth- and falsity-conditions can be used to specify the truth-conditional aspect of the linguistic meaning of a sentence. We receive the *absolute* truth-conditions of a sentence by deleting the used universal quantifiers of (GTC) and by substituting the resulting unbound variables by constants of a specific sort that designate (a) the actual interpretation function of our expressions, (b) the actual world, (c) the present time and (d) a specific single context of use. This leads to the following general form of absolute truth-conditions:

(ATC) s is true relative to $I_@, @, c_1$ iff ... $I_@$ ... @ ... $t_p$ ... $c_1$ ...

In opposition to the generalized truth-conditions, the absolute truth-conditions specify the *semantic content* of a sentence relative to the actual world and a specific occasion of use. The semantic content is the official content that is expressed by a sentence relative to a specific occasion and, hence, the content of the assertion of a declarative sentence.

Kaplan also coined the phrase of a *directly referential term*.[23] In the light of (WMT) and (WMP), we can either characterize a *directly referential term* as a singular term that contributes an individual object as a constituent to a proposition or that makes the truth- and falsity-conditions of a sentence object-dependent. This is a rather popular way to draw the link between Millianism and the notion of *direct reference*. However, in fact the situation is a bit more complicated. For example, Marti proposed to distinguish two different notions of direct reference, a stronger and a weaker notion. The weaker notion corresponds to the introduced Kaplanian notion of direct reference. The stronger notion corresponds to our notion of Strong Millianism:

> However, there is, explicit in the works of Donnellan, Kaplan, Kripke and Marcus, a different and, I contend, stronger conception of direct reference, one that does not appeal to propositions nor truth conditions, one that focuses on the way in which an expression connects to an object. From this point of view, what makes a term directly referential is precisely the lack of a semantic search mechanism, the fact that the term connects to an object without the intervention of a Marcusian prescription semantically associated with the term.[24]

It seems to be a matter of taste whether we want to use the term 'directly referential' for both purposes. However, if we think that Marti is right in claiming that Strong Millianism introduces the strongest possible notion of direct reference with respect to proper names (or singular terms in general), then there is not only *one* weaker version of direct reference, but several. The common denominator of all notions of direct reference is the fact that a directly referential term contributes a single individual object to semantic content or the truth-conditions of a sentence. The strong version holds that the semantic contribution of a term is *thereby* exhausted. However, if singular terms have additional semantic contents or linguistic meanings beside their referents, these additional components may play different explanatory roles. Directly referential indexical expressions such as 'I' and 'here' have a linguistic meaning (a so-called *character*) that determines the semantic referent of such an expression relative to a context of use. In this sense, these directly referential expressions seem to be the closest variant of directly referential terms to not directly referential descriptive terms. However, directly referential terms may have additional semantic contents or an additional linguistic meaning that plays other semantic roles than the determination of reference of such an expression. Let me give two examples to illustrate this point.

Firstly, there are complex demonstratives such as 'that man'. These expressions clearly have a linguistic meaning; however, it does not seem so that the linguistic meaning of these expressions determines the referent of such an expression relative to the context of use of such an expression. The linguistic meaning of 'that man' is the condition of being male and this condition only *filters* or *constrains* the referent of this expression. Secondly, there are individual mental files (or cognitive representation) which may be directly referential in the sense that they represent or refer to on object based on certain causal relations between an object and this file. However, these mental representations also have descriptive contents, but these contents neither determine nor constrain referents. They play other explanatory roles; that is, the descriptive material may play a role when we mentally choose or access a mental file to represent a specific object. This shows that there are different versions of directly referential terms (or presentations) that have different kinds of additional semantic contents or meanings. Maybe, Strong Millianism is some sort of a limiting case, but I think and side with Kaplan that expressions that satisfy Strong Millianism are in no sense *more* directly referential than a Kaplanian indexical or a complex demonstrative. All the mentioned distinctions seem to be additional, but *not* essential. But if one aims to define *direct reference* in such a way that only an expression is directly referential that has a semantic referent that is neither determined nor constrained by additional linguistic meanings or semantic contents (or that even lacks any additional linguistic meaning or semantic content), then she/he may do it this way. However, this then is not only a different variety, but also a different *sense* of a directly referential term. If it is a different sense of direct reference, then it also makes sense to use a different label for this different notion. And I prefer the label 'Strong Millianism' for a view that has such implications concerning the semantics of proper names.

However, there is a more important additional question that concerns Millianism and the direct reference theory in a similar way, namely the question of whether Millian or directly referential terms can lack a semantic referent. The way we have defined these terms seems to suggest a negative answer. Therefore, all versions of Millianism and all versions of direct reference theory for singular terms seem to share the feature that they imply the following additional thesis:

(MM)  Necessarily, for every proper name n: if n is meaningful, then n has a semantic referent.

This thesis says that the *meaningfulness of a proper name* depends on its having a single semantic referent.[25] In the case of Strong Millianism the implication of (MM) is relatively straightforward. However, in combination with two relevant and prima facie plausible principles, we can also derive (MM) from (WMT) or (WMP):

(MT)  Every (simple) sentence that does not express a (singular) proposition is not meaningful.
(MP)  Every sentence that does not have absolute truth-conditions is not meaningful.

We may call a conception of names that is committed to (MM) *Minimal Millianism*. This version of Millianism is, for example, compatible with the thesis that proper names have so-called *de re senses*.[26] *De re* senses are modes of presentation of single objects whose existence depends on the existence of the presented object. A version of the semantic description theory of names is conceivable that holds that these *de re* senses are expressible by certain ordinary definite descriptions. Against this background, it seems to be possible to defend a description theory of names that is committed to (MM). This shows that (MM) is weaker than the central assumptions of a direct reference theory. Therefore, one could be, like Evans, a minimal Millian without committing himself to the central thesis of a direct reference theory.

If we accept that (MM) is the minimal core of Millianism, then the distinction between description theories and Millian theories of names is not only not exhaustive, but also not exclusive. It is, however, more plausible to hold that *orthodox* Millianism with respect to names not only implies (MM), but also that names are directly referential in Kaplan's sense. This observation completes my brief general outline of Millian theories of names.

## Challenging uses of names in natural languages

There are several uses of proper names in natural language that pose a problem for either of the two mentioned orthodox theories. In this section I will introduce thirteen different characteristic uses of proper names in natural language that can be used to formulate different more or less important *material conditions of adequacy* that a correct semantic analysis of names must satisfy. Based on our brief and general overview about the basic assumptions of Millian or semantic description theories of names I will also show in how far these conceptions have difficulties to satisfy these conditions.

### Challenge 1: The problem of empty names

The first four challenges are the familiar puzzles and problematic uses of names that Frege and Russell used as a motivation for their descriptive treatment of names. Our first challenge concerns the apparent existence of meaningful names without a semantic referent in natural languages. There seem to be names that were introduced into use with the intention to refer to a certain single object, but unknown to the users of this name something went wrong during the introduction such that the introductory act failed to identify a single object. Typically, in such cases a definite description (or demonstrative) is used to name a specific object that does not have a unique satisfier (or referent). Nevertheless, the name can subsequently be used in a meaningful way with the false presumption that it refers to a certain object. Such a general scenario seems to provide a plausible case for accepting the claim that there are meaningful names without a bearer that can be used by competent speakers for certain communicative purposes. We may call such names with an established use that were introduced with the aim to name a specific existing object, but whose introduction failed to pick out a single object, *defective empty names*. Examples of names of this kind are 'Vulcan', 'Zeus' or 'Sandy Island'. We cannot only use these names in a meaningful way. Interestingly, it also seems to be possible to use these names in certain sentences that at least intuitively appear to be *true*; such as the following examples:

(1) Vulcan was postulated by Le Verrier.
(2) The Greeks worshipped Zeus.
(3) According to google maps in 2009, Sandy Island is an island in the Pacific Ocean.

Defective empty names provide a difficult challenge for Millian theories of names as the acceptance of defective empty names is incompatible with Minimal Millianism. There are three different notable strategies that defenders of Millianism have pursued to overcome this problem. Firstly, some Millians tried to explain away the data and they opted for the claim that *apparent* defective empty names in fact refer to certain exotic abstract or non-existent objects.[27] Secondly, other Millians claimed that sentences like (1)–(3) are in fact not meaningful, but these sentences can be used to convey true contents that can be expressed by definite descriptions instead of names.[28] Thirdly, some Millians accepted the data, sacrificed all the mentioned key assumptions of Millianism and substituted them with weakened alternative assumptions. So, for example, defenders of (WMP) that committed themselves to a Russellian conception of propositions aim to argue for the thesis that there are, apart from object-dependent singular propositions, also so-called *gappy* singular propositions that contain a *gap* instead of an individual object as a constituent.[29] All of these strategies have their advantages and problems.

The first mentioned strategy makes it relatively easy to account for intuitively true readings of sentences like (1)–(3) in literal terms. However, this strategy has a high prize. It apparently commits one to a questionably abundant ontology or object theory. Furthermore, it has the problem of explaining the introduction of apparently defective empty names in a plausible way. This strategy seems to have some appeal for uses of such names after the error is detected. If we detect that there is no island in the Pacific Ocean that bears the name 'Sandy Island' and this true observation is generally accepted, people who use this name on the basis of this knowledge cannot meaningfully use this name as a name for an actually existing island. Maybe it would then be more adequate to call this use a use of a name for a purely mythical or erroneously accepted object. Therefore, maybe there is at least some plausibility to call such a use a use for a non-existent object. However, the situation seems to be different as long as we are not aware of this error and use this name as a name for a real object. Hence, the strength of the challenge of empty names comes from these initial uses in error. Nevertheless, it is unclear how we can capture both uses on the basis of a single analysis of a name. It also seems to be a bit strange to assume that every unsuccessful attempt to link a new name to an object leads to the creation or naming of a non-existent object. Therefore, this straightforward and simple defence of Millianism seems to owe us a good explanation as to how and when an erroneous naming of an object automatically leads to the creation or naming of a non-existent object. At least to me such an automatic or systematic link does not seem to be natural or straightforward.

The second strategy is a relatively big concession to descriptivism. In this sense, it seems to undermine the status of Millianism as a better and more plausible alternative to description theories of names. This strategy also has non-methodological problems. Firstly, it is not clear which pragmatic mechanism allows us to convey true contents by means of meaningless sentences like (1)–(3). Secondly, it is also not clear how the precise nature of the descriptive contents that sentences like (1)–(3) may convey should be conceived of. It is a generally acknowledged virtue of a Russellian and a Fregean theory of descriptions that they can account for the possibility of meaningful definite descriptions that are not satisfied by any single object. According to a Russellian conception, definite descriptions of the general form 'the F' are interpreted as quantifier phrases that contain a distinctive kind of quantifier 'the', that allows one to express *existence* and *uniqueness*, and the predicate 'F'. Sentences that contain such quantifier phrases can be meaningful even if no object is the unique satisfier of 'F'. According to a Fregean conception, definite descriptions of the general form 'the F' are complex singular terms that consist of the predicate 'F' and the singular term forming operator 'the'. Such expressions refer to an object if 'F' has a singleton as extension. In all other cases, these expressions fail to refer. If someone now assimilates proper names with definite descriptions on the basis of either account, he is able to capture the possibility of meaningful empty names. However, this strategy also has its problems as it is difficult to find definite descriptions that adequately fill the role of defective empty names. For example, if we make use of the nominal description theory, we are faced with the problem that the definite description 'The bearer of "Vulcan"' literally does not apply to a single object, because there is more than one bearer of the name 'Vulcan'. However, this shows that 'The bearer of "Vulcan"' is an empty description for the wrong reasons. The causal description theory of names faces similar problems. It would also be an *ad hoc* move to claim that in the case of defective empty names these names are semantically equivalent to those descriptions that were used to introduce the defective empty name into discourse. It seems to be possible to understand sentences like (1)-(3) without knowing the exact wording of the introductory definite description. But the most difficult part of a description theory of names or any theory that aims to capture the intuitive truth of sentences like (1)-(3) is to explain how such sentences can be true if a description that is substituted for a name in such sentences fails to refer or is not satisfied by a single object. That is, description theories have the resources to account for the meaningfulness of defective empty names, but it is nevertheless very difficult for them to account for the intuitively true contents of sentences like (1)-(3) that contain such names.

The third 'Millian' strategy points, in my opinion, in the right direction. However, I do not think it should be considered as a strategy that still defends Millianism in any strict sense. (MM) is a defining feature of Millianism in general. The theses (WMT) and (WMP) are defining features of Weak Millianism and (SM) is a defining feature of Strong Millianism. A rejection of (MM) is a rejection of Millianism in general. The rejection of the other theses is a rejection of the distinguished sub-varieties of Millianism. Furthermore, I doubt that the assumption of gappy propositions is a coherent and meaningful extension of a Russellian conception of propositions.[30]

In my opinion, the best solution to the problem of empty names makes use of the semantic resources of *single-domain free logic*, rejects (MM) and (WMT) and substitutes (WMT) on the basis of a truth-conditional framework of single-domain free logic with the following conditional alternative, which one may call *Conditional Weak Millianism*:[31]

(POD)   For every proper name n: if n has a semantic referent, then the contribution of n to the truth-conditions of a sentence that contains n = the semantic referent of n.

The broad outlines of such a view are already sketched in Scales (1969) and Sainsbury (2005). In chapters 1, 3, 4 and 7, I will be concerned with the issue of names that lack a semantic referent. I will defend a *synthetic view* on this issue. According to this view, defective empty names lack a semantic referent if they are used in combination with extensional or intensional predicates, but these names may refer to non-existent objects if they are used in the scope of hyper-intensional predicates, which may shift the extensions of embedded expressions. I will make use of the resources of *free logic* and *world semantics* to account for this specific semantic behaviour of defective empty names.[32]

## Challenge 2: The problem of singular negative existential sentences

Let us now focus on the second challenge for a correct semantic analysis of names that is closely related to our first challenge. Intuitively, it is possible to use proper names in singular negative existential sentences that can either be *true* or *false*. So, for example, of the following three claims only the first is intuitively false, while the other two claims are true or at least have true readings:

(4)   Suzanne Vega does not exist.
(5)   Vulcan does not exist.
(6)   James Bond does not exist.

An adequate analysis of this data again seems to provide a challenge for each semantic conception of names. A defender of Millianism has again three different options to react to this challenge. Firstly, he can bite the bullet, stick to his main theses and interpret sentences like (4)–(6) in such a way that all names that (4)–(6) contain refer to some sort of object. If he, on this basis, aims to capture the differences in truth-values between these claims in literal terms, he is forced to conceive of 'exist' as a discriminating predicate that allows one to distinguish two different classes of objects, namely existent and non-existent objects.[33] But this option has two main difficulties. (a) It seems to be difficult to name a plausible and acceptable category of objects that could function as referents of names in true negative existential sentences, and especially of names that appear to be defective empty names like 'Vulcan'. In this respect the second challenge is closely related to our first mentioned challenge. (b) It is difficult to specify the exact nature of the property of existence in an illuminating way if this property is conceived of as a discriminating property that allows one to distinguish two distinct classes of objects. It is not clear which essential features distinguish existent from non-existent objects. The class of non-existent objects seem to be a terribly gerrymandered group of different kinds of objects.[34]

Secondly, the Millian has again the option to capture the difference between (4) and (5) or (4) and (6) in non-literal terms by some conveyed descriptive contents.[35] However, this option again faces three already familiar problems. (a) Such a solution seems to undermine the entitlement of a Millian theory of names to provide an acceptable account of the overall use of names in natural languages. (b) It is again difficult to explain in an adequate way why ordinary speakers are unaware of the literal status of sentences like (4)–(6) and by means of which mechanisms alternative (descriptive) contents are conveyed that are able to capture our truth-value intuitions concerning (4)–(6). (c) It again seems to be difficult to find adequate descriptive contents that are conveyed by sentences like (4)–(6). A sentence like 'The bearer of "Suzanne Vega" does not exist' is for the same reasons literally true as the sentence 'The bearer of "James Bond" does not exist', because there is intuitively more than one bearer of both names. Similar problems concern sentences like 'The individual dubbed at the origin of the name-using practice connected with "James Bond"'. We would need a more fine-grained, but counter-intuitive individuation of proper names to get such an account going. According to such an individuation, there are no two things that literally share a name. I will argue in chapters 2 and 3 against such an alternative individuation.

Thirdly, there is again my own favoured option that sacrifices Millianism, and hence rejects (MM), substitutes (WMT) with (POT) and makes use of the resources of free logic.[36] On the basis of such a view, we account for the semantic difference in truth-value between a sentence like (4), on the one hand, and sentences like (5) and (6), on the other hand, on the basis of the different denotational status of the used names. Sentence (4) contains a name with a semantic referent; (5) and (6) do not. The details of such an account will be presented in chapter 4.[37]

## Challenge 3: The problem of names in attitude contexts

The third challenge that an adequate analysis of names must be able to meet concerns the use of names in *attitude ascriptions* in the scope of the attitude verb. Intuitively, the following two sentences at least have a reading according to which it is possible to assign to them different truth-values, although the names 'Mark Twain' and 'Samuel Clemens' are used as names with the same semantic referent:

(7)   Peter believes that Mark Twain is an author.
(8)   Peter believes that Samuel Clemens is an author.

At first sight, it may appear that the defender of Millianism does not have the resources to account for the mentioned intuitive differences between (7) and (8). However, closer inspection shows that there are much more options in this respect than in respect to the other two problems already mentioned. A quite popular view among Millians concerning attitude ascriptions like (7) or (8) is the view that the verb 'believe' expresses a two-place relation between subjects and propositions and that that-clauses are complex singular terms that refer to Russellian propositions.[38] Against the background of such an analysis, it is impossible to account for the intuitive difference between (7) and (8) in literal semantic terms. Defenders of such an account typically try to explain the difference in purely pragmatic terms. We have already seen what the main problems of this familiar strategy are.

However, in the case of attitude ascriptions a Millian has other alternatives to account for the difference between (7) and (8) in literal terms. One alternative strategy holds that that-clauses are ambiguous. They only refer to Russellian propositions relative to one reading. Relative to another reading they refer to enriched Russellian propositions that additionally to their ordinary constituents also contain modes of presentation of these ordinary constituents.

Another possible alternative is the so-called *hidden indexical theory* of attitude ascriptions that conceives of the verb 'believe' as an expression of a three-place relation between a subject, a proposition and a contextually salient mode of presentation of this proposition.[39]

A third alternative conceives 'x believes that' as a specific sort of modal operator that shifts the extension of certain embedded expressions if specific non-normal worlds that are used to represent intentional states are among the accessible worlds. In chapter 7, I will argue for an analysis of attitude ascriptions that is based on this third option. In this chapter, I will also show why the other two mentioned rival accounts are not plausible alternatives and why this third account has the best resources to capture the difference between *de re* and *de dicto* readings of sentences like (7) and (8). According to their *de re reading*, sentences like (7) and (8) always have the same truth-value if they contain co-referential names. According to their *de dicto reading*, such sentences can have different truth-values, although they contain co-referential names. As far as it concerns attitude ascriptions that contain non-empty names, this account is compatible with Millianism. However, I will defend a version that can also be applied to sentences like (1) or (2) that contain defective empty names. This extended version is incompatible with Millianism.

The description theory of names also has several options to account for the intuitive difference between (7) and (8). One option makes use of the classical analysis of attitude ascriptions that conceives attitude verbs like 'believe' as two-place relations between subjects and propositions and that interprets that-clauses as complex referring expressions that refer to propositions. According to this variant, (8) and (9) can have different truth-values, because the two different that-clauses that (8) and (9) contain can refer to different general Russellian propositions. Another possible option would be a modal operator treatment of attitude verbs in combination with a description theory of names. Against this background, already it seems to be possible to account for the mentioned intuitive difference between (8) and (9) on the basis of a classical possible world semantics. Such a non-rigid treatment of names can be desirable relative to attitude ascriptions to account for different possible truth-values of sentences like (8) and (9). However, such a treatment is not desirable in the case of *de re* attitude ascriptions or relative to an ordinary modal embedding of a proper name. We will also show in chapter 7 that there is a better non-descriptive alternative of the operator treatment of attitude verbs that is compatible with the rigidity of proper names relative to all their embedded and non-embedded uses.

## Challenge 4: Frege's puzzle

The fourth challenge is provided by Frege's puzzle. There is no agreement in the relevant literature about the real nature of Frege's puzzle.[40] However, there are versions of Frege's puzzle that are only variations of the mentioned third challenge concerning uses of proper names in attitude contexts. But it is also possible to formulate a version of Frege's puzzle that is independent from our third challenge. There is a clear intuitive semantic difference between the following identity sentences, even if they are both true:

(9)   Mark Twain is identical with Mark Twain.
(10) Mark Twain is identical with Samuel Clemens.

However, it is difficult to account for a semantic difference between (9) and (10) on the basis of the theory of meaning *and* content that makes use of Russellian propositions and that is also committed to Strong Millianism. If the two sentences (9) and (10) are true, then they express the very same singular Russellian proposition relative to the given theoretical setting. That is an unwelcome consequence of such a conception of names. But this is only half of the story, and the real problem consists in the explanation of the following difference: Frege pointed out that there is not only an intuitive *semantic* difference between (8) and (9), but there is also a significant *cognitive* or *informative* difference between these two identity sentences. A sentence like (10) can be used to convey to a competent speaker important new information that cannot be conveyed by a sentence like (9). How can we account for this informative difference? It is a relatively popular strategy to capture the informative difference between a sentence like (9) and a sentence like (10) on the basis of the different intuitive behaviour of both sentences relative to their embedding in the scope of an attitude verb. So, for example, the substitution of (8) or (9) in the following two constructions for the schematic letter 'p' leads to sentences with intuitively different truth-values:

(11)  It can be known a priori that p.
(12)  It can be informative (to know) that p.

The substitution of (8) for 'p' in (11) leads to a true sentence, while the substitution of (9) for 'p' in (11) leads to a false sentence. In the case of (12), it is the other way round. Understood in such a way, Frege's puzzle would only be a sub-variety of the already mentioned substitution problem of co-referential names in the context of attitude verbs. However, that is not the real essence of Frege's puzzle. The original version of Frege's puzzle concerns *non-embedded uses* of sentences like (9) and (10) and their communicative status. Frege's question was the following: Why is it possible to convey or express different information by means of a sentence like (9) than by means of a sentence like (10) if these sentences are both true? And Frege's answer to this question was: The communicative and informative difference between a sentence like (9) and (10) can be explained by the fact that both sentences express different contents or thoughts. In this sense, Frege accounts for the mentioned intuitive informative difference in cognitive terms. This is only one possible solution to Frege's puzzle, but it is a solution that is congenial to Frege's and Russell's cognitive version of the description theory of names.

Interestingly, this kind of solution is not so easily available for our two distinguished preferable semantic versions of the description theory of names. According to them, (10) is semantically equivalent to one of the following two metalinguistic identity sentences:

(10\*)  The bearer of 'Mark Twain' is identical with the bearer of 'Samuel Clemens'.
(10′)  The origin of the name-using practice connected with 'Mark Twain' is identical with the origin of the name-using practice connected with 'Samuel Clemens'.

At least Frege would protest against such a solution to his puzzle. According to him, the information that is expressed by (10) is more substantial and less conventional than the information that is expressed by (10\*) and (10′), which mostly concerns the contingent and arbitrary co-extensionality of two different names.

In my opinion, we clearly have to distinguish between the two mentioned aspects of Frege's puzzle: (a) the intuitive semantic difference between sentences like (9) and (10), and (b) the mentioned informative difference between sentences of this kind. It is clear that an adequate semantics must be able to draw a semantic difference between sentences like (9) and (10), but it is less clear whether it is necessary to account for the informative difference in purely semantic terms.

The mentioned version of Strong Millianism cannot account for the intuitive semantic difference between the true sentences (9) and (10). So far so bad for this conception. However, the crucial question in this respect is: What exactly consists of the intuitive semantic difference between (9) and (10)? The most remarkable semantic difference between (9) and (10) is reflected by the fact that these sentences have a quite different *inferential potential*. According to a classical logical framework, trivial identity sentences like (9) are tautologies and, therefore, do not have any significant influence on the validity of arguments. An identity sentence like (10), on the other hand, has an important inferential potential and it can be used to derive new premises from a certain given set of assumptions. This important semantic/logical difference between sentences like (9) and (10) is already captured by the truth-conditional semantics of classical first-order predicate logic with identity or classical modal predicate logic with identity. Therefore, a version of Millianism that assimilates proper names to individual constants in classical logic and that makes use of the truth-conditional treatment of these expressions in classical first-order and modal logic is able to capture this significant semantic difference.

Is there any *additional* semantic difference between sentences like (9) and (10) that is not captured on the basis of such a truth-conditional treatment of simple identity sentences and that is required to capture the mentioned informative difference between (9) in (10)? With respect to non-embedded use, I do not think so. (With respect to hyper-intensionally embedded uses, the referents of names can be shifted in the same way as with respect to any sentence that is embedded in a context of hyper-intensional operator or predicate.)

On the one hand, the mentioned inferential difference gives us the resources to account for an important informative difference between sentences like (9) and (10) relative to their un-embedded use. On the other hand, there seems to be an additional important cognitive or informative difference that can be captured on the basis of the given semantic difference by means of additional non-semantic assumptions. A true sentence like (10) is only informative for a specific competent speaker in the desired non-conventional sense if such a person cognitively represents one and the same actual object by means of two different cognitive representations as two different objects and if he, on this basis, associates two different names with these two different representations. On the basis of such a cognitive setting, a true sentence like (10) can be informative for such a person and it can have an important cognitive value, because it can convey important information that leads to an *update* and *correction* of the mental object-representations of this person. A plausible account of such a kind of representational update can only be given based on a more detailed story about how exactly cognitive subjects represent individuals and how these representations can be updated or merged, which will not be given in this book.[41] But it is not necessary to inflate the semantic content of sentences like (9) and (10) to account for this kind of informative value of such sentences. Against this background, I only consider the first mentioned aspect of Frege's puzzle as a challenge for a correct semantic analysis of proper names. The second mentioned aspect does not concern the *semantics* of names in the narrow sense. It is basically a *psychological* problem and it concerns our mental object-representations and the related mental representations of facts that concern the names of these represented objects. Therefore, I think that the core of Frege's puzzle that concerns unembedded uses of identity sentences should not concern us from a purely semantic point of view. Our truth-conditional semantics will give us everything to draw the desired semantic difference between sentences like (9) and (10), but since we are only interested in the semantics and pragmatics of names, we will not investigate the psychological part of the problem in more detail in this book.

Up to now we have only given a brief overview of the four classical challenges of a semantic analysis of names that Frege and Russell have pointed out. The following nine remaining challenges are more recent problems for an adequate semantic analysis of names. These problems were not addressed and discussed by Frege and Russell in their full explicitness.

### Challenge 5: The problem of fictional names

Our fifth challenge concerns so-called *fictional names*. (They are to some extent discussed by Frege and Russell, but the full range of the problems related to this issue were not realized before Kripke's famous John Locke Lecture in 1973.[42])

Fictional names are names with very specific functions and properties but it is not clear whether they are in general names that lack a semantic referent or not. Prototypically, they are *not* introduced by some act of naming, such as ordinary names for real things. Their first and introductory use is essentially connected with certain speech acts of story-telling. In such a context fictional names are used *without* the intention to refer to a specific single thing. If someone tells a story by uttering declarative sentences, he does not thereby make any truth-evaluable assertions and so it also seems to be the case that he does not really refer to things as well. That is, when we use a fictional name as part of acts of story-telling, we probably only pretend that a certain thing exists and we pretend to refer to this thing. This *pretence use* seems to be the primary use of fictional names, but they also have different *secondary uses* in ordinary speech acts such as acts of assertions. Intuitively, there at least seem to be two different sub-varieties of the secondary use of fictional names relative to ordinary speech acts: (a) uses that are part of reports, which report what is the case according to a specific fictional story; and (b) uses that are part of reports that seem to report certain so-called external properties of a fictional object that such an object seems to have independently of what happens or is the case according to a story that features this object.[43] This peculiar status of fictional names poses a severe challenge for any conception of names whether it is a Millian, descriptive or some other sort of theory. The central questions that an adequate conception of fictional names has to answer are the following. Is it correct to conceive of the use of fictional names in acts of story-telling as a pretence use? Should we interpret fictional names relative to this use semantically as names that lack a referent? Is it plausible to conceive of acts of storytelling as acts that create fictional objects? Should we therefore interpret fictional names relative to their secondary use as names of specific fictional objects? In chapter 4 I will argue for the view that fictional names should be conceived of as a specific subvariety of names that lack a semantic referent relative to their primary use. According to this view, fictional names have a uniform semantic status. But unlike defective empty names they are not used with the aim to refer to a specific object. In this sense, fictional names have different derivative functions. Their stipulative function relative to their primary use is derived from the ordinary referential function of names. Relative to their secondary use, fictional names aim to exploit the referential stipulation, which is the consequence of their primary function. Hence, they are used with the presupposition that there is a fictional world relative to which things are as told relative to a specific fictional story. Relative to such a presupposition, fictional names can refer to objects that exist relative to a fictional world. Such a treatment of fictional names faces several delicate problems concerning the correct analysis of ordinary assertions that contain fictional names. These problems will be addressed and discussed in chapter 4.

## Challenge 6: The problem of names in modal contexts

Kripke famously pointed out a sixth challenge that concerns the semantic behaviour of names in the context of metaphysical modal contexts.[44] He has shown that ordinary paradigm names behave very differently than the majority of ordinary definite descriptions and he also gave an explanation based on his previous work on modal logic.

Kripke has drawn our attention to the different semantic behaviour of names and descriptions in the following sentential contexts:

(13a) Barack Obama might not have been Barack Obama.
(13b) The 44th president of the United States of America might not have been the 44th president of the United States of America.

It is important to notice that the name 'Barack Obama' is intuitively co-referential with 'the 44th president of the United States of America'. Nevertheless, the first sentence (13a) does not have an intuitively true reading, while the second has an intuitively true reading. In principle, it seems to be the case that we can distinguish at least two different readings of such metaphysical modal claims like (13a) and (13b). According to a wide-scope reading, both occurrences of the singular term are in the scope of the modal expression. According to the narrow-scope reading, the first occurrence of the singular term is outside the scope of the modal expression, while the second term is inside. Sentence (13a) seems to be intuitively false with respect to both readings, while (13b) seems to be *false* relative to the wide-scope reading and *true* relative to the narrow-scope reading. If we make use of the formal tools of modal logics and extend the language of quantified modal logic by means of a specific version of lambda-abstraction proposed in Fitting and Mendelsohn (1998), we can formally represent these differences as follows:

(13aL1/L2)   ◊a≠a / λx(◊a≠x)[a].
(13bL1/L2)   ◊ιxPx≠ιxPx / λy(◊ιxPx≠y)[ιxPx].

There are different strategies to react to this intuitive data with respect to the special semantic behaviour of names in the context of metaphysical modals.

The first reaction, which was initially proposed by Barcan Marcus and Kripke, takes this data as an important indicator for systematic differences between the *semantics* of names and descriptions. According to this reaction, paradigmatic names like 'Peter', 'London' or 'Germany' are semantically atomic expressions that refer to the same individual as with respect to the actual world relative to all other possible worlds. Such a general semantically rigidity allows one very easily and in a straightforward way to account for the outlined data.

A second reaction to this data that was initially proposed in Dummett (1973) is the so-called wide-scope strategy. According to this view, proper names have the same semantics as definite descriptions, but they always receive by a specific convention a wide-scope reading with respect to metaphysical modal expressions.

A third possible strategy holds that names are special kinds of definite descriptions, namely *rigidified* definite descriptions. There are different possible ways to rigidify a definite description. The most popular way makes use of the modifier 'actual'. Against this background, a definite description has the same but hidden structure as a description of the form 'the actual P'. An alternative version of this strategy makes use of an haecceitas-property, that is a property that applies to an individual and only to this individual relative to every possible world. A third version combines the first strategy with the additional introduction of an indexical expression. According to one example of this reaction, a name is semantically equivalent to an expression like 'The actual P that is identical with that thing'.[45]

A fourth strategy denies that proper names are in general rigid expressions but holds an alternative semantics of modal operators. In opposition to the orthodox view, modal operators do not shift the extension of certain terms to other possible worlds, but they fix the extension of a proper name to the actual world. On this basis, it is possible to explain why proper names appear to be rigid designators in specific modal contexts although they in fact are not expressions of this kind.

A fifth and last strategy that I want to mention denies the mentioned data and tries to explain it in a pragmatic way. The only attempt of carrying out this strategy that I personally know can be found in Bach (1987, 2002). He tried to argue that Kripke's examples neither provide convincing evidence for semantic differences between names and descriptions nor for the rigidity of proper names.

I have a relatively conservative view on this issue and I think that Kripke is basically right. In my opinion, the second option is not viable because it rests on the unfounded *ad hoc* postulation of a so-called scope-convention. The fourth option shares a similar weakness. It seems to be also *ad hoc* and without independent motivation that names and descriptions are semantically alike, while only names interact in a different way with metaphysical modal expressions. Additionally, it also seems to be implausible to claim that expressions with very similar semantics interact with the very same modal expression systematically in a different way. The fifth reaction is desperate, but without any good foundation, as I will show in chapter 1 of this book. The third outlined reaction is in my opinion the second best. Nevertheless, it also seems to be *ad hoc* to postulate a hidden rigidifier or other hidden semantic elements, especially in the case of paradigm names like 'London', 'Peter' or 'Germany'. Furthermore, it seems to be difficult to find the appropriate descriptive matrix-expression 'P' for a description of the form 'the actual P' or alternatively such an expression that expresses a semantically relevant, essential and individual property of the bearer of a name. Hence, in my opinion this option is also not viable.

Furthermore, there also seems to be good more direct evidence for Kripke's strategy. In chapter 1, I will present modified versions of Kripke's test to rebut Bach's doubts. Furthermore, I will show that there are, from a formal semantic point of view, four semantically non-equivalent ways to provide a rigid semantics for proper names. Each of these four versions resets on different metaphysical and semantic assumptions concerning reference and existence, as I will show.

**Challenge 7: The problem of shared names**

Our seventh challenge is the so-called *problem of shared names*. Intuitively, most ordinary proper names have more than one bearer. A large number of names for people, for example, have a large number of different bearers. Our intuitive individuation of proper names poses a problem for Millian and descriptive theories of names. We have to provide an explanation of how it is possible to use a name that has more than one bearer to refer to a single object relative to a specific context of use.

One option would be to reject our intuitive individuation of proper names and defend the claim that different objects that appear to have the same name in fact have different same-spelled names.[46] It is a difficult task to provide a plausible version of such a kind of individuation of proper names that can be applied to empty and non-empty names. In chapters 2 and 3, I will argue *against* such a revisionary individuation of proper names.

A second option accepts the intuitive possibility that different objects may share the very same name, but holds the view that most ordinary proper names are ambiguous. This option seems to be perfectly compatible with a Millian theory of names. A version of this view that assimilates proper names with individual constants in classical first-order or modal predicate logic may represent different meanings or uses of a single ordinary proper name by means of different individual constants that formally represent this ordinary name. There does not seem to be a plausible way to combine this solution with a nominal or causal description theory of names. Defenders of such a view are better advised either to choose the first mentioned option or to treat proper names with more than one bearer as *incomplete definite descriptions*, whose referent is determined by means of an additional implicit restricting condition or by means of some other contextual mechanism. In chapter 2, I will also argue against an ambiguity view as a solution to the problem of shared names.

A third option that I would like to mention here also accepts our intuitive individuation of proper names, but treats proper names as context-sensitive expressions. According to this view, the name-bearer relation is conceived of as a context-insensitive, but time-relative relation, while the relation of semantic reference is interpreted as a context-sensitive relation. This option is compatible with the distinguished two forms of Weak Millianism. It is also compatible with a semantic version of the description theory that either makes use of a Neo-Strawsonian analysis of the definite article and hence assimilates its semantics to the semantics of demonstrative expressions like 'this' and 'that', or that interprets names with different bearers as incomplete definite descriptions and accounts for the completion of these descriptions in use by some context-sensitive semantic or pragmatic mechanism. In chapter 3, I will defend a new version of the view that proper names are context-sensitive expressions and closely semantically related to complex demonstratives and third-person personal pronouns. However, this view does not purport an *assimilation* of proper names to the semantics of these two other expressions. I will argue in detail, in chapter 3, 5 and 6, that there are significant semantic differences between these three kinds of expressions. Nevertheless, they are very close semantic relatives, or at least so I will claim.

## Challenge 8: The problem of past names

The eighth challenge that an adequate semantic conception of names has to address and meet concerns the so-called problem of past names. The name 'Leningrad' was a former official name of St. Petersburg. The use of the name 'Leningrad' in present tense sentences like the following seems odd and unacceptable:

(14)  ? Leningrad has (currently) more than a hundred thousand inhabitants.

On the other hand, it is unproblematic to use the very same name in a sentence that contains a temporal modifier and that shifts the evaluation of a sentence to a time relative to which St. Petersburg was a bearer of 'Leningrad'. The following true sentence is an example of this sort:

(15)  In 1942, Leningrad was the second largest city of the Soviet Union.

The problem of past names now consists in the challenge to explain the mentioned intuitive difference between sentences like (14) and (15). Alternatively, one could also present this problem as a substitution problem. In a sentence like (15) the substitution of 'Leningrad' with 'St. Petersburg' and vice versa neither changes the truth-value nor the *acceptability* of such a sentence. In a sentence like (14) we can substitute the name 'St. Petersburg' for 'Leningrad' and turn the unacceptable (14) into an acceptable and true sentence.

One possible reaction to this problem would consist in a specific ambiguity view that distinguishes between *restricted* and *unrestricted* proper names.[47] An unrestricted name is insensitive to temporal operators and always refers to a certain bearer of this name relative to a context of use. A restricted name in opposition to that is sensitive to temporal operators and can only refer to a thing that is the bearer of a name relative to the time of evaluation of a sentence that contains this name. According to this view, (14) is odd because it contains a restricted name without a semantic referent. This kind of solution is compatible with Weak Millianism and different possible variants of the description theory of names.

Another possible semantic solution to this problem distinguishes two different layers of linguistic meaning of a proper name. According to this view, proper names have a use-conditional meaning that constrains *semantically adequate uses* of a name. This solution characterizes (14) as true, but as a use-conditionally unacceptable sentence that violates the constraining conditions that are associated with proper names. According to this view, temporal operators interact with proper names and modify the use-conditional meaning of a proper name. 'Leningrad' was once a proper name of St. Petersburg. Therefore, it is adequate to use the name 'Leningrad' in an embedded context that restricts the use-conditional meaning of 'Leningrad' to *past* bearers of this name.

A third possibility would be a solution in more pragmatic terms. A sentence like (14) seems to presuppose or pragmatically convey the following false content:

(16)  Leningrad is presently so-called/ is presently a bearer of 'Leningrad'.

We interpret (14) as odd, because we recognize that it conveys or falsely presupposes (16). However, this purely pragmatic explanation also has its problems, because it falsely predicts that the substitution of 'Leningrad' with 'St. Petersburg' in (15) would also lead to an odd sentence that conveys or presupposes a knowingly false assumption, namely:

(17)  St. Petersburg was so-called/a bearer of 'St. Petersburg' in 1942.

Maybe there are other possible pragmatic explanations of the oddness of (14). In any case, it seems to be difficult to find such an explanation that only explains why (14) is odd and not (15) or those sentences that are the result of the substitution of 'Leningrad' with 'St. Petersburg' in (14) and (15).

Weak Millianism is compatible with both mentioned semantic solutions to this problem. The second mentioned semantic solution can also be combined with a description theory of names that interprets the definite article as a demonstrative expression. A descriptive variant of the first semantic strategy is also combinable with a semantic version of the description theory of names. Combined with the nominal description theory this view holds that unrestricted names are semantically equivalent to descriptions of the form 'The present bearer of "N"', while restricted names are equivalent to descriptions of the form 'The bearer of "N"'. I will propose versions of the first and second semantic strategy in chapter 3.

## Challenge 9: The problem of names used in epistemic contexts

Proper names do not only have a very specific behaviour in attitude contexts, but also in the context of epistemic modals like 'might'. Let me explain the semantic problems that arise in connection with names relative to these contexts on the basis of an example. There was a famous series of terrible murders in London (Whitechapel) that was attributed to a single person. Since it was unknown who this person really was, he was called 'Jack the Ripper' for the purpose of communication. There were a lot of different suspects and officially the murderer was never identified. Let us randomly pick out two suspects that were considered as highly suspicious. On the basis of what we all now know, it seems to be possible that the following two claims are both true:

(18) Jack the Ripper might be Aaron Kosminski.
(19) Jack the Ripper might be Montague John Druitt.

But now here comes the problem based on this data. If we assume that all singular terms used in (18) and (19) are rigid designators and that 'might' is an epistemic modal expression that is interpreted on the basis of a standard possible world framework, then we have a serious problem. The names 'Aaron Kosminski' and 'Montague John Druitt' refer to different people and are rigid designators with respect to all possible worlds. 'Jack the Ripper' is also a rigid designator that refers to the actual murderer of the famous Whitechapel murders in every possible world. Against this background, it seems to be impossible that (18) and (19) can both be true. But they are both intuitively true, given our incomplete knowledge about who in fact did the deeds. Hence, we have to change one of our originally made semantic assumptions. It is also important to notice that 'might' is not only polysemous and, hence, has different meanings relative to different uses, but it is also a context-sensitive expression. The truth-value of (18) and (19) depends on the fact, who utters it and from which perspective it is evaluated.

Against this background, we have different options to resolve this problem: One option would be to reject the rigidity of names and allow names like definite descriptions to flip their reference relative to different points of evaluation. In the light of other possible reactions, this is clearly an over-reaction, because we have already seen that names function clearly as right designators in other modal contexts.

A second option is to make use of a two-dimensional possible world semantics relative to which we have at least two different parameters for possible worlds and also correspondingly two different sets of possible worlds. Against this background, proper names refer rigidly relative to all metaphysically possible worlds and they refer non-rigidly relative to the epistemic possible worlds.[48] However, one problem is that this account reserves a second set of possible worlds only for epistemic modals. But there are obvious and possible interactions between epistemic and metaphysical modals and there are certainly a lot of possible meaningful claims that contain both kind of modals. It seems to be difficult to coordinate the interaction between these different sets of possible worlds in a meaningful way. Furthermore, this epistemic interpretation of the second dimension of an evaluation parameter undermines the possibility of providing a more classical Kaplan-style two-dimensional semantics that can be used to account for the semantics of indexical expressions and other context-sensitive expressions. Hence, an alternative would be welcome.

And there also is a third less complex strategy that distinguishes between normal and non-normal worlds. Sentences are evaluated relative to a single world-parameter that can be evaluated in principle relative to all normal and non-normal worlds. Furthermore, it holds that the set of normal worlds represent all metaphysically possible worlds, while the set of all non-normal worlds contains all worlds that, additionally to the possible worlds, are conceivable. Therefore, these worlds can also account for all epistemic possibilities that are not metaphysically possible. Additionally, this semantics assumes that proper names refer rigidly with respect to every *possible* world, but they may refer to different things relative to different epistemic worlds. On this basis it becomes clear how (18) and (19) can come out both as true although these sentences contain only rigid designators. That is the case because, relative to some non-normal world that accounts for the truth of (18) or (19), 'Jack the Ripper' refers to a different object than it actually does. To account for the context-sensitivity of formulas that contain epistemic modals, we will offer different semantics. According to one version, all sentences get evaluated relative to worlds and agents, but the agent parameter will be redundant with respect to all sentences that are not headed by an epistemic modal operator. According to the second version, an assignment function assigns a value to the agent parameter with respect to epistemic modal sentences. Additionally, we will make use of an accessibility relation between worlds that are relativized to agents. On this basis, we can get access to non-normal worlds that are relevant for the evaluation of an epistemic modal sentence, interpreted relative to some agent. I will defend this account in the last chapter of this book and show how we can provide on this basis the required difference between epistemic and metaphysical modals.

## Challenge 10: The problem of apparent predicative uses of names

Let us now focus on our tenth challenge that concerns so-called *predicative* uses of proper names. In Sloat (1969) and Burge (1973), it was pointed out that the very same *nouns* that can be prototypically used as names and hence singular referring expressions can also be used as predicates. We can, for example, use the noun 'Alfred' in a meaningful way in the following sentences:[49]

(20)  There are relatively few Alfreds in Princeton.
(21)  An Alfred joined the club today.
(22)  The Alfred who joined the club today was a baboon.
(23)  Some Alfreds are crazy; some are sane.

But not only that, there seem to be systematic semantic connections between the use of 'Alfred' as a name and 'Alfred' as a predicate. These connections seem to be captured by the following intuitively valid arguments:

Alfred is a nice fellow.
―――――――――――――――――――――
There is an Alfred.

Every Alfred is a nice fellow.
―――――――――――――――――――――
Alfred is a nice fellow.

Defenders of a so-called predicate view of proper names use these data to argue for a semantic treatment of names that is incompatible with Millianism and also to some extent different from the introduced semantic description theories. According to the predicate view, names like 'Alfred' should be primarily conceived of as predicates – that is, not as abbreviations of any other predicates, but as predicates in their own right. The prototypically bare use of a name as a referring expression should be re-interpreted from a logical point of view as the use of a predicate that contains on the level of logical form a specific hidden singular determiner. In this sense, our ordinary names should be conceived as complex referring expressions that contain a predicate and a specific unpronounced determiner. The two most popular accounts with respect to the status of this determiner are:[50] (a) a hidden demonstrative 'that',[51] and (b) a hidden definite article.[52]

In general, there seem to be two possible approaches to capture so-called predicative uses of names and their systematic connections to the prototypically bare singular uses of names as referring expressions: (a) a uniform semantic approach that is proposed by the predicate view and that conceives of a noun like 'Alfred' as a predicate relative to all of it uses; (b) a non-uniform semantic approach that claims that the expression 'Alfred' has at least two different but related meanings and uses. Relative to one of these uses it is an atomic referring expression, relative to the other use it is a predicate. However, the secondary use of such an expression as a predicate is in some sense derived from the primary use as a referring expression. Millianism seems to be committed to the second strategy. A defender of a description theory of names seems to be well-advised in modifying his view in certain respects and change to the camp of the predicate view. In chapter 5, I will defend the second strategy.

### Challenge 11: The problem of apparent anaphoric uses of names

Let us now focus on our eleventh challenge that concerns apparent *anaphoric uses of proper names*. Different authors have relatively recently pointed out that proper names seem to have quite rare and specific *anaphoric uses*.[53] The following two sentences, for example, seem to contain the proper names 'Ernest' and 'Tim' used as an anaphoric device:

(24) There is <u>a gentleman</u> in Hertfordshire by the name of 'Ernest'. **Ernest** is engaged to two women.
(25) Every woman who carries on with <u>a Tim</u> and a Kim should be careful in not addressing **Tim** as Kim.

Especially interesting and challenging is the use of 'Tim' in (25). It at least appears to be the case that this name is used in (25) in a similar way as a so-called donkey pronoun. That is, it seems to be in some sense bound on the level of logical form by the indefinite quantifier phrase 'a Tim', although it is syntactically outside the scope of this quantifier expression. The probably most interesting aspect of this use is that 'Tim' in (25) does not function as rigid designator, because it seems to be bound by some quantifier. Some people have used such kinds of examples to argue for a quite special general semantic treatment of proper names that is also able to account for these uses in literal terms. Elbourne and Matushansky, for example, have argued for the thesis that proper names are definite descriptions that contain hidden variables that can be bound by certain quantifier expressions. Cumming has argued for the thesis that proper names should be formally conceived of as *individual variables* that have unbound and bound uses.

There are at least two possible reactions to this kind of data. Firstly, one can take these uses at face value and accommodate the semantics of proper names in such a way that names can literally be used as anaphoric expressions. Defenders of a semantic description theory of names may for this purpose postulate certain hidden variables that can be bound by quantifiers (like Elbourne and Matushansky). Millians may follow Cumming and formally represent names by means of individual variables that have bound and unbound uses.

Secondly, one may question whether these uses are *literally* anaphoric uses of names. That is, in the case of (23) one seems to have two options to defend this strategy. (a) One may doubt whether the name 'Ernest' is really used as an anaphoric device that is bound by some quantifier. The apparent dependence of the reference of the name 'Ernest' on the previously used indefinite expression might be interpreted as a purely pragmatic phenomenon. (b) One may doubt that the expression 'Ernest' in (24) is at all used as a proper name. Maybe the expression is only used as an elliptic stand-in for a more complex expression that is not literally a name.

In (25), only the second variant of this response seems to be possible, because the expression 'Tim' that is used in (25) indeed seems to share all relevant features with typical donkey anaphora. In chapter 6, I will defend a specific version of this second line of defence. It is to be noticed that examples like (24) and (25) are not only extremely rare, but obviously marked and restricted to certain very specific sentential and discursive constructions. Against this background, it can reasonably be doubted whether they provide relevant data that an adequate semantic conception of names should be able to account for.

**Challenge 12: The problem of apparent descriptive modifiers of proper names**

Our twelfth challenge concerns very special kinds of modifications that can only be made with respect to proper names. These are very special definite descriptions that seem to contain proper names. The first kind of these cases has the general grammatical form *'The [noun] [proper name]'*. Examples of this kind are descriptions like 'The philosopher Saul Kripke', 'The tennis player Andy Murray'. What is interesting about these expressions is that they seem to refer to single objects, but it is unclear whether they literally contain a singular referring expression as semantic constituent or a so-called name-predicate. Therefore, the key question is whether a description like 'The philosopher Saul Kripke' is semantically equivalent to an expression like 'The philosopher that is identical with Saul Kripke' or to an expression like 'The philosopher that is also a Saul Kripke', or even whether it is ambiguous and can have both readings. Let us call the first reading the *identity reading* and the second reading the *predicative reading*.

A second kind of such cases has the general structure *'The [adjective] [proper name]'*. Examples of this sort are 'The famous Bob Dylan', 'The rich Jeff Bezos', 'The former Leningrad', 'The young Mozart', and 'The early Russell'. These cases only contain a single noun, while the other mentioned cases always contain at least two nouns. Nevertheless, a description like 'The rich Jeff Bezos' can have two completely different readings. It can mean roughly the same as 'The rich member of the bearers of 'Jeff Bezos'" (predicative reading), or it can mean roughly the same as 'Jeff Bezos, who is rich' (appositive reading).

Therefore, semantically the situation with respect to our two classes seems, at first sight, to be relatively similar. However, appearances are deceptive. It only appears to be the case that examples of the first distinguished class can have a predicate reading. In fact, sentences that contain these kinds of descriptions can only have an identity reading as we can show on the basis of pertinent examples. Let us start with the following example:

(26)   Most people know the songwriter Bob Dylan, but only a few know the painter Bob Dylan.

With respect to example (26), it might seem that this sentence can have both readings. It is clear that if the conversational context is unmistakably such that the conversation is about one person and his different kinds of artistic work, it is thereby set that the two descriptions in (26) get a co-referential identity reading. One may ask: What is the case if it is clear from the conversational context that (26) is used in a conversation about two different individuals called 'Bob Dylan'? One might think that in such a case a predicate reading with respect to the descriptions contained in (26) is mandatory. But it is not so. An identity reading is again the only possible reading, but the two occurrences of the name 'Bob Dylan' are not co-referential in this case. Why 'the painter Bob Dylan' is in no case semantically equivalent to 'The painter who is also a Bob Dylan' can be shown by an anaphoric test. In the following case that clearly contains the predicative use of the expression 'Bob Dylan', we can get a meaningful anaphoric reading of 'is that too':

(27)   Only a few people know the painter who is a Bob Dylan, but they certainly know the rockstar who is that too.

But in the case of the following similar example that contains a definite description of our described first case, it is impossible to get such an anaphoric reading of 'is that too'.

(28)   Only a few people know the painter Bob Dylan, but I also know the poet that is that too.

I interpret this difference as a clear indication that in a sentence like (28) or (26) the expression 'Bob Dylan' is used twice as a proper name, although with two different referents, and hence the descriptions of our distinguished first kind that (26) and (28) contain can only have an identity reading.[54]

Furthermore, there are sentences that contain a verb that excludes a co-referential identity reading, like the following:

(29)   The footballer Thomas Müller yesterday met the lawyer Thomas Müller.

It is impossible that any person meets himself, hence a co-referential reading in the case of (29) seems to be excluded. Therefore, on the basis of our observation so far, the two descriptions of our distinguished first kind that (29) contains can only have a non-co-referential identity reading.

The situation is different with respect to descriptions that appear to contain names that are of the second distinguished kind. Firstly, there are cases that can only have an appositive reading irrespective of their sentential or conversational context. An example of this sort is 'The early Bertrand Russell', which means roughly the same as 'Bertrand Russell during the early period of his life/work'. Secondly, there are cases that only can have a predicative reading like 'The most famous Thomas Müller' or 'The oldest Nick Jones'. In these cases, the superlative meaning of 'The most famous' and 'The oldest' seems to require a predicative interpretation of the used names. Another example of this sort without a superlative is provided by 'The younger George Bush'. Thirdly, there are expressions of this kind that can have both of the two readings depending on the conversational and sentential context. So, for example, 'The young George Bush' could mean roughly the same as 'The young bearer of the name "George Bush"' if we have a context that requires a contrastive reading of such descriptions as in the following sentence used in 2008:

(30) The young George Bush was longer in charge than the old George Bush.

The situation is different if every indication for a contrastive reading is missing and a statement about a specific time in the life of its bearer is made, as in the following case:

(31) The young George Bush studied at Yale University.

Relative to such a conversational setting and sentential context, 'The young George Bush' means roughly the same as 'George Bush as he was young'. Most descriptions of our second distinguished kind fall into this third and most flexible class.

In my opinion, constructions of the two distinguishing classes do not provide any new challenges for an adequate semantics of names. All reviewed constructions either contain referential or predicative uses of proper names. Therefore, I do not think that they provide a genuine additional challenge. However, there are other people who think that these constructions provide new independent evidence either for the Sloat–Burge-style variety of Predicativism, like Fara (2015) and Matushansky (2008), or the Quinean variety of the predicate view on names, like Rieppel (2020). In Rieppel's paper, an interesting observation is made with respect to our two different distinguished kinds of examples. In descriptions like 'The philosopher Saul Kripke' or 'The earlier Bertrand Russell' we cannot substitute *salva congruitate* with a co-referential singular term that is not a proper name as, for example, in the first case 'the author of *Naming and Necessity*'. It is also true that in the case of the Kripke example, 'The philosopher Saul Kripke' means the same as 'The philosopher identical to Saul Kripke'. However, this is not the case with respect to the Russell example. Hence, 'The philosopher Saul Kripke' might be seen as a syntactic short-cut of 'The philosopher identical to Saul Kripke', but the same syntactic short-cut convention does not hold in the case of 'The philosopher identical to the author of *Naming and Necessity*'. These are only syntactic peculiarities and they also do not hold with respect to the second class of cases. Therefore, I cannot see why such purely syntactic substitution phenomena give us a clear indication for a predicative semantics of proper names. In any case, it would be methodologically very problematic if one aims to justify its preference for a specific semantics by a reference to very peripheral uses of proper names.

## Challenge 13: The problem of apparent names that have the syntactic form of definite descriptions

The thirteenth and last challenge I would like to present here has some relation to our twelfth. This challenge also concerns a specific sort of definite descriptions, but not ones that contain proper names in a special way. These descriptions have apparent similarities with paradigm proper names themselves.[55] These are expressions such as the following: 'The Holy Roman Empire', 'The Morning Star', 'The United States of America', 'The European Union', 'The Netherlands', 'The Mount Everest', 'The Thames'. At first sight, the following seems to be the case: from a syntactic point of view these expressions seem to be definite descriptions, but from a semantic point of view they seem to be more like proper names. With respect to such examples like 'The Netherlands', 'The Mount Everest' and 'The Thames' it seems to be intuitively so that these are special variations of names for countries, mountains and rivers that are descriptions with a very specific syntactic structure. Similar patterns can be observed with respect to names for stars, such as 'the Sun', 'the Pole Star', 'the Sirius Star'.

In this respect, 'the Morning Star' is an interesting and peculiar exception. It was introduced with the intention to name a star. It later turned out that the apparently named star was in fact a planet. Nevertheless, the expression 'the Morning Star' remains in use as a name for the planet Venus. I think this example shows that the apparent descriptive content that the expression seems to express does not play any role concerning the determination of the referent of such an expression. This can also be shown with respect to the famous example 'The Holy Roman Empire'. This expression contains three different descriptive nouns and none of these applies to the referent of this expression.[56] Such exceptional cases shine an interesting light on our apparently descriptive names. There not only seems to be a certain habit of naming natural objects like stars, lakes, mountains, churches and the like with these special 'descriptive' names, but also with respect to some institutional objects like countries, states and confederations. However, these expressions also have other very peculiar grammatical and semantic properties.

The written versions of these constructions contain only expressions that are written in capital letters. That seems to be a syntactic convention to mark these expressions and distinguish them from ordinary descriptions. Another remarkable *semantic* feature of these expressions is that they can be modified in an apparently similar fashion as ordinary definite descriptions, as the following examples show: 'The *famous* Morning Star', 'The *beautiful* Netherlands', 'The *praised* Holy Roman Empire' and 'The *ice-covered* Mount Blanc'.[57] These observations clearly show, I think, that these expressions are semantically different than other *paradigm* names like 'London', 'Germany' and 'Peter', which do not seem to be semantically complex. Hence, it seems that these special descriptions have a compositionally complex semantics. The question now is what kind of semantics. We have already seen that expressions like 'The Morning Star' or 'The Holy Roman Empire' show that these descriptions are special and at least not fully descriptive. However, as one can also easily see, these descriptions are rigid designators unlike the majority of ordinary definite descriptions. Neither of the following two sentences have true literal readings:

(32a) The Morning Star might not have been the Morning Star.
(32b) The Morning Star is such that it is metaphysically possible that it is not identical with the Morning Star.

All apparent definite descriptions of the mentioned kind pass this classical rigidity test.[58] However, there is another interesting difference between a sub-class of the mentioned descriptions that is pointed out in Rabern (2015). He draws our attention to the following example:

(33) When the Brooklyn Bridge is blocked use the Manhattan one.

The expression 'one' seems to have an anaphoric use in this sentence that allows it to pick up the descriptive content of 'Bridge'. This at least seems to show that with respect to such an example the meaning of 'Bridge' contributes in some sense to the truth-conditions of the whole sentence as a self-standing constituent. We can see the same effect with respect to the following additional example:

(34) We first talked about the Holy Roman, then about the German Empire.

However, and interestingly, we do not get these effects in every possible case. Firstly, we certainly do not get such results on the basis of the mentioned description-names that only contain a single capitalized noun like 'The Netherlands', 'The Thames', 'The Arctic' or 'The Sun'. Secondly, and this is the most interesting class, there are also examples that have the apparently same syntactic structure as our examples in (33) and (34), but they do not have the semantic properties that have been pointed out. As it is also shown in Rabern (2015, 312), the following examples are odd and do not have an accessible anaphoric reading:

(35) # We saw the North Star before we saw the Morning one.
(36) # We first visited the North Pole and then the South one.
(37) # We investigated the Mississippi River before the Missouri one.

Interestingly, the ellipsis test provided by Rabern is less sensitive than the anaphoric test. This can be shown by the following acceptable examples.

(38) I showed my son the North and the South Pole on the map.
(39) We have seen the Mississippi and the Missouri River today.

In my opinion, the ellipsis test is not an indicator of semantic complexity it only shows that we can save breath if we have a repetition on a purely syntactic level. Hence, I think the majority of description-names are not in the same way semantically complex definite descriptions as 'the red car'. Furthermore, they are essentially rigid designators and descriptive in a very thin sense, as we have seen. Nevertheless, the 'Bridge' and the 'Empire' cases remain puzzling. One possible way to deal with them, and the way that I prefer, is that we accept the following: it is not only the case that the class of ordinary proper names does not have a uniform semantics. There are *paradigm* names like 'London' and these are the main topic of this book. These are semantically atomic and context-sensitive expressions. Additionally, there are description-names like the presented examples show. However, this sub-class of description-names is also not semantically uniform as there are some description-names that are *more* semantically complex than others. Nevertheless, all these three classes of names have something in common semantically and meta-semantically. They are all rigid designators, and their reference is originally determined by an act of naming or an implicitly established name-using practice.

Even on the basis of this distinction, the main question of this section is: How should we semantically analyse the previously mentioned diverse class of description-names? Here is my proposal to account for all the presented data so far. For the class of description-names with a minimal complex semantics like 'The Thames' I propose the following analysis: 'The Thames' is semantically equivalent to 'The actual bearer of "Thames"' and the capital letters with respect to the matrix-expressions of such descriptions syntactically indicate that (a) a metalinguistic interpretation of 'Thames' is mandatory in this case and (b) the extension of this expression is fixed by an actual naming-convention. This actual name-convention holds that the expression 'Thames', by pure stipulative force, applies to a specific river, which enables one to refer to this river by means of expressions like 'The Thames' or 'The actual bearer of "Thames"' to this object. This view is a *rigidified* version of a metalinguistic description theory that is also briefly suggested in Rabern (2015). For the trickier sub-class of description-names I also have an extension of this analysis: apparently more semantically complex descriptions like 'The Manhattan Bridge' are according to my analysis semantically equivalent to a description of the form 'The actual bearer of "The Manhattan Bridge" that is actually conventionally called "Bridge"'. For this purpose, I distinguish between two different metalinguistic relations.

The first relation of name-bearing is a relation that is established by an explicit or implicit act of naming. The second relation is a relation that is derived from the habit that there is a name-convention that assigns to bridges a name that contains the capitalized expression 'Bridge' to indicate in a more indirect sense than by explicitly using the predicate 'bridge' that the bearer of this name is a bridge. If such a convention or habit is in force, the relation 'x is conventionally called y' can hold between an object and an expression. But this relation is different and weaker than a genuine proper name convention that is constituted by a name-using practice that typically has a naming act as origin. Can we explain on this basis the difference between 'The Morning Star' and 'The Manhattan Bridge'? Isn't there also such a name-convention in force as in the case of names for bridges and in the case of stars? I think not. In my opinion, such a convention is not in force anymore if there are counter-examples like 'The Morning Star' and 'The Evening Star'. These are names that are still in use and can be used to refer to the planet Venus. However, as we all know, Venus is a planet and not a star. But, in my opinion, there are no such prominent exceptions with respect to names of the general form 'The N Bridge', hence it seems to me that in this case the name-convention to refer only by expressions of the form 'The N Bridge' to bridges and to nothing else seems to be still in force. But maybe future investigations show that this sub-class pointed out by Rabern is not as stable as one might think at first sight and maybe it is a more contextual matter. Then we could maybe tell a similar adapted story and use another actualized conventional metalinguistic relation for this purpose. Therefore I think my toy example of a more elaborated version of the rigidified metalinguistic description theory gives us at least a recipe for how we can deal with such exceptional cases.

Surely, one might think that the whole story about description-names is still not told on this basis, because there are other examples of complex names that are not overtly definite descriptions like 'Salt Lake City', 'Montague Street', 'Lake Michigan' and 'Mount Everest'. However, there are interesting differences between these apparently descriptive names and our previously discussed description-names. Firstly, these names cannot be modified as the presented description-names. Secondly, there are no similar anaphoric effects with respect to the apparent descriptive names like 'Salt Lake City' and 'Montague Street' in a similar fashion as in the case of our previously discussed description-names. Thirdly, there is again the phenomenon of elliptical uses with respect to these names as the following example shows:

(40)  Montague and Remsen Street are close to each other.

But as I already have tried to point out in connection with description-names, this shows nothing with respect to the semantic complexity of a term, it only shows that syntactically such ellipsis is always possible with respect to any syntactically complex expression. Fourthly, these expressions do not have an overt definite article and there are no indications that such an article is implicitly present.

Therefore, on this basis I conclude that these new examples are not examples of description-names in the described sense; they are, from a semantic point of view, paradigm semantically atomic names, although they are syntactically complex. However, on the basis of our conception of name-conventions we can provide an explanation why one might think that these names are descriptive. There is name-convention in English to name streets in such a way that indicators like 'Street', 'Avenue', 'Road', 'Way' etc. are included into these names that convey to speakers the information that the specific name is a name for a street, road or something of this kind. But these *indirect* indicators do not contribute to the truth-conditional content of a sentence. From a truth-conditional point of view these expressions provide a non-descriptive contribution. Therefore, I think, it is misleading to claim that there is some descriptive content in play in such cases.[59]

## The two main methodological errors of most philosophical views on names

The first thing I aim to do in this section is to clarify my overall methodology that I have used in this book. In my opinion, this is a crucial issue, which is very often not explicitly considered with enough care. Some semantics with respect to proper names rest on very problematic and questionable methodologies. One can find at least two different kinds of pseudo-scientific methodology in the relevant literature.

The first error consists in a too heavy use of a central scientific norm, namely the norm of *uniformity*. If we have certain phenomena under our focus that are determined by natural laws, it probably makes sense to apply this norm to gain knowledge by means of inductive generalizations. However, it is not clear whether it makes sense to apply this norm of uniformity if one aims to capture all possible uses of proper names and, hence, aims to provide a semantics of *ordinary* proper names. Certainly, there is also uniformity with respect to the overall use and semantics of proper names. However, one should not press the norm of uniformity in this respect too hard as certain accounts do. Therefore, I think an account like the predicate view on proper names makes a significant methodological error if it aims to unify predicative and referential uses of proper names semantically. Natural languages have very productive mechanisms that allow one to change (a) the category and (b) the meaning of an expression.[60] Such derivations follow certain regular patterns and hence an illusion of uniformity may be created. We will focus on such phenomena in more detail in chapters 3, 5 and 6.

The predicative view on proper names also makes a second methodological error that it also shares with other views. A view that makes this error focuses on a specific class of uses of names for which the chosen analysis can easily account for and generalizes from this chosen class to all possible cases. If the chosen class contains paradigm uses of names, if the analysis smoothly applies to all paradigm uses, if the account gives a very good explanation of these paradigm uses and can possibly also extend to non-paradigm uses, then this procedure exemplifies a perfectly adequate methodology. However, several views on names apply this prima facie plausible methodology in an incorrect way to proper names.

Firstly, they focus on uses of proper names that are clearly not paradigm uses of proper names. The paradigm uses of proper names are referential uses, relative to which names are used to pick out a single object that is attached to this name in a conventionalized way. The *predicate view* focuses on predicative uses of proper names and aims to generalize its analysis of these uses to other paradigm uses of proper names as the referential use. However, predicative uses of a proper name are certainly not paradigm uses of a name. Furthermore, it is not clear at all whether they are literally uses of names or whether the uses of these apparent name-like expressions are somehow derivative and derived uses of proper names. The predicative view can easily account for apparent predicative uses of names, but it is unclear whether this simple analysis for predicative uses can be carried over to the paradigm uses of proper names.[61] Additionally, the predicative view faces the problem that its analysis cannot be easily carried over to all apparent predicative uses of proper names. Hence, the predicative view on names makes a second important methodological error. It completely misapplies a plausible methodology to the case of the semantics of proper names.

A second less obvious misapplication is made, in my opinion, by defenders of *the variabilist view*. Although it also makes a similar methodological error, it fares better than the predicate view from a methodological point of view. Let me show why. The variabilist view mainly focuses on two classes of uses of names: referential and apparent anaphoric uses. It observes that variables in standard Tarskian model-theoretic semantics seem to have similar uses as proper names in ordinary languages. Variables in the mentioned formal setting have unbound and bound uses. Relative to their unbound use they have the very same semantics as individual constants, they designate single objects. However, there is an important difference. Individual constants (at least in free logic) may lack a denotation, but individual variables cannot, because that would in spirit undermine their second function for which only defined assignments are required. This second function is their function as bound variables.

Certain operators, namely quantifiers, can manipulate the assignment-parameter with respect to variables in their syntactic scope. That is, quantifiers require the access to all assignments of variables in the scope that are possible with respect to a given domain. Defenders of the variabilist view on names think that there is a striking analogy between variables and their bound and related unbound uses, on the one hand, and names, and their referential and apparently bound uses, on the other hand. At first sight, the analogy might seem striking, but closer inspection shows that something is deeply wrong with this analogy. Firstly, with respect to variables, bound uses are their primary use. Variables were introduced by Frege and Tarski as formal tools into semantics to explain on this basis the peculiar semantics of quantifier expressions. Hence, without the existence of quantifiers and their Frege–Tarski treatment there would not be any variables in formal semantics. That does not only show that bound uses are the primary uses of variables, but also that there would not be any uses of variables in semantics at all if there were no bound uses. Furthermore, the existence of *unbound* uses of variables in Tarskian semantics is only an architectural by-product of the standard version of model-theoretic semantics. In Fregean semantics, there are not any unbound variables. Hence, another difference is that the referential uses of variables only exist by accident in Tarskian semantics. With respect to proper names the situation is the opposite. Referential uses are the *primary* uses of proper names. They are not a purely technical by-product, but a distinctive tool of ordinary language communication. Anaphoric uses of proper names seem to be, on the other hand, a rather special addition. It is not clear whether they are genuine uses of proper names and they are quite rare and marked.

Which brings us to a second important disanalogy. Bound uses of variables are the *raison d'être* of variables and it is, therefore, not only the case that such uses are the dominant uses, but it is also the case that such a use is extremely easy to achieve; one just has to use a variable together with arbitrary predicates to form an open sentence and bind this variable by one of several possible quantifier expressions. It is as easy as that and there are abundant possibilities to formulate sentences that contain bound variables. Hence, bound uses of variables are not only the dominant uses of variables, but also there is a straightforward and universal standard procedure to create such uses, and there are a large number of sentences with different syntactic forms that may contain such bound uses. The situation with respect to names and their apparent anaphoric or bound uses is completely different. These uses are not only very rare, they are also very limited in form. That is, there are only a very few syntactic constructions relative to which an apparent anaphoric use of a name seems to be possible.[62] Therefore, the situation between variables and names with respect to the distributional aspect is also very different.

Thirdly, there seems to be another important difference between names and variables. Proper names seem to have non-referring referential uses. An ordinary name that purports to refer to a single object can fail to refer to an object systematically or accidentally. We have already seen that unbound use of a variable is only an architectural by-product of the basic formal mechanisms of Tarskian semantics. A successful referential interpretation of unbound variables is required by the standard semantics of objectual quantifiers. Therefore, non-referring variables are a conceptual no-go in Tarskian semantics. Certainly, one could allow empty assignments for variables. But then it would be necessary to exclude these empty assignments with respect to the determination of truth-conditions for quantified sentences. Hence, these empty assignments would be a conceptually completely unnecessary addition. With respect to proper names, non-referential uses seem to be a conceptually possible option and consequence of our ordinary use of proper names. Hence, we also have an important functional difference with respect to this topic.

Fourthly, there is another important aspect that distinguishes names and variables. It seems to be part of the nature of ordinary names that names with the same syntactic form can be used to refer to different objects. Certainly, one and the same variable can designate different objects with respect to different assignments. But that is a different case. It at least seems to be the case that the same syntactic form of an ordinary proper name can have two different equally legitimate semantic referents that are at the same time in force. Such an option is not available with respect to variables in formal language. It would undermine the basic idea behind a formal semantics that aims to provide non-ambiguous semantic representations and it would also unnecessarily complicate the role of variables with respect to their primary function as bound variables and their semantic role relative to quantified sentences. Certainly, there are ways to overcome this difficulty: one option would be to claim that appearances are deceptive and there are at first sight in fact different indistinguishable forms in play with respect to ordinary names. On this basis, one could also extend a usual indexing strategy with respect to variables to the case of ordinary names. It is certainly a theoretical option, but it also has a sense of *ad-hoc*-ness because ordinary speakers do not seem to be aware of this syntactic ambiguity and do not treat names in such a way. But maybe the error is on the side of the users. However, on this basis it seems to be a mystery as to how people can nevertheless use the correct name to refer to the correct semantic referents if they are completely unaware of the fact that there are different apparently same-spelled names.

Another option is to add an additional context-parameter with respect to the semantic interpretation of unbound variables. Hence, variables always have a single referent relative to a single context- and assignment-pair, but they might have different referents relative to different contexts of use. One problem with this strategy is that quantified sentences on this basis become context-sensitive, although for them such a context-parameter seems to be in principle irrelevant. However, one has to fix the context-parameter of a variable with respect to a specific context of use such that a possible shifted assignment can deliver the desired infinitely many different values. This shows that such a solution to the problem of shared names is also not without unwelcome consequences with respect to the primary use of variables.

These observations, I think, show that variabilists also make a very similar methodological error as predicativists, but with the important difference that in their case this error is less obvious because their approach, at least on the surface, seems to capture not only accidental but also paradigm uses of proper names. But a closer look shows that also variabilists put the cart before the horse in this respect.[63]

## My alternative linguistically inspired Wittgensteinian methodology

By reviewing the mentioned thirteen challenges we have already seen how variable and multifaceted the overall use of proper names in natural languages is. In my opinion, it is impossible to capture this overall use on the basis of a single and simple semantic representation of names. I think it is more plausible to assume that, in an important number of cases, specific familiar and also not so familiar transformation-, coercion- or modifying mechanisms of syntactic, semantic or pragmatic nature are in play, which are already more familiar from certain other kinds of expressions than proper names like adjectives, verbs and common nouns in natural languages. Therefore, I will only propose a uniform semantics for the *paradigm* referential uses of paradigm proper names, and I will consider all other apparent additional uses of proper names as derivative and derived uses that may rely on different semantic representations other than the primary use. Nevertheless I will try to show that there are, on the basis of the mentioned transformation mechanism, explicit systematic connections between the primary use and the derived uses of 'proper names'. In some cases I will argue that the mentioned transformation leads to a *polysemy* with respect to proper names. In other cases, the contributions to truth-conditions of proper names are converted in kind either in a lexicalized systematic or in an occurrent pragmatic way. That is, relative to specific derived and alternative uses 'proper names' have a different semantic contribution to the truth-conditions of a sentence than with respect to their paradigm referential use.

This general pluralistic and use-sensitive approach towards the semantics and pragmatics of proper names is funded on three pillars: (a) On ample linguistic evidence that such contextual or lexicalized transformation and re-interpretation mechanism can be found in natural languages all over the place and are a key feature for the productive wealth of the expressive resources of natural languages. (b) On the rejection of the two mentioned methodological errors based on too simple-minded and idealized approaches towards the explanation of the overall use of proper names. (c) An alternative *Wittgensteinian methodology* with respect to natural language semantics that is (i) sensitive to important and subtle differences in the overall use of an expression, (ii) against a philosophical tendency of over-generalization and (iii) driven by an awareness for the creative and transformative power of natural languages.

I think I have already clarified the first two pillars in sufficient detail here. The first pillar will be filled with much more details and examples during the whole course of our investigations. But let me here briefly clarify some important aspects of the third pillar. One thing is important in this respect: in this book, I do not buy into a general Wittgensteinian methodology with respect to *philosophy*. I think it is wrong to think as Wittgensteinians do that all philosophical problems rest upon certain confusions about the overall use of specific philosophically interesting expressions. In *some* cases such a diagnosis might be true. However, the Wittgensteinian over-generalizes an original source of problems. In general it is so that a detailed and profound overview of our ordinary overall usage of certain philosophically interpreting expressions gives a good starting base for our philosophical investigations. But followers of this view cannot really provide any good reason why our meaningful philosophical enterprises are exhausted by a completely descriptive analysis of our ordinary use of philosophically interesting expressions. I think, good philosophy must and can have a non-descriptive revisionary dimension. On the other hand, I think Wittgenstein made very interesting and important observations with respect to the structure and nature of natural languages, namely that they are highly complex and sometimes wildly compiled and one must be very careful with respect to the interpretation of the overall use of certain expressions. If one brings (a) this carefulness for differences and details, (b) a caution with respect to simple and tempting over-generalizations together with (c) a detailed survey of data provided by our overall use of languages based on observations and methods provided by linguistics concerning the creative potential of natural languages, then one is at least methodologically on the right track. But surely, as we have seen on the basis of our overview of thirteen challenges with respect to the semantics and pragmatics of names, there are many pitfalls and very tricky issues that have to be solved and sorted out, and there is still no guarantee that one does not get lost in the vagaries of our ordinary usage of proper names. In any case, the most important thing to avoid as many pitfalls as possible is that one constantly reminds oneself about the mentioned guidelines provided by a Wittgensteinian methodology to the analysis of natural languages.

## A brief overview of the main theses of my account on names

In my opinion, this clarification of my methodology will help people to understand in a better way why I will defend such a diverse spectrum of views in the following chapters and on which ground these different views are connected with each other. I will try to give now a brief overview of the main components of my *use-sensitive* philosophical account on names. Interestingly, one can use the expression 'use-sensitive' in two different ways to characterize my views and project: in a more wide sense, to characterize my outlined methodology and in a more narrow sense, to characterize and label my specific semantic analysis of paradigm referential uses of paradigm proper names like 'London', 'Austria' or 'Peter'. In this sense, the central main aim of this book is twofold and has the goal to propagate the correctness of these two related *use-sensitive* approaches.

With respect to the semantics of paradigm referential uses of paradigm proper names, I will defend a new alternative both to any paradigm version of Millianism *and* any version of the description theory of names. This alternative view not only rejects *Strong* and *Weak Millianism* or any assimilation of the semantics of proper names with that of definite descriptions, it also rejects any sort of assimilation of the semantics of proper names with that of any other kind of singular term whatsoever. According to this view, proper names are a genuine class of singular terms with their very own specific semantic features. Nevertheless, proper names have *close* semantic relatives. According to my view, complex demonstratives like 'that man' and simple demonstratives like 'that' are the closest semantic relatives of proper names. Although they share some important semantic features with proper names, there are also significant semantic differences between names and their closest semantic relatives. I will now lay out the main thesis of my view defended in different chapters of this book.

The works of Saul A. Kripke on names have such an important and influential status in the current debate on proper names that every serious analysis of names must have a clear view on its relations to Kripke's views on this issue. The first two chapters of this book are mainly, but not exclusively, concerned with the two (in my opinion) main theses of Kripke with respect to proper names. The first one is the thesis that *proper names are rigid designators*. I agree with Kripke that names are in a certain sense rigid designators and in chapter 1 I will provide an overview of several different possible notions of rigidity. I will assess and adapt Kripke's arguments for the rigidity of names, distinguish four different main accounts towards the rigidity of proper names and show in the remaining book why I prefer the following conception of rigidity with respect to proper names:

(T1)  Proper names are in the following sense rigid expressions. If they actually refer, they refer rigidly to the same object in the actual domain with respect to all possible worlds. If they actually do not refer, they are rigidly without a denotation with respect to all possible worlds.

The second, less precise and more general thesis of Kripke is the topic of my second chapter. Kripke famously argued and proposed the view that the referent of a proper name is not determined by its semantic content or linguistic meaning, but by a meta-semantic process that originates in an initial introduction of a name into use and takes the whole process of the distribution of a name among its users into account.

In chapter 2 I will be concerned with Kripke's famous meta-semantic picture concerning the determination of the semantic referent of a proper name. Kripke proposed the view that the semantic referent of a name is determined by a specific causally connected chain of uses of this name that leads back to an initial stipulative act that connected this name with a certain bearer. Kripke himself only provides a rough outline of this approach, and wisely so, because it is a very tricky issue to develop it in detail. For the purpose of my investigations into this subject, I have, therefore, chosen a more developed version of Kripke's approach that also extends this approach to the use of defective empty names as starting point, namely the approach of Mark Sainsbury. The main reason for this choice is that Sainsbury on the one hand systematizes and develops Kripke's view in a very clear and straightforward way and, on the other hand, he extends it in an interesting way to empty proper names. I will try to show that this suggestive development of Kripke's view is too simplistic. As a result of my critique, I will develop an alternative conception of the determination of the semantic referent of a proper name. My positive view on this issue is based on the following main theses:

(T2)  The semantic referent of a proper name relative to a use of this name is identical with the speaker's referent of this use that satisfies the additional constraining condition that (a) it is a bearer of this name and (b) the user of this name was properly introduced into an already existing name-using practice or has successfully established such a practice.

(T3)  An object is a bearer of a name N iff this object is the constant speaker's referent of an established and connected series of referential uses of N of a specific consistent branch of such a practice with respect to N.

In chapter 3, I develop a use-sensitive formal semantics of proper names. According to this view, proper names are evaluated relative to their uses. Single uses of a name are individuated in a more fine-grained way than contexts of use of an expression. In this sense, proper names can be clearly distinguished from automatic context-sensitive expressions like the indexicals 'I' or 'today', whose referent is determined automatically relative to a context of use. The referent of a *use* of a proper name is determined by specific referential attitudes or intentions of the user. It is in principle possible that each different use of a name has a different referent. Uses of names can either be individuated in an extensional way, that is on the basis of the sameness of their referent or referential status or in a non-extensional way, that is on the basis of the sameness of the accompanying referential intention. According to my view, proper names also have linguistic meanings. The linguistic meaning of the name 'Peter' is the condition of being the bearer of the name 'Peter'. This condition does not determine the referent of a proper name, but it only *constrains* it. That is, the semantic referent of a proper name relative to the use of a name is the speaker's referent of the use of this name that additionally satisfies the semantic constraining condition. The core assumptions of this view can thus be summarized as follows:

(T4)   Proper names are use-sensitive expressions that only have *semantic* referents relative to individual uses of such a name by a competent user.

(T5)   Individual uses of proper names are either individuated by the sameness of speaker's referents or by the sameness of the accompanying referential intentions or attitudes.

(T6)   Proper names have a non-truth-conditional linguistic meaning that constrains the semantic referent of a proper name.

Chapter 4 is mainly concerned with *fictional uses* of proper names, but also with defective names and the semantic behaviour of proper names in existential sentences. I will distinguish three different kinds of fictional uses of proper names. Firstly, there are fictional uses of proper names in acts of story-telling, relative to which a name is used in genuine and very special kinds of speech acts. In my opinion, acts of story-telling considered as acts that are performed by the creator of a story have two different illocutionary forces: the force of stipulating that something is the case with respect to a specific fictional world; and the force of inviting people to assume that this stipulated fact is the case with respect to this fictional world. It is certainly the case that not every illocutionary act that is performed by a story-teller during the process of the creation of a story is an act of story-telling. However, an essential amount of these acts are acts of story-telling in the outlined sense It is a peculiar feature of fictional uses of proper names that their *originating* uses are uses in acts of story-telling. Subsequent uses can be uses in acts of re-telling a story. Secondly, an act of re-telling a story has a different illocutionary force. In such acts a speaker makes relativized assertions that concern states of affairs with respect to fictional worlds only. Thirdly, there are other subsequent fictional uses of proper names in ordinary acts of assertions in the scope of specific hyper-intensional expressions like fictional modifiers or intensional transitive verbs. Relative to such fictional uses, the semantic referents of names are shifted to objects that exist in fictional worlds. In general, fictional uses of proper names are derived uses of ordinary proper names. In this sense, ordinary proper names are polysemous referential devices. The central assumptions of chapter 4 in this respect are:

(T7) Proper names have derived fictional uses relative to which (a) an arbitrary referent is stipulated with respect to a fictional world that is represented by a story, (b) these names lack an actual semantic referent or (c) have a shifted reference towards a single object relative to an accessible fictional world. Most fictional uses of proper names are strictly deferential.

(T8) Beside fictional uses of proper names there are also defective uses of proper names relative to which names lack a semantic referent due to an error in use or with respect to the introduction of this name into discourse.

In chapter 5 I will develop the view that apart from their primary use as proper names, nouns like 'Alfred' or 'London' also have different secondary predicative uses that are derived from their primary use by different pragmatic mechanisms. I will also try to show why such a polysemy view concerning proper nouns should be preferred to a predicate view on proper names. In the relevant chapters about predicative uses of proper names I defend the following three main theses:

(T9) The name-predicate 'is an Alfred' is according to its primary meaning semantically equivalent to 'is a bearer of the name "Alfred"'.

(T10) The primary truth-conditional meaning of 'is an Alfred' is derived by a specific mechanism of meaning transfer from the non-truth-conditional linguistic meaning of the name 'Alfred'.

(T11) Name-predicates like 'is an Alfred' themselves can have several different derived meanings relative to which this expression is non-equivalent to its primary meaning.

The sixth chapter of this book will be concerned with anaphoric uses of proper names. I will distinguish five different classes of apparently anaphoric uses of proper names and I will argue that in only one of these cases do we have a purely pragmatic anaphoric use of a proper name, but no anaphorically bound use. With respect to all other uses I will argue that proper names are not *literally* used as anaphoric or bound expressions. More precisely, I will defend the following main thesis in the chapter:

(T12) All apparently bound uses of proper names are marked and derived meta-linguistic uses of proper names relative to which they function as disguised complex demonstratives, definite or indefinite descriptions with name-predicates.

In the last chapter, I will be concerned with the semantic interactions between attitude verbs or epistemic modals and proper names. I will argue against the orthodox view on attitude ascriptions that interprets attitude verbs as expressions of first-order relations between cognitive subjects and propositions. My alternative view is based on the following two main theses:

(T13) Attitude verbs and epistemic modals are formally represented by non-normal modal operators (predicates) that have access to normal or non-normal worlds that represent the satisfaction conditions of cognitive attitudes of individual subjects.

(T14) Attitude verbs and epistemic modals can shift the referents of proper names that are used inside their scope to objects in non-normal worlds that can either be incomplete, inconsistent or both.

This completes my brief overview of the main theses that are defended in the following chapters of this book.

# 1

# Proper Names and Rigidity[1]

In this chapter I will show that typical formal semantic representations of the rigidity of proper names neglect an essential aspect of the rigidity of *ordinary* names, namely that their rigidity is determined by our ordinary use of a name relative to *the actual world*. This fact was already clearly pointed out by Kripke but ignored by the subsequent formal discussion of this topic. Firstly, I will introduce on this basis two different new varieties of known versions of rigidity; namely, *actualized persistent* and *actualized obstinate* rigidity. Secondly, I will introduce two new and overlooked versions of rigidity, which I will call *actualized restricted* rigidity and *actualized accessible* rigidity. Against this background, I will argue that we have different options to formally model the rigidity of proper names in natural languages. Which option we choose mainly depends on our philosophical background assumptions, as I will show. This chapter also contains a modified version of Kripke's test for the rigidity of proper names.

## Setting the stage: Kripke and his followers on different notions of rigidity

Kripke famously introduced the notion of a *rigid designator* in his essay 'Identity and Necessity' and in the second of a series of lectures published under the title *Naming and Necessity* in the following way:

> What do I mean by 'rigid designator'? I mean a term that designates the same object in all possible worlds.[2]
>
> Let's call something a *rigid designator* if in every possible world it designates the same object, a *nonrigid* or *accidental designator* if that is not the case.[3]

Different interpretations of what exactly is meant by an expression that designates *the same object in every possible world* seem to be possible. Firstly, we will clarify what it means that an expression designates something *in a possible world*. Secondly, we will clarify what exactly Kripke means by *all* possible worlds. As we will see, an unrestricted understanding of this generalization requires certain background assumptions, and given these assumptions, there are also different options on how to spell out the details.

Prima facie there are different explanatory roles that *possible worlds* can play in the formal framework of (possible) world semantics. In connection with the topic of rigidity, possible worlds are mainly conceived of as semantic *points of evaluation* that are sensitive to modal or temporal operators and can be shifted by these operators. Hence, in the quoted passages, Kripke *implicitly* makes use of the conceptual resources of his famous model-theoretic possible world semantics for modal logic.

According to this semantics, every formula is evaluated relative to a possible world and, hence, every formula has truth-values relative to possible worlds. This world-relative evaluation of formulas is based on a world-relative *interpretation function* that assigns world-relative extensions to predicates and individual constants. Furthermore, it can also be based on a world-relative *denotation function* that unifies the semantics of singular terms. Hence, every singular term receives a denotation relative to a possible world. Against this background, we can now first try to formulate Kripke's thesis concerning the rigidity of certain referring expressions in a more precise way if we conceive of 'Den (...,...)' as an expression for the world-relative denotation function:

(RID)   $\varphi$ is a rigid designator iff for every possible world w and w*: Den($\varphi$, w) = Den($\varphi$, w*).

It is not clear whether Kripke himself endorses a conception of rigidity for referring terms that accepts (RID) in its full generality. Which kinds of restriction of (RID) are possible and meaningful? Why should one restrict (RID) at all? What are the background assumptions that are required to accept (RID) in its full generality?

## Obstinate and persistent rigidity

The world-relative interpretation function of model-theoretic possible world semantics presupposes the existence of a so-called *domain of discourse*. Such a domain of discourse basically has two different functions. Firstly, the domain of discourse specifies the possible range of the (first-order) quantifiers. Secondly, it determines the range of possible values of the interpretation or denotation function. There are two fundamentally different conceptions regarding the relations between the domain of discourse, on the one hand, and quantifiers and the interpretation function, on the other hand: a so-called *constant domain* conception and a *variable domain* conception. According to the first conception, there is a single constant domain that determines the range of the quantifiers and the interpretation function relative to all possible worlds.[4] According to the second conception, domains of discourse are also relativized to possible worlds. Hence, there is a *domain function* that assigns exactly one domain of discourse to each possible world. On this basis, quantifiers and the interpretation or denotation function are bound to world-relative domains.[5]

If we introduce a world-relative denotation function to unify the semantics of singular terms and to allow the formulation of a thesis like (RID) as we did, we also have the option either to use a single constant domain of discourse as a possible range of values for this function or to use world-relative variable possible ranges of values. Hence, we can distinguish a constant domain and a variable domain interpretation of the denotation function. Before we focus on the details and possible variants of both interpretations, let us see whether there are clear indications of which of these different possibilities are contained in Kripke's work.

## Proper Names and Rigidity

Kripke seems to endorse different views on this issue in 'Identity and Necessity' and in *Naming and Necessity*. In the first work, he makes the following remarks concerning the details of his conception of rigidity:

> [I]n talking about the notion of a rigid designator, I do not mean to imply that the object referred to has to exist in all possible worlds, that is, that it has to necessarily exist. [...]
>
> All I mean is that in any possible world where the object in question does exist, in any situation where the object would exist, we use the designator in question to designate that object. In a situation where the object does not exist, then we should say that the designator has no referent and that the object in question so designated does not exist.[6]

This quote shows that another important issue for a correct understanding of the notion of a rigid designator is the exact nature of the relation between the extension of the *existence predicate* and the single constant or different variable domains of reference respectively.

Against the background of a constant domain semantics, there seem to be two possible options to determine this relation. Firstly, one might conceive of the existence predicate as a predicate with a constant extension relative to all possible worlds, which is identical to the single domain of discourse. Let us call this view the *necessity variant* of the constant domain view. Secondly, one might conceive of the existence predicate as a world-relative predicate and identify the extension of the existence predicate with different subsets of our single domain of discourse. Let us call this view the *contingency variant* of the constant domain view.

According to the first view, existence is a first-order non-discriminating property. A prima facie implausible consequence of this view is that every object exists according to this view relative to every possible world and hence every object is a necessarily existing object.[7] According to the second view, existence is a first-order discriminating property. This view can account for the intuitive possibility that there are things that exist only contingently.[8]

Against the background of a variable domain semantics, there only seems to be one prima facie plausible view concerning the relation between the extension of the existence predicate and the domain of discourse. This view holds that the extension of the world-relative existence predicate is identical with the respective world-relative domain of discourse. In this sense, the third view can be seen as a compromise between the other two views. According to this view, existence is a first-order non-discriminating property, but it can also account for the distinction between necessarily and contingently existing objects.

Which of these three views does Kripke presuppose in the quote mentioned above? The answer very much depends on how we interpret the following last part of the quote: 'we should say that the designator has no referent and that the object in question so designated does not exist'. Superficially, this claim sounds contradictory, because Kripke speaks *both* about a term without a referent and about an object that is designated by this very term and that does not exist. Here we must be careful; there is a *consistent* interpretation of Kripke's claim. According to the third conception of existence, referential terms can designate an object relative to some worlds, but designate nothing with respect to other worlds. Hence, if we designate an object o relative to a world w with the term t and if this object does not exist relative to world w*, then the term t has no referent relative to w*. I think that this is what Kripke wanted to say. On this basis, it is plausible to assume that Kripke presupposes our third conception of existence relative to the mentioned quote.

If we presuppose such a framework, (RID) cannot generally be accepted in an *unrestricted way* because there are worlds relative to which 'Den' does not assign an object to certain referring terms. Therefore, when we assume our third conception of existence and a variable domain semantics, we have to restrict (RID) to be able to apply the notion of a rigid designator to a referring term that refers to a *contingent* object; an object that does not exist in every possible world.

According to a very natural interpretation of the quoted passage, it proposes the following restriction of (RID): A singular term is a restricted rigid designator iff it designates the same object relative to every possible world *with respect to which this object exists, and it refers to nothing else with respect to those worlds where this object does not exist.*

Nowadays people refer to this notion of rigidity by means of the label 'persistent rigidity'[9] or sometimes also by 'moderate rigidity'.[10] It requires certain adaptions to implement this restriction into (RID). Firstly, we must adapt *Den* to a variable domain semantics framework and conceive of this function as a partial function that may assign nothing to some expressions. Secondly, we have to make use of a particular quantifier in our metalanguage that quantifies over the union of all world-relative domains D*. With these adaptions, we can formulate a variable domain-friendly notion of rigidity in the following way:

(RID*)    φ is a persistent rigid designator iff at least one object x and possible world w is such that (x=Den(φ, w)) and for every possible world w* relative to which x exists: Den(φ, w*)=x, and for every possible world w** relative to which x does not exist: there is no y such that Den(φ, w)=y).

It at least *seems* to be the case that Kripke does not anymore endorse this conception of rigidity in *Naming and Necessity*. What he explicitly says there sounds more as if he would favour the obstinate notion of rigidity, which consists of an unrestricted acceptance of (RID).[11] The following statements by Kripke seem to provide evidence in this respect:

> I say that a proper name rigidly designates its referent even when we speak of counterfactual situations where that referent would not have existed.[12]

> I also don't mean to imply that the thing designated exists in all possible worlds, just that the name refers rigidly to that thing. If you say 'suppose Hitler had never been born' then 'Hitler' refers here, still rigidly, to something that would not exist in the counterfactual situation described.[13]

In informal terms, the difference between *persistent* and *obstinate* rigidity is often marked by the following intuitive characterization of the latter notion that marks the important intuitive contrast between both notions: A singular term is an obstinately rigid designator iff it designates the same object relative to every possible world *irrespective of whether this object exists in a world or not*. Kaplan and Salmon are the most prominent defenders of the notion of *obstinate rigidity*.[14]

Whether my interpretation of Kripke (2011 and 1980) is correct or not,[15] the extracted distinction between *persistent* and *obstinate* rigidity is an important and nowadays widely accepted distinction and we will investigate these two notions in more detail in the main sections of this chapter.

## Weak and bare rigidity

Let us now introduce an additional variety of rigidity that is sometimes confused with persistent rigidity. This notion, which might be called *weak rigidity*,[16] can be characterized as follows: *A singular term is a weakly rigid designator iff it designates the same object relative to every possible world relative to which it designates anything at all*. Hence, weak rigidity seems to be in *at least one respect* similar to persistent rigidity: it also allows that there are possible worlds relative to which a certain singular term does not refer to anything although the term is considered as a rigid designator. This similarity is probably the reason why some people have confused weak rigidity with persistent rigidity.[17] But the crucial difference between these two notions is the following: *only* a weakly rigid singular term can designate a specific object x in certain worlds A, while it does not designate any object in other possible worlds B, even though among these worlds B, there might be worlds where x exists. Therefore, these two notions are not necessarily equivalent. However, persistent rigidity implies weak rigidity. Additionally, there is an even weaker notion of rigidity that is implied by persistent *and* obstinate rigidity: *A singular term is a barely rigid designator iff it designates the same single object relative to every possible world relative to which this object exists*. In so far as the two stronger notions of rigidity (obstinate and persistent rigidity) imply one of the two distinguished weaker notions (bare rigidity), and one stronger notion (persistent rigidity) implies both weaker notions (bare and weak rigidity), we could also in principle introduce *genuine* weaker alternative notions of rigidity on this basis: *a <u>merely</u> bare or <u>merely</u> weak rigid term is a bare or weak rigid term that is in no stronger sense than the sense under discussion a rigid designator*. We will focus in more detail on important differences between *mere weak rigidity* and *persistent rigidity* in the third main section of this chapter.[18]

## *De jure* and *de facto* rigidity

In the famous foreword of *Naming and Necessity* (1980), Kripke not only defends the view that names are rigid designators, he also claims that they are *de jure* rigid, in opposition to *de facto* rigid designators. Kripke draws a

> [...] distinction between '*de jure*' rigidity, where the reference of a designator is *stipulated* to be a single object, whether we are speaking of the actual world or of a counterfactual situation, and mere '*de facto*' rigidity, where a description 'the x such

that 'Fx' happens to use a predicate 'F' that in each possible world is true of one and the same unique object (e.g., 'the smallest prime' rigidly designates the number two).[19]

Let me briefly elucidate this distinction. Are there any uncontroversial candidates for *de jure* rigid expressions? Individual constants relative to a one-dimensional possible world semantics for modal logic are *paradigm* expressions of this kind. The world-relative value of the denotation function for a specific individual constant is determined by the corresponding value of the interpretation function. Therefore, the denotation and rigidity of an individual constant is *stipulated* in the metalanguage.

In opposition to *de jure* rigid designators, the rigidity of a *de facto* rigid designator does not depend on a semantic stipulation in the metalanguage, but on (a) semantic facts of the expression in the object language or (b) metaphysical factors that determine the extension of certain complex expressions relative to all possible worlds. Hence, only complex singular terms can be *de facto* rigid expressions. As Kripke points out, certain rigid definite descriptions are paradigm examples of this sort. We may specify the world-relative denotation of a definite description of the form 'the x: Fx' in the following way:

Den('the x: Fx', w) = the single member of I('F', w).

With respect to a model that has an interpretation function that assigns the very same singleton to the predicate 'F' relative to every possible world, the definite description 'the x: Fx' is a rigid designator, namely a *de facto* rigid designator whose rigidity does not depend on a specific stipulation in the metalanguage, as in the case of individual constants, but on specific properties of the model.

What about definite descriptions like 'the actual F' that are rigidified by an actuality operator? Are these expressions *de jure* or *de facto* rigid designators? They are not in the same sense *de jure* designators as individual constants: their rigidity is not stipulated in the metalanguage. They are rigid because of the specific semantic nature of the actuality operator. In opposition to *metaphysical de facto* rigid designators, the rigidity of *semantical de facto* rigid designators does not exclusively depend on the nature of the models or some more or less arbitrary circumstances.[20, 21]

This completes my brief introduction of the three distinctions concerning the rigidity of referring expressions that summarize the most important findings of the debate on rigidity so far.

## Intuitive tests for the rigidity of proper names

From a purely formal semantic point of view, it is clear and easy to distinguish different notions of rigidity and to determine which formal representations fall under which category. Our task in this section is to determine whether these notions can be applied to names and whether there are any *intuitive tests* to determine whether names are rigid in some of the distinguished senses.

Kripke proposes two similar intuitive tests to determine whether a singular term is a rigid designator or not. According to Kripke, if we substitute in either of the following two schematic sentences a singular term for both occurrences of 'x', and the resulting sentence has only false readings, then the substituted singular term is a rigid designator:[22]

(1)  x might not have been x.
(2)  Someone other than x might have been x.

These two substitution-tests allow us, indeed, to draw certain distinctions concerning singular terms, but they also have their weaknesses and limitations. At first sight, it looks as if they clearly satisfy their task. For example, if we substitute 'the president of the United States of America' for 'x' in (1) and (2), the result for both schemata is a sentence that has a true *and* a false reading. That is, they have a true *wide scope* reading and a false *narrow scope* reading with respect to the first use of the substituted definite description. If we, on the other hand, substitute 'Saul Kripke' for 'x' in (1) and (2), the result is sentences that only have false readings. Given these results, there seems to be some significant differences between the two different examples of singular terms we used. But between which kind of rigid and which kind of non-rigid designator do they distinguish?

One question is whether there are more possible readings of these sentences in play than the desired two. Apart from the scope-ambiguity of 'might' that Kripke himself takes into account, there seem to be two more possible sources of ambiguity in (1) and (2). The first concerns the verb 'to be', the second the repeated use of a singular term. The verb 'to be' in (1) and (2) *can* have different possible meanings. For our purposes we are only interested in uses of the form 'to be N', where 'N' is either a proper name or a definite description. Many philosophers think that 'to be N' can mean the same as 'to be identical with N'. However, that is doubted by linguists and some philosophers. The 'be' in 'to be Kripke' is an expression of a monadic predication. Predications of the form '[copula] + [name]' are a very special sort of predication. What seems to be true, however, is that 'x is Kripke' implies 'x is identical with Kripke'. Nevertheless, it is not completely clear what distinguishes 'to be Kripke' and 'to be identical with Kripke' if 'to be Kripke' is used as an expression of a so-called haecceitas-property. But what makes things more difficult is that 'x is Kripke' can also have a meaning that does not imply 'x is identical with Kripke'. 'Benedict Cumberbatch is Sherlock Holmes' can be used in a way that it means the same as 'Benedict Cumberbatch is an actor that impersonates Sherlock Holmes'. The same holds for 'Benedict Cumberbatch is the famous fictional detective who lives in Baker Street'. Such readings are irrelevant for our test, but they must be excluded to get the test right and applicable to a large number of cases. Therefore, one simple reaction to the first ambiguity problem would be to explicitly substitute 'x might be x' with 'x might be identical with x'.

If we want, we can also get rid of *scope ambiguity* described above by substituting 'might' with the more complicated but also more explicit modal expression 'x is such that there is a possible situation relative to which' which seems to have an unambiguous semantics concerning scope issues. These two adaptions lead to the following new paraphrases of (1) and (2):

(1')  x is such that there is a possible situation relative to which he/she/it is not identical with x.

(2′)   x is such that there is a possible situation relative to which someone other than he/she/it is identical with x.

Let us now focus on the second mentioned ambiguity problem. This problem concerns the possibility that two occurrences of the very same singular term, whether they are names or descriptions, could in principle always have two different readings with two different referents. One cannot solve this problem by any sort of reformulation of a sentence like (1) or (2). We also cannot meaningfully solve this problem just by stipulating that both occurrences must have the same referent. On this basis we would undermine the whole test, whose outcome should be a difference in reference in one of the two compared cases. The best we can do is to stipulate that the expressions must be used twice in the same *context* and with the same *meaning*. That is a bit vague, but it is all that we can do to save the applicability of Kripke's text.

But if we keep this limitation in mind and aim to use the required singular terms twice in the same way with the same meaning, we can use the instances of both schemata as a more reliable and precise, but maybe less intuitive (because of the less colloquial nature of the formulations (1′) and (2′)) test for rigidity. An expression is rigid if the corresponding instance of (1′) or (2′) does not have an accessible true reading relative to the stipulated setting; otherwise, it is non-rigid.

Even on this more precise basis, our slightly modified *Kripkean test* also has its problems. Some people doubted that the notion that we have called *weak rigidity* should count as a variety of rigidity.[23] According to them, any adequate notion of rigidity must be either a sub-variety of one of the two notions considered by Kripke, namely persistent or obstinate rigidity, or at least not weaker than persistent rigidity. If we do not consider mere weak rigidity as a variant of rigidity, it would be more suitable to reserve a different label for this alternative notion, for example the notion of *inflexibility*. Why is such a dispute about the correct extension of the notion of rigidity relevant for the mentioned, intuitive tests for rigidity? If the notion of mere weak rigidity is not a genuine notion of rigidity, then Kripke's intuitive test is not an appropriate test to distinguish non-rigid from rigid expressions because it does not discriminate between merely weakly rigid and persistently or obstinately rigid expressions.

The following three expressions are examples of merely weakly rigid expressions: 'The father of Kripke', 'The bearer of "Kripke" that is identical with Kripke', 'The philosopher that is identical with Kripke'. With respect to every possible world, relative to which they refer at all, these expressions refer to the same thing. However, there are also possible worlds relative to which the referents of these expressions with respect to other worlds, e.g. the actual world, exist, but these expressions do not refer to them. With respect to the first example, these are worlds relative to which Kripke's father has no or other children. With respect to the second example, these are worlds relative to which Kripke is not a bearer of the name 'Kripke'; and in the third case, these are worlds relative to which Kripke is not a philosopher. Nevertheless, these expressions satisfy the outlined tests for the *rigidity* of singular terms. Given this result, at least two questions become pressing. Firstly, is it possible to modify Kripke's test in such a way that it also excludes merely weakly rigid designators and only classifies such expressions as rigid that are *at least* persistently rigid? The answer to this is relatively easy and straightforward. There certainly is a possibility to modify the test in the desired way. The following modified schema does the trick:[24]

(3)  x is such that there is a situation relative to which he/she/it exists without being identical with x.

This schema is suitable to distinguish expressions that are at least persistently rigid designators from any other expressions as (1') or (2'). That is, we need the same kind of stipulations concerning the instances of 'x' in (3) as we needed in the case of (1') and (2') to provide a *reliable test* for the desired purpose. However, if we substitute any merely weakly rigid designator for 'x' in (3) in the mentioned, stipulated sense, then the result is a true sentence, and hence these terms come out as not rigid in the desired stronger sense of rigidity. Our intuitive test concerning at least persistently rigid expressions can also be modified in such a way that we can distinguish persistently rigid from obstinately rigid expressions. An expression t is obstinately rigid iff there is no way to get a true reading of an instance of (3), but there is a way to get a true reading for the corresponding instance of the following schema if we substitute t for 'x':

(4)  x is such that there is a situation relative to which he/she/it is identical with x without existing.

An expression, on the other hand, is a persistently rigid designator iff true readings of instances of (3) and (4) in respect with t are intuitively impossible.

## The application of our (intuitive) test to two different kinds of names

If we now apply our three intuitive test-schemata in the way described above, we get an interesting mixed result. If we apply the test to ordinary *paradigm* proper names for existing objects, proper names seem to come out as *persistently* rigid designators. However, if we apply them, on the other hand, to paradigm names for non-existing objects, they seem to come out as *obstinately* rigid designators.

Let us show the first thing by applying our test to the name 'Kripke'. The substitution of this name into our three schemata has the following sentences as a result:

(1'K)  Kripke is such that there is a possible situation relative to which he is not identical with Kripke.
(3K)  Kripke is such that there is a situation relative to which he exists without being identical with Kripke.
(4K)  Kripke is such that there is a situation relative to which he is identical with Kripke without existing.

Intuitively, all of these three sentences only have false readings. (1'K) seems to show that the name 'Kripke' is not sensitive to a modal expression such as 'there is a possible situation relative to which...' in opposition to certain definite descriptions. Sentence (3K) shows that the name 'Kripke' even refers to the actual Kripke relative to a possible situation with respect to which this object does not bear the name 'Kripke'.

One might think that the intuitive falsity of (4K) shows that we intuitively hold that identity strictly implies existence. But appearances are deceptive. That seems only to be the case if the used name refers to an existing object. If we substitute 'Kripke' with 'Sherlock Holmes' (4S) or 'Sandy Island' (4I) this appearance vanishes. The resulting sentences (4S) and (4I) are intuitively true because the actual world itself verifies these sentences. Therefore, names for non-existing objects seem to come out as *obstinately* rigid expressions.

Another interesting question is what the outcome of our test is if we use description-names like 'The Morning Star' or 'The North Pole' as examples. The result is the very same as in the case of paradigm ordinary names like 'Kripke'. Interestingly, the situation also does not change if we use modified examples of description-names like 'The beautiful Morning Star' that contain perspectival evaluative modifiers. But it certainly changes if we substitute in (1') a modified paradigm name such as 'The poet Kripke' or modified description-names like 'The frozen North Pole' that contain non-perspectival objective modifying adjectives. Hence, our intuitive test seems to clearly show the following: ordinary paradigm names, names for non-existent objects and description-names clearly satisfy the test and should be considered as semantically rigid expressions. However, the question of whether we should treat some or all names as persistently or obstinately rigid expressions cannot be decided in a clear way on the basis of purely linguistic evidence. Additional philosophical and linguistic investigations and considerations are necessary to clarify this aspect in more detail.

## Possible reasons in favour of obstinate rigidity

In this section, we will now review three different philosophical arguments in favour of a general treatment of proper names as obstinately rigid expressions.

### Rigidity and negative existentials

Firstly, there is the argument from modal negative existentials and related claims that Kripke and Kaplan seem to endorse.[25] They draw our attention to the following two sentences:

(5)  Hitler might not have been born.
(6)  Hitler might not have existed.

Both sentences are intuitively true. Kripke and Kaplan seem to suggest that the best compositional semantics of sentences like (5) and (6), to account for their intuitive truth-value, assumes that 'Hitler' refers the same object as in the actual world with respect to a possible world in which Hitler neither exists nor was born there.

Why is a semantics of (5) and (6) that conceives of 'Hitler' as an obstinate rigid designator the best kind of semantics with respect to such claims like (5) or (6)? The truth-value of (6), according to a Kripke-style semantics, depends on the fact of whether or not the sentence 'Hitler does not exist' is true relative to some possible world.

However, there are two possible different accounts to provide truth-conditions for existential sentences with respect to possible worlds. Firstly, a negative existential sentence of the logical form '¬E!a' is true relative to a possible world w iff 'a' has no denotation relative to w. Secondly, a negative existential sentence of the form '¬E!a' is true relative to a possible world w iff the referent of 'a' relative to w is not an element of the extension of 'E!' with respect to w. The second option is the option proposed by Kripke and Kaplan. The first option is suggested by negative free logic and it is compatible with the view that names are persistently rigid designators.

Since a sentence like (5) intuitively entails (6), it is plausible to apply a similar strategy to (6). Negative free logic provides all the necessary resources to account for its intuitive truth-value. According to negative free logic, every atomic sentence of the form 'Fa' is false relative to a possible world w if 'a' does not have a denotation relative to w. Did Kaplan overlook this possibility in the mentioned quote, because he claims that '¬E!a' does not get a classical truth-value if 'a' has no referent? I am not sure. What Kaplan and Kripke could do is to press negative free logic on the issue of compositionality. Their analysis is fully compositional because every constituent expression of '¬E!a' contributes a semantic value to the determination of the truth-value of the whole sentence. That is not the case with respect to the free semantics if 'a' lacks a semantic referent relative to some possible word. But maybe existential sentences are an exception and do not have a fully compositional semantics. However, even if someone concedes that they have a fully compositional semantics, there are two alternative options that are not committed to an obstinately rigid treatment of proper names.

There is a third kind of semantics that treats atomic constants as expressions that rigidly refer to the very same object in the actual world. On this basis, a sentence of the form '¬E!a' is true relative to a possible world w iff the *actual* referent of 'a' is not an element of the extension of 'E!' with respect to w. Such a semantics provides fully compositional truth-conditions for sentences like (5) and (6) without a commitment to obstinate rigidity. There is even a fourth alternative that I have recently proposed. In Rami (2020), I suggested a distinction between the semantic value of a name and the semantic referent of a name to overcome the mentioned problem of compositionality. According to this view, the semantic values of individual constants are singletons that contain the semantic referent of a name or the empty set if these constants lack a referent. The semantically fixed extension of the existence predicate relative to a world w is the set of all singletons that contain only objects that are part of the domain of discourse relative to w. On this basis, we can provide the following fully compositional semantics for a sentence like (5): A sentence of the form '¬E!a' is true relative to a possible world w iff the semantic value of 'a' with respect to w is not an element of the extension of 'E!' with respect to w. Hence, I think that the issue of the correct semantics of singular existential sentences by itself does not provide any good reasons in favour of obstinate rigidity.[26]

## Rigidity and the necessary truth of identity sentences

Let us focus on another related issue that concerns the semantic status of true identity sentences of the logical form 'a=a'. It is widely accepted that the law of self-identity is a logical law, and therefore the following truth should be conceived as a logically necessary truth:

(7)   □∀x(x=x).

But if this generalization is a logically necessary truth, it is intuitively quite plausible to assume that the following instance of (7) is also a logically necessary truth:

(8)   It is necessary that Kripke is identical with Kripke.

For a defender of obstinate rigidity for proper names, it is quite easy to account for this special logical status of (7) and (8), but a defender of persistent rigidity does not have the resources to assign the same logical status to (7) and (8). A defender of the latter view has difficulties to account for the intuitive truth of (8).

It is certainly the case that we cannot account for the necessary truth of (8) on the basis of a standard semantics of (a) necessity and (b) identity, and (c) a persistent interpretation of the rigidity of proper names. However, there seem to be alternative semantics that lead to equal results as do the standard semantics based on an obstinate conception of rigidity of individual constants. One option would certainly be to fiddle around with different notions of necessity. One could postulate a weak notion of necessity: A formula φ is *weakly necessarily true* according to a S5 setting iff there is no possible world relative to which φ is false. If one then also assumes that 'a=a' is neither true nor false if 'a' does not refer, then one could account for the intuitive truth of (8).[27] However, this strategy pays a high prize: (a) it comes with a commitment to a three-valued neutral free logic, which is logically very weak; (b) it is committed to an *ad hoc* ambiguity of the notion of necessity; (c) it is not fully compositional; and (d) it seems to cheat because the explanation of the truth of (7) is on this basis still completely independent from the truth of (8).

But there are better alternative semantics. One could try to apply the two alternative strategies we know from the last section. Firstly, there is again the possibility to conceive the rigidity of 'a' in such a way that it refers constantly to an object in the actual world. Hence, 'a=a' is true iff the actual referent of 'a' is identical with the actual referent of 'a'. On this basis, we can easily explain the necessary truth of (8) and also the link between the truth of (7) and (8). Secondly, it is a bit more difficult to apply the other strategy to our case. We again assume that the semantic value of a referring name is a singleton that contains the referent as its extension. Identity is on this basis conceived as a relation between semantic values. However, we have to fiddle around a bit to get the desired and correct truth-values for at least most identity sentences.[28] For trivial identity sentences, such a result is easy to achieve: 'a=a' is true iff the semantic value of 'a' is identical with the semantic value of 'a'. However, these two alternative semantics also show that the problem of providing a plausible semantic explanation of the intuitive truth of sentences like (8) does not provide a direct argument in favour of the obstinate rigidity of names. It is also by no means clear that the semantic standard interpretation, which makes use of the obstinately rigid conception of names, provides the best overall semantics for identity sentences with names.

## Rigidity and names for merely possible objects

The third issue that defenders of obstinate rigidity have used to argue for their view concerns the issue of whether or not we can name objects that do not actually exist.

Kaplan and Salmon have suggested such examples.[29] Their examples have several additional complications and unnecessary controversial background assumptions.[30] I will use an alternative example, which, I think, is the most simple and straightforward example of the mentioned kind. It is possible, although we usually do not do it, to give a *single knife* a name. Consider two different knives that have wooden handles and steel blades of the same kind, but with different colours. Let us name the handle of the first knife A, of the second A* and the respective blades B and B*. There exist two objects with two parts, but it is also possible to combine the parts of these two objects and create two new objects. Some people think that two new non-existent combinations of the parts A, A*, B and B* correspond to two different *merely possible objects*. On this basis, it seems to be possible to name the merely possible object that is constituted by the possible combination of A and B*. Let us name this object 'Rambo'. If we accept this kind of scenario, we are committed to the existence of names that actually refer to non-existent objects. Based on such a commitment, it also seems to be plausible to conceive of actual objects as non-existent objects with respect to other possible worlds. Hence, we have all the resources we need to reject instances of (4) and opt for the obstinate rigidity of proper names.

I agree that this kind of reasoning has some appeal, but there are also reasonable ways to resist it. The possibility of a new combination of actual parts of two different objects might indeed be sufficient to be able to speak of a possible object that possibly has these parts. However, a merely possible object is not literally an *object*, namely in the same sense as a merely possible child is not literally a child. Given the two knives that exist there is also the possibility to recombine these two knives and there is also the possibility to create two new knives. But there literally are not any kind of knives as long as the recombination is not literally carried out. The assumption of possible knives as ordinary objects is the result of a linguistic confusion. Hence, the move from the assumption of a possible F to an F is the problematic step in this kind of argument. But philosophers who accept this kind of step might use such examples to favour an obstinate conception of rigidity over a persistent one.

I have doubts concerning the plausibility of the given argumentation and I am therefore inclined to reject the possibility that we can literally name merely possible objects.[31] It is also interesting to note that in actual languages there do not exist any names for merely possible objects. Is this really a coincidence? Or is there a good reason for this restriction?

As we will see in the next section, the restriction of the actual reference of proper names to actually existing objects is not only a feature of a conception of persistent rigidity but that there are formal frameworks where persistent rigidity and the reference to non-actual objects are compatible. Hence, it is questionable whether there are really any serious problems that seem to speak in favour of the acceptance of the instances of (4) based on independent semantic reasons.

## Actualized accounts of rigidity

Whether or not we favour a formal account of the semantics of proper names that interprets them as persistently or obstinately rigid, there is an often overlooked independent problem of standard formal accounts to capture the rigidity of proper names based on a one-dimensional modal logic. Typically, names are represented as *individual constants* in such a formal framework. The rigidity of such individual constants can be stipulated, as we have already seen, in at least two possibly different ways in our metalanguage. However, these stipulations are in a certain sense problematic because they do not represent that the reference of a name is fixed relative to the actual world and projected from there to all other possible worlds.

Kripke is quite explicit about this: the *actual* referent of a proper name is stipulated with respect to the *actual* world by means of an explicit act of naming or other more implicit procedures that have the same outcome as an explicit act of naming. The semantic rigidity of proper names seems to be based on this kind of stipulation with respect to the *actual* world. Hence, it seems to be a *metasemantic feature of proper names* that their actual referent is *projected* to all other possible worlds than the actual world. This is exactly the link between our ordinary practice of naming and rigidity that is proposed by Kripke in *Naming and Necessity* and expressed by the following two quotes:

> Our intuitive idea of *naming* suggests that names are rigid[.][32]

> In the present case I imagined a hypothetical formal language in which a rigid designator 'a' is introduced with the ceremony, 'Let "a" (rigidly) denote the unique object that actually has the property F, when talking about any situation, actual or counterfactual'.[33]

However, this specific and distinctive feature that the rigidity of proper names is fixed relative to the actual world and, hence, depends on certain facts in the actual world, is completely missing relative to the standard formal ways to capture persistent or obstinate rigidity of ordinary names.

A standard approach in philosophy to formally represent ordinary proper names interprets them as individual constants. The most typical way to introduce obstinately rigid individual constants into a possible-world semantic framework makes use of a *total world-relative* interpretation or denotation function that assigns world-relative referents to these constants. We get *obstinately* rigid individual constants on this basis by adding the following additional denotation-restriction:

(ORR)  For every possible world w and w* and every individual constant $\varphi$: I/Den($\varphi$, w)= I/Den($\varphi$, w*).

There are two alternative ways to get the same result technically. The first assumes a technically constant domain of (a) reference, (b) quantification and (c) predicate-interpretation D. On this basis, a total *absolute* interpretation or denotation function assigns elements of D to the individual constants of the language. Nothing like (ORR) is required because the interpretation by an *absolute* interpretation or denotation function makes individual constants insensitive to any world-shifting operators like the standard modal operators. Therefore, such expressions would also invalidate (4) if a world-relative existence predicate is used in this respect. The second alternative distinguishes between a constant domain of reference D* and world-relative variable domains of quantification and predicate-interpretation D(w). Individual constants are again interpreted by an absolute interpretation or denotation function, but now based on D*. The only difference between this and the first alternative concerns the use of individual constants in quantified sentences. We have a constant domain semantics in the first case, and a variable domain semantics in the second case.

There is a single standard way of introducing *persistently* rigid individual constants into the formal framework of a standard intensional semantics. Apart from two exceptions, it makes the very same model-theoretic assumptions as the standard way of introducing obstinately rigid individual constants. The first exception is that it makes use of a *partial* world-relative interpretation or denotation function; the second is that instead of (ORR) it makes use of the following alternative additional restriction:

(PRR)  For every possible world w and w* and every individual constant φ: (If I/Den (φ, w) and I/Den (φ, w*) are defined, then I/Den(φ, w) = I/Den (φ, w*)) and I/Den (φ, w) is undefined iff I/Den (φ, w*) is undefined.

There are not any interesting alternative ways of introducing *persistently* rigid individual constants.

Relative to all four distinguished different ways to account for the rigidity of individual constants it is not the case that their reference is at first determined with respect to the actual world and then projected to all other possible worlds. All these methods just tried to keep the referent constant across all possible worlds by different meta-semantic assumptions. For this purpose, it is completely irrelevant which world is the actual world. The actual world completely drops out of the picture as the grounds for rigidity.

This shows that standard formal representations of rigidity do not capture the *specific rigidity* that proper names have according to Kripke's correct observations with respect to natural languages. However, a correct formal semantics of *ordinary* proper names should capture this specific *actual dependence* of the rigidity of proper names.

It is relatively easy to satisfy this additional requirement. Nevertheless, it is surprising that the differences that have been pointed out are constantly overlooked in the relevant literature. For this purpose, we simply must add the actual world @ as additional constituent to our modal-structures. Furthermore, we must choose a framework that makes use of a world-relative interpretation or denotation function. As we have seen, such frameworks are available for both distinguished kinds of rigidity. Therefore, we now finally add to each of these two different frameworks one of the following two alternative restrictions:

(AORR) For every possible world w and every individual constant φ: I/Den(φ, w)= I/Den(φ, @).

(APRR) For every non-actual possible world w and every individual constant φ:

(a) if I/Den(φ, @) is defined, then I/Den(φ, w) = I/Den(φ, @), if I/Den(φ, @) ∈ D(w), otherwise: I/Den(φ, w) is undefined;

(b) if I/Den(φ,@) is undefined, then I/Den (φ, w) is undefined.

On this basis we now have notions of rigidity in the original sense of Kripke. The restriction (AORR) now delivers the desired version of *actualized* obstinately rigid individual constants; the restriction (APRR) delivers *actualized* persistently rigid individual constants.

In both cases, the reference of expression relative to the actual world is projected to all possible worlds, however, in two different ways. From a purely formal point of view, the difference between the two original and the two new restrictions seems to be insignificant. However, philosophically the two new formalizations provide the more adequate way to capture the *specific* rigidity of proper names.

## Two new additional actualized accounts of rigidity

This new way of looking at the rigidity of proper names, namely as a reference-projection from the actual world to all other possible worlds, opens up the whole horizon and allows one to search for new interesting alternative notions of rigidity with respect to proper names.

### Actualized restricted rigidity

In response to two of the three discussed arguments in favour of obstinate rigidity, we have *implicitly* already made use of one of these new notions. The basic idea behind it is the following: individual constants should receive a similar semantics as actualized descriptions such as 'The actual winner of ATP Finals 2020' to overcome two of the three mentioned problems. In the latter case, the reference of this description gets relative to each sentential context of use always redirected to the reference of the description 'The winner of ATP Finals 2020' relative to the actual world. However, our new desired notion of rigidity is only analogous because we do not want a redirection of the reference of some individual constant to the actual referent of some related expression. What we *literally* want is that the reference of an individual constant is redirected relative to *all* non-actual possible worlds to its reference relative to the actual world. This idea provides an interesting alternative interpretation of the idea of reference projection from the actual to non-actual worlds. In the original sense of rigidity, we exported the actual reference to every other possible world in one or the other way. In this new sense, we just redirect the reference back to the actual world. In the original sense, *rigid terms could only refer with respect to non-actual worlds to objects that exist or are also elements of the domain of these non-actual worlds*. In the new sense, *we can refer with respect to every non-actual possible world w\* to the objects in the actual domain, irrespective of whether they are part of the domain of w\* or not.*

How can we introduce individual constants with such properties into our formal framework? What structural changes are required for this purpose? Two important changes are necessary. Firstly, we have to reject an important implicit restriction that is typically assumed with respect to standard possible-world frameworks, namely the following:[34]

(LOC)  For every individual constant $\varphi$ and every possible world w: $I(\varphi, w) \in D(w)$/ $Den(\varphi, w) \in D(w)$.

This restriction pairs the world-relative interpretation of individual constants with the respective world-relative domains. We must give up this pairing to make the desired redirection possible. However, it is not our aim to give this constraint up for all possible worlds. At least relative to our first new version of rigidity described above, we aim to keep this restriction in play with respect to actual worlds but reject it with respect to all other worlds. Hence, we substituted (LOC) with the following more local restriction:

(LOC@) For every individual constant $\varphi$: $I(\varphi,@) \in D(@)/Den(\varphi,@) \in D(@)$.

Secondly, we now have to add a new projective restriction with respect to the interpretation of individual constants that adds the desired redirection of reference to our semantic architecture. This can be done quite nicely and smoothly in the following way:

(ARR) For every possible world w and every individual constant $\varphi$:

    (a) if $I/Den(\varphi, @)$ is defined, then $I/Den(\varphi, w) = I/Den(\varphi, @)$;
    (b) if $I/Den(\varphi, @)$ is undefined, then $I/Den(\varphi, w)$ is undefined.

This restriction gives us the desired result. According to it, (a) the reference of every individual constant is fixed with respect to the actual world, (b) it is restricted to objects that are part of the actual domain of reference and (c) it is projected to all other possible worlds by redirecting all reference relations that are relativized to non-actual possible worlds to the respective referents in the actual world.

This new notion of rigidity is weaker than (actualized) obstinate rigidity but stronger than (actualized) persistent rigidity. Why is it weaker than actualized obstinate rigidity? Actualized obstinate rigidity does not have the restriction (b). It allows us to refer, relative to the actual world, to every object that is part of the total domain of reference, whether this object exists in the actual world or not. Why is it stronger than actualized obstinate rigidity? It is stronger because it allows us to refer to actual referents with respect to every possible world irrespective of whether the corresponding world-relative domain contains this object or not. This feature makes our new notion of rigidity very attractive concerning the two problems already mentioned that a standard account of persistent rigidity of individual constants has to face with respect to singular negative existential sentences and necessarily true trivial identity sentences.

Firstly, on the basis of our new notion of rigidity, we can now formulate modified standard truth-conditions for singular existential sentences that make it possible to provide compositional truth-conditions relative to all possible worlds for singular negative existential sentences that contain *referring* names. Explicitly, we can formulate these conditions as follows: 'E!a' is true with respect to w iff Den(a, w) $\in$ D(w). This view also provides correct truth-conditions with respect to *non-referring* names. (Although, these truth-conditions are not fully compositional in such a case.)[35]

Secondly, we can also account for the truth of sentences of the form '□(a=a)' in a straight forward way on the basis of a (i) standard analysis of modal operators and (ii) the following standard truth-conditions for trivial identity sentences: 'a=a' is true with respect to w iff Den(a, w) = Den(a, w). (Nevertheless, this solution also has its limitations: it only works properly with respect to names that refer to things that are elements of the actual domain and, hence, are things that exist with respect to the actual world. We do not get intuitively correct truth-conditions of identity sentences of the form 'a=a' that contain non-referring terms.)

A third advantage of this notion is that we get a nice *symmetric* treatment of referring and non-referring rigid expressions. One can read off this feature almost directly from (ARR). Both kinds of expressions project their denotational status to *every* possible world. Hence, we now have the same uniformity as in the case of pure obstinate rigidity, while there is a strange asymmetry between referring and non-referring rigid expressions if we interpret these expressions as *persistently* rigid. To use a new and apt label for the new notion of rigidity let us call it *actualized restricted rigidity*.

Such a notion of rigidity seems to be very attractive for philosophers that: (i) think that the set of actual things exhausts the set of all things and who additionally believe, therefore, that (ii) one can only refer to actually existing things. It is also attractive for philosophers that believe for other reasons only in the limitation expressed by (ii).

## Actualized accessible rigidity

But there is also a second interesting modification of this new account of rigidity for people who believe in non-existent objects and who also believe that it is possible to refer to these things by proper names. It is, in my opinion, often overlooked that the standard conception of obstinate rigidity makes too naïve assumptions about the possibility of reference to non-existent objects.

There only seem to be *four* different ways to determine the referent of a proper name: (a) on the basis of some direct causal contact, (b) on the basis of some kind of demonstration, (c) by a description or descriptive content that exclusively identifies an individual, or (d) in a deferential way by some act of reference from a previously used referring device. However, there are many apparently merely possible non-existent objects to which we cannot attach a name on the basis of these four ways. My infinitely many merely possible sisters cannot be identified in any such way. If they are metaphysically complete objects, it is very difficult to distinguish them. Maybe, only someone who possesses all complete individual concepts[36] of all my possible sisters is able to distinguish them all and to single a specific one out on this basis. However, only divine beings might possess such complete individual concepts.

A similar problem arises with respect to extremely under-determined fictional objects. In their respect, it even seems metaphysically impossible to have complete individual concepts of these objects. Nevertheless, they are out of reach of our ordinary reference-fixing devices and possibilities. The number of non-existent objects that cannot be assigned to a proper name relative to our available procedures to determine the referent of such a name is probably much larger than the class of non-existent objects that are referentially accessible to us. If non-existent objects are at all metaphysically possible objects or objects of some kind, there in fact seems to be ways to talk about *all* of them or very large classes of them in a more *indirect* way, namely by quantifying over them. For this purpose, the satisfaction of a *general* descriptive condition by an object is sufficient and this goal is easier to achieve than to identify an object individually. Certainly, there are sub-classes of non-existent objects about which we cannot even quantify in very specific ways from our current perspective because of conceptual limitations. However, we at least seem to be in the position to quantify over them by using very general predicates. The picture that emerges on the basis of these observations is the following. We have to distinguish a *constant* domain of quantification that may contain all existent and non-existent objects from *variable* domains of reference that are only subsets of the constant domain of reference. These world-relative domains contain all those objects that are *referentially accessible* in the senses described above relative to a specific possible world. This referential accessibility may change from world to world and these world-relative domains may contain existent and non-existent objects.

Against this background, we can now introduce our second new variation of rigidity for proper names. For this purpose, we make use of a function ACC(), which assigns to every possible world a set of referentially accessible objects relative to this possible world. This function is also added as a new component to our new projection principle (ARR) from above.

Against this background, we can now substitute (LOC@) with the following new local restriction principle:

(LOC-ACC@)   For every individual constant φ: I(φ,@) ∈ ACC(@)/Den(φ,@) ∈ ACC(@).

We can now use this principle in combination with our new projection principle (ARR) and we get on this basis another *new* version of rigidity, which we may call *actualized accessible rigidity*, but which is more difficult to locate in logical space. It is clearly not as strong as the notion of actualized restricted rigidity and it would only be stronger if we assume that every actually existing object is, in principle, referentially accessible from the actual world. Maybe this assumption is too naïve. Nevertheless, it is an interesting alternative option, which is clearly weaker than obstinate rigidity, but not clearly stronger than actually restricted rigidity. In any case it rejects, like typical defenders of obstinate rigidity, *actualism* about existence and reference. Therefore, it can account for the possibility of names that refer to non-existent objects and it also allows us to extend the outlined solutions with respect to existential and identity sentences to a reasonable class of cases that concern proper names that refer to non-existent objects. This conception also shares with the conception of obstinate rigidity the validation of (4) with respect to all kinds of names, whether they refer to existent or non-existent objects.

I think the outlined two new alternative notions provide, from a philosophical and semantic point of view, interesting alternatives to the more familiar notions of rigidity and they seem to be in a reasonable sense applicable to *ordinary* proper names.

## Four possible conceptions of rigidity and their application to names

The four distinguished accounts of rigidity: (a) obstinate, (b) persistent, (c) restricted and (d) accessible rigidity, can all be used in a reasonable way to account for the rigidity of ordinary proper names. They are either largely or fully vindicated by our new version of Kripke's intuitive test for the rigidity of proper names. However, which of these notions is in fact the best fit for a formal semantics of ordinary proper names depends on certain philosophical and linguistic background assumptions.

*Option 1*
This option is for philosophers that: (a) are convinced that existence is a first-order discriminating property of individuals[37] (or a necessary property of everything), (b) accept the possibility of proper names that *actually* refer to non-existent objects, (c) hold that all instances of the law of identity are necessary truths, (d) accept the intuitively problematic instances of (4) in general for systematic reasons, and (e) reject the idea that there are any meaningful restrictions with respect to the referential accessibility of existent or non-existent objects. For these philosophers, the *best option* to capture the rigidity of proper names is to hold the view that proper names are **actualized obstinately rigid designators**.

*Option 2*
This option is for philosophers that share all views with Option 1 concerning (a)–(d), but that have clear doubts with respect to (e) based on the outlined reasons and think that any correct conception of names has to take into account important restrictions with respect to the referential accessibility of non-existent objects relative to the actual world. These philosophers are advised to hold the view that proper names are **actualized accessible rigid designators**.

*Option 3*
This option is for philosophers that reject (a), (b) and (d) of Option 1 and have doubts concerning (e). They reject (a) because they believe that existence is only a discriminating property with respect to semantic values or individual concepts, and they have doubts concerning (b) because they believe that we cannot name, for the outlined reasons relative to the actual world in a meaningful way, so-called merely possible objects. These philosophers also have to reject the intuitive falsity of claims like (4K) if they aim to capture the intuition that the true instances of the law of identity are, like the law itself, logically necessary truths. With respect to the notion of referential accessibility, they think this notion is not applicable to so-called non-existent objects. They typically do not have doubts that proper names cannot be found for all actually existing objects.[38] (But maybe this is an illusion if one takes quarks and other individual microphysical particles into account.) For these philosophers the best option to capture the rigidity of proper names is to hold the view that proper names are **actualized restricted rigid designators**.

*Option 4*
This option is for philosophers that aim to reject (a) and (b) of Option 1 for the same reasons as followers of Option 3. They also share the same view concerning (e), but are strictly inclined to accept our intuitive verdict concerning sentences like (4K) with respect to names that refer to *existing* objects. (However, they have to reject the data

with respect to (4) that concerns instances of names for apparently non-existing objects. One way to do so is to point out that there are not any uncontroversial examples of names for non-existent objects.) These philosophers have either to swallow the outlined problem concerning the true instances of the law of identity or may alternatively adopt the second outlined solution strategy to the identity-sentences problem that distinguishes between the semantic referent and the semantic value of a name. For them, the best option to capture the rigidity of proper names is to hold the view that proper names are **actualized persistently rigid designators**.

All four outlined views share Kripke's opinion that proper names are *de jure* rigid designators. However, if one believes in the existence of names without a denotation, he/she may hold a slightly weaker view than Kripke: proper names are *de jure* rigid *expressions*. An expression is rigid iff it is a rigid designator or a rigid non-designator. A rigid non-designator has no denotation with respect to every possible world.

In my opinion, our investigations so far have clearly vindicated Kripke's general view on rigidity, but they have also shown that there are very tricky issues with respect to the details of a correct conception of the rigidity of ordinary names that depends on a number of other issues. Some of these we will again address and discuss in the remaining chapters of this book.

2

# Proper Names and Reference Determination[1]

In this chapter, I will defend a novel pluralist conception of the determination of the reference of proper names and the constitution of the name-bearer relation. I will argue for the thesis that the semantic reference relation in the case of names is *context-sensitive* and for the Neo-Strawsonian claim that the use-sensitive semantic referent of a name is identical with the speaker's referent of this use that satisfies certain additional constraining conditions that are imposed by the linguistic meaning of the name or its meta-semantics. Furthermore, I will defend the view that the name-bearer relation is in opposition to the relation of semantic reference, a time-relative *context-insensitive* relation. According to my view, there are different possible mechanisms or facts that determine (a) the semantic referent of a name relative to a context of use, and (b) the name-bearer relation between a name and its possible semantic or speaker's referent.

## Introduction: the development of Kripke's picture of reference into a theory

In *Naming and Necessity*, Kripke introduced a currently still popular *picture* of the determination of the reference of a proper name. The following two passages contain a brief outline of this picture:

> A rough statement of a theory might be the following: An initial 'baptism' takes place. Here the object may be named by ostension, or the reference of the name may be fixed by a description. When the name is 'passed from link to link', the receiver of the name must, I think, intend when he learns it to use it with the same reference as the man from whom he heard it.[2]

> In the case of proper names, the reference can be fixed in various ways. In an initial baptism it is typically fixed by an ostension or a description. Otherwise, the reference is usually determined by a chain, passing the name from link to link.[3]

Several philosophers have tried to develop Kripke's 'rough statement of a theory' into an elaborated theory about the determination of the reference of a proper name.[4] In my opinion, Sainsbury provided the best developed version that he also extended to the problem of empty names, which is also of great importance for our investigations. For these reasons I have chosen a more developed version of Kripke's picture as a starting point for the development of my own views on this topic. Sainsbury proposed the following generalization and *extension* of Kripke's picture concerning the determination of the reference of proper names:

> A use of a name counts as referring to an object just if that object was baptized in the baptism from which the current use derives. [...] [T]he notion of a baptism is extended to include cases in which no object is baptized. These will be the kinds of baptism involved in empty-name-using practices. It is also extended to include unwitting baptisms: events which originate a new name-using practice, even though the agent of the event had no such intention. A baptism has at most one referent. Each name-using practice involves exactly one baptism; baptisms metaphysically individuate practices, and thus fix the referent, if any, of a practice[.][5]

Sainsbury's development of Kripke's picture consists of three different main classes of theses: firstly, a thesis about the determination of the referent of a use of a name; secondly, two theses about the constitution and individuation of name-using practices and names; and thirdly, two extensions that modify and extend Kripke's picture to account for names that lack a semantic referent and intuitive implicit changes of the semantic referent of a name.

The single main thesis of the first class can be formulated in more explicit terms in the following way:

(T1)  A *use* of a proper name N has a (semantic) referent x iff this use is part of a single name-using practice that originates in a single act of naming that has x as its target and this use exploits (a) a previous use that has x as its referent and is part of the same practice or (b) the originating event of this practice.

Name-using practices consist of single uses of a name that are connected in a specific way. The first event of a name-using practice is, according to Sainsbury, always a single act of naming. Subsequent uses are deferential uses of a name. The first referential act in a name-using practice that follows an initial act of naming is the use of a name that is *parasitic* on the initial act of naming. There are different ways to spell out the *parasitic* (or deferential) nature of these acts. A popular way makes use of specific intentions for this purpose (like Kripke in the first quoted passage above). The first or initial referential use of a name is, according to this view, a referential use with the intention to use the name to refer to the object of the initial baptism. Subsequent referential uses are parasitic on preceding referential uses. They might be conceived of as uses with the intention to use a name in a similar way as it was done relative to a certain previous use of the very same name by the user himself or other users.

We can extract the following thesis about the constitution and individuation of name-using practices from the quoted passage of Sainsbury (2005) above:

(T2)  Name-using practices originate in single acts of naming and are individuated by their originating events.

Kripke seems to agree with Sainsbury about the individuation of name-using practices by means of their origin.[6] But there are clear indications that Kripke thinks the identification of these originating events with acts of naming oversimplifies the real situation:[7]

> Analogously for proper names, of course I recognize that there need not always be an identifiable initial baptism; so the picture is oversimplified. [...] It is probably true, however, that in the case of proper names, examples with no identifiable initial baptism are rarer than in the species case.[8]

Furthermore, there are two extensions of Kripke's picture that are proposed by Sainsbury, which Kripke at least does not explicitly consider. These two extensions can be captured by the following thesis:

(T3)  Not every name-using practice orignates in a successful intentional act of naming: (a) name-using practices of empty names originate in firstly unrecognized *unsuccessful* acts of naming, (b) some non-empty name-using practices originate in *unwitting* acts of naming.

We will later focus in more detail on these two extensions.

There is one additional essential component of Kripke's picture concerning the determination of the reference of a proper name that is not explicitly discussed and only briefly mentioned in Sainsbury (2005), it concerns the *individuation of proper names*:

> [E]ach practice has at most one referent. This makes name-using practices like uses of names, and so enables us to say more about what makes for different uses of single (syntactic) name, namely, different practices. 'Aristotle' is used for the philosopher and for the tycoon. On the proposed view, that means there are two name-using practices.[9]

Kripke also does not mention or discuss this topic in those passages of his lectures where he outlines his picture of the determination of the reference of names, but he makes it explicit in the following passage of the foreword of Kripke (1980):

> For language as we have it, we could speak of names as having a unique referent if we adopted a terminology, analogous to the practice of calling homonyms distinct 'words', according to which uses of phonetically the same sounds to name distinct objects count as distinct names.[10]

> Thus, on the picture advocated in this monograph, two totally distinct 'historical chains' that by sheer accident assign phonetically the same name to the same man should probably count as creating distinct names despite the identity of the referents. [...] But distinctness of the referents will be a sufficient condition for distinctness of the names.[11]

If we combine the views of Kripke and Sainsbury on the *individuation of names* and name-using practices in the quoted passages, we can extract the following last main thesis of Sainsbury's development of Kripke's picture:

(T4)  Names are individuated in a very fine-grained way by means of single name-using practices and every such practice has at most one referent.

Based on this brief outline of the key components of Kripke's picture of the determination of the reference of names, according to Sainsbury's development of it, I will provide a detailed critique of different key components of this view in the next sections. In this context, I will also develop an alternative conception concerning the explanatory role of *acts of naming* and *name-using practices*. More specifically, I will proceed as follows.

Firstly, I will discuss and criticize (T4), the mentioned fine-grained historic individuation of proper names, and argue for a more coarse-grained historic individuation of names. Secondly, I will argue against (T1) and the view that *each* semantically correct non-introductory use of a proper name is parasitic or deferential. In this connection, I will also introduce an alternative pluralist conception of the determination of the reference of a proper name. Following Strawson (1950), I will conceive of *semantic reference* in the case of names as a sub-variety of speaker's reference that satisfies certain additional constraining conditions that are constituted by the linguistic meaning or the meta-semantics of a name. The basic idea behind my alternative conception of the determination of semantic reference of proper names can be expressed as follows:

(SC)   A (use of a) name n has a semantic referent x relative to a context of use c iff there is an act of speaker's reference relative to c that uses n and that has x as referent and this referent is a bearer of the name n relative to the time of c.

Against this background, the main parts of this essay will be concerned with two questions: (Q1) Are there any (semantic or pragmatic) restrictions concerning the acts of a speaker's reference that ultimately determine the semantic referent of a proper name? (Q2) Which kind of facts ultimately determine the name-bearer relation and, hence, also *constrain* semantically correct uses of names? I will defend a *pluralist* conception of reference determination in respect of (Q1) and a *disjunctivist* conception of the constitution of the name-bearer relation with respect to (Q2).

Thirdly, I will be concerned in more detail with the nature and explanatory function of acts of naming and, hence, the correctness of (T2). In this respect, I will argue for the thesis that a successful performance of an act of naming is not always a sufficient condition for the obtaining of the name-bearer relation and it is never a sufficient condition for the existence of a name-using practice.

Finally, I will focus in more detail on the nature and explanatory role of name-using practices and the correctness of the second part of Sainsbury's extension thesis (T3). In this respect, I will also argue against the existence of unwitting baptisms that are proposed by Sainsbury to account for intuitively possible implicit changes of reference.

# On the individuation of proper names

### Against a too fine-grained individuation of proper names

The fine-grained individuation of names that Kripke's picture of the determination of reference presupposes is mainly based on an analogy with homophonic ambiguous predicates. The English predicate 'is a bank' is ambiguous in a non-systematic way: it has different extensions relative to its different meanings. Not only is the representation of the predicate 'is a bank' in a formal language provided by two separate entries, there also seem to be two different words in English that are spelled 'bank' and which have two completely different origins and histories. According to Kripke's picture, names are quite similar in this respect: the extension of a proper name is its semantic referent. Different referents correspond to different 'meanings' of a name; every act that assigns a new object to a certain name is an originating event of a new name; and names are individuated by their histories of use and histories of use by originating events. Therefore, there are no two different objects that bear the *very same* name.

This consequence seems intuitively problematic. It concerns one important difference between names and non-systematically ambiguous predicates: names can intuitively be shared by different objects. We accept sentences like the following as true:[12]

(1) There are many different bearers of the name 'Alfred'.
(2) In honour of David Hume, his parents gave David Kaplan the same first name as the former.

The defender of Kripke's picture has to react to this data in some way. A radical way would be to deny that sentences like (1) and (2) have a true reading at all. According to this view, ordinary users of names and certain linguists and philosophers of language are massively ignorant about the true nature of names, but such a view strikes me as implausible. It might be defended in the case of natural kinds, but names are social artefacts and their nature essentially depends on how we think about them and how we use them. It is implausible to assume that we are massively ignorant about the individuation conditions of names. I think that is the main reason why most defenders of Kripke's picture aim to capture our intuitions about shared names and the sameness of names in some way.

The most popular move to account for our data is based on an ontological distinction between *generic* and *specific (or common currency)*[13] names. Kaplan famously draws this distinction as follows:

> There is the generic name 'David', and then there is my [common currency] name 'David', there is David Lewis' [common currency] name 'David', and so on. These are all three distinct words. The latter two have – and here I speak carefully – a semantic function: They *name* someone. The first, the generic name doesn't name anyone (doesn't name any*one*, perhaps it names or is an unnatural kind).[14]

> Generic names are the genera, or species, of our individual common currency names.[15]

The properties that names intuitively exemplify are on this basis divided between generic and specific names. Specific names capture the semantic and communicative role of names, while generic names are introduced to capture certain intuitions about the sameness and shared-ness of names. Such a strategy seems to be problematic in several ways and there are two methodological problems. Firstly, this distinction leads to an ambiguity of the ordinary notion of a name and ordinary speakers are not aware of this ambiguity that concerns sentences like (1) and (2). This view seems to be in danger of multiplying meanings beyond necessity.[16] Secondly, it also seems to be methodologically questionable to draw such an *ontological* distinction just to fill an obvious *explanatory weakness* of the proposed historic individuation of names. This view seems to be in danger of multiplying entities beyond necessity.

It is not only necessary to postulate a distinction between generic and specific names to solve the outlined aspect of the problem of shared names, but also to postulate that generic names can also have name-bearers in a certain sense and that they can have more than one bearer in this sense. Only on this basis can we interpret sentences like (1) or (2) as true. The best way to meet this requirement is to postulate that the notion of a bearer of a name is systematically ambiguous:[17] A generic name x has a bearer (in a derived sense) iff at least one of all specific names that are instances[18] of x has a bearer.[19, 20] But such a view seems to face a dilemma. If we want to account for the intuitively true readings of (1) and (2), we have to regard generic names as *names* and *words*. Kripke's picture identifies the bearers of a name with the referents and extensions of names. If generic names have bearers in a derived sense that is systematically related to the bearers of specific names, then generic names also have in a derived sense semantic referents and extensions. But then they cannot be conceived as *names* in a meaningful way because they have *multiple* referents and extensions and therefore would require disambiguation. But this would undermine the whole motivation for the distinction between generic and specific names. It is also unclear for which semantic and communicative purpose we could use generic names *qua* words that have multiple referents and extensions.[21] So maybe it is better to regard them not as words, as Kaplan also considers in our quote, but as some abstract unnatural kinds that function as templates for the creation of new specific names. But if generic names are conceived as unnatural kinds that function as templates concerning the linguistic form of expressions, it does not make sense to treat them as representational devices that have name-bearers or extensions. Therefore, on this basis, we again cannot account for the desired readings of (1) and (2). Hence, the sketched view seems to face a dilemma and so it is questionable whether we can assign to generic names a coherent and meaningful explanatory status.

Another problem concerns the nature of the relation between generic and specific names. It is completely unclear how generic and specific names are exactly related but what is clear is that generic names are individuated in a more coarse-grained way than specific names. There are people that suggest that generic and specific names are related in the same way as species and specimen.[22] Another suggestion might be that they are related like types and tokens.[23] But this latter suggestion does not work if we individuate specific names by their origin, and therefore resemblance in form is neither a necessary nor a sufficient condition for their identity. Normally, different specimens of one species share a certain essential and common feature that is independent of their origin, but it is not clear what this feature should be in the case of specific names if different specific names that are instances of the same generic name may completely differ in their form, might have different origins and might also have different bearers or no bearer at all.

These observations show, I think, that the distinction between specific and generic names provides no plausible solution to the mentioned problem. And that is not only a problem for a strategy that holds that sentences like (1) and (2) can have literally true readings. It is even a problem for a strategy that conceives of (1) and (2) as literally false but thinks that there are true contents that could be pragmatically conveyed by (1) and (2). However, if we do not have a distinction like the distinction between specific and generic names at hand, we cannot model these conveyed contents in a plausible way. Therefore, if there are no plausible ways to draw this distinction, then it also seems to be impossible to account for any true readings of (1) or (2) whether literally expressed or only conveyed.

**An alternative coarse-grained historic individuation of names**

What are the main options with respect to the individuation of names? There are two main types of a fine-grained individuation of proper names: the first one individuates names by means of their bearers, the second one individuates names by acts of naming. Both accounts have their problems: the first account cannot be applied or extended to meaningful names that lack a semantic referent, the second account falls short of covering cases of gradual introductions of names that lack an initial act of naming. The standard examples for such a case are the typical procedures of introducing a nickname into use. However, ordinary proper names can also be introduced without an act of naming. For example, there might be a dispute between two parties about the introduction of a certain name and it may take some time until this dispute is resolved and one expression is established as a new name for a certain object.

In opposition to such views, a more coarse-grained individuation holds the view that a single name might have more than one bearer. Such a view on the individuation of names must be either combined with a context-sensitive or an ambiguity view with respect to the semantics of proper names. The standard version of such a coarse-grained individuation aims to individuate names by their spelling or pronunciation.[24] However, there are also problems with this account: the very same name can have different spellings. There is, for example, a Russian tennis player whose name is sometimes spelled 'Juschni' and in other contexts 'Youzhny'. The very same name can have different pronunciations. Furthermore, there are different forms of the same name in a single language and different forms in different languages. 'Jack', 'Ian', 'Sean' are different variations of the name 'John' in English. 'Giovanni' is the Italian version of this name, 'Johann' the German and 'Evan' the Welsh version. All of these versions have different spellings and different pronunciations. Additionally, different people from different regions with different accents or mother tongues can pronounce the very same name in different ways. Therefore, a coarse-grained individuation of names is also a quite tricky endeavour. It is important to notice that the following sentence has different true and false readings:[25]

(3)    John and Sean Lennon bear the same name.

This sentence is true if we interpret it as a statement about the shared *family name* of father and son or any two different bearers of this name. It is also true if we interpret it as a statement about the same etymological forename. However, it would nevertheless be semantically incorrect to refer to John Lennon by using the name 'Sean' of his younger son. Hence, there is also a reading relative to which (3) is false. This example teaches us an important lesson, I think. Even if we favour a coarse-grained individuation of names as bearers of specific semantic properties, we have to clearly distinguish between at least two notions of names: (i) a purely etymological conception of names and (ii) a semantic conception of names. In my opinion, we have to combine a more sophisticated version of the linguistic form account with a version of the historic individuation of names to get the desired result in both cases. In these two cases, we should identify a name with a single linguistic form, but with time-relative clusters of different spellings or pronunciations. But the semantic-clusters seem to contain a smaller number of members and are, therefore, more restrictive than the etymological-clusters. On this basis, we can account for the fact why 'Juschni' and 'Youzhny' are two expressions of the same semantic name for a specific former tennis player, while 'Sean' and 'John' are not in a semantic, but only in an etymological sense variations of the very same name.

There are two different possible simple strategies to provide an account of the *synchronic* individuation of these clusters. According to the internalist account, *an expression (linguistic form) A belongs to the same semantic cluster-name as expression B at time t iff the majority of the users of A and B at t interpret A and B as the very same name at t*. The externalist alternative substitutes 'interpret' in the specified condition with 'uses'.

The first version has the problem that it neglects cases where competent users are not aware of what they are in fact doing. Maybe one can overcome this problem by making the condition dispositional and we, hence, substitute 'interpret' by 'has a disposition to accept'. On this basis, some people might not be aware of their more fundamental and unconditional disposition. However, another error problem is lurking on this basis. People might be fundamentally mistaken about the status of a specific expression. Hence, they may even lack the required disposition and, nevertheless, this specific expression may in fact be the same name as some other expression and nobody is aware of this identity.

The second version can overcome this problem but has itself the problem that is ambiguous between the two readings: it has a dispositional and an occurrentist interpretation. The first version makes 'uses' more precise by substituting it with 'has the disposition to use'; the second version means 'uses' literally and relativizes them to the time of use. One might think that the dispositional account has the so-called tabu-problem:[26] in a certain community, there might be a tabu to use a certain name for a certain thing or person. Hence, certain people might not only lack the disposition to use a specific name to refer to a specific object but also lack the disposition to use this expression and some other unproblematic expressions as the very same name. It seems to be difficult to find a satisfying account that determines such name-clusters diachronically on the basis of necessary and sufficient conditions. Maybe there is a clever fix with respect to the briefly outlined accounts or a better alternative account. I will not go into the details of developing such an account in full detail; nevertheless, my view on names presupposes such a type of account.

However, the problem of the synchronic identity of the name-clusters relative to a specific time is only one part of two identity problems. The second part concerns the diachronic individuation. In my opinion, a good account should also be very flexible in this respect. Hence, the components of a name-cluster might change in the semantic version from time to time. Maybe, in the case of the etymological-clusters these changes are less common, because of the specific nature and function of these clusters. Maybe in their case, we only have clusters that grow over time and, therefore, have a constant kernel from the beginning. But in the case of the semantic-clusters more changes seem to be possible. Hence, I think, in their case to purport a conception that allows overlaps and strict identity between clusters relative to two different times, but also allows the possibility of a continuity of the cluster on the basis of complete change with respect to its members. Therefore, one could say that such semantic name-clusters are individuated in a similar way as football teams that mostly change gradually, sometimes do not change at all, but that on rare occasions also may change completely. Against this background, I would opt for the following historic-cluster conception with respect to the individuation of ordinary names. Semantic name-clusters are subsets of etymological name-clusters. These clusters contain different expressions that might differ in spelling and pronunciation to some extent and that also might have different semantic properties. Their synchronic identity heavily depends on certain dispositions of use of competent speakers of these expressions and their diachronic identity is similar to the identity over time of social artefacts, especially of sports teams. Therefore, in this sense their individuation is historic. That is the type of a conception of the identity that I favour. However, I am not able to provide all the details of such an account in this book, which is mainly focused on the semantic and pragmatic properties of names.

Against this background, one might object that such an account of the individuation of proper names that distinguishes between clusters of expressions and expressions themselves is quite similar to an account that distinguishes between generic and specific names. It may appear so at first sight, because I have not made every detail clear so far. On the new outlined account, the so-called clusters of expressions should be more precisely called clusters of linguistic forms. The genuine bearers of semantic properties are, according to this account, the clusters of forms and these forms are therefore literally the constituents of the logical forms of sentences that contain a proper name. On this basis, a specific linguistic form that is used as a name is only used as a stand-in for the name-cluster, which is the ultimate bearer of semantic properties. Certainly, it would be possible to transfer the semantic properties of the expressions conceived as clusters to the forms that they represent. Hence, while a version of the Kaplan–Sainsbury account is a bottom-up account with respect to the transform of semantic properties, this account is top-down. Furthermore, the other account seems to have problems if there is more than one linguistic form that can be used to express a single specific name. Therefore, if the Kaplan–Sainsbury view takes these problems into account, it would also have to say something about, on the one hand, the relation between linguistic forms (as *Gestalt*) and, on the other hand, generic and specific names. If one is aware of these differences, I think it becomes clear that appearances are deceptive, and our favoured type of account is quite different from the Kaplan–Sainsbury account and does not face similar problems.

# On the determination of reference of names

### Against a purely parasitic determination of reference of names

In this section, I will focus on Kripke's idea that the semantic referent of a single use of a proper name is always determined in a parasitic or deferential way. That is, that every new use of a name that aims to refer to a specific thing can only achieve this goal by borrowing the reference for this new use from a referent of a previous use.

Let me now give three different kinds of examples to show that the use of different names might be determined in a meaningful non-deferential way.

### *Demonstrative determinations of referential uses of names*

In specific situations, it is possible to determine the reference of a use of a proper name in a *demonstrative* way. We may consider a situation where someone enters a stage, a spotlight shines on him and he gets announced by another person that utters the following sentence:

(4)   We are very proud to present you Peter James.

In such a situation, it seems to be possible to use a name and determine the referent of this use of the name in a demonstrative way. That is, either by intending to refer to an object by means of the name 'Peter James' that is in the focus of one's attention relative to a certain time or by mentally or literally pointing to a certain person or thing.

Alternatively, we may consider a business meeting of a certain company, where someone explicitly points to a certain person and utters:

(5)   Peter James is our representative in London.

In such a situation, it again seems to be plausible to assume that the referent of such a use of a name 'Peter James' is determined in a demonstrative way.

### *Descriptive determinations of referential uses of names*

Furthermore, if a person *only* knows by description which object is the bearer of a certain name and this person is, therefore, only in the position to identify this object in a descriptive way, it also seems to be possible to determine the referent of a name in this way.

Let us imagine the following situation. A person S overhears a conversation about the name of the inventor of the computer. Some people claim it is 'Richard Zuse', some claim 'Reinhard Zuse' and a third party claims 'Konrad Zuse'. After some discussion and after checking the name via google the group agrees that 'Konrad Zuse' is the name of the inventor of the computer. S memorizes the conclusion of this overheard conversation. On some other later occasion, S takes part in a TV quiz show. The quizmaster asks S the question 'Who invented the computer?' S answers in the following way:

(5)   Konrad Zuse is the inventor of the computer.

S cannot remember anymore from where he has this information. He also cannot rely explicitly or implicitly on previous referential uses of the name 'Konrad Zuse' itself. He never had direct contact to such a use, he was only lisening to a conversation about the name itself. Therefore, I think the best explanation for such a use of the mentioned name in a sentence like (5) on the basis of the given background seems to be that this user determined the referent of his use by means of the mentally associated content of the description 'the inventor of the computer'.

The following is important to note in this respect: the idea that the referent of the use of 'Konrad Zuse' is determined by an associated description is completely compatible with the rigidity of (5). Such a descriptive determination of the referent of the use of a name is a meta-semantic issue that does change the status of 'Konrad Zuse' as a *de jure* rigid name. It is also compatible with Kripke's argument from ignorance and error. There might also be other uses of names that are (a) descriptive and fail to designate a bearer of the used name or (b) non-descriptive. Our case only provides an example for *one possible* way to determine the referent of a name; it does not opt for a general unified conception.

## Cognitive determinations of referential uses of names

Another possible way to determine the use of a single name seems to exploit specific individual mental representations of objects. Let me justify this option on the basis of an example. I am in constant direct causal contact with my son and I collect a lot of information about him. It seems quite plausible to assume that I have a specific mental storage that contains only collected information about him. One might call such a storage an *individual mental representation* (or as some colleagues do, *a mental file*). This storage about my son also contains the information that his name is 'Florian'. Therefore, if I think about a specific afternoon and Florian and say out of the blue to my wife the following:

(6)  I will bring Florian to the football training today,

it is quite plausible to assume that the referent of my use of 'Florian' is determined by exploiting the individual mental representation about him that only has him as the causal source. Therefore, I think we should consider this as another possibility to determine the referent of a use of a name, which is clearly not parasitic in the outlined sense.[27]

## Erroneous determinations of referential uses of names

Additionally, there are also non-parasitic uses of names, that even the defender of Kripke's picture has to admit, to be able to account for certain data about possible scenarios of reference changes in the case of names. Evans (1973), for example, has famously pointed out that the name 'Madagascar' was once used as a name for a certain part of the African mainland. It is now used as a name for a certain big island near to the African mainland. The reference change was the result of a firstly unnoticed erroneous transmission of the use of the name from certain Arabic sailors to Marco Polo. But if really *every* use of a proper name is parasitic, then such transmission errors cannot take place. How should, on this basis only, every *correct* use be parasitic?

Consider, for example, a certain tribe that uses the name 'Ateb' to refer to a certain mountain. An ethnologist visits the tribe and aims to learn more about this tribe and the environment in which they live. He also learns that the tribe uses the name 'Ateb' for a certain mountain, but he misunderstands the pointing gesture that a member of the tribe makes towards a whole series of mountains that can be seen from a high plateau. The ethnologist uses the name for the first time with the intention to use it in the same way as the ethnic and with the additional intention to refer to the object that he has identified as the referent of the pointing gesture. He on this basis utters the following sentence:

(7)   Ateb is a very high mountain.

There are three different possible ways to interpret such an utterance. Firstly, it is an utterance that does not refer to anything, because it was uttered with conflicting referential intentions. Secondly, it is an utterance that refers to the mountain that is the bearer of the name 'Ateb' according to the tribe, because the parasitic intention triumphs over the explicit referential intention of the utterer of (7). Thirdly, it is an utterance that refers to the mountain that the ethnologist has confused with the bearer of the name 'Ateb' according to the tribe, because an explicit referential intention triumphs over a parasitic intention.

Let us further assume that the ethnologist travels back to his homeland and spreads the name 'Ateb' as a name for a certain mountain. Furthermore, let us assume that subsequent uses of this name are only parasitic uses. In this case, according to the first scenario, the ethnologist has spread a corrupt name without any referent. According to the second interpretation, no reference change took place and the ethnologist was able to participate in an already existing practice. According to the third interpretation, he has initiated a reference change concerning the name 'Ateb' and has thereby, according to Sainsbury, created a new name. We will focus in more detail on these different cases in the fifth section of this chapter. For our purpose now it is enough to notice that a defender of Kripke's picture has to admit acceptable non-parasitic uses of names to account for the intuitive possibility of implicit reference changes anyway.

### *How a defender of Kripke's picture might react to our four counter-examples*

A defender of Kripke's picture might react to all our proposed *counter-examples* against (T1) in the following way: granted there are many different ways to determine the referent of a *use* of a proper name, but only *semantically correct* uses of a name are those uses that are parasitic uses of a name. Other non-parasitic uses of names are only so-called examples of a *speaker's reference* that may only be pragmatically acceptable.

A distinction between those uses of a proper name that are licenced by the semantics of a name and those uses that are only in a wider pragmatic sense acceptable is certainly meaningful. However, we have already seen that the conception that every use of a name can be conceived of as a parasitic use becomes problematic in cases where certain people use same-spelled names to refer to different things. If someone aims to exploit a certain use of a name of such a person to determine the referent of her use, she must be in the position to identify a single previous use of such a name. But often we are not in the position to identify such a single use, we are only able to identify a user or source of such a use. But the identification of a previous user of such a name is very often not sufficient to identify a single name-using practice or a single use of a name. Therefore, we have to make use of certain extra conditions to pick out a single use or practice in such cases. If we make use of the mentioned fine-grained individuation of proper names, this extra condition is provided by the use of a certain specific name that only belongs to one of the practices to which a certain user might have access.

Superficially, such a restriction provides a solution to our problem, but closer inspection shows that such a solution is only viable if we are able to identify the correct specific name in such a context of use. Different specific names may have the same form – that is, the same spelling or pronunciation – there is no intrinsic criterion that distinguishes different same-spelled specific names. Therefore, it is necessary to distinguish such names in an *external* way by means of the name-using practice to which they belong. Some people, like Sainsbury, think that every name-using practice can be identified by its originating event. Maybe at least some name-using practices can be identified by their referent. But in the situations described, we are neither in the position to identify the origin nor the referent of the relevant name-using practice in a parasitic way. Therefore, it is not possible to use a name to refer to a certain object in a semantically adequate way relative to such a situation. But intuitively it seems to be possible to use a name in a semantically correct way relative to such a scenario.

This shows that it is an illusion that the commitment to a fine-grained individuation can be used to extend Kripke's picture of the determination of reference of names to *all* possible uses of a name. On the other hand, semantically correct uses of names in the described situations are possible. Firstly, someone might not be in a position to identify a single name-using practice in a parasitic way, but she might be in a position to identify such a practice in a partially descriptive and partially parasitic way, if she knows a property that distinguishes a certain bearer of a certain same-spelled name from other bearers of this name. Or secondly, if she is in a position to identify this object purely demonstratively or descriptively, she can also use a name relative to such a situation. In the latter case, she has identified a certain name-using practice in an *indirect* way, but the name-using practice itself plays no essential role with respect to the determination of the referent of a use of a name. The defender of Kripke's picture must exclude such uses from the semantically correct uses of a name. But we are very often in the situation that we *cannot* identify a certain referent of a name in a purely parasitic way.[28] Therefore, I think Kripke's picture provides an incorrect distinction between semantically and pragmatically correct uses of a name. (This problem is also a further reason to question the correctness of the proposed fine-grained individuation of proper names.)

However, it seems to be possible to hold a version of Kripke's picture that makes use of our mentioned coarse-grained historic individuation of proper names. This *moderate version* rejects the claim that every act of naming leads to the creation of a new name, but it supports the thesis that every act of naming leads to the creation of a new *name-using practice*. That is required to be able to exploit a name-using practice for the purpose of reference determination. Furthermore, this moderate version weakens (T1) and holds that it is not necessary that every single semantically correct use of a name is a purely parasitic use. That is, every semantically correct single use of a name is still necessarily a *partially* parasitic use, but there might be additional non-parasitic elements that help us to identify the desired *unique* name-using practice. Against this background, we can at least account for some intuitively acceptable, but not purely parasitic uses of names. But even on this basis the question remains whether it is really *always necessary* to exploit a name-using practice to determine the semantic referent of a name. In the case of bare demonstratives and personal pronouns, for example, deferential (parasitic) uses of these expressions are also possible. However, these uses are not the paradigmatic uses of these expressions. Why should the situation in the name-case be completely different? Why should we conceive of only deferential (parasitic) uses of names as the *paradigmatic* uses and the only uses that are semantically correct?

**An alternative neo-Strawsonian picture of reference determination**

An *alternative picture*, which is more liberal and flexible in respect to mechanisms of reference determination in the case of names is the following. Names are individuated in the mentioned coarse-grained way by historic chains of clusters of linguistic forms. Every name-using practice might contain more than one act of naming and also different uses of the same name with different referents. We can distinguish different *branches* of a single complex name-using practice that historically constitutes the temporal existence of a name in the semantic sense. All uses of a name that belongs to a name-using practice and that has the *same object* as the referent constitute an *individual branch* of such a name-using practice. The more bearers a single name-using practice has the more *branches* of such a practice we can distinguish. According to this alternative picture, the participation into a name-using practice does not necessarily require a parasitic referential use of a name that borrows its referent from some previous use of the same name, it only requires that a use of a name counts as the use of a name that already exists and belongs to an already existing practice. Every participation into an already existing name-using practice requires *specific intentions*. In the most explicit case, I pick up an already used name with the intention to use the very same name as others did. But an intention of this kind is not really necessary for a successful participation as we have already seen on the basis of our given counter-examples to Kripke's deferential picture of reference borrowing.

Not every use of a name that has a referent and is part of an already existing name-using practice is a semantically correct use of this name. The basic idea of our alternative picture concerning the distinction between semantically correct and incorrect uses is: only such uses with a referent that are part of a *conventionalized branch* of a name-using practice[29] are semantically correct uses of a name. What are conventionalized branches of name-using practices? Inspired by Kripke, we could say that each conventionalized branch of name-using practice originates in an explicit act of naming and continues with a series of connected uses of a name with the same referent. However, our conception is in one important respect different from Kripke's: these uses are causally and intentionally connected and the intention to use a certain name in the same way or with the same referent as it was used before can be conceived of as a *connecting intention*. But in opposition to Kripke we do not conceive of such intentions as a *reference determining* intention. We only conceive it as a *reference constraining intention* that either constrains the semantic or speaker's reference. According to this conception, we are only then able to determine the referent of a use of a name with a connecting intention if this intention is accompanied by an additional genuine reference determining intention or some other reference determining mechanism. This additional intention might be parasitic, in the sense that I not only intend to use a name with the same referent as someone else, but that I really intend to *borrow* the referent of my use from a previous use. But it may also be demonstrative, descriptive, cognitive or of any possible sort. That is, our *pluralistic* conception of reference determination assumes no constraints at all concerning the determination of the speaker's referent of a use of a name; any possible and suitable reference determining intention or mechanism might be used for this purpose. On the other hand, our conception assumes different clear constraints that a speaker's referent must satisfy to become a semantically correct referent of a name. Hence, such a use of a name with a connecting and a genuine reference determining intention has a *semantically correct* referent if the determined referent is identical to the referent of those uses to which this use is intentionally connected. On this basis, we can now formulate a first possible conception of conventionalized branches of a name-using practice:

(A)  x is a conventionalized branch of a name-using practice *if* x originates in an explicit act of naming and x continues with subsequent connected uses of this name that are used with satisfied connecting and reference determining intentions and each use has the named object as referent.

In the following two sections, we will consider a second, alternative conception of conventionalized branches of a name-using practice that (a) rejects the condition that such a branch necessarily originates in an explicit act of naming and that (b) does not *require* the satisfaction of the connecting intention of a use of a name. But until then, we will rely on the more conservative and Kripke-inspired (A).

Against this background, we can now formulate our alternative *Strawsonian picture of reference determination*[30] that conceives of semantic reference (a) as context-dependent and (b) as a specific variety of speaker's reference in the following way:

(T1*)  A (use of a) name n has a semantic referent x relative to a context of use c iff
(c1) there is an act of speaker's reference relative to c that uses n and that has x as referent and (c2) this act of reference is part of a conventionalized branch of an already existing name-using practice that has x as its referent.

Why Kripke's idea that the participation in an existing name-using practice is essential for a semantically correct use of a name is also important for our alternative pluralistic account can be shown as follows.[31] Initially, I thought it is sufficient to combine (c1) in (T1*) just with the relatively simple condition (c2*): *x is a bearer of n*, to get a linguistically correct account. Why such a view might be problematic can be shown by a counter-example. Let us assume that Bob Dylan has an imposter that also is a bearer of the name 'Bob Dylan'. This imposter gives a concert in Germany. I stand in front of a poster that advertises this concert and that contains a picture of the imposter and the name 'Bob Dylan', and I say to my wife the following:[32]

(8)     Wow, Bob Dylan will soon give a concert in Bochum.

Now, two questions arise: To whom did I refer as I asserted (8)? Does my use of the name 'Bob Dylan' have a semantic referent? In the outlined scenario, I might have used the name 'Bob Dylan' with the intention to refer to the person depicted on the poster in front of me. Alternatively, I might have activated my mental representation of the famous singer Bob Dylan and determined the referent on this basis. In the first case, my use of the name refers to the imposter; in the second case, to the famous singer/songwriter. In the latter case, it also seems to be plausible to assume that this person is also the semantic referent of my use because (c2) and (c2*) are satisfied in this case. However, one might doubt whether the imposter is the semantic referent of my use of 'Bob Dylan' in the first case. Condition (c2*) is satisfied in this case, but (c2) is not because it might be doubted that I am already a participant of the conventionalized *branch* of a name-using practice that uses 'Bob Dylan' to refer to the imposter. Hence, (c2) seems to be a slightly more plausible option that (c2*) for our purposes. However, one might claim that this counter-example is relatively controversial and highly artificial, and, therefore, we may distinguish a *simplified* version of our new view that relies on (c1) and (c2*), a more *sophisticated* version that makes use of (c1) and (c2).

The most significant difference between this alternative picture and the moderate version of Kripke's picture mentioned above is that according to it, neither name-using practices as a whole nor their conventionalized branches play a role concerning the *determination* of the referents of a name, they only provide *constraints* for uses of a name such that we can distinguish semantically incorrect from correct uses of a name.

According to this picture, there can certainly also be *purely parasitic* and *partially parasitic* uses of names. A *purely parasitic* use is a use that exploits a *single* previous use of a name by some person by directly identifying such a use. For example, if someone overhears a conversation about a certain person that bears the name 'John Perry', but she does not know who that person is, she might use the name 'John Perry' in a purely parasitic way and utter the following question:

(9)     Who is John Perry?

She thereby exploits a single previous use that was performed by someone else who participated in the mentioned conversation about John Perry.

But there can also be only *partially parasitic* uses of a name; for example if one uses the name 'Cicero' with the intention to use it the same way as those Roman people did who used it to refer to a famous roman orator. If one succeeds on this basis in referring to a single bearer of the name 'Cicero', such an act of reference was successful and semantically correct.[33]

The important difference between our alternative picture and the moderate version of Kripke's picture is that the former is more liberal concerning those acts that can be used in a semantically correct way to determine the referent of a use of a name.

# On the nature and explanatory role of acts of naming

## Against a too broad conception of acts of naming

We have already seen that Kripke, on the one hand, is rather sceptical whether really every name-using practice originates in an act of naming or baptism. While Sainsbury, on the other hand, explicitly says in the quote mentioned above that he aims to *extend* our ordinary notion of a baptism in such a way that *empty* and *unwitting* baptisms are also possible. An *empty baptism* is a failed attempt to attach a name to an object because the identification of a single object fails. An *unwitting baptism* is a single act that leads to an unintentional introduction of a new name or at least the assignment of an 'old' name to an object. Sainsbury (2005, 111) distinguishes between two kinds of unwitting or inadvertent baptisms. Firstly, those cases where a certain *name that already has a referent* is used to refer to a thing that is not a bearer of this name and as a consequence of this use a new name-using practice is initiated. And secondly, a scenario where a *common noun* is used and accidentally a nickname is created:

> Inadvertent baptism is common, for example with nicknames: a parent calls a spindly child a beanpole, using the word as a common noun and with no intention to originate a practice, but it sticks as a nickname and for years is used as a proper name of the child.

Sainsbury (2005, 111) also thinks that acts of baptism should be conceived as the first *uses* of a name relative to a certain name-using practice: 'A baptism is an event in which a name is bestowed and which originates a practice (in the limiting case, it is the only use in the practice).'

One question is now whether Sainsbury's extensions are plausible and whether they are sufficient to dispel Kripke's doubts about the general status of acts of naming.

Before we discuss this question in more detail let us focus more explicitly on the nature of acts of naming *in the narrow Kripkean sense*. For the sake of simplicity I will use, in the following, 'acts of naming' only for acts of naming in the narrow sense and I will use the phrase 'originating acts of a name-using practice' for acts of naming and their proposed extensions by Sainsbury.

### *The nature of acts of naming in the narrow sense*

We can distinguish two different kinds of acts of naming. The paradigm variety are *explicit* acts of naming. These are intentional speech acts that make use of a performative naming verb like 'name', 'baptism', 'christen' or 'call' and some singular term to identify the object that should be named. A sentence like the following can be used to perform an explicit act of naming:

(10)   I (hereby) name her *Mary*.

Kripke distinguishes two different sub-varieties of explicit acts of naming, namely explicit *ostensive* acts of naming, where we use some demonstrative expression like 'her' or 'this woman' to fix the referent of an act of naming, and *descriptive* acts of naming, where we use some attributively used definite descriptions like 'the inventor of the computer' to fix the referent of our act of naming. The distinction drawn by Kripke is obviously not an exclusive one. We can intuitively also use a lot of other singular or plural terms to fix the referent(s) of an act of naming.

It is important to note that if an explicit act of naming is performed, names are not used, but mentioned. This is not completely obvious in the case of a claim like (10), because the semantic status of the name 'Mary' in (10) seems to be rather peculiar. Linguists and philosophers disagree about whether 'Mary' is used or mentioned in (10), because we cannot substitute *salva congruitate* 'Mary' in (8) with 'the name "Mary"'. I think the main reason why this is not possible is that constructions like 'is named Peter' or 'is called Peter' are elliptical constructions and a sentence like (10) is semantically equivalent to the following more explicit counterparts:

(10*) I (hereby) name you by the name 'Mary'.

Relative to such a sentence, it is obvious that the name 'Mary' is mentioned, but not used: Even in this case, we cannot, for good reasons, substitute 'Mary' *salva congruitate* with 'the name "Mary"'. This observation is relevant for Sainsbury's claim that acts of naming can always be conceived as uses of a specific name. In the case of paradigm acts of naming, that is not the case. Therefore, we have found one reason why it is questionable whether we should consider acts of naming as essential constituents of a name-using practice.

According to the standard analysis of explicit speech acts of naming, these acts form a sub-variety of so-called *declarations*[34] (which are sometimes also called *effectives*[35] or *exercitives*).[36] We can distinguish *effect-expressions* that describe a wide range of social statuses from *bringing-about-expressions* that can be used in a performative way to bring about the corresponding social status of affairs. Relative to certain contexts of use the utterance of bringing-about-expressions by certain persons is a sufficient condition for the bringing about of the corresponding social status of affairs. If we accept the prima facie plausible claim that expressions of the name-of-relation are effect-expressions like expressions of the being-married-with-relation, then we can specify an act of naming in the following way as a sub-variety of a declaration:

(DN)   For every person s, every x, every name y and every time t: s names x by the name y at t iff s declares at t that y is a name of x.

Declarations satisfy the following declaration schema, if we substitute for 'p' any sentence that contains a verb with a performative potential:

(DS)   (For all suitable substitutions for 'p':) If s declares at t that p, then p (at t).

According to this standard analysis, the performance of an act of naming *seems* to be a sufficient condition for the obtaining of the name-of-relation. But that is not true in every case. If acts of naming are declarations, then they should be in significant respects similar to acts of marrying, acts of hiring or acts of nominating. But the successful performance of an act of marrying at a certain time is not sufficient for the state of affairs that someone is married to someone *for all times*, because it is possible that after the marriage an act of divorce was performed that cancels the consequence of the initial act. And in the case of the act of hiring, things are similar.

There is no verb like 'to fire' or 'to divorce' that designates such cancellation-acts in the naming-case and we are also not really familiar with acts of withdrawing a name.[37] But there is another sort of *established* act in connection with naming that has the same consequences as an act of withdrawing a name, namely an act of re-naming. People may acquire apart from their 'official' names *additional* names, for example nicknames or stage names; these are not cases of name-changes.[38] But people that marry or that have a gender re-assignment very often *change* their names. The names of countries, cities and streets may also be changed for certain ideological or political reasons. Therefore, there are cases where a certain object acquires a *new* name *in place* of its old one. And these acts of re-naming have the same consequences as acts of withdrawing a name. As a reaction to this diagnosis, we can now formulate a principle to provide at least more adequate *sufficient conditions* for the obtaining of the name-of-relation based on the performance of an act of naming:

(SC)   For every person s, every name x, every y and every time t: If there is a time t′ before (or identical with) t and s named y x (at t′) and there is no time t″ after (or identical with) t′ relative to which an act or a series of acts was performed that have the same consequences as an act of name-withdrawal, then x is a name of y at t.

Apart from these similarities, there also seems to be an important difference between acts of naming and other prototypical declarations like hiring or marrying. In the case of the two latter acts, the successful performance of such a declarative act is always bound to a specific *authority* of the performer. Only a person with a specific *social status* that is equipped with specific *rights* can hire a person or marry two people. In the case of acts of naming the situation is more messy. There is a certain sub-variety of acts of naming where a specific authority is required for the successful performance. Only certain authorities can assign in a *legal or religious sense* names to certain persons. Furthermore, people who are responsible for certain things (e.g. their children) or own certain things (e.g. their pets) have a certain *privilege* to assign a name to these things. This kind of privilege is defeasible and it is linked with an authority that is weaker than the mentioned legal authority. But, on the other hand, every competent speaker of a language can introduce names for each object he desires to name. Nicknames are paradigm examples of names that can be introduced by everyone and no specific authority seems to be required for the successful performance of such an act of naming. In this sense, acts of naming are special. These observations also cast doubt on the universal correctness of (DN). Maybe only acts of naming in the strict and legal sense are really declarations, and acts of naming in a looser sense are acts of a different kind. For example, it does not seem to be implausible to claim that the performance of an act of naming in the loose sense is only a personal commitment on the side of the performer of such an act to use a certain expression as a name of some object in the future. And in some cases such acts might be accompanied by an *invitation* to other people to follow the lead of the performer:

(CN)  For every person s, every x, every name y, every time t: s names x by the name y at t (in the weak sense) iff s commits himself to using y as a name for x.

The acceptance of such an alternative conception of acts of naming has important consequences.[39] On the basis of (CN), (SC) would come out as false. It requires much more than the performance of an act of naming in the loose sense to establish a social fact that a certain thing bears a certain name. According to (CN), acts of naming might *initiate* certain name-using practices, but only an established name-using practice would be a sufficient condition for the obtaining of the name-of-relation.

Are there any good reasons to favour (CN) over (DN)? Or should we at least distinguish two completely different kinds of acts that we may perform by using performative verbs like 'name' and 'baptise'? Acts of the introduction of nicknames seem to be paradigm cases that may favour a distinction between two different kinds of acts of naming. There are at least two different ways to coin a nickname. The first has already been mentioned by Sainsbury: a common noun might be transformed into a nickname. Alternatively, some pre-existing name is introduced as a nickname for a certain person. Nicknames are typically not introduced by an act of naming. Nicknames are normally just used to refer to a certain person on a certain occasion and this person becomes a bearer of this name if a specific name-using practice in respect to the used name is established. But it also seems to be possible that nicknames are introduced by an act of naming. I might point to a friend and say 'I (hereby) name you *Milky*'. I do not have the authority in the two mentioned senses nor in any meaningful sense to assign a new name to my friend. My successful utterance on its own also does not seem to be sufficient to establish the fact that my friend bears a certain new nickname. My utterance can at most be considered as an invitation to use the name 'Milky' as a name for a certain person. Therefore, we seem to have a good case in favour of (CN).

The defender of (DN) could react to such a case as follows: an utterance of a sentence like (10) is only then a successful act of naming, if the utterer has the authority to name someone. In a situation where it is obvious that the utterer of a sentence like (10) does not have this authority, the act is unsuccessful, but might be interpreted as the performance of a different act that can explicitly be performed by a literal utterance of the following sentence:

(11)  Let's call her *Mary*.

A successful utterance of a sentence like (11) is an invitation to use the name 'Mary' to refer to a certain person, but not an act of naming in the strict sense.

Based on the observations made so far, I have the tendency to regard only *legal acts of naming* as acts of naming in the narrow sense that satisfy (DN) and (DS). All other acts that can be performed by uttering sentences like (10), (10*) or (11) are not genuine declarations. That either means that we have to distinguish two different sorts of acts of naming, or at least it means that the sentence that we typically use to perform genuine acts of naming can also be used (indirectly) to perform other illocutionary acts.

If one accepts this conception of so-called explicit (non-legal) acts of naming, this has important consequences for Sainsbury's conception of acts of naming. He aims to stretch the notion of an act of naming or baptism to capture by this notion other *single* acts than explicit acts of naming that have the same institutional consequences as acts of naming. But our examples have shown that there are certain introductions of names that cannot be identified with a *single* act. And more importantly not in every case does the determination of the semantic referent of a name ultimately depend on a *single* act of naming, but on a whole series of uses of a specific name.[40]

These observations pose a problem for Sainsbury's conception of name-using practices, but interestingly they do *not* pose a problem for our alternative picture of reference determination and our proposed much more liberal conception (A) of conventionalized branches of name-using practices. But for Sainsbury these acts (a) ultimately individuate name-using practices and (b) ultimately determine the referent of such practices.

However, there are also other possible ways to introduce a new name or new bearer of an existing name that *also pose* a problem for our conception based on (A). We will focus on two examples of this kind in the following.

## *Implicit introductions of names*

There are other alternative ways to introduce a new name that are completely independent of any explicit acts of naming or utterances of sentence like (10), (10*) or (11). There are cases where people introduce names for objects just *by starting on the fly* to use a certain name to refer to this object. Consider, for example, a case where a family finds a cat and they bring the cat to their home. After a while back home, the father asks the son, who is already very fond of the cat, where the cat is. The son answers in the following way:

(12)   Whiskers is in the kitchen.

Let us further assume that the son uses (12) with the intention to refer by 'Whiskers' to the cat he has seen in the kitchen. The son might use this name with or without the intention to establish this name as a name for the cat. In the described situation it seems to be in any case implausible to assume that the utterance of (12) is sufficient to assign 'Whiskers' as a name to the mentioned cat. However, the use of (12) in the given scenario is acceptable (at least in a pragmatic sense), but further actions seem to be required to establish the obtaining of the name-of-relation and also to make this use the *first use* of a certain name-using practice or a conventionalized branch of such a practice. So, for example, it depends on how the parents react to this use, whether they accept the proposal, whether the son himself uses the same name on further occasions and in some case it may also depend on the fact of whether the family is allowed to keep the cat and whether there is not another person who owns the cat and aims to get it back. There might be an explicit act by the parents that licences the use of the son. But such an explicit acceptance is not always necessary. The establishment of a new name might be a gradual process. Think of the case of 'Karl-Marx-Stadt' and the inhabitants of this town that only gradually will change their habit of referring to their city by its old name to the new one of Chemnitz. Therefore, it seems that a certain *series of connected acts* is often required to establish a name-using practice or a conventionalized branch of such a practice. In my opinion, these more or less *ad hoc introductions* of a name without the performance of an explicit act of naming are not exceptional cases. And they seem to be speaking in favour of a view that is also significantly different from our conception (A). Sainsbury's view, on the other hand, seems to be motivated by considering explicit acts of naming as the standard cases and by the aim to generalize such cases in a plausible way. But such a generalization that postulates in each case a *single originating event* that individuates a name-using practice and determines its referent seems to be an over-generalization and a simplification of the actual situation concerning the introduction of names into use.

## *Plural legal acts of naming*

There is also a different sort of case that concerns explicit acts of naming that poses a problem for Sainsbury's approach and our slight modification of this approach. If we accept that an explicit act might be performed by using an attributively used definite description, and I do not see any good reason why we should exclude such cases, then the way from such cases to certain other less familiar cases is not a far one. In certain contexts, legal acts of *mass baptisms* seem to be possible. Consider, for example, a country that is ruled by a dictator that has the authority to assign names in a legal sense to its citizens. Assume that on a certain day this dictator publicly makes the following announcement:[41]

(13)   I hereby name every male child that was born today in my empire *Vladimir*.

Such a legal act of naming is a single act that may lead to the initiation of a considerable number of very different name-using practices. It seems to be implausible to claim that the dictator has not only performed one act by uttering (13), but as many acts as people have been named by means of (13), because there is no direct causal or intentional connection between the act that is performed by the dictator and the named object. It also seems to be implausible to claim that only one act was performed, as many events happened as people were named. But against this background and on the basis of his view that acts of naming are the originating events of name-using practices, Sainsbury would have to concede that there are different name-using practices that have a *single* originating event. In the case of such name-using practices it would not be possible anymore to determine the referent of a single use of a name by exploiting the referent of such a practice if the referent of the practice is ultimately determined by an originating act of naming. In such a case, there is no single object that could be transferred to such a specific use of a name.

To circumvent this problem, Sainsbury might claim that the dictator not only named many different people, but also that he created many different names and therefore also either performed a whole *series* of actions or at least made a whole series of events happen. Hence, Sainsbury might use this kind of case as another independent motivation for his proposed fine-grained individuation of names.[42] However, we have already seen that such a conception leads to counter-intuitive consequences. Furthermore, such a reaction to plural acts of naming also seems to be *ad hoc* and theory-driven.

## An adaptation of the alternative neo-Strawsonian picture with respect to naming

How should a defender of the outlined *alternative picture* react to the two kinds of cases of the introduction of a name discussed above? The first case might be called a *case of introduction of a new bearer of a name on the fly*. Such cases, if taken seriously, require a significant modification of our conception of conventionalized branches of name-using practices.

The situation is a bit different concerning the mentioned cases of legal acts of naming in their single and plural form. There seem to be three different options as to how we could react to them. What is the most plausible reaction? This partly also depends on how we modify our conception of conventionalized branches of name-using practices in reaction to the first kind of case. To cover cases like the Whiskers case we need to allow conventionalized branches of a name-using practice that originate not in an act of naming, but in a *referential use* of a name where the referent is determined in a non-parasitic way and that is accompanied by an *introductory intention*. That is, an intention of the user to introduce a new bearer of the user's name that is identical with the speaker's referent of its use. However, neither a non-legal act of naming nor such an *introductory referential* use of a name is intuitively sufficient to constitute a new name-bearer. Additionally, a series of connected and co-referring users of the very same name is required to constitute a new *referential* practice and, hence, a new name-bearer. In this sense, the notion of a name-bearer is a vague notion, because it is indeterminate how many instances of such a series of uses are required to constitute a new name-bearer; it might be different from case to case. These additional modifications now lead to the second conception of *conventionalized branches of name-using practices*:

(B)    x is a conventionalized branch of a name-using practice if either (a) x originates in a non-parasitic referential use of a name that is accompanied by the intention to introduce a new bearer of a name (or a new name) or (b) x originates in a non-legal act of naming and x continues with a *series* of uses of this name that are used with satisfied connecting and reference-determining intentions and each use has the introduced/named object as referent.

In the light of this modification of the notion of a conventionalized branch of a name-using practice and if we accept the difference that has been pointed out between legal and non-legal acts of naming, only one of the three distinguished reactions to a mass-baptism case seems to be plausible. We have argued that in opposition to non-legal acts of naming, legal acts of naming are sufficient to constitute new bearers of names. However, legal acts of naming are intuitively not sufficient to constitute a new conventionalized branch of a name-using practice, because during an act of naming it is not essential that a *name* is *used* at all; it could also only be *mentioned*. Therefore, the most plausible option is to distinguish two different standards of correctness for a semantic referent of a name: (a) uses that are part of a conventionalized branch of a name-using practice, and (b) uses that *exploit* a successful legal act of naming.

There are different ways to *exploit* a legal act of naming. One way this can be done is by a *parasitic referential* use of a name that borrows its referent from the legal act of naming. One might make use of a parasitic referential intention for this purpose and use a name with the intention to refer to the object that was named by a specific official legal act of naming. However, such parasitic uses can only be successful if the user of a name aims to borrow its referent in the described way from a *singular* legal act of naming. One cannot borrow a referent from an act of *mass baptism* in the same way. But there are other options to also exploit *plural* legal acts of naming. This can be done by a non-parasitic referential use of a name that is accompanied by a *connecting intention* that aims to refer to one of the objects that were named by a certain legal act of naming. With this conception of referential uses of names that exploit legal acts of naming at hand, we can now also modify (T1*) in the following way to also cover semantically correct uses of a proper name that exploit singular or plural legal acts of naming:

(T1**)  A (use of a) name n has a semantic referent x relative to a context of use c iff there is an act of speaker's reference relative to c that uses n and that has x as referent and this act of reference is either (a) part of a conventionalized branch of an already existing name-using practice that has x as its referent or it (b) exploits a legal act of naming in force that concerns the used name and that constitutes a name-bearer relation between this name and x.

The discussion so far has shown that the nature and constitution of the name-bearing-relation is a complicated matter and that it is a *gruesomely gerrymandered* relation that can be characterized in the following way:

(NR)  For every name x and object y: x is a name of y at t iff either there exists at t a conventionalized branch of a name-using practice of x and this practice has y as referent *or* at t there is an explicit legal act of naming *in force* that assigned the name x to y and that is exploited by users of x.

However, (B), (T1**) and (NR) are not the end of the story. Further adaptions seem to be necessary if we also take into account possible cases of an *unintentional* and *implicit* constitution of a conventionalized branch of a name-using practice. We will now focus on this additional phenomenon in the following section.

## On the implicit and unintentional constitution of name-using practices

### The problem of implicit reference changes

In this section, we will discuss the often so-called phenomenon of *implicit reference change* and we will consider the option of whether it is possible to establish a new name-using practice or a conventionalized branch of such a practice in an unintentional way.

### Different possible ways to use Evans' famous examples

It is well-known that Gareth Evans introduced several examples of implicit reference change to provide a challenge for Kripke's picture of reference. According to Evans,

Kripke's picture cannot plausibly account for the intuitive fact that a name may change its referent accidentally and unintentionally. The following quote contains Evans' two classical examples of implicit reference change:

> Not only are changes of denotation imaginable, but it appears that they actually occur. We learn from Isaac Taylor's Names and their History (1898):
>
>> In the case of 'Madagascar' a hearsay report of Malay or Arab sailors misunderstood by Marco Polo ... has had the effect of transferring a corrupt form of the name of a portion of the African mainland to the great African Island.
>
> A simple imaginary case would be this: two babies are born, and their mothers bestow names upon them. A nurse inadvertently switches them and the error is never discovered. It will henceforth undeniably be the case that the man universally known as 'Jack' is so called because a woman dubbed some other baby with the name.[43]

Let us focus in more detail on these two examples: the first case introduces two different name-using practices that concern the name 'Madagascar'; the second practice was accidentally initiated by an erroneous attempt to participate in the first practice. In the second case we have on the one hand an act of naming that can be conceived of as a failed attempt to initiate a specific name-using practice, and on the other hand a name-using practice that was initiated by some confusion. Are these differences significant?

The second example is only then an example of a reference change of a name, if we accept two things. Firstly, that the two acts of naming performed by the two mothers in the story are sufficient for the obtaining of the name-of-relation between the two mentioned names and the two babies. Secondly, it is possible that the establishment of a new (conventionalized branch of a) naming practice can cancel the consequences of a successful act of naming.

We already had doubts as to whether the performance of normal non-legal acts of naming are sufficient for the obtaining of the name-of-relation. But that is not a significant point in respect to Evans' example, because we could easily change the example in such a way that two *legal* acts of naming were performed before the baby switch. On the other hand, if we change the example in this way, it becomes relatively obvious that the establishment of a certain name-using practice that uses the name whose reference was initially fixed by a legal act of naming is also not sufficient to cancel the consequences of this legal act of naming. Against this background, this modified baby-switch case could not be considered as an example of a reference change, but only as an example of an unintentional introduction of a new name for a certain object. However, as an example of the latter kind it is fairly plausible and acceptable.

The first example *as it is presented by Evans* is also not a genuine example of reference change. According to his presentation, things are as follows. There are three groups of people. There is a group of people G (= the original inhabitants of certain parts of Africa) who use the name 'Madagascar' to refer to a certain portion of the mainland of Africa. There is the second group of people G' of Malay or Arab sailors that report the use of the people of group G to a certain member of a third group G". This third group

G″ is the group of Spanish sailors that does not have any use of the name 'Madagascar' in their repertoire, before they get in touch with members of group G′. As things happened, Marco Polo, a member of group G″, gets in contact with members of group G′ and misunderstands the report of these members concerning the use of the name 'Madagascar' of members of group G. Marco Polo distributes this use of 'Madagascar' (that is based on a misunderstanding) among the members of group G″ and later this use becomes the primary use of the name 'Madagascar' of a much larger class of people than group G″. According to this reconstruction, Evans' Madagascar example is of the same kind as our modified baby-switch example. It is an example of an *unintentional establishment* of a new (conventionalized branch of a) name-using practice. A genuine reference-change example would require that a certain person already participates in an established practice before a transmission error happens. We could, for example, modify the baby-switch case in such a way that we postulate an already existing name-using practice for the name 'Jack' before the baby switch takes place. Then we would have a clear example of an *implicit reference change*.

Let us use this modified example as an example of an *implicit reference change*. And let us use the *original* Madagascar example as an example of an *unintentional constitution of a new (conventionalized branch of a) name-using practice*, which is the result of a failed attempt to participate in an already existing (conventionalized branch of a) name-using practice.

The original Madagascar case is also presented by Evans in a more complicated way than required. The main reason for this complexity is that Evans wanted to provide an *actual* and not just an *imaginary* example. What are really *essential features* of any example of an unrecognized unsuccessful attempt to participate in a certain existing name-using practice that led to the creation of a new name-using practice and a new name-bearer? The following three components seem to be essential. The first component is an already established (conventionalized branch of a) name-using practice of a certain person or group of people concerning a specific name. The second component is a speaker that does not already use this name, but who aims to participate in this existing (conventionalized branch of a) practice *or* a speaker that already uses this name, but aims to add a new use of this name to his repertoire. As a third component there must be a *very specific failed attempt* of participation in the original practice that implicitly leads to the creation of a new (conventionalized branch of a) name-using practice and on this basis a new name-bearer.[44]

## The implicit determination of conventionalized branches of name-using practices

If we want to understand and capture cases like the original Madagascar case, we have to answer the following question: *Which conditions must be satisfied such that a failed attempt of participation in an existing (conventionalized branch of a) name-using practice leads to the creation of a new (conventionalized branch of a) name-using practice?*

There are different *ways* to participate in an already existing name-using practice and there are also different kinds of *errors* that one might make in connection with such an attempt. We have already seen that an intentional participation in such a practice requires a *connecting intention*. That is, a competent speaker intends to use a name in the same way or with the same purpose as (a) himself, (b) a single other user, or (c) a group of users did before. Such an intended participating use can be accompanied by a parasitic or a non-parasitic referential intention. Against this background, we may distinguish two different kinds of error that may occur relative to such a use: (a) a transmission error, (b) a meta-representational error. Applied to the Madagascar example, this leads to the following two types of cases:

*Case 1: Transmission error*
Speaker A uses the name 'Madagascar' with the intention to use it in the same way as members of the group G.
Speaker A uses the name 'Madagascar' with the intention to refer to a certain African island.
A believes that 'Madagascar' refers to a certain African island.
The group G uses 'Madagascar' to refer to a certain part of the African mainland.

*Case 2: Meta-representation error*
Speaker A uses the name 'Madagascar' with the intention to use it in the same way as members of the group G.
Speaker A uses the name 'Madagascar' with the intention to refer to the same object as members of G.
A believes that 'Madagascar' refers to a certain African island.
The group G uses 'Madagascar' to refer to a certain part of the African mainland.

On this basis, we can now answer our question. An implicit unintentional constitution of a new (conventionalized branch of a) name-using practice can only take place if a certain sequence of uses of a name occurs. A necessary condition for such a sequence is *at least one* use that exemplifies a transmission error. A uniform series of uses that consists only of uses that exemplify meta-represenation errors may lead to a massive number of false beliefs, but not to a reference change or constitution of a new name-bearer. The mentioned necessary condition can only be satisfied if we accept that speakers who aim to use a name in a semantically correct way are allowed to determine the referent of such a use in a *non-parasitic* way. That is, we need to distinguish in opposition to Kripke between a (parasitic) *connecting intention* that is not satisfied in a case of a transmission error and a possible accompanied non-parasitic referential intention that is satisfied.

In the light of the plausibility of such cases like the Madagascar case, these cases do not only provide further evidence for the thesis that not all uses of a proper name that intend to be semantically correct uses should be considered as parasitic uses, but they also provide evidence for the thesis that *connecting intentions* and their satisfaction should only be considered as necessary conditions for the *successful* participating with a referential use of a name in an existing (conventionalized) name-using practice. That is, it should be possible that such a use can have a speaker's referent although the connecting intention is not satisfied and the use is, therefore, a failed attempt to participate in an existing conventionalized branch of a name-using practice.

What is, apart from a *transmission error*, required to get a genuine case of an implicit constitution of a new conventionalized branch of a name-using practice? We also need a *connected series* of uses of the very same name with the very same speaker's referent. However, these uses need not to be *intentionally* connected by means of satisfied connecting intentions, they may only be *causally* connected and the user must be in some sense mentally or intentionally directed towards previous uses in such a series. In a case with the fewest possible accidental elements, we have *only one* use with a transmission error in a series of uses that are intentionally connected uses with the same speaker's referent as the use with the transmission error. Such a series is only then possible if the connecting intentions and possible parasitic referential intentions of uses of the very same name that succeed the use with the transmission are very local such that they only concern a single or very few previous uses. This is necessary because only very local connecting and parasitic referential intentions can be satisfied after such a transmission error. However, more likely is a series of uses with *more than one* transmission error. Such series can only then constitute a new name-bearer of a specific name if the uses of this series are causally connected, they are performed with connecting intentions that are directed towards previous uses in the series although they sometimes mischaracterize these previous uses and there also must be an identical speaker's referent of all these uses.

This shows that the Madagascar case and similar examples,[45] if they are taken seriously, require another adaptation of our proposed conception of conventionalized branches of name-using practices. Hence, we get the following already relatively complicated and messy constitution of those branches of name-using practices that constrain semantically correct use of a name:

(C)  x is a conventionalized branch of a name-using practice *if* x either (i) originates (a) in a non-parasitic referential use of a name that is accompanied by the intention to introduce a new bearer of a name (or a new name) or (b) in a non-legal act of naming and x continues with a *series* of uses of this name that are used with satisfied connecting and reference-determining intentions and each use has the introduced/named object as referent or (ii) x originates in the use of a name with a transmission error and x continues with a subsequent *series* of causally and intentionally connected uses of this name that are used with (not necessarily satisfied) connecting and (constantly satisfied, but not necessarily parasitic) reference-determining intentions and each of these uses has the same speaker's referent as the originating use.

This second correction of our initial conception of conventionalized branches of name-using practices (A) completes our search for adequate constraining conditions for semantically correct uses of a proper name.

## Summary: the main theses of my pluralist conception of reference determination

The pluralist conception of reference determination of proper names that I have introduced and defended in this essay is based on the following main theses.

Firstly, I argued for the thesis that we should *individuate* proper names in a relatively coarse-grained way such that a single name can literally have many bearers; nevertheless names are individuated by means of their history and hence in most cases there exists very long, old and big name-using practices of the very same name.

Secondly, I proposed to conceive of the relation of semantic reference in the case of names as a context-sensitive relation, in a similar way as in the case of bare demonstratives or third-person personal pronouns. This comparison led to an additional thesis that I have argued for, namely that we should conceive of semantic reference in the case of names by following Strawson (1950) as a sub-variety of a speaker's reference that satisfies certain additional constraining conditions that are constituted by the linguistic meaning of a name. These constraining conditions are in the case of proper names provided by the *name-bearer relation*. In this respect, names are similar to the third-person personal pronoun 'he', for example, which expresses the constraining condition of *being male* as part of this linguistic meaning. But as in the case of names, this constraining condition is not a consituent of semantic content. Hence, the basic idea behind the proposed conception of the determination of semantic reference of proper names can be expressed by the following bi-conditional:

(SC) A (use of a) name n has a semantic referent x relative to a context of use c iff there is an act of speaker's reference relative to c that uses n and that has x as referent and this referent is a bearer of the name n relative to the time of c.

Against the background of this path breaking bi-conditional, the main parts of this chapter were concerned with two questions: (Q1) Are there any restrictions concerning the acts of a speaker's reference that ultimately determine the semantic referent of a proper name? (Q2) Which kind of facts ultimately determine the name-bearer relation and, hence, also constrain semantically correct uses of names? I defended a *pluralist* conception of reference determination in respect of (Q1) and a *disjunctivist* conception of the constitution of the name-bearer relation in respect of (Q2).

More precisely, I argued, thirdly, in connection with (Q1) that the semantic referent of a name interpreted as a speaker's referent of a use of a name that satisfies additional constraining conditions can ultimately be determined by a variety of different mechanisms. More exactly, there are no restrictions concerning the determination of the speaker's referent of a name that are imposed by the linguistic meaning of a name. Against the background of a conception of speaker's reference that makes use of referential intentions and that I have used as an example in this chapter, this means that any *kind* of referential intention can be used for this purpose, for example, parasitic, demonstrative or purely descriptive referential intentions. Such a conception rejects the famous Kripkean dictum that the semantic referent of a name is essentially determined in a parasitic or deferential way.[46]

Fourthly and finally, I argued in connection with (Q2) that we have to clearly distinguish between the context-sensitive relation of semantic reference in respect with names and the context-insensitive but time-relative name-bearer relation. The name-bearer relation only *constrains* but does not *determine* semantic reference. However, this relation is a gruesomely gerrymandered relation that is metaphysically constituted by different sorts of facts. More precisely, facts about name-bearing can be determined (a) by an exploited legal act of naming that is in force, or (b) by the establishment of a conventionalized branch of a name-using practice. I also showed that such conventionalized branches of a name-using practice can be constituted in quite different ways: (i) in an explicit intentional and (ii) in an implicit unintentional way. Our conception (C) aims to capture three different ways – two intentional and one unintentional – of how a conventionalized branch of a name-using practice can be established.

There is one important topic that I bracketed in this chapter and that motivated one of the two mentioned extensions of Kripke's picture of reference determination made by Sainsbury. It concerns the meaningful use of empty names and the specific nature of conventionalized branches of name-using practices of empty names. We need further adaptation of the here presented conception of conventionalized branches of name-using practices to cover such uses as well. I leave this topic for chapter 4 that deals explicitly with empty and fictional names.

# 3

# Proper Names as Use-Sensitive Expressions[1]

This chapter will be concerned with semantic approaches to proper names that conceive of names as context-sensitive expressions. Firstly, I will present, discuss and criticize two different kinds of approaches of this variety, namely (a) the indexical view of names and (b) the variabilist view of names. Based on my critique, I will in a first step propose a new version of the indexical view and in a second step a completely new version of context-sensitive semantics for names.

## Setting the stage: proper names as context-sensitive expressions

There are two important sorts of conceptions in the relevant literature that treat proper names as context-sensitive expressions: *indexical* and *variabilist* views of names. The first kind of conception semantically assimilates proper names to indexical expressions like 'I' and 'today'. The second kind of conception semantically assimilates them to third-person personal pronouns or variables in (modal) predicate logic. There are significant semantic differences between both kinds of views. In this section, I will briefly present the core ideas behind both views in some detail.

### Indexical conceptions of proper names

Indexicals are linguistic expressions whose semantic reference depends in a certain way on specific parameters of the context of use. Therefore, an indexical expression can have different semantic referents relative to different contexts of use. Prototypical and uncontroversial examples of indexicals are expressions like 'I', 'here', 'now', 'this' and 'today'. The view that proper names are indexical expressions is controversial.[2] Nevertheless, there is a group of philosophers and linguists that have proposed such a view.[3]

We can distinguish between two different general varieties of an indexical view on proper names that can be found in the relevant literature: *informal* and *formal variants*. A defender of the first kind of variant identifies certain natural language expressions that are unquestionably indexical and claims that they are semantically equivalent to proper names. Typically, such an equivalence claim is put forward without providing a formal semantic representation of the proposed equivalent indexical expression.[4] The following claim is an example of such a view: 'Alfred' is semantically equivalent to 'the present bearer of "Alfred"'.

A *formal variant* of the indexical view on proper names makes use of a formal semantic framework that is suitable for the representation of indexical expressions and conceives of proper names as indexical expressions according to this framework.

It is a defining feature of formal indexical views of proper names that they treat proper names as *non-logical constants* of a specific kind. We can distinguish two different main versions of this kind: proper names are either conceived of as *simple*[5] or as *complex*[6] non-logical constants with an indexical semantics. The best-known formal semantic framework amenable to such an approach is Kaplan's logic of demonstratives – in the following abbreviated as KLD.[7]

It is nowadays a common feature in philosophy of language and linguistics to distinguish different layers or levels of linguistic meaning. An important distinction of this kind is the distinction between truth-conditional and non-truth-conditional meanings. The truth-conditional meaning of expressions *constitutes* the contribution of an expression to the truth-conditions of a sentence. Non-truth-conditional meanings provide either further additional contents that are only conveyed but not directly expressed by sentence or they only *constrain* **or** *determine* the truth-conditional meaning of an expression.

However, if we are concerned with the truth-conditional meanings of indexical expressions, Kaplan introduced an important distinction that is nowadays widely accepted, namely the distinction between *character* and *content*. Following Kaplan, I will call those aspects of truth-conditional meaning that only *determine* (or constrain), but do not constitute the truth-conditional contribution of an expression, the *character* of an expression; and those aspects of meaning that really *constitute* the truth-conditional contribution of an expression I will call the *semantic content* of an expression. More generally, contents are a certain kind of generalization of what is classically called an *intension*. An intension is a (total or partial) function from possible worlds into extensions.

Contents are functions from circumstances of evaluation into extensions. In the minimal sense of circumstances of evaluation, they are just possible worlds. But a circumstance of evaluation can contain additional parameters; for example, also a time parameter. In the case of a singular term, the extension is identical to the referent of this term. A content of a singular term is *rigid* if the output of this function is the same relative to every possible world. *Character* is a second layer of truth-conditional meaning additional to contents. It is a total function from contexts of use into contents. Kaplan conceives *contexts of use* as ordered quadruples consisting of (a) the agent, (b) the place, (c) the time and (d) the possible world of the context of use of a specific expression. It might be necessary to extend these parameters to capture the character of specific indexical expressions in an adequate way.[8] A character is non-indexical if it has the same output relative to every context of use; it is indexical if not.

In addition to these two truth-conditional layers of meaning, one could add a third use-conditional layer. I will call this additional layer (*contextual*) *constraint*.[9] A *constraint* is a (proper) subset of the set of all contexts of use. That is, the contextual constraint of an expression *e* restricts the set of all possible contexts of use of *e* to the set of all contexts of use of *e* relative to which *e* is used in an *acceptable* or *felicitous* way.

According to the version of the indexical view on names that I will propose as a first alternative to the standard accounts, proper names are non-logical constant expressions, with a rigid content, a very *specific* indexical *character*.

Those formal versions of the indexical view of proper names that I will discuss and criticize in the third section of this chapter make use in more or less extent of the semantic resources of KLD. These versions are represented by Zimmermann and Lerner (1991), Recanati (1993), Haas-Spohn (1995), Pelczar and Rainsbury (1998) and Pelczar (2001).

**Variabilist conceptions of proper names**

Variabilism concerning proper names assimilates names semantically *informally* to third-person personal pronouns and *formally* to individual variables in formal languages like first-order predicate or modal predicate logic.[10] According to this view, proper names are not formally represented as simple or complex constant expressions, but as atomic individual variable expressions. In predicate first-order logic or modal logic, individual variables are typically semantically interpreted by an assignment function that assigns to each variable of the language an object that is an element of the domain of discourse of the logical framework. Variabilists concerning proper names modify this treatment in one significant respect; they either relativize the assignment function to contexts of use *or* they relativize the extensions of names to contexts of use and make use of different assignment functions relative to different contexts of use to interpret the extension of a name. Contexts of use are formally interpreted in a similar fashion as in KLD.

There are two important distinctions that allow us to distinguish different versions of variabilism. Typically, variables in predicate first-order or modal logic have two different semantic functions. They can either be used as *unbound* individual variables in open sentences or as *bound* individual variables in quantified sentences. A *monist* version of variabilism restricts the function of names conceived as variables to one of these two functions, typically to the function of unbound variables, as, for example, in Dever (1998). However, there also is the monist view defended in Sommers (1980) that interprets proper names as bound special-duty pronouns. *Dualist* versions assign both mentioned functions of variables to proper names. Different versions of this view are proposed in Cumming (2008) and Schoubye (2017, 2020).

The second distinction concerns the individuation of proper names. *Fine-grained* versions of variabilism individuate proper names by their referents. Hence, the name 'Peter' corresponds to different variables on the level of logical form with respect to different uses and bearers of this name. The most important defenders of this version are Dever (1998) and Cumming (2008). *Coarse-grained* versions individuate proper names like pronouns and allow for the possibility of a single name with different semantic referents relative to different contexts of use. Most notably, this version is defended in Sommers (1980) and Schoubye (2017, 2020).

This completes my first brief overview of the two standard versions of contextualist views of proper names.

## Four motivations for context-sensitive views on proper names

In this section, I will briefly discuss and present different motivations to adopt at least one of different possible versions of a context-sensitive view concerning the semantic reference of names. I will show none of these motivations by itself is sufficient to motivate such a view, but there is a plausible combination of three of these four motivations that seem to favour a specific version of a contextualist view on proper names.

**Motivation 1: Pluralism about the determination of reference**

There are two different views about the determination of the referent of a proper name that have dominated the discussion in the last decades: the *descriptivist* and the *communication chain* conception of reference determination. Both views share the general assumption that there is a *single general mechanism* that accounts for the determination of the reference of a name. But they disagree about the nature of this general mechanism.

According to descriptivism, there is an object-identifying descriptive meaning or content that is associated with a name (or use of a name), and the referent of this name (or use of this name) is determined by means of the satisfaction of this descriptive content. For example, if a condition of the general form 'the unique object that has property P' is associated with a proper name and is satisfied by an object, then this object is the semantic referent of this name.

According to the communication chain picture, there is an initial act of naming that conventionally links a name with its bearer and after that initiating act a name is typically passed on from user to user. The referent of such a name (or use of this name) is determined by an act of participation in such a communication network that links the name (or use of this name) to the referent of the initial act of introduction.

But both general views seem to *over-generalize*. In the case of descriptivism that is very well-known. It is possible to use a name and refer to an object even if one is not in a position to associate a specific definite description with a bearer of this name (ignorance case); or if the description that is associated with a specific name is not satisfied by a bearer of this name (error case).[11] But the communication chain view seems to over-generalize as well. It is also not true that a proper name with an established use can only be used in a parasitic way and therefore only with the intention to use this name like some person or group of people that have used this name previously (in a certain situation) in a certain way.

In fact, there seem to be quite *different* ways to determine the reference of a proper name in an adequate way. Therefore, I propose to reject the general assumption made by both views and hold a *pluralist view* about reference determination with respect to names instead.

One thing also has to be noted: the two classical approaches mentioned primarily give an account of what determines the referent of a single *use* of a proper name. The semantic referent of the name itself is only determined in a secondary and derived way. I think that this is no coincidence. It is a specific semantic feature of proper names that in the case of each single use of a proper name the question arises *how* the referent of this specific use is determined. In this respect, proper names resemble indexicals, demonstratives and pronouns, where this question also arises. Furthermore, in the case of proper names there seem to be different possible ways to determine the referent of a single *use* of a name. This fact speaks in favour of pluralism. Nevertheless, not every referent of a single use of a proper name is the semantic referent of a proper name relative to a single use or context of use. I can use any proper name to refer to nearly any single object, but only some of these uses are linguistically correct or licenced.

We can make use of the jargon of *reference fixing referential intentions or attitudes* to draw distinctions that are required to formulate the version of pluralism that I aim to propose. According to this view, the referent of a name can be determined: (a) by means of demonstrative referential intentions, (b) by means of cognitive referential intentions, (c) by means of descriptive referential intentions, (d) by means of parasitic referential intentions, or (e) by means of mixed referential intentions that are combinations of at least two of the four other kinds of intentions.

We have already shown intuitively in chapter 2 how uses of names in these distinguished five ways are possible. I will now try to provide a more systematic account of how these different uses can be analysed.

There are *temporary* and *constant* mental representations of individual objects which we make use of. For example, if we see a specific object, a *temporary* or *occurrent* mental representation seems to be created that is used to think about it as long as we have direct contact with such an object. Furthermore, we also have more constant mental representations of individual objects that are important to us *or* with which we very often causally interact. We also make use of these constant representations to (re-) identify familiar objects. In such cases, a temporary and a constant mental representation of the same object can be present and linked. Both kinds of representations primarily represent objects on the basis of a causal connection between the objects and their representations.[12] Such a causal representational relation is exploited if the referent of a use of a proper name is determined by means of an *object-related* referential intention. That is, such a referential intention mainly activates or uses a mental individual representation to refer to an object by means of a proper name in a non-satisfactional way. The determination of the referent of the *use* of a name by means of temporary mental representation corresponds with a *demonstrative* use of a name. This use can be made manifest by a pointing gesture or something similar.[13] The determination by means of a constant mental representation corresponds with a *cognitive* use of a name.

Let us now turn to the class of descriptive determinations of the referents of uses of a proper name. Two different cases seem to be possible. On the one hand, a constant mental representation of an object that is grounded in different objects, and hence defective, might be used in a descriptive way. That is, the information contained in such a representation might be joined to designate the singular or dominant satisfier of this information or a certain subset of the collected information. Such a *descriptively* used representation that may also contain a specific name-information can also be exploited by a single use of this stored name. On the other hand, the use of a single name can also be determined in the classical way by an associated definite description or a uniquely determining descriptive condition. For example, in a situation where somebody believes to *know* that a specific bearer of a name has a specific individuating property and this individuating property is the *topic* of a certain conversation, a single use of a name can also be determined by a descriptive condition. However, such uses are not paradigm cases, but only exceptional uses of a proper name. Nevertheless, they seem to be possible.

Furthermore, we have cases that are also quite common and made famous by Kripke, namely *parasitic* or *deferential* uses. Beside the mentioned cognitive determinations, I think these cases constitute the most common uses of proper names. It is very likely that a proper name will be used accompanied by a parasitic referential intention if someone aims to participate in a conversation where people talk about a person or thing he does not know, and where he aims to gain more knowledge about this person or thing and therefore asks certain questions about it.[14] Schematically we may characterize such a case as follows: If a speaker S intends to use the name 'N' in the same way and with the same referent as 'T', where 'T' stands for a certain person or a certain group of people, then the referent of 'N' is determined by means of a *parasitic referential intention*.[15]

A proper name can be used accompanied by an object-related referential intention if a bearer of this name (or at least a representation of this bearer) is present in the context of use of this name. This use can be made manifest by a pointing gesture or something similar.[16]

Finally, there might also be cases where a person uses a name accompanied by several kinds of intentions or attitudes and in certain cases they may also be incompatible such that we have to decide which intention trumps the others.[17]

*Pluralism* concerning the determination of a use of a proper name ascribes on this basis to the following central theses. Firstly, the notion of reference concerning the *use* of a proper name is the primary notion of reference concerning names. The notion of the semantic referent of the name itself is a derived notion. Secondly, there are different mechanisms to determine the referent of a use of a proper name, namely those different options that I have briefly sketched. The two most notable mechanisms are the mentioned *cognitive* and *parasitic* uses of proper names; but there are also occasional *descriptive* and *demonstrative* uses. Thirdly, the semantic referent of a name is use-relative. That is, the referent of a use of a name becomes the semantic referent of such an expression if the use-referent is also a *bearer* of the used name and the use is linked to a specific branch of a name-using practice. An object is a bearer of a proper name basically if there is an established practice of connected uses of a name that refer to the very same object.

Pluralism seems to offer a realistic description of our *ordinary use* of proper names. The central question now is in how far the acceptance of pluralism provides an argument in favour of a context-sensitive view of proper names. The distinguished mechanisms are undoubtedly mechanisms that determine the referent of a *single use* of a proper name. The crucial assumption of the outlined version of pluralism that forces one to adopt the view that proper names have a context-sensitive semantics is the third mentioned thesis. One could accept the first and second theses and make use of Kripke's distinction between a speaker's reference and semantic reference. According to this distinction, a speaker's reference and semantic reference can be related, but semantic reference is neither relativized to uses or contexts of use nor a specific sub-variety of a speaker's reference, as it is according to pluralism. Based on such a distinction one could identify the referent of a use of a proper name with the speaker's referent of the name and the semantic referent of a name with the referent of an established practice of connected uses of a specific name. Hence, the core of pluralism also seems to be compatible with a context-insensitive view concerning semantic reference. This shows that further additional motivations are required to get the intended *full-flagged* version of pluralism. The question of the correct semantic individuation of proper names may provide this required additional evidence in favour of a context-sensitive view.

**Motivation 2: The problem of shared names**

The correct semantic individuation of proper names is a very tricky and controversial issue. One can find more fine-grained and more course-grained proposals concerning the individuation of proper names in the relevant philosophical literature as we have already seen in chapter 2. According to the more fine-grained proposals, there are literally no proper names (that bear the primary semantic properties associated with names) that share the same semantic referent. That is, intuitively there are different bearers of a popular name like 'Peter', but in fact each bearer of this kind of name has its own *proper* name. To be able to account for this kind of intuitive data, the fine-grained view distinguishes two different *kinds* of names. Namely, name-types and name-tokens, or as some defenders say: *generic* and *specific* names. Generic names account for the mentioned intuitive data concerning name-sharing. Specific names are the primary bearers of the semantic properties of names. The most important feature of such a view, in the context of our discussion, is that it can easily be used to combine the two core theses of pluralism with a context-insensitive semantics of proper names that treats them formally as individual constants or variables. However, this view, which is mainly driven by the theoretical desire to assimilate names either to individual constants or to individual mental representations of objects, has severe problems and it is very difficult to motivate this view in a plausible way. The mentioned distinction between generic and specific names seems questionable not only from a methodological, but also from a metaphysical point of view as we have already shown.[18] Methodologically, it is problematic to insist on the existence of generic proper names in addition to specific names *just* to account for some intuitive data concerning name-sharing. Metaphysically, it is problematic, because there is no independent plausible metaphysical or explanatory motivation for the postulation of two different *kinds* of names. However, the most serious problem of this view is that it is linguistically inadequate. Here is another new argument for this claim: if this view were correct, it predicts that sentences like the following have a true and a false reading:

(1)　John Wayne is a bearer of the name 'John', but John Lennon is not.
(2)　Paul McCartney has the same first name as Paul Newman.

However, intuitively, a sentence like (1) *only* has a false reading. The true reading of (1) that is proposed by the fine-grained individuation is not accessible. Furthermore, intuitively a sentence like (2) has only a true reading. The proposed false reading is again inaccessible. Therefore, if a semantic conception of names aims to capture our intuitive *ordinary* notion and uses of names, then the proposed fine-grained conception is inadequate.

The defender of the fine-grained view of names could argue that our ordinary *folk-conception of names* is mistaken and should be replaced by a more adequate one. However, in fact there is no good and independent theoretical motivation for such a replacement. We can stick to our ordinary *notion* of names and capture all desired semantic properties of names based on a *context-sensitive* semantics of names.

A coarse-grained conception of the individuation of names in any version is committed to the view that the very same proper name conceived as a bearer of semantic properties can have more than one bearer. Against this background and taking into account the two mentioned assumptions of pluralism, a context-sensitive view concerning the semantic reference of names seems to be the most plausible. Names could on this basis be semantically assimilated to demonstratives or pronouns, at least to some extent. With respect to these expressions, we also seem to have multiple different options to determine the referent of a *single use* of such an expression. Furthermore, the semantic referent seems to be dependent on this use-referent in some way.

The combination of the two core theses of pluralism with a coarse-grained individuation of proper names seems to exclude a plausible version of the ambiguity view of proper names. There only seem to be *two* remaining options of this view on this basis: either one claims that proper names have as many meanings as there are different individual ways to determine the referent of a single use of a name; or one claims that each proper name has a single linguistic meaning but a multitude of different semantic referents. The first option makes the notion of ambiguity vacuous. On this basis, a name is not in a *linguistic* sense ambiguous. It cannot be seen as a kind of linguistic competence to know all the possible uses of a single name. The second option seems to make use of a terminological trick.[19] It admits that each proper name has only one linguistic meaning, but that such a name has multiple semantic referents. However, it does not make sense to say that a name *qua* singular term that has only one linguistic meaning has multiple semantic referents. Names would on this basis either become predicates or plural terms. Relative to the first option, names would apply to multiple different things. Relative to the second option, names would refer to a multitude of single objects like plural terms. However, both views do not lead to the desired result of preserving that status of names as *semantically singular* terms. This can only be done on the basis of the given assumptions, if the semantic reference relation in the case of names is relativized to uses or contexts of use. Therefore, I conclude, that full-flagged pluralism is the only *meaningful* way to combine the core of pluralism with a coarse-grained individuation of proper names.

A coarse-grained individuation of proper names seems to be the natural option for someone who aims to capture our ordinary notion of names in natural languages. However, it is not a trivial matter to spell out the details of such an account. Especially because our ordinary notion of names is not as straightforward and simple as the examples mentioned above suggest. The right way to individuate proper names seems to be in *historic* terms. There are many different correct spellings or pronunciations that a single name can have and there can also be different versions of a single name in one language or in different languages. What counts as such a variation of a single name is basically a matter of historical conventionalization. That is, what counts as an expression or linguistic form that represents one and the same name is a matter of an established convention by a series of uses of such an expression for a specific purpose. In this sense, names are rather complex entities, whose individuation strictly depends on the history of the conventionalized use of certain expressions for a certain purpose. However, this complex notion of a name is also *polysemous*. We sometimes use the expression 'name' to denote the whole historically evolved bundle of possible versions, spellings and pronunciations of a single name. On other occasions, we use it to denote a specific subset of all the variations, spellings and pronunciations of a single name. Or we use it to denote the semantically relevant class of variations. The following two examples show this difference:[20]

(3)   Johannes and Hans bear in fact the very same name.
(4)   There are two bearers of the name 'Jon' and two bearers of the name 'John' that attend my seminar on proper names.

Both sentences have at least two readings. It is important to be aware of this polysemy and the possibility to narrow down the extension of our ordinary (basically etymological) notion of a *name* to a subset relative to different contexts of use of the expression 'name'. However, this variation *only* concerns the possibility to *narrow down* the extension of the notion of names to a specific sub-class of possible expressive variations of a single name. The dimension that a single linguistic name-form can have different bearers is not a possible dimension of variation of this kind. Therefore, the mechanism that allows us to narrow down our ordinary coarse-grained notion of a name to certain variations of a name does not include the fine-grained notion of names proposed by some philosophers. For semantic purposes, only a specific subset of the etymological cluster of different variations, spellings and pronunciations of names seems to be a relevant notion of a name and name-bearing. Hence, we should only make use of this notion of names when we specify the semantics of a *name* in natural language. The other less or more restricted notions are only relevant for the semantics of the expression 'name' and its counterparts in natural languages itself and that concern its uses in sentences like (4).

In my opinion, the two mentioned motivations already provide relatively good evidence for a context-sensitive treatment of the semantics of proper names. However, there are people who think that there are even two more additional motivations for such a view.

## Motivation 3: Predicative uses of proper names

Beside their paradigm uses as singular referential devices in a sentence like the following:

(5)   John loves Mary,

proper names also seem to have a couple of derived uses, most notably they seem to have derived predicative uses in sentences like the following:

(6)   Peters tend to be nice.
(7)   Every Peter I know is funny.

From a semantic point of view, it is clear that the name-like expressions in (6) and (7) behave quite different than the name in (5). However, although theses expressions clearly are of a different semantic type, there also seem to be intuitive systematic connections between these two different name-like expressions.

Some authors have suggested that the best explanation for this kind of systematic connection is provided by a comparison to a similar phenomenon in the case of third-person personal pronouns.[21] Interestingly, third-person personal pronouns, which are also referring expressions, seem to have similar derived uses. The third-person personal pronouns 'she' is used as a singular referential term in the following example:

(8)   She is the nicest person that I know.

However, third-person personal pronouns like 'she' also have, apart from a referential use, a predicative use as the following additional example demonstrates:

(9)   It is obviously a she.

In the case of a referential use of 'she' in a sentence like (8), it is uncontroversial that this expression is use-sensitive and that it therefore only has a semantic referent relative to a context of use. Furthermore, the semantic referent of such an expression is constrained (but not determined) by the condition of being female. Full-flagged pluralism concerning proper names proposes an important semantic similarity of names and pronouns like 'she' with respect to the referential use of this expression.

In the case of a referential use of 'she' in a sentence like (8) it is clear that the condition of being female only constrains the semantic referent of this expression and that it does not contribute directly to the truth-conditional content of a sentence like (8). However, the situation is different in the case of a predicative use of 'she' in a sentence like (9). In this case, the condition of being female constitutes the truth-conditional contribution of 'is a she' in (9). Hence, it seems there is some kind of semantic transfer between the *character* or *constraint* of 'she' in a sentence like (8) and the *truth-conditional meaning* of 'is a she' in a sentence like (9). It seems that the constraining condition of 'she' is transferred from the pre-semantic or use-conditional level of meaning to the truth-conditional level of meaning. Such conversions in meaning are a typical productive feature of natural languages.

Now it also seems that in cases like (5) and (6) something similar is going on. According to full-flagged pluralism, proper names are use-sensitive expressions and have context-sensitive semantic referents. The condition of bearing the name 'N' constrains the semantic referent of the name 'N'. Furthermore, this constraining condition is not part of the truth-conditional content that is expressed by a sentence like (5), but it is part of this content in a sentence like (6) or (7). Hence, the same kind of meanings-transfer seems to be operative as in the case of third-person personal pronouns. This interesting similarity seems to provide further indirect evidence for a close semantic relationship between names and third-person personal pronouns. However, it also must be noticed that the analogy has some limitations.[22] In the case of names, predicative and other derived uses seem to be less restricted and more productive as in the case of third-person personal pronouns. In English and several other languages there is no established predicative use of the counterparts of 'she' and 'he' in combination with most quantifier expressions. There are also cross-linguistic variations relative to different languages. In different languages, more or less of these combinations are possible. However, in the case of names there is a greater variation of predicative uses of proper names and there is also a greater variety of other derived uses of names as verbs or adjectives.[23] These disanalogies do not necessarily show that there is a principle difference between the name- and the pronoun-case. What they show is that all these kinds of derived uses are a matter of convention and use. In principle, such derivations are possible because they are typical processes of natural language modulation. However, it really depends on the actual establishment of such derivations, as to whether such uses really become conventionalized and part of the lexicon of a language. In the case of names, there seems to be a greater expressive need for such derivations. This instrumental difference is the root of the difference in frequency and type concerning the derived uses of names and pronouns. But these differences do not show that there are necessarily different mechanisms operative in both kinds of cases.

## Motivation 4: Anaphoric uses of proper names

I want to briefly mention a final indirect motivation for the semantic assimilation of proper names and third-person personal pronouns. These kinds of pronouns do not only have referential and predicative uses, but they also have anaphoric or bound uses. The combination of referential and anaphoric uses seems to be a distinctive semantic feature of these kinds of expressions. Now the question arises as to whether names also have anaphoric or bound uses. A positive answer would provide further evidence for a close semantic relationship between this kind of pronouns and proper names. In fact, there are also certain uses of proper names where they seem to be used as bound or anaphoric expressions as the following examples show:

(10) A Mary and a Paul joined the Diogenes Club yesterday. **Mary** is a very nice person.[24]
(11) If a boy loves a girl with the name 'Mary', **Mary** ends up being admired by him.[25]

However, these kinds of uses of proper names are quite rare and they seem to be marked. Proper names cannot be bound in the same flexible and typical way as third-person personal pronouns. It is in fact one of the most difficult riddles concerning the semantics of proper names as to why there seems to be anaphoric and bound uses and why these apparent uses are much more restricted as in the case of third-person personal pronouns. These extremely restricted seemingly bound and anaphoric uses of proper names only provide very weak evidence for the semantic assimilation of proper names and pronouns of the mentioned kind. However, if it really can be shown that proper names can be bound by a quantifier, even if only in very specific sentential contexts of the case, this data would nevertheless provide a further reason to assume a close semantic relationship between names and third-person personal pronouns. In the next section I will focus in a bit more detail on these kinds of uses and in chapter 6 I will defend a view that denies that proper names can be bound by quantifiers.

## Against the two most popular formal versions of a context-sensitive view on names

Before I develop and defend my own context-sensitive view of the semantics of proper names in more detail, I will provide a critical overview of the two most popular versions of a context-sensitive semantics of proper names, namely the variabilist and the indexical views on this issue. In this context, I will also show why the analogy between names and complex demonstratives or names and third-person pronouns should not be taken too seriously. Furthermore, I will argue against the view that the notion of *salience* or *prominence* can be used to unify different reference-determining mechanisms in the case of names.

### Against formal variable indexical views on names

The main motivation for formal variabilist views on names is provided by certain examples of seemingly anaphoric uses of proper names. (I use the expression 'anaphoric use' in a very broad sense such that it covers proforms of laziness, prototypical bound anaphora, discursive anaphora, and donkey anaphora.[26]) It is a well-known fact that third-person personal pronouns and complex demonstratives can be used in a referential and an anaphoric way. There also seem to be anaphoric uses of proper names in addition to the more familiar referential uses. Prima facie the two already mentioned discourse fragments (10) and (11) seem to have readings according to which the name 'Mary' is used in an anaphoric way; namely in (10) as a discursive anaphora and in (11) as a donkey anaphora.

There are people who have used examples like (10) to argue for a view that is called *variabilism* and that holds that names can be represented by individual variables in a formal semantic framework. According to this view, the use of 'Mary' in (10) is an example of a bound use of such a name-variable.[27]

Other people have used examples like (11) to argue for the view that a proper name like 'Mary' can be represented by a complex descriptive phrase like '(ιx)(Mary(x) ∧ x=y)' that contains the predicate 'Mary', the free variable 'y' and that such a phrase is interpreted on the basis of a Fregean[28] theory of the description-operator '(ιx)'.[29] According to this view, the use of 'Mary' in (10) can be interpreted as a use of '(ιx)(Mary(x) ∧ x=y)', where the free variable 'y' is bound by a universal quantifier.[30]

The first view is based on an analogy between proper names and third-person pronouns.[31] The second view is inspired by an analogy between proper names and complex demonstratives.[32]

Do examples like (10) and (11) provide good motivations for the proposed variable formal indexical views on names? I do not think so. Firstly, there is a significant difference between third-person personal pronouns on the one hand, and complex demonstratives and proper names on the other hand. Third-person personal pronouns have prototypical bound anaphoric uses. These are uses where the pronoun is in the scope of a quantifier expression *and* is bound by this quantifier.[33] Third-person personal pronouns also have deviant bound anaphoric uses, where the pronoun *seems* to be outside of the scope of a certain quantifier and nevertheless *seems* to be bound by this quantifier.[34] Discursive or donkey anaphora are examples of this sort.[35] If names have anaphoric uses at all, they *only* have deviant bound anaphoric uses, a feature that they would share with complex demonstratives. This shows that variabilism is in danger of over-generalizing the possibility of anaphoric uses of names. It needs to provide a rationale as to why certain bound uses of name-variables are appropriate and others are not. It seems to be difficult to provide such a rationale on the basis of the proposed formal representations of proper names.

Secondly, the view is also not restrictive enough concerning so-called unbound uses of proper names. In a formal theory, we can assign any arbitrary object via an assignment function to an unbound individual variable. Intuitively, we cannot use any name in a correct and felicitous way to refer to any object, but prima facie only to the bearers of a name. Therefore, an additional restriction of the assignment function is needed. But such an adaption would lead to an ambiguity, because the semantics of names relative to their unbound uses would differ from the semantics relative to their bound uses. In the case of unbound uses the values of a name-variable are *always* restricted to the bearers of a certain name relative to the domain of discourse of the actual world. In the case of bound uses, the values of a name-variable are restricted to the bearers of a certain name relative to the domain of discourse of the quantifier that binds such a variable. And these domains can differ between a quantifier that is modally unembedded and a quantifier that is modally embedded.[36]

Thirdly, the really challenging apparent anaphoric uses of proper names that are provided by examples like (11) are relatively rare and restricted to very specific sentential contexts.[37] But it seems to be methodologically questionable to make use of such a rare and special use of an expression – as Elbourne does – to motivate a general semantic analysis of proper names.

Fourthly, the semantic analysis proposed by Elbourne is problematic if we apply it to non-anaphoric, referential uses of a proper name. A phrase like '$(\iota x)(Mary(x) \land x=y)$' is only a *weakly* rigid designator.[38] It only refers to the very same object in respect to those possible worlds relative to which this object is a bearer of the name 'Mary'.[39] But intuitively 'Mary' refers to the very same object in respect to every possible world relative to which this object exists. Hence, we cannot account for the true reading of a sentence like 'It is possible that Mary is not identical to any bearer of "Mary"' according to the proposed analysis. Therefore, in some way we need to rigidify the expression '$(\iota x)(Mary(x) \land x=y)$' for this purpose, either by using an actuality- or a dthat-operator. But this kind of rigidity is not welcome if we use an expression like '$(\iota x)(Mary(x) \land x=y)$' in a bound way and in a context like (11). In such cases, a non-rigid interpretation of '$Mary(x)$' is desired. And it is even required if we use (11) within the scope of a modal operator like 'It is possible that' and want to account for the correct truth-conditions of such a sentence. Therefore, Elbourne's analysis cannot provide a *uniform* analysis of so-called anaphoric and referential uses of a proper name that he aims to provide. If he wants to make use of the given analysis of (4), he must accept that names have different semantic interpretations relative to so-called anaphoric and referential uses.

Fifthly, as we have already noticed, names seem to have more in common with complex demonstratives than with personal pronouns. In the light of this similarity, some people have claimed that a proper name like 'Alfred' should be treated as semantically equivalent to a complex demonstrative like 'This Alfred' or 'That Alfred'.[40] There is one observation that seems to provide some evidence in favour of this view. We can substitute a proper name 'N' relative to every seemingly deviant anaphoric use with the corresponding complex demonstrative 'this N' or 'that N' *salva veritate*, and without changing the content of such a claim. But things are different if we focus on non-anaphoric referential uses of names. In these cases, it is not in general possible to substitute a name *salva veritate* for a complex demonstrative 'this N' or 'that N'.[41] There are significant differences between these two kinds of expressions: the determination of the reference of a complex demonstrative of the form 'this F' or 'that F' *requires* an act of demonstrative identification. Such a *requirement* does not exist in the case of names.[42] Furthermore, a sentence like 'That Alfred is a nice guy, but the other one isn't' is perfectly meaningful, but if we substitute 'That Alfred' with the name 'Alfred' the result is an odd sentence.[43] These differences also seem to confirm the thesis that if names are indexicals, they are indexicals of a distinctive kind.

Our five observations suggest being sceptical whether examples like (10) or (11) provide a very good and strong motivation for a variabilist view on names. If we also take into account our additional more general methodological worries concerning this view in the 'Prolegomenon' of this book, variabilist views on names do not seem to be such a quite appealing option at all. (Chapter 6 contains more arguments against this view.)

### Against the most popular indexical views on names

There are at least three different formal constant indexical views based on KLD that have been proposed in the relevant literature. According to KLD, every expression has an extension that is relativized to two different kinds of parameters: contexts of use and circumstances of evaluation. Following Kaplan, we consider circumstances of evaluation to be ordered pairs consisting of a possible world and a time parameter. I use the abbreviation '$[e]_{c,<w,t>}$' for *'the extension of "e" relative to the context of use c and the circumstance of evaluation consisting of the possible world w and the time t'*. We can specify the conditions φ that determine the extensions of expressions in KLD by certain equations of the general form '$[e]_{c,<w,t>} = \varphi$'.[44] From such statements one can also read off the *character* and *content* of an expression in KLD, because the following additional equation holds: $[e]_{c,<w,t>} = char(e)(c)(w,t)$.[45] Against this background, we can now capture the indexical semantics of a name like 'Alfred' according to the three mentioned indexical views in the following way:

(IC1)   $[Alfred]_{c,<w,t>}$ = the object of the originating event of the most salient **name-using practice** that concerns the name 'Alfred' relative to $c_w$.[46]

(IC2)   $[Alfred]_{c,<w,t>}$ = the object of the most salient **naming-convention** relative to $c_w$ that concerns the name 'Alfred'.[47]

(IC3)   $[Alfred]_{c,<w,t>}$ = the object of the most salient **dubbing in force** relative to $c_w$ that concerns the name 'Alfred'.[48]

There are obvious similarities and differences between these three views. Firstly, these are three at least superficially different variations of a *specific kind* of formal constant indexical view. All three theories can be generated from the general schema 'The object of the most salient F relative to $c_w$ that concerns the name "N"', where 'F' is placeholder for an expression that denotes some common factor about the use of a name 'N' that relates 'N' to its bearers. The three accounts use at least superficially different expressions to classify these common relating factors. Secondly, all three views make use of the notion of *salience* (or *prominence*) to provide a functional correspondence between a name and a bearer of this name relative to a certain context of use.

Before we can evaluate these three views, we have to clarify the contents of the three listed reference fixing conditions. A *name-using practice* consists of individual uses of a specific proper name that are in a specific way connected with each other. According to the orthodox conception of name-using practices or so-called chains of communication, introduced by Kripke, each name-using practice has an originating event that assigns a specific name to a specific object.[49] Prototypically, these acts are acts of naming. The first explicit use of such a name is parasitic on the originating act: it is used with the intention to refer to the named object. Subsequent uses of a name are parasitic on their preceding uses. According to this view, the referent of an individual use of a name is the object of the originating act to which this use is connected via a chain of uses of this name that constitute a certain name-using practice. Prototypically, this kind of view about reference determination is combined with an ambiguity view on names and therefore a fine-grained individuation of names that holds that there are literally no two different objects that share the same name. As we have seen, one motivation for an indexical view is the rejection of such a fine-grained individuation of names. The three listed standard versions of a formal constant indexical view respect this motivation and are committed to a more coarse-grained individuation of names that allows a single name to have more than one bearer. But this combination of a coarse-grained individuation of names and a Kripkean determination of reference leads to a specific problem for the view (IC1). Such a view has the consequence that there can be different name-using practices that involve the very same name. Therefore, fission cases and fusion cases concerning name-using practices are possible and these lead to trouble. There are fission cases where one name belongs to a name-using practice that has a single origin relative to which a name is assigned to more than one object. Single acts of naming that assign one name to different objects are also possible.[50] But that means that there can be originating events of name-using practices with more than one object or target. Furthermore, it is also possible that a single name-using practice has more than one origin, because such a practice might be the product of a fusion of two name-using practices with two different origins with different or identical objects.[51] This shows that in certain cases the salience of a specific name-using practice might not provide a sufficient condition for determination of the reference of a proper name relative to a specific context of use.

The view (IC3) shares this problem with (IC1), but this view also has an additional problem if dubbings in force are conceived of in a certain way. The notion of a *dubbing in force* can be understood in a *narrow* and in a *wide* sense. In the narrow sense, a dubbing is identical to a single speech act of naming. In the wide sense, the notion of dubbing describes an act or series of acts that has the same consequence as a single act of naming, namely that a certain object becomes the bearer of a certain name. A dubbing D concerning a name 'N' is *in force* relative to a time t if 'N' still has the bearer or the bearers at t that were assigned to 'N' by D and therefore no other act was performed between the time of the performance of D and t that was able to change the naming status of 'N'. Pelzcar and Rainsbury prefer to understand the notion of dubbing in the narrow sense.[52] But that is problematic, because not every name is introduced by means of an act of naming. Probably, a large number of names are introduced in a more implicit way. But that is only an additional problem. Whether we understand dubbings in a wide or narrow sense, such a view faces a similar problem as (IC1). A single act of naming can make it the case that a certain name receives more than one bearer. Therefore, the salience of a specific dubbing in force might not be a sufficient condition for the determination of the referent of a proper name relative to a context of use.

A *naming-convention* is a convention that links names with their bearers. In agreement with Perry, Recanati holds the view that there might be different individual naming-conventions that link the very same name to different bearers of this name. On this basis, the indexical view based on (IC2) does not face the mentioned problem of (IC1) and (IC3) concerning the insufficiency of reference determination. There is a dispute between Perry and Recanati as to whether these conventions are semantic or non-semantic conventions.[53] An indexical view like (IC2) is committed to the view that these conventions are non-semantic, because otherwise it would collapse into a specific variant of the ambiguity view. These conventions can be established by acts of naming or acts with the same institutional consequences as acts of naming. Against this background, it makes sense to call such conventions non-semantic. But on the other hand, these non-semantic conventions could be constitutive for *semantic* naming-conventions. Therefore, a defender of the view (IC2) must not only reject the thesis that those naming-conventions that are constituted by certain institutional acts are semantic, but must also hold that these conventions do not constitute specific semantic naming-conventions that might be identified with the meanings of a proper name. And it is not clear whether there are any good reasons to resist such a kind of view if these conventions really constitute the name-bearer relation between names and objects. Therefore, the indexical view based on (IC2) seems to be in danger of collapsing into a certain version of the ambiguity view.[54]

Apart from these specific problems of the three mentioned views, there are also certain general problems that our three salience-based views share. Firstly, all these accounts use the notion of salience in a rather peculiar way. They do not apply the notion of salience to objects that are bearers of a certain name and therefore potential referents, they apply it to certain *instances* of relations that relate names and their bearers. It might be doubted whether our ordinary acts of the determination of a referent of a name relative to a context of use can be captured in an adequate way on this basis. A specific F can only become the most salient F relative to a certain context of use if there is a certain mechanism that raises the salience of F to the maximum. Most ordinary competent users of a proper name are not aware of the existence of name-using practices, naming-conventions and dubbings in general. It is unclear which kind of mechanisms ordinary speakers may use to raise the salience of abstract entities like name-using practices or naming-conventions. It is even more mysterious how concrete events in the past like dubbings, can be raised to salience. It seems to be more plausible to hold that the only kind of salience that matters in the case of the determination of the referent of a name is the salience of a certain bearer of a name. Therefore, a more plausible variant of the salience-based approach would be a variant that identifies the referent of a proper name relative to a specific context of use with *the most salient bearer of this name relative to this context of use*. Such a variant would also avoid the individual problems of the three mentioned views.

Secondly, it seems to be necessary to restrict the mechanisms that determine the salience of a bearer of a name or instances of a certain relation that connects names and their bearers in a certain way. Intuitively, the *user* of a proper name has in a certain sense the *control* to which object he refers by means of his use of a name. He can *decide* in which way he wants to use a name and determine the referent of its use; and as we have seen there are multiple ways to determine the referent of a use of a name. Even in the case of a parasitic use of a name, such a use is controlled by the user of this name. He can *decide* to use the name in a parasitic way and he can determine which pre-existing use of a name he aims to exploit. This important controlling aspect is missing in the case of our distinguished variants of the indexical view on names. According to them, the most salient bearer of a name relative to a context of use is conceived of as the referent of this name, whether the salience of this object depends on actions of the user of this name or not. That is too one-sided and simple-minded.

Thirdly, and most damaging for salience-based approaches concerning the determination of reference of a name: the salience of a certain bearer of a name, or the salience of an instance of a certain relation that connects names and their bearers, is neither necessary nor sufficient for the determination of the reference of a name. It does not seem to be the case that the referent of a name relative to a context of use needs to be salient in any plausible sense. I can use a name in a context, where no bearer of this name is salient at all, and refer to a specific object in a felicitous way, although my audience might not immediately be able to figure out to which object I am referring, because no object is raised to the maximum of salience relative to such a context of use by me or anyone else.[55] Furthermore, there might be a certain bearer of a name that is made most salient by a user of this name or someone else in a context of use, but it is nevertheless possible that the user of this name *refers* to a completely different object in this context. One may think of a situation where a user of a name takes his audience on a ride concerning the referent of this name, before he reveals the real referent. Or a user might, for example, refer to different objects by different uses of the same name in the very same context and only one of these objects might be the object whose salience is raised to the relative maximum by the user of this name. Salience-based indexical accounts seem to confuse facts about the determination of the reference of a name with *evidence* for such facts that is available to an interpreter.

These observations show, in my opinion, that salience-based indexical views on names provide a fundamentally wrong view of the determination of the reference of names relative to a specific context of use. Let us investigate in the next section of this chapter whether an approach based on the proposed variant of pluralism about the determination of reference fairs better.

## Towards a new context-sensitive semantics for proper names

In this section, I will propose and discuss some alternative versions of a context-sensitive semantics of proper names. The *first alternative* makes use of pluralism and implements it into KLD. According to pluralism, there are different ways and mechanisms to determine the referent of a single (referential) *use* of a proper name. This referent of a single use of a name, however it is determined, then functions as one of two inputs to determine the semantic referent of a name relative to a context of use. The second additional input is the name-bearer condition, which has to be satisfied relative to time of use of the name. This leads to the following *first alternative* context-sensitive semantics for proper names based on KLD:

(IC4)　　[Alfred]$_{c,<w,t>}$ = the referent of the use of 'Alfred' by $c_a$ in $c_w$ that is a bearer of 'Alfred' at $c_t$.[56]

I will now confront this view with four different objections. These objections lead to a stepwise modification of the proposed semantics. The final version of this stepwise modification is my own favoured context-sensitive semantics of proper names.

More specifically, I will discuss the following four problems: (i) the problem of empty and incorrect uses of proper names, (ii) the problem of non-literal uses of proper names, (iii) the problem of temporal modification with respect to past names, (iv) the problem of multiple occurrences of the same name with different referents.

### The problem of empty and incorrect uses of proper names

KLD is a classical logic. Therefore, for pure logical reasons, it is impossible that there are singular terms without a semantic referent. However, intuitively there is the possibility to use a proper name without a semantic referent in a meaningful way. Firstly, there are *defective* uses of a proper name. For example, if one makes use of (a) an individual concept, or (b) an individual singular condition that fails to pick out a single object, or (c) a demonstration that fails to pick out a single object to determine the use of a specific proper name, then neither the use of this name will have a referent nor will there be a semantic referent of this name relative to such a use. Secondly, there are *incorrect* uses of ordinary proper names. I might use a single proper name to refer to an object that is not a bearer of this name. In such a case the constraining condition is not satisfied. Hence, the use of the name has a referent, but there is no semantic referent of the name relative to this use. In this sense, the use of the name is *semantically* empty. Thirdly, there are *defective name using practices* that are either initiated by an unsuccessful act of naming or by a series of non-referring uses of the very same name. If one aims to exploit such a defective practice by a single use of this name, then such a use has neither a speaker's nor a semantic referent. Good examples are name-using practices that aim to establish a name for a phantom island (like the name 'Sandy Island').

We have to modify KLD by means of the tools provided by *free logic* to be able to account for such cases. Therefore, we must substitute (IC4) by the following more sophisticated reference-determining condition:[57]

(IC5)  If (the referent of the use of 'Alfred' by $c_a$ in $c_w$ that is a bearer of 'Alfred' at $c_t$) is defined, then $[Alfred]_{c,<w,t>}$ = the referent of the use of 'Alfred' by $c_a$ in $c_w$ that is a bearer of 'Alfred' at $c_t$; otherwise ($[Alfred]_{c,<w,t>}$) is undefined.

## The problem of non-literal uses of proper names

We have seen that there are incorrect uses of proper names that may lack a semantic referent for different kinds of reasons. Such uses are infelicitous uses and the lack of a semantic referent is a consequence of the lack of felicity. However, there is also a class of *felicitous* uses that, strictly speaking, either seem to lack a semantic referent or that force us to *relax* the notion of a semantic referent in a certain way. Let me exemplify such cases by means of four examples that share an important feature, but that are also different in certain respects. They share the feature that they are all *stressed* uses of a proper name. The addition of *stress* seems to transform or relax the constraining condition of the proper name in a certain sense. Consequently, the use is felicitous although the constraining condition is literally not satisfied.

*Case 1*
The first example I want to introduce concerns the intentional introduction of a new name by using this name and aiming to establish a new name-using practice. Imagine a case where someone finds a cat and decides after a while to keep it. The new owner of this cat does not yet have a name for the cat. He is at first undecided which name he should give the cat. On some occasion, someone asks the new owner 'Where is the new cat?' And he responds by uttering the following sentence with a stressed name:[58]

(12)  WHISKERS is in the kitchen.

Such an utterance is perfectly acceptable if (a) it is accompanied by the intention to establish a new name for the new cat and (b) the used name is stressed to indicate that the use is non-literal; and (12) is also true if the new cat is in fact in the kitchen. But the utterance of (12) need not be conceived of as an explicit or implicit act of naming. There might be a dispute about the name of the new cat after the utterance of (12) and it may take a while until there is some agreement about the new name of the cat. And even if it turns out that the cat in the end receives a different name than 'Whiskers', the *initial* utterance of (12) remains flawless and the use of the name 'Whiskers' remains a proper use of the name although the cat to which the utterer of (12) referred was not a bearer of this name relative to the time of utterance. Therefore, there seem to be acceptable uses of a name that refer to potential future bearers of a name. But a use of 'Whiskers' in a context like CASE 1 would be *infelicitous* if (a) it is not accompanied by the mentioned manifested intention or (b) the name is not stressed to indicate the non-literalness of the use. It seems to be unquestionable that the use of the name in (12) is felicitous. However, what is not completely clear is whether we should say that the name 'Whiskers' only has a speaker's referent with respect to its specific use in (12) or whether we should assign to him a (non-literal) semantic referent.

*Case 2*
The second case of a non-literal use of a name concerns the implicit correction of an incorrect use of a proper name by another speaker. Assume, for example, that a speaker A erroneously thinks that person P is a bearer of the name 'Peter Sanders', but in fact this person has a completely different name. Imagine now that A utters the assertoric sentence 'I know Peter Sanders from school'. Now to this utterance B, who knows that P is not a bearer of the name 'Peter Sanders' responds as follows:

(13)   PETER SANDERS, who is not a bearer of this name, is ten years older than you.[59]

We again have a stressed use of a name that refers to an object that is not a bearer of this name and nevertheless this use of this name is felicitous and there is no semantic or pragmatic norm that is violated by this use. Therefore, we again are forced to take a stand in how far the situation is compatible with (IC5) or not.

*Case 3*
The third case concerns a stressed use of a *former* name for a certain object, where the speaker makes sure by stressing the name that the use is non-literal. Imagine a situation where someone talks about a person that is a big fan of the Soviet Union and has the tendency to use all names for cities of the former Soviet Union as they were used during the existence of the Soviet Union. This person makes use on this occasion of the following sentence:

(14)   My wife is a big fan of the Soviet Union and she would love to join me during my next trip to LENINGRAD.

The user of (14) uses the stressed name 'Leningrad' to refer to St. Petersburg, which was named 'Leningrad' during the existence of the Soviet Union. We again have a completely felicitous stressed use of a name that refers to a former, but not a current bearer of this name. This is the third case that forces us to take a stand on the issue of whether or not such specific non-literal uses are compatible with (IC5).

*Case 4*
The fourth case concerns the referential use of a proper name to an object that *only resembles* a famous bearer of this name. Imagine someone that looks like Jürgen Klopp regularly visits the football ground of a local and very small football club. Someone can report this kind of activity in a proper way by uttering a sentence like:

(15) JÜRGEN KLOPP regularly visits.

A proper use of this kind of sentence relative to the given scenario seems to require a *stressed demonstrative* use of the name 'Jürgen Klopp'. The stress is again required to indicate non-literalness. A demonstrative use seems to be required to indicate that the resemblance between the use referent of the name and some famous bearer of this name is at issue. It is again a challenge to explain how such a use can be infelicitous although it violates (IC5).

What exactly is the role of stress in all of these presented cases? It not only seems to indicate non-literalness, it also seems to suspend the ordinary constraining condition of proper names that is captured by (IC4) or (IC5) and it seems to licence certain alternative uses of a name that does not satisfy this condition. In principle, there seem to be two different strategies to account for such perfectly correct literal uses of proper names.

A *purely pragmatic* approach could describe the role of stress in such cases in such a way that it overrides or suspends the linguist norms that guide the use of proper names relative to a certain use and substitutes these linguist norms by some purely local pragmatic norms. That is, in the first case the stressed use of 'Whiskers' is correct, because the user intends to establish a new use by this name and the object to which he refers is the intended new referent. In the second, the stressed use of 'Peter Sanders' is correct because the user intends to correct a false use of a name and the object to which he refers is the erroneously assumed or alleged bearer of this name. In the third case, the stressed use of 'Leningrad' is correct because the user intends to use a former name of an object to a former bearer of this name. Alternatively, someone could question that the distinction between semantics and pragmatics is as clear as the first proposal suggests. According to this alternative model, there are pragmatic intrusions into the semantics of expressions that modulate or transform the linguistic meanings of an expression on the occasion of a specific use. Therefore, contextual factors together with stress as an indicator of non-literalness are used to mark a modulating use of an expression that makes it possible that the constraining condition that is captured by (IC4) and (IC5) is locally modulated such that on the occasion of the mentioned three uses the used names have the following four different modulated linguistic meanings:[60]

$M_1[[\text{Whiskers}]]_{c,<w,t>}$ = the referent of the use of 'Whiskers' by $c_a$ in $c_w$ that is an intended future bearer of 'Whiskers' by $c_a$.

$M_2[[\text{Peter Sanders}]]_{c,<w,t>}$ = the referent of the use of 'Peter Sanders' by $c_a$ in $c_w$ that is the assumed bearer of 'Sanders' by $c_{ad}$.[61]

$M_3[[\text{Leningrad}]]_{c,<w,t>}$ = the referent of the use of 'Leningrad' by $c_a$ in $c_w$ that is former bearer of 'Leningrad' relative to $c_t$.

$M_4[[\text{Jürgen Klopp}]]_{c,<w,t>}$ = the referent of the use of 'Jürgen Klopp' by $c_a$ in $c_w$ that resembles a famous bearer of 'Jürgen Klopp' relative to $c_t$.

I leave it to the reader as to which of these two approaches he/she prefers; whether he/she opts for a more conservative occasional suspension of semantic norms, or whether he/she opts for a more progressive pragmatic intrusion into semantics. In any case, the outlined felicitous non-literal uses of proper names provide a challenge for an approach that aims to capture *all possible felicitous* use of proper names.

## The problem of temporal modification with respect to past names

There is another problem that is to some extent related to our third example of a non-literal use of proper names. Former names cannot only be used in a felicitous way if they are stressed and used on a specific occasion, but can also be used unstressed if they are embedded under an appropriate temporal operator.

In (14) we have already used 'Leningrad', with stress. This was once the name of St. Petersburg, but it is not the official name of this city anymore. But a proper use of 'Leningrad' in a present tense sentence without the addition of stress or other indicators of non-literalness is not possible. An utterance of a sentence like the following seems to be unacceptable or odd:

(16)   ? Currently, Leningrad has more than a hundred thousand inhabitants.

But interestingly there are also felicitous uses of the name 'Leningrad' without stress. It can be used in *past tense sentences* that refer to times relative to which 'Leningrad' was the name of the second largest city of Russia. The following sentence is an example of an acceptable and true sentence of this kind:

(17)   In 1944, Leningrad had more than a hundred thousand inhabitants.

Furthermore, there is a significant and important difference between the present name of the second largest city of Russia 'St. Petersburg' and its former name 'Leningrad'. We can substitute the name 'St. Petersburg' for 'Leningrad' in (16) and (17) and we get two true and acceptable sentences as a result.[62]

This interesting additional observation excludes the possibility of the simplest solution to the problem. If we would only focus our attention on (16) and (17), a simple modification of the time-parameter in (IC5) would provide the desired solution. We could relativize the name-bearer condition to the time of evaluation instead of the time of the context of use. Against this background, (16) would be semantically incorrect because the referent of 'Leningrad' with respect to (16) is not a bearer of this name relative to the present time. However, (17) would come out as correct because the referent of 'Leningrad' with respect to (17) was a bearer of this name in 1944. So far, so good. But this solution predicts that the substitution of 'Leningrad' in (17) with 'St. Petersburg' delivers an infelicitous use of 'St. Petersburg'. In fact, this substitution has a semantically correct and true sentence as a result. This shows that this simple solution of our problem makes false predications with respect to temporally embedded uses of names that are currently in use.

An alternative semantic solution to the problem has been proposed that postulates a specific ambiguity concerning proper names and distinguishes *restricted* from *unrestricted names*.[63] According to this solution, a former name of a certain thing has a different semantics than a current name of a certain thing. Here is my version of this view: current, unrestricted names have the semantics that is proposed by (IC5). In their case, the constraining condition is relativized to *the time of the context of use*. Former, restricted names, on the other hand, have a slightly different semantics. In their case, the constraining condition is relativized to *the time of evaluation*. Against this background we have to add to (IC5), which can only be applied to unrestricted names, the following further additional semantics for restricted names:

*Semantics for restricted (former) names*

(IC5*)     If (the referent of the use of 'Alfred' by $c_a$ in $c_w$ that is a bearer of 'Alfred' at t) is defined, then [Alfred]$_{c,<w,t>}$ = the referent of the use of 'Alfred' by $c_a$ in $c_w$ that is a bearer of 'Alfred' at t; otherwise ([Alfred]$_{c,<w,t>}$) is undefined.

On this basis, we can now explain why (17) is a semantically correct and true claim; and why, on the other hand, (16) is in some sense true, but semantically odd because the name 'Leningrad' does not satisfy the required constraining condition that guides the use of this name. Furthermore, the significant difference between (IC5) and (IC5*) explains why the substitution of 'St. Petersburg' for 'Leningrad' in (16) and (17) leads to sentences that are true and semantically correct. This solution can also be extended to evaluate sentences like the following:

(18)    In 1850, Leningrad had more than a hundred thousand inhabitants.

Intuitively, this sentence is as odd as (16). The semantics (IC5*) can account for this oddness because 'Leningrad' was not a name for St. Petersburg in 1850, therefore the required constraining condition is violated in the case of (18).

    I think this solution is the best available solution to our problem and the generally overlooked ambiguity of ordinary names is justified by a different systematic semantic behaviour between present and past names. However, people who do not like to postulate such an ambiguity could also treat (IC5*) as the result of a purely pragmatic modulation process. Probably, such a modulation process is the ultimate source of the difference between past and present names; that has already been pointed out but I think this modulation is already *lexicalized* and leads thereby to a genuine semantic ambiguity.

## The problem of multiple occurrences of the same name with different referents

Let me now come to a final problem that is a well-known problem for certain indexicals semantically modelled on the basis of KLD. I will show that this problem has certain important dimensions that are generally overlooked.

    Intuitively, different occurrences of a single name can be used in a single sentence or utterance to refer to *different* things relative to a single context of use. A good example of this kind is provided by the following sentence:[64]

(19)    Alfred could not hear what Alfred was saying.

This sentence *can* be used relative to a single context of use in such a way that it expresses a truth although the the two occurrences of 'Alfred' in (19) refer to two different people. We cannot account for this kind of data on the basis of our current semantics (IC5). If we interpret (19) relative to a single context of use, we *must* assign on the basis of (IC5) to both occurrences of 'Alfred' in (19) the very same extension (referent).

The standard solution to this problem is to introduce an additional evaluation parameter for proper names. This parameter can change relative to the very same context of use. Inspired by an example like (19), the easiest and most natural way is to introduce *indices* as parameters that mark the syntactic occurrence of a name in a sentence. On this basis we can distinguish two uses of 'Alfred' in (19) in the following way:

(19*) Alfred$_1$ could not hear what Alfred$_2$ was saying.

This strategy leads to the following slight modification of our semantics (IC5):[65]

(IC6)   If (the referent of the use of 'Alfred' by $c_a$ in $c_w$ that is a bearer of 'Alfred' at $c_t$) is defined, then [Alfred$_x$]$_{c,<w,t>}$ = the referent of the use of 'Alfred' relative to the occurrence x by $c_a$ in $c_w$ that is a bearer of 'Alfred' at $c_t$; otherwise ([Alfred$_x$]$_{c,<w,t>}$) is undefined.

According to this proposal, names are syntactically represented at the level of logical form as ordered pairs consisting of the ordinary proper name 'N' and an index that marks the terminal nodes of a syntactic tree that represents the structure of a certain sentence.

The idea of relativizing the referent of a use of a name to the *syntactic occurrences* of this name in a sentence also seems to be empirically adequate. Ordinary speakers are implicitly aware of the fact that the use of different occurrences of the same use-sensitive expression in a sentence requires specific individual attitudes and intentions concerning the use of this expression. However, there are different *default expectations* concerning multiple uses of different kinds of expressions. In the case of demonstratives, there is the default expectation that different occurrences of the same demonstrative in different subsequent sentences correspond with different demonstrative acts of identification that identify different objects.[66] In the case of names, there is the default expectation that if the first occurrence of a name in a discourse situation is identified in a certain way, subsequent uses of the same name in different subsequent sentences are identified in a parasitic way that relies on the identification of the first occurrence.[67] These default expectations can be undermined by contextual counter-evidence. A use of (19) relative to a contextual setting where it is obvious that a speaker aims to refer to two different bearers of the name 'Alfred' is an example of this kind. These different expectations mainly concern communicative roles of different kinds of expressions and need not be explicitly captured on the level of the truth-conditional contribution of such an expression.[68, 69]

This standard solution allows us to capture simple examples of multiple uses of a single name in single sentences like (19). However, this solution has severe problems when it comes to the formal representation of more complex patterns of communication like *inferences*. Especially, if these indices are standardly used to mark the syntactic position of a name in a sentence, then we cannot account anymore for the logical validity of very simple intuitively valid inferences as the following two:

Mark Twain$_1$ is an author.
Mark Twain$_1$ is Samuel Clemens$_2$.

---

Samuel Clemens$_1$ is an author.

Mark Twain$_1$ is Samuel Clemens$_2$.

Samuel Clemens$_1$ is Mark Twain$_2$.

Therefore, if we are forced to index names relative to their *absolute occurrences* in a sentence, simple inferences like the given two cannot be represented as valid inferences anymore.

However, this problem can be solved if we make use of expression-relative indices that only index the relative occurrence of an expression in a sentence. Against this background, we can assign the index 1 to both used names in our inferences; and, hence, we can account for the validity of both inferences.

Nevertheless, this new indexing strategy does not solve all problems. We can construct a similar problem for *multiple* uses of a single name, where expression-relative indices do not have the desired purely syntactic function. Arguments like the following seem to be possible and valid:

Alfred$_1$ ≠ Alfred$_2$.

Alfred$_2$ ≠ Alfred$_1$.

Alfred Merker$_1$ [pointing to a man] is the only winner of the Rolf Schock Prize in 2018.
Alfred Merker$_1$ [pointing to a man] ≠ Alfred Merker$_2$ [pointing to a picture].

Alfred Merker$_2$ [pointing to a picture] is not a winner of the Rolf Schock Prize in 2018.[70]

According to the proposed expression-relative indexing, it is not possible to assign the required indices to the conclusions of both toy examples. In the first case, the order of the indices must be the reverse. On this basis the argument becomes an argument of the form 'a≠b; ∴ a≠b' although it was intended as an argument of the form 'a≠b; ∴ b≠a'. In the second case, we are not allowed to index the name in the conclusion with 2. We are only allowed to assign the index 1 to this occurrence. But on this basis the argument becomes invalid.

This shows that there is something fundamentally mistaken in choosing *syntactic* indices to solve our initial problem. What we in fact need are indices that are *semantic* in nature and that mark *same* or *different* uses of the very same name. Against the background of such an alternative semantic indexing strategy, our two toy examples would be possible, correct and valid.

However, the use of such a *semantic* indexing strategy is in tension with the general idea that the semantics of proper names depends on the context of use. According to the proposed strategy, proper names are relativized to *single uses of the name* and to *contexts of use*. That is much more than required and it seems to be an unnecessary duplication. Therefore, much more fundamental revisions are required to overcome the apparently minor problem of multiple uses of a single name in a sentence or discourse fragment as our two toy examples show.

## My alternative context-sensitive semantics for proper names

In my opinion, there is a fundamental distinction between two different kinds of context-sensitive expressions whose importance is often underestimated in the relevant literature. There are, on the one hand, what I want to call *use-sensitive expressions*, and, on the other hand, what I want to call *occasion-sensitive expressions*. There are two general features that distinguish these two different kinds of context-sensitive expressions. Firstly, only in the case of a use-sensitive expression is it metaphysically possible that each *single* use of such an expression has a *different* (semantic) referent. For example, this is definitely true for expressions like 'that', 'that man' and 'she' if they are used as referring terms. We are completely free to use these expressions to refer to different things from one use to another. That is not true of terms like 'I', 'today' or 'now'. The use of these expressions is much more bound and limited by their character or linguistic meaning and depends on certain more objective properties of the context of use. If these properties do not change, then the referent of these expressions also does not change. Secondly, only use-sensitive expressions are completely under the control of a user of this expression. That is, they only get a referent relative to a use if they are accompanied by a certain intention, attitude or action of the user. They indeed require this addition, and this kind of addition makes them so flexible. This typical feature is again exemplified by expressions like 'that', 'that man' or 'she' if they are used as referring terms. But it is not exemplified by such terms like 'I', 'today' and 'now'. In their case, the determination of reference does not require any accompanying attitude, intention or action; they can have context-sensitive referents just on the basis of their linguistic meaning (character).

With this distinction at hand, I now want to defend two different theses. Firstly, proper names are use-sensitive expressions. This is a more or less direct consequence of full-flagged pluralism. Secondly, KLD is a logical framework that allows one to provide a formal semantics for occasion-sensitive expression in a quite accurate way. However, KLD is not a very good choice to formally model the semantics of use-sensitive expressions. Hence, we need a new and more adequate formal semantic framework for this purpose. The problem of multiple uses of a single name in the same sentence with different referents is only one important indicator of this problem. In fact, the difficulties with KLD applied to use-sensitive expressions are more fundamental in nature.

KLD is basically designed to capture a form of context-sensitivity that is utterance- or sentence-relative. According to KLD, whole sentences are relativized to contexts of use and sentence-types get assigned truth-values relative to contexts of use. However, the formal representation of use-sensitive expressions requires a context-relativization that is *expression-relative* and that not only provides a semantic interpretation of a sentence relative to a context, but interpretations that also provide different contextual interpretations of constituent expressions of a sentence. There already exists a more fine-grained semantics for context-sensitive expressions due to Reichenbach and it relativizes semantic interpretation to single expressions.[71] However, for our purposes, this alternative model would be too fine-grained. A Reichenbach-semantics relativizes token-expressions to token-contexts. On this basis, no expression of the same type can be used twice relative to the same context of use. Hence, we need a *new* semantic framework that is a compromise between the existing frameworks of Reichenbach and Kaplan. It should be a type-semantics in Kaplan's spirit, it should allow us to relativize every expression to a context of its use and these contexts of use should be type-contexts. I will call such a kind of semantics *a use-sensitive type-semantics*.

## A new formal semantics for use-sensitive expressions

I will now outline a formal semantic framework for such a kind of semantics that is simply an extension of classical first-order modal logic of an S5-type. This logic makes use of a structure that contains (a) a set of possible worlds W, (b) a total domain D, (c) a world-relative interpretation function I, (d) an absolute denotation function Den and (e) an absolute assignment function δ.

Additionally, this framework makes use of an infinite set of numerical constants: 1, 2, 3 and so on. These numerical constants formally represent single uses of an expression and the sameness of numerical constants indicates sameness in use. There are two different possible ways to individuate the uses of referring expressions that are use-sensitive. Firstly, there is the Russellian coarse-grained individuation of uses that individuates them on the basis of *the sameness of their referents*. Secondly, there is the Fregean fine-grained individuation that individuates them on the basis of the sameness of their accompanying reference-determining attitudes, intentions or actions. Therefore, there are also two different possible semantic interpretations for our numerical indices. According to the first version, *Den* assigns to each index numeral a different single individual of the domain D. Hence, there are no different indices that get assigned the same value. The referent of a use of an expression is the object assigned to the index that represents the use. On this basis, it is impossible that different uses have the same referents. According to the second version, we additionally make use of an infinite set of indexed functions: $f_1()$, $f_2()$ and so on. These functions formally represent reference-determining attitudes, intentions or actions. As their inputs function our use-indices and they assign relative to each index an object of D. The denotation function *Den* assigns to each index an indexed function. The referent of a use is, therefore, the *output* of a function assigned to an index that represents a use. On this basis, it is now possible that different uses have the same referents.

According to this framework, proper names are interpreted as *functional expressions* whose inputs are their possible uses and whose outputs are objects of the domain D. The partial functions that represent the meanings of proper names are conditions that constrain the semantic referent of a proper name relative to the possible uses of this name. That is, if the referent of the *use* of a name is a bearer of this name, then our function assigns this object as *semantic* referent to the use-relativized name. If this condition is not satisfied, the use-relativized name receives no semantic referent.

In principle, this formal system has an *infinite* number of functional expressions that formally represent proper names. For illustrative purposes, I will explicitly introduce only the following three examples:

peter(), michael(), florian().

These functions only yield an output relative to a use-index if the referent at the use-index is also a bearer of this name.[72] To be able to formally model this kind of dependence, we also introduce corresponding name-predicates that all have bearers of a certain name in their extension. For our illustrative purposes, these are the following three predicates:

Peter [], Michael [], Florian [].

The world-relative interpretation function assigns to the name-predicates relative to each world a subset of the domain D that contains the bearers of the corresponding name. These predicates are intuitively roughly equivalent to expressions of the form 'x is a bearer of the name "N"'.

Name-function expressions can only be meaningfully combined with use-indices. *Ordinary uses of a proper name* are now formally represented by a name-function expression and a use-index. These are expressions like 'peter(1)', 'peter(100)', 'florian(2)' and so on.

In the following, I will use the functional expressions 'n()' as schematic stand-in for *name-function expressions* and the predicate 'N[]' as schematic stand-in for *name-predicates*. At first, I will introduce name-function expressions into our formal language. The Russellian or coarse-grained version of our semantics provides the following semantic rule to determine the denotation/extension of name-function-expressions:

*The coarse-grained semantics for name-functions and name-uses*

For every use-index i there is exactly one object $x \in D$ such that: Den (n()) = <i, x> if $x \in I(N[], @)$, otherwise (n(i) is undefined).

More informally, our semantics work as follows. The coarse-grained version assigns to name-functions ordered pairs that consist relative to the first position of *natural numbers* that are denoted by numerical index expressions that formally represent uses of proper names and relative to the second position consists of an *object* that is on element of the domain of discourse D. Every object in D is a potential referent of a use of a proper name. However, only those use-referents of names that are bearers of this name relative to the actual world are semantic referents of a name relative to a semantically correct use of this name. Relative to our system, bearers of names are members of the extension of the corresponding name-predicate 'N[]' of a name-function expression 'n()'. The interpretation function assigns extensions to these name-predicates. A name-function remains undefined relative to those possible pairs of indices and objects that contain an object that is not a bearer of the name that denotes the respective function.

The Fregean or fine-grained version of our semantic is slightly more complicated. On this basis, the semantic values of name-function expressions do not any more capture the semantic denotations of uses of proper names, but only their semantic values. Hence, we can now distinguish between the semantic *value* of a name relative to a use and the semantic *denotation* of a name relative to a use. The semantic value of a name relative to a use is, according to the Fregean version of our semantics, formally represented by indexed-functions that are the formal counterparts of reference determining attitudes, intentions or actions. The semantic denotation of a name relative to a use is the value of the assigned indexed-function. There are different possible ways to capture the two-fold distinction already mentioned. I will now introduce a version that interprets indexed-name-function expressions like 'florian(1)' as singular terms for indexed-functions and I will use the operator '[]' to transform such a name of a function into a name of an individual. Hence, '[florian (1)]' denotes the value of the indexed-function that is denoted by 'florian (1)'. Against this background, expressions of the schematic form '[n(1)]' are the proper semantic counterparts of use-relativized ordinary proper names. We therefore now need two different but connected semantic rules to specify the Fregean version of our use-sensitive semantics for proper names:

*The fine-grained semantics for name-functions and name-uses*

For every use-index i there is exactly one indexed-function f such that: Den(n()) = <i, f> if there is at least one i such that f(i) ∈ I(N[], @), otherwise (n(i) is undefined).

For every name-function-expression $\varphi$ and every use-index i: Den([$\varphi$(i)]) = the value of the denotation of $\varphi$(i) relative to the index i, if (Den ($\varphi$(i)) is defined, otherwise (Den([$\varphi$(i)]) is undefined).

This second version of our semantics assigns to name-function expressions ordered pairs that consist relative to the first position of *natural numbers* that are denoted by numerical index expressions that formally represent uses of proper names, and relative to the second position by an *indexed-function* from use-indices to objects of the domain D. However, only those index-functions can be in the extension of a name-function expression 'n()' that have a bearer of 'n()' relative to the actual world as their output value. Those use-referents of names that have bearers of this name relative to the actual world are semantic referents of a name relative to a semantically correct use of this name. The name-function remains undefined with respect to uses that have a use-referent that is not a bearer of the respective name. Name-function-index combinations denote indexed-functions. So, for example, 'florian(1)' denotes a function that assigns some individual named 'Florian' to the use-index 1. *Extended* name-function-index combinations of the general logical form '[n(i)]' denote on the other hand individual objects that are use-referent relative to index i of the name 'N'. These expressions are without a denotation if 'n(i)' denotes an indexed-function that assigns an object to i that is not a bearer of 'N'.

Against the background of these two versions of our semantics, we can now provide two different semantic representations of *atomic sentences that contain proper names only*. Relative to the Russellian version of our semantics, atomic sentences have the following logical forms and truth- and falsity-conditions:

For any predicate P, any name-function-expression $n_1 \ldots n_n$, and any indices $i_1 \ldots i_n$:

$V(P[n_1(i_1), n_2(i_2), \ldots, n_n(i_n)], w) = T$ iff for (Den $(n_1(i_1))$ is defined ... and Den $(n_n(i_n))$ is defined) and $<n_1(i_1), n_2(i_2), \ldots, n_n(i_n)> \in I(P, w)$.

$V(P[n_1(i_1), n_2(i_2), \ldots, n_n(i_n)], w) = F$ iff it is not the case that ((Den $(n_1(i_1))$ is defined ... and Den $(n_n(i_n))$ is defined) and $<n_1(i_1), n_2(i_2), \ldots, n_n(i_n)> \notin I(P, w)$).

According to the Fregean version, we get the following alternative and slightly different logical forms and truth- and falsity-conditions for atomic sentences with proper names:

$V(P[[n_1(i_1)], [n_2(i_2)], \ldots, [n_n(i_n)]], w) = T$ iff for (Den $([n_1(i_1)])$ is defined ... and Den $([n_n(i_n)])$ is defined) and $<[n_1(i_1)], [n_2(i_2)], \ldots, [n_n(i_n)]> \in I(P, w)$.

$V(P[[n_1(i_1)], [n_2(i_2)], \ldots, [n_n(i_n)]], w) = F$ iff it is not the case that $((\text{Den } [(n_1(i_1)]) \text{ is defined} \ldots \text{and Den } ([n_n(i_n))] \text{ is defined})$ and $<[n_1(i_1)], [n_2(i_2)], \ldots, [n_n(i_n)]> \notin I(P, w))$.

This kind of semantics is relatively close to the standard-semantics of atomic sentences in modal predicate logic. The only main difference is that in our new semantics proper names are treated as functional expressions that are relativized to their uses, which are formally represented by numerical indices.

It is important to note that both *names* treated as functional expressions and *name-uses* represented by name-function-index combinations have rigid extensions. That is, both kinds of expressions have the same denotation with respect to all possible circumstances of evaluation. We have used an absolute denotation function to specify the semantics of both expressions. Against this background, names and name-uses are *obstinately* rigid expressions. They either have the same extension with respect to every possible circumstances of evaluation, or they have no extension with respect to every possible circumstances of evaluation. The main reason for this choice was simply to keep the semantics as simple as possible. Alternatively, we could also use a world-relative denotation function and project the denotation of names and name-uses relative to the actual world to all other non-actual worlds.

The provided semantics is mainly a semantics for unrestricted names. If we also want to model restricted proper names on this basis, we have to introduce an additional time-index to our semantics and a set of times to our structure. On this basis, we could then also introduce world- and time-relative name-predicates and filter the denotation of name-functions and name-function-index combinations in a more restrictive way. I leave it as an exercise to the reader to provide this relatively easy additional modification of our two proposed semantics for proper names.

Before I compare our new semantics with our proposed semantics based on KLD, I want to say more about the relevant differences between the *coarse-grained* and the *fine-grained* versions of our new semantics. The coarse-grained semantics is completely transparent with respect to proper names that have a semantic referent. That is, if a use has a semantic referent, then different indices guarantee a difference in semantic referents. However, there is still the possibility that a name has no semantic referent relative to a certain use and, hence, a difference with respect to indices. Therefore, uses do not guarantee a difference concerning the extensions of the names used. But on this basis, we cannot semantically capture the possibility of a user that standardly uses two different mental representations of the same object to determine the referent of a name relative to different occasions of use based on the false belief that these two representations represent two different objects. Therefore, only the fine-grained semantics allows uses to formally model such uses, which are known as Paderewski-cases.[73] It is not clear whether these cases at all require a semantics that allows for the possibility of different uses of a name with the same referent. However, if one thinks a semantics must be able to account for such cases, our fine-grained semantics provides the desired resources for this purpose.

Another related motivation for the fine-grained semantics are demonstrative uses of proper names. If demonstrative uses are possible, then it is also possible to use the very same name twice in an informative identity sentence and accompanying both uses of the same name by different co-referential pointing gestures. For example, I might use the name 'Mark Twain' twice in such a sentence and, relative to the first use, I point to an early photograph of Mark Twain and, relative to the second use, I point to a later photograph of Mark Twain. Against this basis we can also account for the validity of arguments that make use of such informative identity sentences with the very same name, whether the two uses are accompanied by demonstrations or not:

Mark Twain$_1$ is an author.
Mark Twain$_1$ is Mark Twain$_2$.
---
Mark Twain$_2$ is an author.

If we want to account for such possible uses of proper names, the fine-grained version of our semantics is our choice.

The main difference between our new semantics and semantics based on KLD is not only that single uses of proper names can be individuated in a more fine-grained way. According to our framework, proper names are use-sensitive expressions that could in principle have a different referent with respect to every different use. But there are also additional important semantic differences.

Firstly, according to KLD, every sentence gets a truth-value that is not only relativized to a world and a time, but also to a context of use. That is, *contexts of use* are standardly not represented at the level of logical form, but only relative to the metalanguage. In the case of our semantics, uses are only expressions-relative, the relativization is represented at the level of logical form, hence, context-sensitivity gets resolved on this level and so, no additional relativization of truth-values to contexts of use (or to uses) are required. In this sense, our new semantics is a use-semantics that represents uses of proper names, it is not *primarily* a semantics of names. Nevertheless, it is not a token-semantics, it is a type-semantics for uses of names. In my opinion it is an advantage of our semantics that additional relativizations of truth-values are not necessary. Therefore, I consider it as a virtue of our formal language that although it is simpler than KLD, it nevertheless is able to capture all essential semantic features of names if they are treated as context-sensitive expressions.

Secondly, given the relativization to worlds and contexts of use, KLD has the resources to introduce two completely different notions of entailment and truths that are constant with respect to different relativizations or dimensions. In KLD, the standard procedure is to distinguish between *analytic truths* that are true relative to every context of use, and *necessary truths* that are true relative to every possible world. Additionally, we can have truth-preservation relative to interpretations, contexts of use and possible worlds. Most notably, on the basis of a semantics like (IC4), sentences of the following kind come out as contingent *analytic truths*:

(20)    Peter is a Peter/bearer of the name 'Peter'.

This is the case because relative to (IC4) every use of 'Peter' refers to something and it can only refer to a Peter or bearer of the name 'Peter'. In this sense, (20) is true relative to all contexts of use. However, (20) is not necessarily true, because a thing could have a different name in a different possible world (or not exist).

Relative to (IC5), (20) is not an analytic truth, because it is possible that 'Peter' does not refer relative to some contexts of use. However, on this basis, there is the following weaker claim that functions as ersatz for (20):

(21)   If Peter exists, Peter is a Peter/bearer of the name 'Peter'.

This claim is also an analytic truth in the mentioned sense.

Relative to our new formal semantics, a sentence like (21) has a different formal representation as in KLD, therefore, we cannot account for the analytic truth of (21) in literal terms. Nevertheless, we have the resources to represent certain *uses* of the name 'Peter' in sentences like (21) in such a way that every use of this kind leads to truth structurally similar to (21). Furthermore, we have the logical resources to distinguish logical, analytic and necessary truths. According to our framework, a sentence is a logical truth if it is true with respect to all interpretations and all possible worlds. A sentence is a necessary truth if is true with respect to all possible worlds. Furthermore, a sentence is an analytic truth if it is true with respect to all interpretations relative to the actual world. On this basis, sentences that satisfy the following general schema are *analytic truths* according to our logical framework, if we conceive of 'n' as a schematic letter for name-function-expressions, 'N' as a schematic letter for name-predicates and 'i' as a schematic letter for use-indices:

(22)   If Exist [n(i)], then N[n(i)].[74]   [or: If Exist [[n(i)]], then N[[n(i)]]].[75]

An example of this kind would be the sentence: *If Peter¹ exists, then Peter¹ is a Peter.*

This shows that our semantic framework, although significantly different from KLD, has the logical resources to capture all the desired advantages of the framework KLD. And additionally, it can in opposition to KLD also solve and capture *all* aspects of the problem of multiple occurrences of the same name in the same sentence with different referents. Therefore, I think that our semantics is the best choice to provide a formal semantics of proper names conceived of as context-sensitive expressions.

**A more progressive two-dimensional version**

There is also a last modification that one could make if one aims to distinguish uses of names without a use-referent from those uses that have a use-referent, but no semantic referent. One might have a more relaxed attitude towards a truth-conditional semantics of the uses of expressions. Our semantics is a type-semantics that concerns uses of proper names. But it only captures *semantically* correct uses of proper names. Against this background, it is impossible to express with a sentence in a direct way a truth-evaluable content that contains a name that is not used in a semantically correct way. However, one might argue that we often use sentences to *directly* express truth-evaluable contents that contain names that are not used in a semantically correct way. Hence, semantic correctness can be seen as an additional use-conditional feature, but not as a feature that is required to express a content directly by sentence relative to a context of use. For example, there is a significant difference between the following two incorrect uses of a name. (i) a use of the name 'Peter', where I refer to someone of whom I erroneously think is a bearer of the name 'Peter', and (ii) a use of the very same name, where I refer to a thing that I confuse with a bearer of this name. In the first case, it seems clear that I can use the sentence 'Peter is my friend' to directly express a content about a man to whom I have referred and who is not a bearer of the used name. In the second case, at least some people think that I have directly expressed a content about a specific bearer of the name 'Peter' and only indirectly a content about the man to which I have referred to with 'Peter'. However, even in the second case it depends on how exactly the reference of the name was determined. If I, for example, have a direct mental representation of a person in front of me, I additionally activate a constant mental representation of a bearer of the name 'Peter' that I confuse with the directly represented thing and I determine the use of my name based on both representations, then my use has no use-referent at all and, hence, no content is expressed by the use of the sentence itself. However, I might only make use of *one* of my two representations to determine the referent of my use of the name 'Peter'. Both options seem possible, and in one case it also seems possible to directly express a content that is about an object that is not a bearer of the used name, but I think the combined determination is the most plausible. On this basis, the first outlined case is the more convincing for a more relaxed conception of truth-conditional contents that are expressed by the uses of sentences.

If one takes such examples seriously and accepts a more relaxed attitude towards the expression of truth-conditional contents by uses of sentences, one could also provide an alternative version of our semantics that strictly distinguishes between a now *more minimal* truth-conditional meaning (content) and an additional use conditional meaning (constraint). This additional use-conditional meaning functions as a semantic sieve that restricts the set of all possible uses of an expression to the set of all semantically correct uses. Therefore, we can formally represent the semantically correct uses of a name by the set of those indices of use of this name that satisfy a certain constraining condition; in the case of names the constraining condition says that extensions of the indices must be bearers of the name used. With this recipe at hand, we can now formulate a more progressive version of our *coarse-grained* semantics for proper names as follows:

*The use-conditional coarse-grained semantics for name-functions and name-uses*

*Truth-conditional meaning*
For every use-index i there is exactly one object $x \in D$ and it is such that: Den (n()) = <i, x>.

*Use-conditional meaning*
$C_n$ = The set of all use-indices that have a bearer of 'N' as its extension.

I leave it to the reader to formulate the *fine-grained* alternative from what I have said so far.

Additionally, we could also plausibly extend this strategy to the problem of non-literal uses of proper names. With respect to our mentioned three cases, one could claim that, as in the case of erroneous uses of proper names in the case of non-literal correct uses of names, the sentences that contain these names directly express truth-conditional contents that are not literally their semantic contents. However, in the case of the mentioned non-literal uses, *contextual factors* in combination with *stress* do not modify the semantic content of a proper name anymore, but, now, according to the progressive version of my theory, they temporally modify the use-conditional meaning of a proper name. In our three different cases, the following *occurrent* modified use-conditional meanings regulate our outlined four different non-literal uses of names:

$M_1[C_n]$ = The set of all use-indices that have as its extension an object that the speaker of this use intends to be a bearer of 'N'.

$M_2[C_n]$ = The set of all use-indices that have as its extension an object that the addressee of this use assumed to be a bearer of 'N'.

$M_3[C_n]$ = The set of all use-indices that have as its extension an object that is a former bearer of 'N'.

$M_4[C_n]$ = The set of all use-indices that have as its extension an object that resembles a famous bearer of 'N' relative to $c_t$.[76]

On this basis, the modification does not affect the truth-conditional, but only the use-conditional level of meaning. I leave it to the reader to choose between the more conservative and the more progressive version of my alternative contextual semantics for names.[77]

# 4

# The Fictional Uses of Proper Names

In this chapter, I will mainly be concerned with fictional uses of proper names. I will argue for the view that there are three different fictional uses of proper names. Firstly, there are fictional uses of proper names in acts of story-telling. The specific illocutionary force of these acts modifies the semantic contribution of a name in such a way that the name does not refer relative to such uses. The main purpose of a name relative to such a use is either to stipulate the existence of certain fictional objects or to purely confirm previous stipulations of this kind. Secondly, there are fictional uses of proper names in assertoric sentences and in the scope of extensional or intensional predicates. Relative to these uses, proper names fail to refer to objects, but not because they fail to satisfy their referential function relative to such uses; they fail to refer because they are unable to exploit previous fictional stipulations that constitute the origin of a name-using practice of a fictional name. Thirdly, there are fictional uses of proper names in assertoric sentences and in the scope of specific hyper-intensional predicates or expressions. Relative to such fictional uses, names refer to objects in fictional worlds; with respect to these shifted uses, fictional names exploit those fictional stipulations that are relevant and necessary for a referential use of a fictional name. Hence, I will argue for a synthetic view of fictional proper names that holds that they have at least three different kinds of uses and that they only refer to fictional objects with respect to one of these three different kinds of uses.

## Setting the stage: key features of fictional names

In general, philosophers agree that fictional names have specific features that distinguish them from ordinary proper names, but they disagree about the nature of these distinctive features. There are at least *two dimensions* that philosophers have used to distinguish fictional from ordinary names. The *first dimension* concerns the referential status of proper names. Some people think that at least one thing that distinguishes fictional names from ordinary names is that fictional names do not have semantic referents. Other philosophers think that the distinguishing feature is not a lacking semantic referent, but a referent of a very specific ontological kind. According to this view, only fictional names refer to fictional objects.[1] The *second dimension* concerns the introduction of fictional names into use. Some people think that fictional names are unlike ordinary proper names not introduced into use by some explicit act of naming or by the implicit establishment of a referent by a connected series of referential uses of a name, but introduced by very specific acts that concern the use of a name in fictional works. A popular version of this view assumes that we only pretend to refer to some objects if we use a fictional name relative to an act of story-telling. Other philosophers disagree and hold that there is no significant difference between the introduction of ordinary and fictional proper names.

Against this background, we can distinguish *three different orthodox views* on this issue. Firstly, we might call a view that sees the only significant difference between fictional and ordinary proper names in the ontological status of their referents *Millianism about fictional names*. On this view, fictional names are a specific sub-variety of referring proper names that refer to specific fictional objects. Secondly, there is the view that acknowledges the mentioned difference concerning the introduction of fictional and ordinary proper names. But they additionally assume a second use of fictional names in ordinary assertions and non-fictional speech acts relative to which they refer to fictional objects. By calling this view *Kripkeanism about fictional names*, we recognize that Kripke was the famous initial defender of this kind of view.[2] That is, relative to their introductory uses fictional names only pretend to refer, but as a consequence of these kind of uses new objects are created to which fictional names can refer relative to their ordinary uses in assertoric sentences. Thirdly, there is the view that assumes that fictional names are names without a semantic referent relative to all of their uses. We may call this view *naïve irrealism about fictional names*.[3]

In this chapter, I aim to defend a new view concerning the semantics of fictional names. This view might be called the *pluralistic view* of fictional names. It aims to combine different elements of the three distinguished views into a single view. According to this view, the primary fictional use of a name is the use in acts of story-telling. Relative to this use, fictional names do not refer to any object, but they also do not merely pretend to refer to something relative to this use. A secondary fictional use of a name is a derived referential use in different but very specific kinds of assertoric sentences. In purely extensional contexts, fictional names fail to refer. In certain hyper-intensional contexts, they refer to things in fictional worlds.[4] The development of this view will proceed by dealing with three different general worries about fictional names if they are at least relative to one of their uses conceived of as names that lack a semantic referent.

Firstly, people have argued that names that do not refer to anything cannot be regarded as meaningful expressions. This worry will be discussed in the next section of this chapter. I will show why it is based on an incorrect universalist conception of the nature of proper names and why a *functionalist* conception of the nature of names is more adequate and suitable.

Secondly, there is a tension between the general intuitive function of names, which have the function or purpose to refer to something, and the use of fictional names if they are conceived of as names without a referent. I will present an argument that aims to use this tension to argue for a realist position concerning fictional names; and I will argue for a specific response to this argument that pleads for the thesis that names are *polysemous expressions* that have a primary referential function and a secondary stipulative function that is in a certain sense derived from the primary referential function.

Thirdly, a challenge will be addressed that concerns the specific nature and structure of name-using practices that concern the use of names relative to their secondary stipulative function. These name-using practices are in several respects different from those name-using practices that are constituted by uses of names with a referential function. On the one hand, the initial uses of such practices are not uses that aim to fix a certain referent of a specific name. On the other hand, there are different ways to participate in an already existing name-using practice of a fictional name: uses that are part of acts of story-telling have a significantly different function from those uses that are part of ordinary speech acts, like the speech act of assertion. Our third challenge consists in a specification of possible initial and subsequent uses of fictional names and the relations between these uses that constitute a fictional name-using practice.

## The meaningfulness of names without a semantic referent

Several people have argued that names without a semantic referent cannot be meaningful. I will argue in this section that this view is incorrect because it is based on an implausible conception of the nature and semantics of names.

It is quite common and popular to hold the view that proper names are (a) a semantic natural kind (b) with a *universal* nature that satisfies the following universal metaphysical truth:

(UN)　　Essentially, every proper name names or refers to something.

This universal metaphysical assumption is often backed up by either one of two relatively popular theses about the semantics of names that are mainly inspired by the views of Mill on names. These are the following two main theses of the *strong* and the *weak* version of Millianism:

(SM)　　The meaning of a name is exhausted by its referent.
(WM)　　The meaningfulness of a name essentially depends on its having a referent.

The views that are the result of the combination of (UN) and (SM) or (WM) had a strong impact on the philosophical discussion of proper names in the last few decades. The main initiators of this trend are Mill, Russell and Kripke. We may call any view of the nature of names that is based on (UN) a *universalist view of names*.[5]

### The functionalist conception of proper names

In my opinion, each of the three listed theses is false if they are applied to *ordinary* proper names. They are based on over-generalizations and simplifications that concern the overall use of names in natural language. Before I show why they are false, let me briefly sketch an alternative picture, which we may call *the functionalist view of names*. According to this view, names are specific social artefacts and like other artefacts their nature is determined by their function, or at least by their *intended* function. A gun, for example, roughly has the function to fire bullets with a certain speed in a certain direction that allows one to kill or wound creatures in a relatively reliable way.[6] A name, on the other hand, is designed in such a way that it is possible to refer to a single object by using this name. This is the general functional feature that names share with other singular terms. What distinguishes names from other singular terms is the specific feature that proper names have their referential function either *in virtue of* some stipulation or a certain referential habit; that is, either in virtue of a successful act of naming or an established name-using practice. Like other singular terms proper names might fail to satisfy their function, for example because of an unsuccessful attempt to establish a certain object as the bearer of a name.

Why should names be fundamentally different from any other natural language singular referring expressions? Definite descriptions might fail to refer to something relative to a context of use, as might personal pronouns and demonstrative expressions. Why should not a name also fail to refer? In general, personal pronouns and complex demonstratives seem to share many features with proper names. Firstly, the very same name (according to our pretheoretic individuation of proper names) can be used to refer to different objects. Secondly, the correct semantic use of a name seems to be constrained by the obtaining of the name-of-relation. That is, only those uses of a name that are semantically correct relative to which a competent speaker uses this name to refer to a bearer of this name. Hence, this relation seems to play a similar constraining role as the property of being male in the case of the personal pronoun 'he'. Furthermore, the referent of a correct use of a name on a given occasion can be determined in different ways: it can be determined by a demonstrative act of identification, by means of an associated mental representation or descriptive condition or by means of exploiting a preceding use of the very same name by the user itself or some other user.[7]

If we conceive of names as social artefacts that have a specific function in analogy to, for example, such social artefacts as a gun, we can conceive of a name without a referent, either in analogy to a gun that has a *stoppage* or in analogy to a gun that has a *manufacturing defect*. In the first case, these artefacts *temporarily* do not satisfy their function, while in the latter case, they do not satisfy their function in a more *systematic way*. Like any other singular term, names have the function to refer to a single object. However, there might be reasons why a name cannot satisfy this function temporarily or systematically. If, for example, we accept that the referent of a name can be determined by exploiting a pre-existing use of this name, then such an attempt of exploiting a pre-existing use might fail if someone fails to identify any pre-existing single use or a specific pre-existing name-using practice. In this sense, we have a case of *misfiring* in analogy to the case of a gun that has a stoppage. However, if the referent of a use of a name can be determined in different ways, and the semantic referent is the referent of a use of a name that satisfies additional constraining conditions, then a name can fail to have a semantic referent on the basis of different failed attempts to refer to a single individual.

But the more interesting cases are uses of names with a more *systematic defect* concerning the satisfaction of their function. These indeed seem to be analogous to a gun that has a manufacturing defect and therefore *cannot* be used to satisfy its function. We may introduce a name by means of an act of naming that makes use of an attributively used definite description to determine the referent of this name.[8]

Unfortunately, the definite description is not satisfied with respect to the actual world. But the users of this name (at least) at first do not recognize that the act of naming was unsuccessful. They use this name with the *erroneous belief* that it refers to something. After a while they may recognize that the name is defective, but nevertheless between the introduction and this recognition this name can be used in different meaningful sentences. Such a name seems to have a meaningful use and it can even be used to formulate *true* assertions of some sort. That is, we can at least formulate certain true attitude ascriptions that contain such names.

**Two kinds of defective empty names**

What are the standard examples of systematically empty names? Very prominent examples are the names 'Vulcan' and 'Zeus'.[9] It may seem that both are names that were once introduced to name an object whose existence was erroneously assumed. However, in the case of 'Vulcan' it can be doubted whether this is really an apt description. Le Verrier assumed that a good explanation for the perturbations in the orbit of Mercury was the postulation of a new yet unobserved planet that causes these perturbations. Hence, he formulated the hypothesis that there is a planet, which we might call 'Vulcan' and that causes the mentioned perturbations. However, Le Verrier did not *assume* that such a planet existed and he, therefore, did not make an attempt to name an object that already was assumed to exist. But it would also not be an apt description to say that Le Verrier named a non-existent object 'Vulcan'. All he did was to *postulate* a certain object and he used the name 'Vulcan' to talk about this postulated object. A postulated object might turn out to be a real and existing object or no object at all. Hence, in the end, Le Verrier introduced a name into use that had no referent, because there was no such planet in the orbit of Mercury as postulated. But this introduction was not based on an erroneous assumption of the existence of a certain object. We may, therefore, hold that 'Vulcan' is a different sort of empty name than the kind we were searching for. It is a name that was introduced by mistakenly postulating the existence of a specific object. This is a different sort of error than the one mentioned above.

Our present use of 'Zeus' is also not a good example for an empty name that was introduced on the basis of an erroneous assumption of existence. It is plausible to assume that the old Greeks believed in the existence of a god, which they aimed to name 'Zeus'. Hence, they introduced this name for an object of which they assumed exists. Most present users of 'Zeus' do not believe in the existence of this God anymore. We assume that this God is part of Greek mythology and, therefore, we use it as a name for a mythological object. But a name of such a kind is not a good example for the use of a name without a referent based on a false existential assumption. In this sense, our use of this name is more like the use of a fictional name than the mentioned kind of empty name.

In my opinion, the best examples of the desired sort are names for *phantom islands*. In the case of phantom islands, it is erroneously assumed that there is a specific island. Human history is full of names for phantom islands, which trace back to unsuccessful attempts to name a certain island that was assumed to exist in a certain part of the sea, but which turned out to be an illusion or the source of a navigation error. A recent example of this kind is the name 'Sandy Island', which is a name for a phantom island in the Pacific Ocean.

Therefore, we can distinguish two kinds of *defective empty names*. Names like 'Vulcan' that were introduced on the basis of a *postulation or hypothesis* that turned out to be false, or names for phantom islands like 'Sandy Island' that were introduced on the basis of a mistaken *belief about the existence* of a certain island.

It is very difficult for a defender of the essential view of names to account for such cases. To capture them, such a defender would be forced to either claim (a) that the mentioned acts of naming were successful attempts to name an exotic object *or* (b) that two different acts of naming were performed, an explicit act that failed, and an implicit one that did not fail. However, both reactions seem to be *ad hoc* and implausible. If someone uses the definite descriptions 'the island that is located at longitude X and latitude Y' to determine a referent of a name in an act of naming, then this description can only be satisfied by an *actual* and *concrete* island, because at least relative to its use in a sentence that can be used to perform a act of naming, 'the island …' is necessarily equivalent to 'the actual and concrete island'. Furthermore, it would be *ad hoc* to postulate a second implicit act of naming that makes use of a definite description that does not aim to refer to an actual and concrete object. Therefore, the best way to account for the mentioned examples of descriptive acts of naming is to admit that there are meaningful names without a semantic referent.

## Defective uses of ordinary names

Additionally, every account concerning the determination of the referent of *a single use* of a name should admit the possibility that such an act might fail to identify a single object. So, for example, if we make the popular assumption, for the sake of argument, that every semantically correct use of a proper name exploits some preceding use or an act of naming, then there might be attempts to exploit a single use that fail. And nevertheless, such uses are in some sense meaningful, because one aimed to determine the referent of a name in the correct way. This shows that it is not only plausible to accept meaningful uses of systematically empty names, but also meaningful uses of accidentally empty names. In this respect, names are very similar to personal pronouns and complex demonstratives. If I aim, for example, to use the pronoun 'he' to refer to a certain male person, but I fail to identify a *single male* person, my use can be meaningful in the outlined sense.

## The best semantic framework to account for defective empty names

What is an adequate formal semantic framework to account for the possibility of meaningful names without a semantic referent? The resources provided by a *single-domain free logic* can be implemented into any formal semantic framework and adapted for any formal semantic treatment of names. Relative to its simplest form a single-domain free logic is a slight modification of classical first-order predicate logic.[10] In opposition to classical first-order predicate logic, it conceives of the interpretation function as a *partial function* and it also allows for the possibility of complex singular terms without a denotation. According to the most conservative version of such a free logic, atomic sentences that contain at least one individual constant *or* complex singular term without a denotation are interpreted as false. Alternatively, one could make use of a three-valued logical framework and conceive of such sentences as neither true nor false.[11] Hence, there are different ways to implement names without a semantic referent into a formal semantic framework. This shows that the technical issue is not an obstacle for admitting names without a semantic referent.[12]

Therefore, I opt for replacing the quite radical universalist view of names with the more moderate functionalist view. That is, names only *typically* name something. The meaning of a proper name is not exhausted by its referent and the meaningfulness of a name does not depend on whether a name has a semantic referent.

## The semantic status of fictional names

In the last section, we have argued for the meaningfulness of names without a semantic referent. Our defence of this thesis mainly focused on two different *uses* of proper names without a semantic referent in natural languages: occasionally empty uses of names and uses of defective empty names. However, fictional names are arguably of neither kind. If fictional names are empty names, they are not without a semantic referent because of occasional unsuccessful referential uses *or* because they were introduced into use by means of an unsuccessful attempt to name an object of any kind. It is the task of this section to show in which sense it is possible to conceive of fictional names as names without a semantic referent and whether such a view is compatible with the outlined functionalist conception of proper names.

Intuitively, there seems to be a certain tension between the outlined functionalist view of names and the thesis that fictional names are names without a semantic referent. Ordinary proper names, whether they are defective or non-defective, are introduced in a specific way into use. They are either introduced by an explicit act of naming that aims to fix the referent of a name for future uses or a referential use that is accompanied by the intention or aim to introduce and establish a new name-using practice with a specific semantic referent. That is, the initial uses of ordinary name-using practices are uses that *aim* to fix a new referent of a specific name.

Fictional names seem to be introduced into use in a completely different way. The initial uses of fictional names are uses by authors of fictional works that are part of specific acts of story-telling. A *sophisticated* irrealist conception of fictional names may aim to do justice to this specific feature of fictional names by claiming that the initial uses of fictional names are neither uses that aim to fix a new referent of a specific name nor uses that aim to use a name to refer to an already established referent of this name. Subsequent uses of fictional names relative to acts of story-telling or other kinds of speech acts are uses that aim to be in accordance with the initial uses of a specific fictional name. In this sense, subsequent uses of fictional names seem to be *essentially deferential*. Against this background, at least two questions arise. (a) Which positive purpose or aim is constitutive for initial or introductory uses of fictional names according to an irrealist conception of fictional names? (b) In which sense are subsequent uses of fictional names, according to such a conception, related to the initial uses and what is the aim of these uses relative to acts of story-telling and other kinds of speech acts? We will address these two questions in detail in the next two sections of this chapter. For the aim of this section the mentioned negative findings are sufficient to construe a tension between the conceptual setting of an irrealist conception of fictional names and the outlined functionalist view of names.

This tension allows us to formulate an objection against an irrealist conception of fictional names in the following way:

(P1)  If fictional names are names without a semantic referent, then the introductory or initial uses of fictional names neither have the purpose to fix a new referent of a name nor the purpose to refer to an already established referent of this name, and the subsequent uses of a fictional name aim to use such a name in accordance with the introductory uses.

(P2)  If the introductory or initial uses of fictional names neither have the purpose to fix a new referent of a name nor the purpose to refer to an already established referent of this name and the subsequent uses of a fictional name aim to use such a name in accordance with the introductory uses, then it is not the function of a fictional name to refer to a single object.

(P3)  Every fictional name is (literally) a proper name.

(P4)  It is the function of every proper name to refer to a single object.[13]

(C)  Fictional names are not names without a semantic referent.

What is the best way to react to this kind of argument? A defender of a realist conception of fictional names might use the argument as a *reductio ad absurdum* of an irrealist conception of fictional names. That is the most obvious use of the argument. Are there any plausible ways *for the irrealist* to react to this kind of argument?

It does not seem to be a plausible option to reject (P1) and conceive of fictional names as defective proper names. Firstly, no fictional name is introduced into use on the basis of a false postulation of an object or a false belief about the existence of an object. Secondly, it is part of the correct understanding of a fictional name to know that such a name does not typically refer to a pre-existing thing. But defective names are initially used with the false assumption that they refer or might refer to an existing thing. One would have the burden to explain away this tension. Thirdly, this conception seems to neglect the fact that the primary use of a fictional name is the use of this name in acts of story-telling. Empty names can only be used in a meaningful way relative to such acts if they are used under the pretence that they refer to something. Hence, we also would have the burden of proof to explain away all the important intuitive differences between ordinary and fictional names. It seems to be impossible to meet this requirement in a plausible way.

The key premise of our argument is premise (P2) because it points out the tension between the general conceptual setting of irrealism concerning fictional names and the functionalist view on names. It seems to be the only premise of our argument that cannot rationally be denied. Therefore, the irrealist mainly seems to have the option to reject one of the other two remaining premises.

At first sight, (P3) might seem to be a trivial, conceptual truth, but closer inspection shows that there are different possible readings of (P3) and only according to some of them is (P3) a trivial, logical truth. The reason for the possibility of different readings of (P3) is that it is unclear whether the adjective 'fictional' is used in (P3) as an intersective or a modifying adjective. Relative to the first reading (P3) would be true for logical reasons. But relative to the second reading it could be false in a similar way as 'A false friend is a friend' is false or 'A fake bomb is a bomb' is literally false. Therefore, the rejection of premise (P3) seems to be a first possible option.

What about premise (P4)? In a certain sense one could conceive of the functionalist view of names as a *modification* of the essential view of names that allows us to capture the meaningful use of defective empty names. The common factor between ordinary proper names and defective empty names is their common *functional purpose* to refer to a single object. Is there also a way to modify the functionalist view in such a way that we can additionally also integrate an irrealist conception of fictional names? That does not seem to be the case. There is no plausible way to find a common functional purpose or purpose of some common kind to integrate non-empty names and all distinguished sorts of empty names. There is no general common denominator between fictional names and defective empty names concerning their semantic and communicative purpose. That is basically because the function of fictional names is the result of a *modification* of the function of ordinary proper names. Therefore, the only viable rejection and modification of premise (P4) assumes at least *two different* functions of ordinary proper names. There are two different notable versions of this kind of solution: (a) a version that assigns to names two different but systematically *unrelated* functions, and (b) a version that assigns to names two different systematically related functions.

In this respect, an important distinction between different kinds of social artefacts is relevant, namely the distinction between those that have a specific institutional function that essentially depends on their physical realization (like cars, screwdrivers and guns) and those that have such an institutional function on a purely conventional basis (like flags, traffic lights and traffic signs). Artefacts are designed for a specific purpose that determines the nature of this artefact. There are artefacts with a physical realization that are designed to fulfil different purposes or functions. Most knives, for example, are designed in such a way that they can be used to cut things and also to poke holes into things. These two functions do not essentially depend on each other. However, in the case of artefacts with a function on *a purely conventional basis* it seems to be unlikely that an artefact of a specific kind has two completely different and unrelated functions. Therefore, in the case of names it seems to be prima facie more plausible to consider only variant (b) as a solution to our problem that rejects (P4).

## Different kinds of uses of fictional proper names in sentential contexts

We have seen that there seem to be two different possible options to react to our outlined argument. The first reaction is to reject premise (P3), the second to reject (P4). Which of these two options is the more plausible?

Is there any plausible way to make sense of a rejection of (P3)? Our gun analogy might help us in this respect again: there are guns that can be used to satisfy their purpose, namely, they can be used to fire off bullets. There are defective guns that were designed to fulfil their purpose as guns, but because of some sort of defect they cannot satisfy their function. But on the other hand, there are also *mock guns* or *toy guns*. A mock gun looks like a gun, but is not a gun. It is produced with the purpose to look like a gun and to pretend in a deceptive way that it is a real gun, but it is not its purpose to function like a gun. A toy gun is also not in the literal functional sense a gun, but it looks like a gun and it is produced to function as some kind of prop in a pretence game as representative of a real gun.

Against this background, we might conceive of fictional names either in analogy to (b) toy guns or in analogy to (b) mock guns. It is clear that we cannot take the analogy with the mock guns too seriously, because if fictional names at all pretend to be proper names according to some of their uses, they pretend to be names in a non-deceptive way. However, *both* conceptions of fictional names have to face several delicate difficulties. Firstly, according to both conceptions, fictional names are not literally names from a semantic point of view; they only pretend to be names or they are only props that can be used in certain pretence games. Therefore, these conceptions seem to face the challenge to specify what kind of expressions fictional names in fact are. Secondly, it seems to be difficult to deny that fictional names can be used in genuine assertions. However, it is unclear how expressions that only pretend to be names or that are special devices that can be used in specific pretence games could contribute in a meaningful way to the truth- and falsity-conditions of genuine assertions. Thirdly, fictional names are syntactically indistinguishable from ordinary proper names and can be used in a meaningful way in the very same sentential contexts as ordinary proper names. Furthermore, a competent speaker seems to be in the position to understand a sentence that contains a fictional proper name in a certain minimal sense without knowing that this name is a fictional name. A defender of the proposed rejection of premise (P3) must find a way to accommodate this kind of data. Maybe this is all possible, but I will not follow this thorny way.[14]

Let us now investigate the question whether the rejection of (P4) is a more fruitful option. This question can only be answered in a meaningful way if we can say more about the positive function of fictional names. For this purpose, it is also necessary to draw our attention to different kinds of uses of fictional names as part of different kinds of speech acts. Typically, *three* different uses of fictional names are distinguished: Firstly, uses of fictional names as part of acts of story-telling. Secondly, uses of fictional names as part of reports about what is the case according to fictional stories. Thirdly, uses of fictional names as part of apparent assertions that seem to ascribe properties to fictional objects that these objects have, independently of what happens according to a specific story that makes use of them. Let us review these three kinds of uses case by case.

### Acts of story-telling and acts of re-telling a story

There is much controversy about the specific nature of acts of *story-telling*. We must in this respect distinguish at least two kinds of acts: those acts that authors perform when they *create* a story or play in an explicit linguistic form, and those acts that people perform when they *re-tell* a story or perform a play on stage. Let us for the sake of simplicity here focus on stories and not plays. I will call the first kind of act an act of *story-telling* and the second kind of act an act of *re-telling a story*. (Alternatively, one could reserve the term 'fiction-making' for the former and 'fiction-telling' for the latter.)

Some people claim that these kinds of acts are not genuine illocutionary acts. Frege and Searle are famous examples. Searle holds the view that if an author of a novel uses the following declarative sentence as part of an act of story-telling, he thereby only pretends that he performs an assertion of the content of this sentence:

(1)   Sherlock Holmes lives in London.

However, this conception does not seem to be correct. I can non-deceptively pretend to assert (1) without thereby performing an act of story-telling (fiction-making), if I utter a certain declarative sentence, for example, as part of a parody of a specific person. It is also not clear whether an act of pretended assertion is a necessary constituent of an act of story-telling. Acts of story-telling seem to have consequences and lead to commitments that go far beyond merely pretended acts of assertion. These acts at least intend to create new fictional states of affairs. They also have a specific communicative dimension and they intend to create a very specific reaction by addresses of such acts.

Against this background, other people have claimed that the two distinguished kinds of acts are *genuine illocutionary acts*. There are two notable variants of this view. The first version conceives of acts of *story-telling or creating a story* and *re-telling of a story* as acts of a primitive additional kind of speech act that has to be clearly distinguished from those kinds of speech acts that are standardly distinguished, like assertive, directive or commissive speech acts. The second version holds that these acts are complex or simple acts that have one or more illocutionary purposes that are of a specific sub-variety of those kinds of speech acts that are standardly distinguished. I personally prefer a view of the second variety.

The first view seems to be some sort of a last resort if a specification of these acts in terms of a specific sub-species of standardly distinguished speech acts is not possible. According to my view on this issue, acts of story-telling/creating a story have *two* different illocutionary forces; in this respect (but only in this respect) they are similar to Searle's famous assertive declarations.[15] That is, they have the force of (i) a *directive* speech act and (ii) of a *declaration*. According to my view, if someone utters (1) as part of an act of story-telling (fiction-making), he performs the following two different kinds of actions:

(T1)   he invites possible addressees to fictionally assume that Sherlock Holmes lives in London;
(T2)   he stipulates that Sherlock Holmes lives in London is the case relative to some fictional world that is represented by the presently created/actualized story.

By *fictionally assuming that p* I mean the following: assuming that p is the case relative to some (purely) fictional world.

As it stands, this conception might seem to be too simple-minded. However, I do not want to assume that the *process* of creating a story consists *only* of acts of story-telling. It may also consist of plain assertions. Furthermore, in the case of an (external) unreliable narrator,[16] some acts performed by the story-teller might only be invitations to *pretend* or *assume* that something is the case relative to a fictional world without the normative force of (T2). Furthermore, I only want to claim that *typical* stories are mostly created by acts of story-telling that have force (T1) and (T2). But stories may also consist (at least partially) of *open* acts of story-telling, where the creator, instead of performing (T1) and (T2), invites the addressee to stipulate or determine by themselves whether a certain state of affairs that is p is the case relative to some fictional world. These are cases where different interpretations of a story are *intended* by the author. I think, with these qualifications at hand, we can cover most cases of creating a story. There might also be further additions that are required. Maybe, *some* truths about what is the case relative to certain fictional worlds are also settled by some kind of agreement between a group of recipients. However, I only want to insist on one important point about the introduction of fictional names that is used in a fictional work: the successful introduction of a *new fictional name* relative to such a setting requires the performance of an act with force (T1) and (T2). Hence, a new fictional use of a proper name can only be established if certain fictional facts are created, whose creation require the use of this very name.

Acts of *re-telling a story* may share with acts of *story-telling* the force (T1), but they have, in my opinion, also a second additional force, namely an assertoric force of a specific variety. If someone utters (1) relative to an act of *re-telling a story*,

(T3)  he informs possible addressees that it is the case *according to the story he is presently re-telling* that Sherlock Holmes lives in London.

This feature seems to be, apart from the shared feature (T1), an essential feature of acts of re-telling a story. People who know the content of a story typically protest when someone re-tells a story in an incorrect way and they then aim to correct this mistake. Therefore, it is plausible to assume that an act of re-telling a story is more than a *pure invitation* to pretend that something is the case.

This conception of acts of story-telling and re-telling provides a very good foundation for a proper semantics of reports about the contents of fictional works and other assertoric sentences about fictional objects. The mentioned stipulations also fix the semantic interpretation of fictional names relative to fictional worlds. Two different alternative views seem to be possible as to how these stipulations determine the relevant uses of fictional names.

The first view makes use of an *irrealist conception* of fictional names that holds that proper names lack a semantic referent relative to all of their uses. The second *synthetic conception* holds that proper names lack a semantic referent relative to all of their uses in extensional and intensional contexts; that is, their uses that are evaluated relative to the actual world or any other metaphysically possible world, but they can refer to fictional individuals if they are evaluated relative to those non-normal worlds that formally represent fictional worlds. A normal (possible) world is complete and consistent and captures a metaphysically possible alternative to the actual world. A non-normal (fictional) world can be incomplete, or inconsistent, or both and it is *irrelevant* whether these fictional worlds could be in some sense metaphysically realized. We use the tools provided by world semantics to give an account of the mentioned kinds of stipulations. In this light, they can be interpreted in two significantly different ways.

Firstly, they can be interpreted relative to a so-called story-semantics. A *story-semantics*, as I interpret it, is a world semantics that distinguishes between normal and non-normal worlds. Relative to normal worlds, different kinds of sentences receive their truth-values on the basis of the standard compositional procedures. Relative to non-normal worlds, the interpretation function directly assigns truth-values to sentences in a non-compositional way. Against this background, an atomic sentence of the form 'Fa', for example, can receive the truth value TRUE relative to a non-normal world, even if 'a' lacks a semantic referent. Relative to this framework, every sentence (and each translation of this sentence into a different language) that is used in a genuine act of story-telling receives the truth value TRUE by the interpretation function relative to some non-normal world that represents the content of the fictional story that is told by means of this act of story-telling.

Alternatively, such acts can be interpreted on the background of a *noneist semantics*. On this basis, the stipulations provided by acts of story-telling do not *directly* determine the truth-value of those sentences (and its translations) that are used in acts of story-telling in a non-compositional way. These acts also stipulate the existence of certain objects if the right kinds of singular terms are used for this purpose. And additionally, certain properties of these stipulated objects are also stipulated. Hence, according to this second framework, both the existence of certain objects relative to fictional worlds are stipulated and the properties of or relations between these kinds of objects. So for example, if an act of story-telling says that Sherlock Holmes is a detective, then this leads to the stipulation of an object named 'Sherlock Holmes' relative to a fictional world that represents the content of the told story and also to the stipulation relative to the very same world that this object bears the property of being a detective. Such stipulations need not stipulate the existence of the *very same* object relative to different fictional worlds that represent the contents of fictional stories. It is only necessary that, relative to each fictional world that represents a certain story or parts of it, the correct and required number and kinds of objects are stipulated. In this sense, fictional names that only refer relative to fictional worlds may literally refer to different objects relative to different fictional worlds. Therefore, they are non-rigid with respect to non-normal/fictional worlds. However, they are rigid expressions in the classical sense, in so far as they are rigidly without a semantic referent relative to all *possible* worlds. This different semantic treatment of fictional names with respect to normal and non-normal worlds is a key feature of the *synthetic* approach concerning fictional names.

## Reports about the content of fictional stories

There is a significant intuitive difference between the use of a sentence like (1) as part of an act of story-telling and a use of (1) as part of a conversation about what is the case according to a specific story or fictional work. Such uses are assertions of a very specific kind. They are specific in respect that the literal semantic content of (1) is *only part* of the content of an assertion of (1) if this sentence is used as a report about what is the case according to a fictional story or work. The remaining part of the asserted content of a sentence like (1) relative to such a report is more *implicitly* provided. There are different possible options to characterize the mechanism that adds this implicit part of the asserted content.

The most simple and straightforward option holds that the additional content is provided by some implicit pragmatic enrichment. That is, in the context of conversation, speaker and hearer are aware of this implicit addition and for the sake of convenience it is implicitly assumed, but not explicitly expressed. According to this view, the implicit addition of content is a *local* phenomenon that concerns the discourse about fictional stories of work. Typically, if a conversation clearly focuses on what is the case according to a fictional story or work such implicit enrichments are made. And only if there is the desire of more explicitness are they made explicit.

However, in principle, there would also be another more *global* way to draw the distinction between implicit and explicit contents of uses of (1) as reports about fictional stories or works. We could distinguish two different general layers of common ground or discursive 'scoreboards' or commitment boxes. One part of this *scoreboard* concerns commitments about what is actually the case relative to the actual world. The second part of this scoreboard concerns commitments about what is the case only relative to fictional worlds or purely fictional alternatives to the actual world. Relative to both parts, the part of commitments about the actual world and the part of the commitments relative to fictional worlds, there is a three-part division of commitments: (a) commitments that are only commitments of the speaker, (b) commitments that are only commitments of the hearer, and (c) commitments that are shared by speaker and hearer. From a point of view of formal representation, we only have to distinguish two different commitment boxes. The box that concerns commitments of the speaker and the box that concerns commitments of the hearer with respect to a single content. If there is a match of commitments with respect to the same content between speaker and hearer with respect to the same scoreboard of commitments, then we have a case of shared commitments. The desired goal of an assertion of a sentence like 'Peter is a nice guy' is to achieve a shared commitment to the truth of the content of this sentence relative to the actual world between speaker and hearer. However, the hearer always has three possible reactions to such an assertive attempt by the speaker: (a) explicit or implicit acceptance, (b) explicit or implicit rejection, or (c) explicit or implicit abstention. Hence, in an ideal case an ordinary reality-related assertion leads to the mutual commitment of speaker and hearer to the truth of the asserted content relative to the actual world. However, an assertion is also then successful if at least the speaker commits himself to the truth of the asserted content relative to the actual world.

The same general model can now also be applied to assertions or use of (1) that attempt to assert something about what is the case according to a story or relative to a fictional world that is licenced by a story. The only difference between these two cases is that the commitment to the truth of the asserted content by the speaker, hearer or both does not concern actual truth, but truth relative to a set of worlds licenced by a specific fictional story or truth according to a specific story or work. This second way of capturing two different uses of a sentence like (1) provides a more global account and assumes that we in general always must be aware or decide whether a certain sentence is meant to be an assertion about what actually is the case or about what only is fictionally the case. It is a difficult issue to provide evidence in favour or against such a global account. I just only want to point out that such a more global conception of providing the mentioned additional implicit content with respect to reports about fictional stories or works, seems to be in principle a possibility that we should seriously consider. For our purposes here, we do not have to decide between the global and the local account, because the differences only concern the *mechanisms* that provide the implicit content, but the implicit contents themselves can be modelled on the basis of both accounts in a similar and translatable fashion. Therefore, for the sake of simplicity, I will now only assume that the mentioned *local* account concerning implicit content enrichment is correct and will leave the more detailed development and comparison of the global and local account for another occasion.

If we assume that there is a local pragmatic mechanism that provides additional parts of the asserted content of (1) relative to a use of (1) as a fictional report, we still have to face the important question concerning the exact nature of the additional provided account relative to such a use of (1). It is very often assumed in the relevant literature that these implicit additions are always of the same kind and can be made explicit by adding the modifying phrase 'according to fiction' to (1). But such a view is too simplistic. Reports about fictional stories or works mostly do not only concern the totality of all fictional works, but also specific fictional works or stories. Hence, our modifier should be in some sense relativized to fictional stories or works. It is a standard procedure in natural languages to use the title of a fictional story or work to refer to this story. 'According to *Anna Karenina*' can be used to mean roughly the same as 'According to the fiction work with the title "Anna Karenina"'. Alternatively, one could also use the modifier 'According to the fictional work *Anna Karenina*'. In a case like the present one, where there are more and different fictional works with the same title, for example a novel and different screen adaptions of this novel, one would also use, if relevant and necessary, more specific modifiers to pick out the right kind of fictional work; for example, especially if one compares the novel to a specific screen adaption of it. Therefore, the explicit counterparts of the often implicitly made additions relative to uses of a sentence like (1) as a fictional report can be less or more specific. In this sense, there is a multitude of different more or less specific content-modifiers whose contributions to the contents of fictional reports can be provided in an explicit or implicit way.

Beside these possible additions to make the nominal content of 'fiction' in the modifier 'according to fiction' more specific, there is also the question of whether there are some interesting and significantly different *prepositional* alternatives to 'according to'. Some authors have argued for a systematic difference in content between 'In fiction X', and 'According to fiction X'.[17] I do not think that these prepositions systematically differ concerning their semantic contributions relative to all their possible uses. However, I agree that there are some differences. In some cases, 'in' constructions provide more access to other literal and non-literal readings than the corresponding 'according to' constructions. So, for example, one might have the impression that:

(2)  According to the fictional story *The Hound of the Baskervilles*, Sherlock Holmes has a brother,

is false, because the content of the fictional work mentioned does not settle the issue whether Sherlock Holmes has a brother according to this story or not. On the other hand, someone who knows that *The Hound of the Baskervilles* is one of many different Sherlock Holmes stories that describe the very same fictional world or at least a certain part of this fictional world, may get a reading of the sentence:

(3)    In the fiction *The Hound of the Baskervilles,* Sherlock Holmes has a brother,

relative to which is true. Maybe this is not a literal reading of (3). It is in any case an accessible reading, because Sherlock Holmes does not lose his fictional brother that was introduced in a story that was published before *The Hound of the Baskervilles* just because this brother is not mentioned in the later novel. Nevertheless, even in the case of the in-fiction-variant such a reading seems to be a bit forced and highly dependent on the context of conversation of the use of a sentence like (3).

Interestingly, the difference that Sainsbury pointed out becomes more apparent if we make use of more specific nouns than 'fiction' that denote sub-kinds of fictional works like 'novel', 'film' or 'play' in our modifiers. The sentence

(4)    In the novel *The Hound of the Baskervilles*, different fictional characters are portrayed, like Holmes or Watson,

clearly has a true reading and relative to this reading the prefix 'In the novel X' seems to provide a natural access to the acts of story-telling that constitute the mentioned novel and its content. On the other hand, the following sentence does not have a reading that has access to the speech-act-dimension of a novel:

(5)    According to the novel *The Hound of the Baskervilles*, different fictional characters are portrayed, like Holmes or Watson.

In this sentence the 'according to' construction only seems to provide an access to the content-dimension of this novel and says something about the fictional truth of this content. Hence, only the 'in novel' construction seems to provide a meaningful access to certain aspects of a novel that do not concern its explicit content. The situation is similar if we use other related prefixes like 'in the opera' or 'in the drama' or 'in the poem'. However, there is an important semantic difference between (4) and (5) that is overlooked by Sainsbury. In (5) we have a genuine sentential content modifier 'according to the novel *The Hound of the Baskervilles*' that modifies the whole content of 'different fictional characters are portrayed'. In (4), on the other hand, 'in the novel *The Hound of the Baskervilles*' is not a sentential modifier of a whole sentence and its whole content, it is only a *locative* addition to the verb 'portray'. That is, it only modifies the verb and provides an additional argument position for it. Sentence (4) and the following sentence are only stylistic syntactic variants:

(4*)   Different fictional characters are portrayed in the novel *The Hound of the Baskervilles*, like Holmes or Watson.

This shows that (4) and (5) are not semantically on a par. Therefore, the pointed-out differences should not be surprising at all. For our purpose, sentences like (4) are completely irrelevant because only sentences like (4) can be *literally* used to make fictional reports. The situation is different with respect to the construction 'In fiction X'. This expression can, like 'According to fiction X', be used as a sentential modifier. Therefore, it is no surprise that there are only minimal and purely pragmatic differences between these two constructions as mentioned above.

But there are other more interesting differences between a fictional operator that uses the 'in' construction and an operator that uses the 'according to' construction. However, these differences are not only due to the use of different presuppositions, but also due to different nominal additions. So, for example, there is a clear and important difference between two ways to make a possibly implicit additional content of a fictional report explicit if we compare (2) to the following alternative fictional report:

(6) In the fictional world that is described or portrayed by *The Hound of the Baskervilles*, Sherlock Holmes has a brother.

In opposition to (2), (6) has a clearly true reading and in opposition to (3), this reading is a *literal* reading of (6). Hence, on the basis of the pair of examples (2) and (6), we have now made explicit an important difference concerning possibly implicit content-additions of a fictional report like (1): the fictional operator that a sentence like (6) contains has a different contribution to the truth-conditions of (6) than the corresponding fictional operator in (2). The operator in (2) is only sensitive to the literal content of a specific fictional story, while the operator in (6) is more liberal with respect to additions to this literal content that are (a) either licenced by some related fictional work(s) or (b) by the specific genre of a certain fictional work. Sentence (6) provides an example of the first variety, the following sentence one of the second variety:

(7) In the fictional world that is described or portrayed by *The Hound of the Baskervilles*, Sherlock Holmes has a blood group.[18]

It is neither explicitly settled in the mentioned novel nor in any other Sherlock Holmes story, as far as I know, whether Sherlock Holmes has a blood group. Nevertheless, (7) seems clearly true because the Sherlock Holmes stories are of a *realistic* variety and Holmes is characterized in these stories as an ordinary human being. In this sense, certain facts about what is literally the case according to the stories plus the genre of these stories are responsible for the truth of (7). Therefore, we at least have to distinguish three different implicit or explicit additions to a sentence like (1) used as a report about a fictional work represented by the examples (2), (6) and (7).

There is a further possible alternative to these additions that should also be mentioned. This addition concerns the possibility of interpretations of fictional stories by interpreters and, therefore, facts about fictions that are only settled by an interpretation. As an example of this sort we can use the following explicit fictional report.

(8) According to Peter's interpretation of *A Scandal in Bohemia*, Sherlock Holmes fell in love with Irene Adler.

Arthur Conan Doyle gave some hints that, according to the story mentioned, Sherlock Holmes fell in love with Irene Adler, but it is never explicitly said in the story nor can it be settled by additional assumptions as in the case of (6) and (7). It is a plausible option to assume that according to *A Scandal in Bohemia*, Sherlock Holmes fell in love with Irene Adler, but the establishment of the fictional truth that Sherlock Holmes fell in love with Irene Adler requires an additional stance or interpretation by a recipient that interprets the hints given by Doyle in a certain way. Such examples of interpretative fictional facts cannot only concern facts about a single story, they can also concern the part of a fictional world that is described by a story. In this sense, we can also distinguish two sub-varieties of interpretive readings of fictional reports: they are additional sub-varieties of examples like (2) or (6).

This shows that the matter concerning fictional reports and the fictional truths of stories that they report is much more differentiated and complex than it is very often assumed in the relevant literature. I think that even the mentioned distinctions are not exhaustive. But it is not our goal to provide an exhaustive overview. The provided distinctions give us a recipe of how other alternative variations can be construed or handled.

The last goal of this section is now to offer a formal semantics of different kinds of fictional reports as they are represented by (2), (6), (7) and (8). I interpret all the mentioned fictional modifiers that provide implicit or explicit additions to a fictional report by means of a sentence like (1) as non-normal modal operators that make use of very specific accessibility relations to non-normal worlds. The notion of a non-normal world has already been introduced. In principle, there are three possible types of modal operators with respect to a modal logic that distinguishes normal and non-normal worlds: (a) modal operators that have access to both kinds of worlds, (b) modal operators that only have access to normal worlds, (c) modal operators that only have access to non-normal worlds. In my opinion, all distinguished fictional modifiers should formally be modelled as non-normal modal operators of the third variety. Intuitively, if it is metaphysically possible that p, that p could be actualized. However, purely fictional states of affairs can *per definition* not be actualized and they need not to be metaphysically possible. Hence, if it is fictionally the case that p, then this neither implies that it is metaphysically possible that p nor that the state of affairs could be actualized. Alternatively, one could also interpret our fictional modifiers as fictional operators of the first kind mentioned and exclude the actual world from the range of accessible worlds.

The formal semantics for fictional reports that I will use makes use of a non-normal modal logic based on the formal system FDE with a relational semantics. (Concerning the choice of the system, I mainly follow Priest (2005).) The version of this kind of formal framework that I favour makes use of the following structure: $<W, N, O, D, D^*, I, F^*, @>$. W is the (non-empty) set of all worlds, normal and non-normal. N is the (non-empty) set of all normal worlds. O is the (non-empty) set of all non-normal worlds. Every formula can, in principle, arbitrarily be either true or false relative to non-normal worlds. Individual constants that either refer to the same individual with respect to all normal worlds or lack a referent with respect to all these worlds, can have different denotations with respect to non-normal worlds. D is a function from worlds into domains of discourse. $D^*$ is the union of all domains of all worlds. (In your system,

D is more fundamental than D*.) I is our interpretation function. F* is (the non-empty) set of all fictional worlds, which are a subset of O. @ is the actual world.

Against this background, we can now introduce four different kinds of fictional operators. These non-normal modal operators have different kinds of *accessibility relations* that are relativized to different entities. These specific accessibility relations are assigned to operators by means of the interpretation function.

Our first fictional modifier that we aim to interpret formally can be informally expressed by the modifying expression 'According to the fictional work x it is the case that'. The formal equivalent of this expression is the following sentential operator: FC<x>[p]. This sentential operator is relativized to fictional works x that are elements of F*. In our metalanguage, this operator is interpreted as a non-normal modal operator with a specific accessibility relation: I(FC, <α>)(w,w'). We can informally paraphrase this relation as follows: The accessibility relation that is assigned by I to FC and the fictional work α provides access from w to a fictional world w' that respresents the literal contents of α. Against this background, we can now define the truth- and falsity-conditions for fictional reports that make use of 'FC' by using a relational world-relative valuation function V as follows:

V(<FC<α>[φ], w>, T)   iff   for every world w* ∈ F*: such that I(FC, <α>)(w, w*), V(<φ, w*>,T).

V(<FC<α>[φ], w>, F)   iff   for some world w* ∈ F*: such that I(FC, <α>)(w, w*), V(<φ, w*>, F).

Informally, a sentence 'φ' is true according to a fictional work iff it is true with respect to all fictional worlds that represent the literal content of this work. Hence, it is important to notice that this fictional operator is only relevant for those implicit or explicit fictional reports that concern the *literal* content of a fictional work; that is, the content that is literally expressed by a work, but not only conveyed by this work. For other kinds of fictional reports that also concern more implicit aspects of the content of a fictional work, we have three other alternative fictional operators. This general semantics for fictional reports can either be based on a *story-semantics* for the embedded sentences or a *noneist semantics*. For the sake of brevity, I will only explicitly outline the differences between these two versions of our semantics with respect to atomic sentences. I leave it for another occasion to work out the differences in detail for other kinds of sentences. According to a *story-semantics* for our framework, atomic sentences have the following truth- and falsity-conditions if we use a world-relative interpretation function that assigns to each predicate an extension + and an anti-extension − and that relates atomic sentences relative to non-normal worlds to an element of the classical set of truth-values {T, F}, and world-relative partial denotation function d(x,w) that assigns elements of D* to our individual constants:

V(<Pt$_1$...t$_n$, w>,T)   iff   if w ∈ N, <d(t$_1$,w),..., d(t$_n$,w)> ∈ I(P,+,w), or
If w ∈ O, I(Pt$_1$...t$_n$, w) = T.

V(<Pt$_1$...t$_n$, w>,F)   iff   if w ∈ N, <d(t$_1$,w),..., d(t$_n$,w)> ∈ I(P,−,w), or
If w ∈ O, I(Pt$_1$...t$_n$, w) = F.

Against this background, our example sentence

(2)     According to the fictional story *The Hound of the Baskervilles*, Sherlock Holmes has a brother,

is formally represented as 'FC<h>[Bs]', if 'h' is a name for the fictional story mentioned, 's' is a formal counterpart of the name 'Sherlock Holmes' and 'B' is the formalization of '… has a brother'. The formula 'FC<h>[Bs]' is true relative to a world iff relative to those non-normal worlds that formally represent the literal content of h the sentence 'Bs' receives the truth-value T. Based on our truth- and falsity-conditions for atomic semantics the sentence 'Bs' can receive the truth-value relative to a non-normal world, even if 's' does not refer to any individual with respect to this world.

The situation is different if we alternatively make use of a noneist semantics for atomic sentences. According to my version of this semantics, fictional names lack a referent with respect to all normal worlds, but refer to objects that represent fictional characters relative to non-normal worlds. Atomic sentences receive on this basis, the following more uniform and simple truth- and falsity-conditions:

$V(<Pt_1…t_n, w>, T)$   iff   $<d(t_1,w),…,d(t_n,w)> \in I(P,+,w)$.
$V(<Pt_1…t_n, w>, F)$   iff   $<d(t_1,w),…,d(t_n,w)> \in I(P,-,w)$.

According to this second version of our semantics, 'FC<h>[Bs]' is true relative to a world iff relative to those non-normal worlds that formally represent the literal content of h the object that represents the fictional character Sherlock Holmes in this world is an element of the extension of 'B' relative to this world. In opposition to our story-semantics, the noneist semantics is fully compositional with respect to atomic sentences but has assumed fictional objects in the metalanguage to be able to provide compositionality also with respect to non-normal worlds.

Let us now extend our semantics to the three other fictional operators that are represented by our example sentences (6), (7) and (8). We formally represent the fictional modifier 'In the fictional world that is depicted by the fictional work x it is the case that' if it is used with the presupposition of a whole set of fictional works that depict the very same fictional world as follows: FW<x>[p]. This sentential operator is relativized to fictional works x that are elements of F*. In opposition to 'FC', this operator has more complicated truth- and falsity-conditions. For this purpose, we also make use in our metalanguage of a relation that compares different fictional works concerning their representational status. 'WM(x,y)' means the same as 'the fictional story x depicts the very same fictional world as the fictional story y'. I will leave the explication of the philosophical and metaphysical foundations of this relation for another occasion. However, it seems to be a meaningful relation that has a plausible intuitive background. For example, all the Holmes stories by Conan Doyle seem to depict without any doubt the very same fictional world or larger part of this world. With this relation at hand, we can now add the set S of fictional stories to our model and specify the truth- and falsity-conditions of fictional reports that use our second fictional operator in the following way:

$V(<FW<\alpha>[\varphi], w>, T)$   iff   for every world $w^* \in F^*$ such that there is an $x \in S$ and $WM(x, \alpha)$ and $I(FW, <x>)(w, w^*)$, $V(<\varphi, w^*>, T)$.

$V(<FW<α>[φ], w>, F)$ iff for at least one world $w^* \in F^*$ such that there is an $x \in S$ and $WM(x, α)$ and $I(FW, <x>)(w, w^*), V(<φ, w^*>, F)$.

More informally, a sentence of the logical form 'FW<h>[φ]' is true relative to a world w iff 'φ' is true relative to every non-normal world that represents the literal content of some story that represents the same fictional world as h. We again now have the option, as in the case of our example sentence (2), to interpret (6) if it is understood as a sentence about a whole set of fictional works that are related to *The Hound of the Baskervilles* relative to our two base semantics for the embedded sentences 'φ' with respect to 'FW<h>[φ]'.

A third formal fictional operator can be introduced to capture example sentences like (7). Informally, I follow here the idea of Friend, who holds that the *genre* of a fictional work determines a certain range of additional fictional truths based on what is literally said in this fictional work.[19] We can now implement this idea into our formal framework. We formally represent the expression 'In the fictional world that is depicted by the fictional work x it is the case that' if it is understood on the background of factors that concern the genre of this work by the sentential operator: FG<α>[φ]. The semantic interpretation of this operator requires an alternative kind of accessibility than 'FC' and 'FW'. This accessibility relation is relativized to pairs consisting of a work and its genre. We formally represent this kind of relation as follows: $I(FG, <α, G(α)>)(w, w^*)$. Informally, we can interpret this relation as follows: The accessibility relation that is assigned by I to FG, the fictional work α and the genre of α, provides access from w to a fictional world w' that respresents the content of a relative to the genre rules provided by G for α. The basic idea behind this modification is that an accessibility relation that is relativized to fictional work *and* its genre is more liberal with respect to the accessed worlds than an accessibility relation that is only relativized to fictional work. This idea leads to the following formal truth- and falsity-conditions for fictional reports that make use of 'FG':

$V(<FG<α>[φ], w>, T)$ iff for every world $w^* \in F^*$: such that $I(FG, <α, G(α)>)(w, w^*), V(<φ, w^*>, T)$.

$V(<FG<α>[φ], w>, F)$ iff for some world $w^* \in F^*$: such that $I(FG, <α, G(α)>)(w, w^*), V(<φ, w^*>, F)$.

More informally, a sentence of the logical form 'FG<h>[φ]' is true relative to a world w iff 'φ' is true relative to every non-normal world that represents the content of h based on the conventions of the genre of h. My account for 'FG' provides only the basic idea for such a genre-specific fictional operator. Probably, there is more fine-tuning necessary to get an account that delivers results for all relevant cases. Genre-conventions may change from time to time and they might be interpreted by different people in different ways. Therefore, additional modifications of the outlined account seem to be plausible and necessary.

The last thing I want to do in this section is to introduce a transformed version of 'FC' that is additionally relativized to an interpreter. In principle, this addition could be made with respect to all the three fictional operators introduced so far. But I will only explicitly make this addition concerning 'FC'. Our example sentence (8) provides the intuitive basis for the introduction of a possible modification of 'FC'. We formally represent the intuitive fictional modifier 'According to U' interpretation of the fictional work x it is the case that' by means of FCI<x, y>[p]. This sentential operator is relativized to pairs of fictional works x that are elements of F* and interpreters of this work y relative to w. In our metalanguage, we make use of a world-relative set of interpreters U of a fictional work α and therefore we are able to specify the truth- and falsity-conditions of fictional reports that explicitly or implicitly make use of 'FCI' as follows:

V(<FCI<α,β >[φ], w>, T)  iff  for every world w* ∈ F* such that β ∈ U(α, w) & I(FG, <α,β>)(w, w*), V(<φ, w*>,T).

V(<FCI<α>[φ], w>, F)  iff  for some world w* ∈ F* such that β ∈ U(α, w) & I(FG, <α,β>)(w, w*), V(<φ, w*>, F).

More informally, a sentence of the logical form 'FCI<h,A>[φ]' is true relative to a world w iff 'φ' is true relative to every non-normal world that represents the interpretation of A of the literal content of h. Again, as in the case of 'FG' our semantics for 'FCI' only provides the basic idea for a formal interpretation of a modifier as it is used in (8). Also in this case more fine-tuning might be required to apply this account to all relevant cases of interpretation. I will leave this fine-tuning for another occasion.

As a general upshot of this section, we can say the following. If we use sentences like (1) as fictional reports in natural languages, there is a big variety of possible implicit content-additions that transform a use of the sentence (1) into a genuine fictional report. In this section, I have outlined a formal semantic framework that allows us to capture and introduce such different kinds of implicit and explicit additions. However, it is not intended to provide the *full* range of possible additions. Our introduced four fictional operators should only be understood as examples to capture the variety of fictional reports that natural languages have to offer on the basis of a formal semantics for such reports.

**Assertoric sentences with fictional names**

There is a third and last class of uses of fictional names in natural languages sentences that I will now focus on. These are uses in plain and explicit assertions that contain at least one fictional name. The most important difference between these assertions and fictional reports that have been discussed before are the following two. Firstly, these assertions are not concerned with the truth-evaluable content of fictional works or what is the case relative to a fictional world. These assertions primarily concern states of affairs in the actual world. Secondly, these assertions do not require an implicit content-addition to express their purported truth-evaluable content. These assertions literally express those contents that concern their primary use or function. We can distinguish three important classes of assertoric sentences that can be used to make the mentioned literal assertions: (a) sentences that only contain extensional predicates, (b) sentences that only contain intensional predicates, and (c) sentences that only contain hyper-intensional predicates.

With respect to the first class, the most important sentences that can contain a fictional name and nevertheless be true are negative singular existential sentences like:

(9)   Sherlock Holmes does not exist.

Intuitively, every negative singular existential sentence of the form 'x does not exist' is true if 'x' is substituted by a fictional name. Hence, it is important that a proper semantics of fictional names can also account for this important data. Our formal semantic framework has the resources to account for this semantic data relative to both proposed versions, the version with a *story-semantics* and that with a *noneist semantics*. In general, positive existential sentences have the logical form 'E!t' and their negative counterparts the logical form '¬E!t'.

According to the first of these two semantics, singular existential sentences have the following truth- and falsity-conditions:

V(<E!t, w>,T)   iff   if w ∈ N, d(t,w) ∈ D(w), or if w ∈ O, I(E!t, w) = T.

V(<E!t, w>,F)   iff   if w ∈ N, it is not the case that d(t,w) ∈ D(w), or
                      if w ∈ O, I(E!t, w) = F.

If the world-relative and partial denotation function d() can, as mentioned above, assign any element of D* to an individual constant relative to a possible world, then it is also possible to assign an object relative to a world w to a constant x that is not an element of D(w). This shows that there are in principle two different reasons why an existential sentence of the form 'E!t' can be false. Firstly, it can be false because the partial function d() fails to assign an object to the constant 't'; secondly, it can be false because the function d() assigns relative to w an object that is not an element of D(w). In the case of fictional names, only the first condition can be the reason for the falsity of 'E!t' relative to normal worlds because we have assumed that these names lack a semantic referent with respect to all normal worlds. However, this is sufficient to account for the mentioned linguistic data concerning the truth-values of sentences of the form 'E!t' that contain fictional names. If we combine the mentioned semantics of positive existential sentences with the following standard semantics for negation, we can account for the intuitive truth-value of sentences like (9):

V(<¬A, w>,T)   iff   V(<A, w>, F).
V(<¬A, w>,F)   iff   V(<A, w>, T).

Relative to a story-semantics, sentences of the form 'E!t' can be true or false for arbitrary reasons relative to non-normal worlds. However, these truth- and falsity-conditions should only be relevant for a restricted purpose, namely for specific embedded uses of sentences in the scope of non-normal modal operators.

The alternative noneist semantics of singular existential sentences is simpler and more uniform and has the following truth- and falsity-conditions:

V(<E!t, w>,T)   iff   d(t,w) ∈ D(w).
V(<E!t, w>,F)   iff   it is not the case that d(t,w) ∈ D(w).

Relative to this kind of semantics, there are again the mentioned two different alternative reasons why a sentence of the form 'E!t' can fail to be true. However, the main difference to the story-semantic approach is that we have these two alternatives relative to all worlds. If desired, the truth- and falsity-conditions can be slightly altered in such a way that objects can be elements of D(w) without existing relative to this world. For this purpose, we would have to substitute the condition '∈ D(w)' by the condition '∈ I(E!,w)'. Relative to both variations of the noneist semantics for existential sentences in combination with the outlined standard semantics for negation, we have the resources to account for the desired intuitive truth-values of sentences like (9).

What also has to be mentioned is that our semantics for the fictional operator 'According to fiction x' in combination with either of our two variants for singular existential sentences also allows us to account for a significant difference in truth-value between (9) and:

(10) According to the fiction *The Hound of the Baskervilles*, Sherlock Holmes does not exist.

While (9) is intuitively true, (10) is intuitively false. Our semantics also allow us to capture this additional linguistic data.

Singular negative existential sentences are certainly the most important and most discussed examples of true sentences that contain fictional proper names and only extensional predicates. I will not discuss any other examples of this kind and move on to an example of the second variety: an assertoric sentence that contains fictional names and intensional expressions. The most important examples of this kind certainly are sentences that contain modal expressions. Against the background of examples like (9) and (10) the most obvious examples of these second kind are sentences like:

(11) Sherlock Holmes could not have existed.

I share with Kripke the intuition that this sentence is true if it is understood as a claim about a metaphysical possibility. We can account for this true reading of (11) on the basis of our conception of fictional names in combination with our outlined two accounts of existential sentences and the following standard account concerning metaphysical possibility:

$V(<\Diamond A, w>, T)$ iff for some $w^* \in N, V(<A, w^*>, T)$.
$V(<\Diamond A, w>, F)$ iff for every $w^* \in N, V(<A, w^*>, F)$.

Against this background, we can assign to (11) the following logical form:

(11*) ¬◊E!h.

This logical form is false because 'h' lacks a referent with respect to every possible world and, hence, 'E!h' is false with respect to every possible world. There are other interesting assertoric sentences that contain fictional names and intensional predicates, but we will not discuss any additional examples of this kind here.

We will now move on to probably the most interesting class of assertoric sentences that contain fictional names, namely those that contain only hyper-intensional predicates. In my opinion, the following often discussed examples for true assertoric sentences that contain fictional names are of this third variety:

(12)  Arthur Conan Doyle created the fictional character Sherlock Holmes.
(13)  Sherlock Holmes is a fictional character.

In my opinion, sentence (12) is true because it is used as a short-cut or simplified version of the following more explicit claim.

(12*)  Arthur Conan Doyle created a fictional work that features the fictional character Sherlock Holmes.

Relative to our outlined framework, a sentence like (12*) has the following informal truth-conditions: (12*) is actually true iff there is actually a fictional story that is created by Arthur Conan Doyle and relative to all non-normal fictional worlds that represent the literal content of this story it is true that Sherlock Holmes exists and it is false relative to all non fictional worlds. In this sense, (12*) contains hyper-intensional expressions because the truth-conditions of (12*) require an access to non-normal possible worlds.

In a very similar fashion, (13) can be analysed and should also be considered as a sentence that contains the hyper-intensional expression 'is a fictional character'. Informally spoken, (13) is actually true iff there is an actual fictional story that is such that relative to all worlds that represent the literal content of this story Sherlock Holmes exists and it is false relative to all non fictional worlds. For the sake of brevity, I will not elaborate the formal details of both analyses here. However, it should be obvious that our outlined semantic framework has the resources to provide an analysis of sentences like (12*) and (13).

The remaining question now is whether our account can also be extended to more classical and obvious assertoric sentences that contain fictional names and hyper-intensional expressions, namely those that contain intentional transitive verbs[20] like 'fear', 'admire' and 'hate'. Intuitively, a sentence like the following has a true reading if the mentioned person has the described mental state:

(14)  Peter Hanks admires Sherlock Holmes.

Our formal semantic framework can also be used to analyse ascriptions of these specific kinds of objectual attitudes. In a nutshell, this account goes like this. Like attitude verbs intentional transitives are also formally represented as non-normal modal operators. In a certain sense they can be formally treated as attitude verbs of a quite specific sort. Verbs like 'admire' treated as non-normal modal operators also come equipped with a specific accessibility relation that is assigned to the operator 'ADMIRE<x>[y]' by the interpretation function. In opposition to fictional operators, these kinds of operators can have access to all worlds, that is, normal and non-normal worlds. Intuitively, an operator like 'ADMIRE<x>[y]' has access to those worlds that represent the objects that are admired by a certain person S and that bear, relative to these worlds, the properties that provide the reasons for S' admiration of these objects. Hence, the sentence (14) is actually true iff from the actual world all worlds that represent the mental states of admiration of Peter Hanks can be accessed and these worlds are all such that Sherlock Holmes exists relative to these worlds. Unfortunately,

I cannot work out all the necessary formal details of these accounts in this chapter and I leave the detailed exposition of this account for another occasion.

These brief remarks about intentional transitive verbs complete my brief overview about the use of fictional names in genuine and fully explicit assertions. I have briefly outlined a formal semantic framework to capture the uses of these names relative to such assertoric sentences relative to a truth-conditional semantics. In the next section, we will come back to the issue of the semantic function of fictional names against the background of the proposed semantic treatment of names in different sentential environments.

## The semantic and pragmatic functions of fictional names

According to both outlined versions of our view, (a) sophisticated irrealism and (b) the synthetic view, genuine fictional names lack a semantic referent with respect to all possible worlds. However, according to the first version they also lack a semantic referent with respect to all non-normal worlds, while according to the second version they can have a semantic referent with respect to non-normal worlds.

Uses of fictional names by the creators of fictional stories in genuine acts of story-telling are *introductory uses* of fictional names. All subsequent uses of a fictional name seem to be in some sense *parasitic* on these initial uses. Based on the outlined role of fictional names in acts of story-telling there are now different options to capture the semantic function of fictional names relative to these initial uses in acts of story-telling and their dependent uses in other speech acts, most notably in speech acts of assertions.

According to our view of acts of story-telling, introductory uses of fictional names can neither be attempts to name a specific already existing object nor attempts to create a specific new real object. We said that a full-flagged genuine act of story-telling that concerns a content that p has two different purposes: (a) to invite a potential addressee to fictionally assume that p, and (b) to stipulate that p is the case relative to a fictional world that is represented by the told story. Someone who fictionally assumes that p, assumes that p is the case relative to some fictional world. Someone who fictionally stipulates that p, stipulates that p is the case relative to some fictional world.

Against this background, we only seem to have *one* plausible choice to specify the role of fictional proper name relative to acts of story-telling, namely by contributing their fair share to the acts of *stipulation* mentioned. The details of this contribution very much depend on how we interpret the mentioned acts of stipulation, whether relative to that variant of our view based on story semantics or on a noneist semantics.

Let us begin by examining the role of proper names in acts of story-telling relative to the second setting because it is easier on this basis to identify a specific role of proper names relative to these acts. Relative to this setting, it makes sense to hold the view that by using a fictional name 'N' in an act of story-telling someone *stipulates that 'N' refers to N* relative to those fictional worlds that are aimed to represent the content of the story that is created by this very act of story-telling. More precisely, such an act of referential stipulation has two aspects: (a) the stipulation of the existence of a specific object relative to a certain fictional world, and (b) the stipulation that this object bears a specific name. However, if we assume that certain uses of fictional names have this specific function, it would be strange to hold that *every* use of the very same fictional name relative to the process of creating a story has this very same use. It is intuitively not possible to stipulate the existence of the very same single object more than once. It also does not seem plausible to assume that we again and again stipulate that a certain object bears a certain name. The mentioned function for our use of fictional proper names should be restricted to the *introductory* use of a fictional name relative to an act of story-telling; and we should assign to *subsequent* uses of the very same fictional name a different role or function. Which function should we assign? These uses are dependent on the introductory use and in this sense *exploit* the result of the introductory use.

What does it mean to exploit a stipulation? A use of a fictional name that *exploits* a fictional stipulation aims to use this name *in accordance* with this stipulation. Against this background, we either have the option to assume that these subsequent uses *refer* to the stipulated object or that they only *confirm* or *update* the initial stipulation. In my opinion, it makes more sense to hold the second view. If a single use of a fictional name in an act of story-telling can stipulate the existence of an object relative to a certain class of fictional worlds, then the result of this stipulation is a rather *thin* or *purely formal object* that has at most the property(ies) that an act of story-telling that uses this name stipulates of this object. I have the tendency to conceive of a series of acts of story-telling that lead to the creation of a fictional work as constant process of updating information about a stipulated object. Therefore, because of the very peculiar nature of those speech acts that lead to the creation of a fictional work, I think, it is more appropriate to assume that introductory uses of fictional names in acts of story-telling stipulate the existence of an object, and subsequent uses only *confirm* this object-related stipulation. In this sense, the uses of *fictional* names in acts of story-telling are extremely specific and significantly differ from the range of uses of *ordinary* proper names.

It is more difficult to specify a distinctive role of proper names relative to acts of story-telling on the basis of the version of our view that assumes a story-semantics. According to this view, acts of story-telling are constituted by acts of stipulations that merely stipulate the truth-value of the logical form of a sentence relative to certain non-normal worlds. Hence, there is not much room for a distinctive function of proper names relative to such kinds of acts. I think, the best we can do against this background is to assume that names only *pretend* to refer to objects in fictional worlds relative to introductory and subsequent uses and there is some kind of coordination between these different acts of pretence. Hence, the noneist variant of our view seems in this respect to be in a position to offer a more informative story about the distinctive role of proper names in acts of story-telling.

However, as we already know, fictional names cannot only be used in a meaningful way in acts of story-telling, they can also be used in (a) acts of re-telling a story, (b) fictional reports and (c) ordinary explicit assertions. How should we understand these kinds of uses? Are they referential uses of fictional names? There is an important overlap between fictional reports that concern the literal content of a fictional story and acts of re-telling a story. Both kinds of acts have a very similar assertive component. In the first case, this component is exhaustive, in the second case we have an additional directive component. However, the core element of both kinds of acts is the assertive component. It now very much depends on whether we interpret these kinds of acts in the first or second version of our view. According to the story-semantics version, proper names relative to none of their uses refer to any kinds of objects. Therefore, even if they are used in the scope of non-normal modal operators, they cannot refer to any objects. However, if they also do not refer relative to this kind of use, what is their distinctive function in assertoric sentences that contain these fictional names in the scope of non-normal modal operators? It seems to be difficult to find a plausible answer to this question. It would be strange to assume that they again only *pretend* to refer to things in fictional worlds, because (a) such a use of a name seems to be inappropriate relative to acts of assertions and (b) it is implausible to assume that fictional names have the same use in assertions and acts of story-telling. The best we could do is to say that such uses are in some sense parasitic on the pretence-use in acts of story-telling. But it is very unclear in which sense they could depend, relative to uses in assertoric sentences, on these uses in acts of story-telling and how we should describe the nature of these dependent uses in an informative way.

The situation seems to be much better in this respect for the noneist variety of our semantics. This view cannot only provide a plausible story concerning the truth- and falsity-conditions of such kinds of assertions that contain fictional names, it also can offer a plausible story concerning the function of proper names relative to such assertoric sentences. Relative to both kinds of mentioned cases, fictional names are uses in the scope of non-normal modal operators and these operators in some sense *shift*, according to our analysis the sematic interpretation of proper names to non-normal fictional worlds. Therefore, although fictional names do not refer relative to normal worlds, because in such cases they cannot exploit the mentioned stipulated fictional facts, they can refer relative to fictional worlds. That is, the noneist version of our framework does not only account for the specific referential function of fictional names in the scope of fictional operators, it also provides a nice story of how these shifted referential uses of fictional names are connected and dependent on previous stipulative uses. Therefore, our synthetic view fairs in this respect much better than its irrealist counterpart.

The only remaining class of uses of fictional names are those uses relative to *explicit* assertions that do not report what is the case according to fictional stories. We have seen that there are important sub-kinds of such uses. If we use a fictional name in an assertoric sentence as the argument of an extensional or intensional predicate, then fictional names remain without a semantic referent, but not because they fail to refer or they do not satisfy their referential function. They lack a semantic referent relative to those uses because it is impossible relative to such uses to *exploit* those kinds of stipulations that are relevant for the referential status of fictional names with respect to fictional worlds. But the situation is different relative to uses of fictional names in assertoric sentences and in the argument position of a hyper-intensional expression that provides access to fictional worlds. Relative to such contexts, fictional names can exploit the relevant stipulations that fix their referential status relative to non-normal worlds and hence they function as rather extraordinary referential devices relative to such uses. The story about the use of fictional names in the mentioned two different kinds of sentential contexts in assertoric sentences is therefore straightforward on the basis of the synthetic version of our view. It again seems to be very different for the irrealist variant of our view to provide an equally plausible story. This shows that questions that concern the functional status of fictional names relative to their different kinds of uses in different kinds of sentences and speech acts clearly favour the synthetic version of our semantic view on fictional names over its irrealist rival.

Against this background, we also can now answer the challenge provided by our above-mentioned argument against irrealist views of fictional names. Even if we give up premise (P4) and, hence, the view that fictional names have, like ordinary names, the function to refer to objects relative to all of their uses, to block the mentioned argument, it is difficult to find a plausible replacement for (P4) on the basis of a full-flagged irrealist view on fictional names. Our synthetic view also rejects (P4) in its too simplistic generality, but it shows that a plausible and so far overlooked compromise between a full-flagged realist view and a full-flagged irrealist view exists and has earned more careful attention and future investigation.

# 5

# Apparent Predicative Uses of Proper Names[1]

In this chapter, I will defend the thesis that proper nouns are primarily used as proper names – as atomic singular referring expressions – and different possible predicative uses of proper nouns are derived from this primary use or an already derived secondary predicative use of proper nouns. There is a general linguistic phenomenon of the derivation of new meanings from already existing meanings of an expression. This phenomenon has different manifestations and different linguistic mechanisms can be used to establish derived meanings of different kinds of expressions. One prominent variation of these mechanisms was dubbed *meaning transfer* in Nunberg (1979, 1995, 2004). In this chapter I will distinguish two different sub-varieties of this mechanism: *occurrent* and *lexical* meaning transfer. Nunberg conceives of meaning transfer as a mechanism that allows us to derive a new truth-conditional meaning of an expression from an already existing truth-conditional meaning of this expression. I will argue that *most* predicative uses of proper nouns can be captured by the mentioned two varieties of *truth-conditional* meaning transfer. But there are also important exceptions like the predicative use of the proper noun 'Alfred' in a sentence like 'Every Alfred that I met was a nice guy'. I will try to show that we cannot make use of truth-conditional meaning transfer to account for such uses and I will argue for the existence of a second variant of meaning transfer that I will call *non-truth-conditional meaning transfer* and that allows us also to capture these derived meanings of proper nouns.

## Setting the stage: referential and predicative uses of proper names

A capitalized noun like 'Alfred' is prototypically used as a proper name with the purpose of referring to a single object, as in the following sentence:

(1)    Alfred is a nice guy.

The only literal correct use of 'Alfred' in (1) uses this expression to refer to a single bearer of the name 'Alfred'. Apart from its *referential use*, this noun also seems to have a *predicative use*. The following sentence provides an example of this kind:

(2)    Every Alfred in our club is a nice guy.

Relative to the default reading of 'Alfred' in (2), this predicate is used in such a way that it satisfies the following general equivalence schema:[2]

(PE)   For every x: x is an N iff x is a bearer of the name 'N'.

Nevertheless, it is not clear which semantic status the instances of (PE) in fact have. We will try to clarify the explanatory status of (PE) in the following. It seems that either the use of 'Alfred' in (2) is in some sense *derived* from the use (1), or the other way round. In any case, there seem to be systematic semantic connections between the use of 'Alfred' as a name in (1) and as a predicate in (2). Let us call predicative uses of proper nouns that satisfy equivalences like (PE) *original examples*, because these examples were originally used by certain philosophers and linguists to motivate the thesis that the noun 'Alfred' has in a sentence like (1) exactly the same semantics as a *predicate* in (2).[3]

Apart from these original examples, there are at least three different classes of *additional examples* of predicative uses of proper nouns that all share the negative feature that they do *not* satisfy the equivalence schema (PE).

Firstly, there are so-called *dynasty* or *family examples*. A prominent example of this sort is:[4]

(3)   Waldo Cox is a Romanov.

In an appropriate conversational context, the predicate 'is a Romanov' can be used in a way such that it is roughly equivalent to the predicate 'is a member of the Romanov family/dynasty'.

Secondly, we can also distinguish so-called *production examples*. Here is one example of this sort:[5]

(4)   Linda bought three Picassos yesterday.

This sentence seems to have a reading relative to which 'is a Picasso' is intuitively equivalent to 'is a work produced by Picasso', where 'Picasso' refers to the famous artist with this name.

Thirdly, we can distinguish from the other cases highly context-sensitive *resemblance examples*. Let us focus on the following example of this sort:[6]

(5)   Two Napoleons were at the party yesterday.

There are contexts of use where (5) can be used to express or convey the thought that two people that resemble Napoleon in the way they are dressed were at a certain party on a certain day. In the case of such examples, a contextually salient mode of resemblance seems to be operative, and certain objects are compared on this basis with a specific contextually salient bearer of the used proper name.

These three classes of additional examples of predicative uses of proper nouns are undoubtedly examples of *derived* uses; these uses are derived from other *primary* uses of the very same expression. In some cases, the result is a new derived meaning of the expression. In other cases, we only have a highly context-sensitive and purely pragmatic derived use of this expression. The relevant literature on these issues provides a good explanation of the additional examples. Nunberg's so-called mechanism of *meaning transfer* can be used to explain such uses.[7] In the next section, I will introduce this mechanism as it is characterized in Nunberg (1979, 1995, 2004) and I will distinguish two important varieties of this mechanism: *occurrent* and *lexical* meaning transfer. I will use these two varieties to account for all the distinguished three additional kinds of examples. After that, I will argue for the positive thesis that the instances of (PE) should be conceived of as semantic equivalences and the negative thesis that the mechanism of meaning transfer described by Nunberg cannot be used in a meaningful way to account for our original examples.[8]

In the third section, I will propose an alternative kind of derivational mechanism to account for these cases. Meaning transfer, in Nunberg's sense, only concerns the truth-conditional level of meaning, but I will show that in the case of the original examples there is a transfer from the meta-semantic level of meaning of the name 'Alfred' to the truth-conditional level of meaning of the predicate 'Alfred'.

## The linguistic mechanism of meaning transfer

Meaning transfer, as this mechanism is called by Nunberg, is a general linguistic mechanism that can be operative in the case of different linguistic phenomena like metonymy, metaphors or polysemy.[9] It can be used to derive certain new correct uses or meanings of a specific target expression from an already established meaning of this expression. Meaning transfer allows us to assign an additional meaning to an expression in a systematic, more or less context-sensitive way. According to Nunberg, it is a defining feature of each case of meaning transfer that there is a direct correspondence between the original extension (property) and the derived extension (property) of the target expression based on a functional mapping.[10] In paradigm cases,[11] this correspondence is based on a so-called *transfer relation* that holds between elements of the original extension and elements of the derived extension.[12]

We can distinguish two important sub-classes of meaning transfer: *occurrent* and *lexical* meaning transfer. In the first case, we have got a *contextually salient* transfer relation that can only be exploited relative to a restricted range of situations. In this sense, meaning transfer is a purely pragmatic phenomenon. In the case of a lexical meaning transfer, on the other hand, we have a stable, contextually invariant transfer relation that is licenced by a lexical rule and can be exploited relative to a large class of different situations. We therefore have in this case an initial pragmatic phenomenon that is transformed into a semantic one by a certain sort of conventionalization.[13]

A standard example of a case of occurrent meaning transfer can be provided by making use of the following sentence:[14]

(6)   The ham sandwich is at table 7.

In a situation where a visitor of a restaurant has ordered a ham sandwich, (6) can be used to convey the thought that this specific visitor sits at table 7. The original extension of 'ham sandwich' is the set of ham sandwiches. The derived extension is the set of orderers of a ham sandwich. The contextually salient transfer relation is the relation expressed by 'x ordered y', it obtains between a specific element of the derived extension and some element of the original extension. The meaning transfer in such a case is only occurrent, because it is not part of the lexical meaning of 'ham sandwich' that can be applied to orders of ham sandwiches and this use is restricted to a very specific conversational setting.

The situation is different if lexical meaning transfer is operative in cases of polysemy.[15] A standard example of a polysemic expression is the expression 'maple'. According to its primary meaning, this expression can be correctly applied to trees of a specific kind; according to its secondary derived meaning, it also applies to the wood of these trees. The fact that the expression 'maple' has a primary and a derived secondary meaning can also be captured by a semantic equivalence in the following way, if we use 'maple$_1$' to express the primary and 'maple$_2$' to express the secondary meaning of 'maple':

(E1)   For every x: x is a unit of maple$_2$ iff x is a unit of the wood of a maple$_1$.

The truth of (E1) is licenced by a *general higher-order lexical rule* that does not only concern a specific predicate for trees like the predicate 'is a maple', but predicates of this kind in general. This lexical rule can be formulated in the following way:

(G1)   If 'N' is a noun that is used as predicate for a certain sort of trees, then 'N' can also be used as a mass term for the wood of these trees.[16]

Such a lexical rule establishes a specific *stable* transfer relation in connection with predicates for trees. Against this background, these predicates receive a secondary meaning that can be captured by a semantic equivalence like (E1). In the maple case, the transfer relation is the relation expressed by 'x is the wood of y' and this relation obtains between members of the original and the derived extension of the expression 'maple'.

## Meaning transfer and resemblance examples

Let us now show how the mechanism of meaning transfer can be applied to our family, production and resemblance examples. We will start with the *resemblance examples*. They are examples of occurrent meaning transfer. In each case of this class of examples a certain *resemblance relation* is operative as a meaning transfer relation. The specific form and prominence of such a resemblance relation is highly context-dependent. We can distinguish two important sub-classes of resemblance examples based on different resemblance relations: *specificity* and *typicality* examples. In the former cases the meaning transfer is a resemblance relation that can be expressed by an expression of the form 'x resembles y in the respect of C'. This relation provides a comparison between different objects relative to some specific way of resemblance. So, for example, if we use

(5)   Two Napoleons were at the party yesterday,

in a situation that concerns a certain costume party, it may turn out that the most adequate interpretation of such a sentence makes use of a meaning transfer relation that can be expressed by 'x resembles y in the way y is dressed'. And therefore, our example sentence (5) conveys in such a context that two people that were dressed as Napoleon were at a certain party. We might use the very same sentence (5) in a different situation that, for example, concerns a party where no costumes are worn. In such a context it is possible to make use of a different salient resemblance relation as our meaning transfer relation. One prominent candidate in such a context is the relation expressed by 'x resembles y in certain/every respect(s) that we typically associate with y'. According to this reading, (5) is an example of the typicality variant of resemblance cases. In such a case, we compare a certain person or persons with a salient object in more than one respect, namely in those respects that are typically associated with this salient object.[17] There might be other variations of the resemblance examples, other contextually salient procedures to make different respects of resemblance salient. But all these different kinds of resemblance examples share one general feature. They all satisfy the following schema:

(S1)   For every x and every context c: x is a $N_2$ (relative to c) iff x resembles $N_1$ in every respect that is (made) salient by the utterer of 'N' in c.

Against this background, I think it makes sense to classify resemblance examples as a distinctive class of examples of occurrent meaning transfer.

## Meaning transfer and production examples

Let us now focus on *production examples*. There seems to be at least two different clear-cut classes of nouns that can be used as proper names and that also have a secondary meaning relative to which they can be used as predicates for certain products of the bearers of the corresponding names. Firstly, we have those cases like (4), where we can use a noun that is used as a name for an artist as a predicate for the works of this artist. Secondly, we have cases like the following, where we can use a noun that is used as a name for a company as a predicate for the products of this company:

(7)   This car is a Chevrolet.

Examples like (4) and (7) seem to be closely related to our mentioned maple case. These sentences contain predicates with a stable meaning that is not in the same way dependent on the situation of use as in cases of occurrent meaning transfer. Furthermore, we can find the very same systematic use of expressions like 'Chevrolet' and 'Picasso' in different natural languages. As in the maple case there seem to be *lexical rules* operative that define the two mentioned sub-classes of production examples. We can formulate them roughly[18] in the following way:[19]

(G2)   If 'N' is a noun that is used as proper name for an artist, then 'N' can also be used as a predicate for the works of this artist.
(G3)   If 'N' is a noun that is used as a proper name for a company, then 'N' can also be used as a predicate for the products of this company.

Applied to our examples (4) and (7) we can capture on this basis the specific predicate uses of 'Picasso' and 'Chevrolet'. Therefore, it seems to be plausible to assume that names for *artists* and names for *companies* are in the same way *systematically ambiguous* as predicates for kinds of trees. In both cases a transfer relation holds between elements of the original and elements of the derived extension of our target notion. Therefore, they are both *paradigm* cases of lexical meaning transfer.

But there are also purely pragmatic production examples that are clearly examples of occurrent meaning transfer. For example, a sentence like the following can be used to convey that a certain cake is a typical product of (the actions of) a certain man named 'Nick':

(8)  This cake is a typical Nick.

Such a use of (9) is highly context-sensitive and it clearly depends on the conversational setting of a situation relative to which (9) is used, which meaning transfer relation is operative and relevant. Hence, there are also production examples that are the result of occurrent meaning transfer.

## Meaning transfer and family examples

Beside our lexical production examples, dynasty or family examples are also examples of derived uses of names that can be captured by *lexical* meaning transfer. A dynasty is a specific sub-species of a (human) family. In this sense, a dynasty case like (3) that concerns the Romanov dynasty is only a specific sub-variety of a larger class of cases that concern family names. A family example that is not a dynasty example is the following:[20]

(9)  Billy Jones is in reality a Smith.

There seem to be at least two different predicative uses of family names that have to be distinguished. We can distinguish *institutional* uses from *biological* uses, because there is a legal or institutional notion of a family and a biological notion. In the first case, a person's membership of a family depends on certain institutional properties like marriage or adoption. In the second case, the membership is determined by genetic code. Our example sentences (3) and (9) can be interpreted relative to both readings. Which of these two readings is relevant depends on the context of use. But this does not mean that our family cases are examples of occurrent meaning transfer. On the contrary, these two readings are stable across a very large number of different situations and the very same systematically derived predicative use of nouns that can be used as family names can be found in different natural languages. We can distinguish the following two different *lexical rules* to capture these two meanings of family names:

(G4.1/2)  If 'N' is a noun that is used as a (human) family name, then 'N' can also be used as a predicate for the institutional/biological members of the corresponding family.

A lexical rule like (G4.1/2) constitutes a derived meaning for the class of human family names and therefore also accounts for the meaning of the name-like predicates in (3) and (9). The expression 'the Romanov family' refers to a specific family whose core members are bearers of the name 'Romanov'.[21] Therefore, we can define a secondary meaning of a predicate like 'is a Romanov' licenced by the lexical rule (G4.1/2) in the following way:

(E1*)  For every x: x is a $Romanov_2$ iff x is a biological member of a certain family whose core members are $Romanovs_1$.

This shows that our family examples are again *paradigm* cases of lexical meaning transfer. In their case, the meaning transfer relation is expressed by 'x is a biological descendant of a core member y of a certain family'. And this relation holds between elements of the extension of the derived and secondary meaning of 'is a Romanov' and elements of the extension of the primary meaning of the very same expression. But (E1*) also provides reasons to assume that the original examples of predicative uses of proper names are examples of a systematic use with a stable meaning. Lexical semantic transfer is only then possible if there is an already established meaning from which an additional meaning can be derived.

## Meaning transfer and the original examples

Two different accounts have been proposed in the literature to capture our *original examples* by means of Nunberg's mechanism of meaning transfer. Firstly, there is a metalinguistic version that aims to capture our original examples by means of occurrent semantic transfer.[22]

### *Metalinguistic meaning transfer*

According to this approach, (2) is not really an accurate semantic representation of the desired reading of the noun 'Alfred', because in fact the use of 'Alfred' in (2) is of a specific metalinguistic kind and therefore the correct representation would be something like the following:

(2') Every 'Alfred' in our club is a nice guy.

On the basis of this reformulation, it seems to be possible to apply the mechanism of meaning transfer to the example (2'). The expression '"Alfred"' has an original use relative to which it functions as a name of a proper name. Hence, the extension of such expressions is a specific *name*. We can now make use of the meaning transfer relation expressed by 'x is a bearer of y' and constitute on this basis a new shifted extension for the expression '"Alfred"'. This new extension is the set of bearers of the name 'Alfred'. Hence, we get the desired reading of (2'). However, there are several reasons that speak against such a simple analysis of the original examples.

Firstly, it might be doubted that all competent speakers are confused about the correct semantic representation of (2), and the correct representation of 'Alfred' in such a context discovered by certain philosophers would in fact require the use of quotation marks. The expression 'is an Alfred' seems to be a perfectly legitimate predicate in its own right. Therefore, a correction or reformulation of sentences like (2) along the lines of (2') neither seem to be necessary nor appropriate.

There are other examples where the correct and most explicit semantic representation seems to require the use of quotations or some other quotation-indicating device. Competent speakers seem to be clearly aware of the fact that such devices are required to formulate a sentence like the following in its most explicit and correct way.

(10) I counted three 'terrific' and two 'awesome'.

However, there seems to be a clear and intuitively obvious difference between cases like (2) and cases like (10) with respect to the dimension of correct and explicit semantic representation.

Secondly, our original predicative uses of proper nouns seem to be more stable and context-insensitive than those special uses of implicitly or explicitly quoted expressions in combination with determiners like (10). We have already pointed out that these uses are quite systematic across different languages and that they can also function as *inputs* of lexical semantic transfer. The situation would be different if the proposed analysis were correct. The following sentence, for example, has at least two different readings, and it can be used with both readings relative to the very same situation:

(11)  There are two 'Alfred'(s) in this room.

There might be a situation where we find two inscriptions of the word 'Alfred' on a blackboard in a certain room and where two bearers of the name 'Alfred' are also present. If the given interpretation of (2′) is correct, then one might use the sentence (11) relative to such a situation with two different readings: one can either convey that there are two inscriptions of the name 'Alfred' in the mentioned room or that there are two bearers of the name 'Alfred' in this room. In general, a sentence like (11) can have a number of different readings that depend on the specific contextually salient transfer relation. Hence, these are examples of occurrent meaning transfer. But intuitively the mentioned original uses of proper nouns do not have this kind of flexibility and contextual variability.

Thirdly, one additional problem of a metalinguistic interpretation of original uses of a noun like 'Alfred' has to do with the plural of 'Alfred' that seems to be required to interpret a sentence like 'Some Alfreds are nice' in an adequate way. It is not clear how we account for an explicitly used plural in sentences like (2) in an adequate way by applying the metalinguistic strategy.[23] One can see this problem more clearly on the basis of a comparison with an explicit metalinguistic example like the following:

(10*)  I counted some 'terrific' and some 'awesome'.

This sentence can clearly be used to talk about the result of some word-counting activity with respect to a specific text and it is not required to use any plurals for this purpose. Furthermore, to my ears it sounds odd to add in such a case a plural 's' to the mentioned adjectives. However, I am not a native speaker. In any case, if my impression is wrong, there is at least no cross-linguistic evidence for such plural uses of the mentioned expressions. In German, the following translation of (10*) is not only completely adequate as it stands, but it would also be incorrect to add any plural markers to the quoted adjectives:

(10*G)  Ich habe einige 'großartig' und einige 'fantastisch' gezählt.

On the other hand, plural uses of name-predicates like 'einige Friedas' are common and also completely adequate in German.

Fourthly, it seems to be clear that with respect to a very large number of names there exist lexicalized versions of name-predicates that apply to all bearers of a specific name in different natural languages. In these languages, we also always have the possibility to use different kinds of expressions in a metalinguistic way on a given occasion. Hence, for example if I use the following sentence:

(12)   This and that is a bank,

while I am pointing to a bank-institute and a river-bank, the contextual metalinguistic re-interpretation of 'bank' in (12) helps us to turn this use of (12) into a meaningful and truth-evaluable statement. However, this mechanism is standardly available and there are no familiar examples of lexicalized versions of such highly contextual metalinguistic uses. Hence, it seems to be *ad hoc* to claim that name predicates would be examples of specific lexicalized metalinguistic uses of names. Therefore, I think there are good reasons to reject the proposed metalinguistic account.

## Non-metalinguistic meaning transfer

There is also another, non-metalinguistic proposal that aims to make use of lexical meaning transfer to account for our original examples. This view was defended under the label *polysemy view*.[24] The basic idea behind this account is that we can capture the meaning of the noun 'Alfred' used in (2) as a secondary meaning that is derived from the meaning of the proper name 'Alfred'. There is a certain transfer relation that holds between the extensions of these two expressions and we can formulate on this basis a lexical rule to establish this kind of transfer in a conventionalized way. Furthermore, it is claimed that on the basis of this lexical rule that it is possible to explain why the following semantic equivalence holds:

(E2)   For every x: x is an Alfred iff x is bearer of the name 'Alfred'.

That is the basic idea behind this account. And on the basis of this *general* description, one may think that original examples are on par with production examples. In the latter case, we indeed have derived a specific meaning of a predicate like 'Picasso' from the meaning of the corresponding name 'Picasso'. But closer inspection shows that these two cases are different. The name 'Picasso' is used relative to the respective bi-conditional, while the name 'Alfred' is mentioned in (E2). Therefore, the proposed account is based on a confusion. If we want to carry out the proposed idea, we need a transfer-relation between the extension of the name 'Alfred' and the extension of the predicate 'Alfred'. One important problem of this proposal is that the extension of the name 'Alfred' is rigid with respect to all possible worlds, while the extension of the predicate 'Alfred' is non-rigid, and may change from world to world. Therefore, it is especially difficult to get in the proposed way an intensionally correct substitute for (E2). That is the main reason why a superficially promising assimilation of (E2) to the Picasso case that uses the relational expression 'x shares the name "Alfred" with Alfred$_1$'[25] for this purpose fails.[26] However, in the light of this problem it seems to be difficult to get any interesting substitute for (E2). The best we can get on this basis is the following substitute for our necessary and sufficient condition in (E2): 'x and Alfred$_1$ are such that x bears the name "Alfred" and Alfred$_1$ actually bears the name "Alfred"'. This condition literally consists of two components: (a) the condition 'x bears the name "Alfred"', and (b) the condition 'Alfred$_1$ actually bears the name "Alfred"'. The second condition expresses an analytic truth and is completely redundant for the desired purpose. The first condition carries all the work and is also contained in (E2). I think this shows that one might construe some artificial relation that apparently holds between the extension of the name 'Alfred' and the predicate 'Alfred', but there is no interesting explanatory substitute for the metalinguistic relation expressed by condition (a). Therefore, I conclude that the second version of meaning transfer proposed in Leckie (2013) as the polysemy view is a dead end. Nevertheless, we can learn something important from this account: namely, that it does not seem promising to propose a semantic transfer between the extension of a name and the corresponding predicate, but it might be more fruitful to look for a transfer between some other meaning-component or a meta-semantic feature of a name to get going an alternative version of semantic transfer.

## The derived nature of the meaning of the original examples

The linguistic mechanism of meaning transfer that Nunberg describes concerns the truth-conditional meaning of an expression. He gives an account that explains how the extension of a secondary occasional or lexical truth-conditional meaning of an expression can be derived in a *systematic way* from the extension of the primary truth-conditional lexical meaning of the very same expression (linguistic form). The systematic connection is provided by a specific transfer relation that obtains between members of the two different extensions. However, there seem to be other possible ways to derive the truth-conditional contribution of an expression in a systematic way from some level of meaning or content of another expression.

If we mean by *semantics* compositional truth-conditional semantics, then we can distinguish at least two other aspects of the meaning of an ordinary expression: (a) pre-semantic and (b) trans-semantic aspects. Two prominent examples of pre-semantic meanings are the following: (i) the character of indexical expressions, (ii) the constraining conditions of pronouns. If I use an expression like 'you' this expression can only be used to refer to *the addressee of the producer/user of this expression in the context of use*. This highlighted condition is the so-called *character* of the indexical 'you': it determines the referent of this expression in a context of use. The referent is the contribution to the truth-condition of a sentence. Therefore, the character is pre-semantic because it only determines the truth-conditional contribution.

A second example is provided by the constraining conditions of a third person personal pronoun. Relative to a referential use of such a pronoun like 'he' or 'she', the meta-semantic meaning of these expressions *constrains* the semantic referent of these expressions, without determining it. 'He' can only be used to refer to *a male object*, 'she' only to refer to a *female* object. However, these conditions are not part of the semantic content or truth-conditional meaning of these pronouns.

Let me also give two examples of post- or trans-semantic meanings that constrain the use of certain expressions. A first case is provided by examples of expressive meaning. The expression 'Oops' can be used as an expressive modifier of any assertoric sentence. This expression does not contribute to the truth-conditional content of a sentence. 'Oops, I dropped the glass' and 'I dropped the glass' have the same truth-conditional content. However, 'Oops' adds an additional expressive meaning and this additional expressive meaning also comes with certain use-conditional restrictions. 'Oops, p' can only be used *in a conversational context, where the agent in this context has witnessed a minor mishap in this context, some time immediately after the mishap.*[27] Such conditions might be called *use-conditions* for sentences with an additional expressive meaning. This use-conditional meaning conventionally linked with 'Oops' is a non-truth-conditional additional layer of meaning.

Another important example of expressions with a non-truth-conditional meaning are expressions that fall under the phenomenon of *social deixis*. If one aims to address a person that one does not know by a personal pronoun in German, she/he has to use the *formal* expression 'Sie' instead of the *informal* 'du'. The use of 'du' is only then allowed if speaker and addressee have agreed to use it in one or both directions. Hence, in German there exist two different second person personal pronouns that have exactly the same truth-conditional meaning and function in exactly the same way in this respect as the English 'you', but on top of this they have a different *use-conditional* meaning. This use-conditional meaning restricts the use of these pronouns with respect to the application to people on the basis of some given and rather complex restriction conditions that depend on *social relations* between speaker and addressee. Hence, this phenomenon provides another and interesting example of a trans-semantic additional meaning of a referring expression.

Interestingly, with respect to all our four examples of expressions with non-truth-conditional meanings there exist additionally to the mentioned primary uses derived uses that seem to resemble in important respects our *original examples* of derived uses of proper names.

Let us start with the case of *third person personal pronouns*. These expressions seem to resemble in a very high degree our case with respect to names. These pronouns also have, apart from their familiar and above-mentioned referential use a predicative use as the following example shows:

(13)   Leslie is a her/she, but not a him/he.[28]

This use is also cross-linguistically stable in a similar way as in the name-case. That is, such predicative uses of pronouns also exist in other natural languages than English. As for example, the following German translation of (13) shows:

(13G) Leslie ist eine Sie, aber kein Er.

What is especially interesting about this case is that 'is a she' or 'ist eine Sie' means roughly the same as 'is female'. Hence, we have here a case of a non-truth-conditional meaning transfer, where a non-truth-conditional constraining condition of an expression of type $T_1$ is transferred to a same or similar spelled expression of type $T_2$, where the main descriptive content of this constraining condition now functions as the truth-conditional meaning of the second expression. This case provides a clear example that meaning transfer is not exhausted by Nunberg's proposed mechanism of truth-conditional semantic transfer.

A somewhat similar case also exists with respect to the *second-person personal pronouns*. However, these examples have a less widespread distribution. There are certain German philosophers of the twentieth century, such as Heidegger, Buber and Gadamer, that were relatively creative in introducing new derived uses of words. Buber famously discusses in his philosophy the relation between *I* and *You*. In this respect, Buber also established a new predicative use of the German pronoun 'du' ('you'). This use is not very widespread in ordinary German, but it nevertheless found its way into the ordinary German language. The following sentence provides a famous example of this use:

(14)   Ihr ewiges Du haben die Menschen mit vielen Namen angesprochen.

There are also philosophers that discuss Buber's views in English and that transferred this predicative use of second person pronouns also to the English language. Therefore, the best literal translation of (14) would be:

(14E) Human Beings have addressed their eternal You with many different names.

The predicate 'x is a You' used in (14E) as the German translation of 'ist ein Du' in (14) means roughly the same as 'personal counterpart'. The expression 'the eternal You' certainly refers to God. This predicate is also used in the very same way by Gadamer:

(15)   Jedes Du ist ein Alter Ego.
(15E) Every You is an alter ego.

There is a very interesting difference between this predicative use of 'you' and the more familiar predicate use of 'he' or 'she'. In the former case, the semantic transfer is a product of two different processes of the modulation of meaning. Firstly it is, as in the case of 'he' and 'she', a transfer from the non-truth-conditional meaning of the pronoun 'you' to the truth-conditional meaning of the predicate 'You'. In this respect, the condition 'x is an addressee of y' is transferred from one level to the other. Secondly, the extension of 'addressee' is loosened (extended) such that it now receives the same extension as the predicate 'personal counterpart'. Extensional loosening is a familiar more classical mechanism of semantic modulation.[29] But for our purpose, the most important lesson is that this case gives us a second example of a semantic transfer from the non-truth-conditional to the truth-conditional level.

A third example is provided by the interjective 'oops' introduced above. This expression also has a derived predicative use. A sentence like the following provides an example for this kind of use:[30]

(16)   That is not an oops; it is a major disaster.

In a sentence like (16) the expression 'is an oops' is used as semantically equivalent to 'is a minor mishap'. As we have already seen, the condition that 'oops' should only be used in a context where a minor mishap happened constitutes the expressive meaning of this expression. In the case of a predicative use of 'oops', the main descriptive part of the expressive meaning of the interjective 'oops' is transferred to the predicate use of 'oops' and functions as its truth-conditional meaning. This case provides another example of our proposed alternative mechanism of non-truth-conditional semantic transfer.

Let us provide a last example of this sort on the basis of the distinguished two different German second-person personal pronouns that are represented by 'Sie' and 'du' and have two different use-conditional meanings. There are derived lexicalized uses of these two expressions that are exemplified by the two verbs 'siezen' and 'duzen'. An example of their use is the following:

(17)  Wir siezen uns noch, die anderen duzen sich schon.[31]

These are two reflexive verbs that require plural subjects. The verb 'siezen' applies to a group of at least two people iff these two people address each other only with the word 'Sie' based on the use-conditions associated with 'Sie'. In the case of the verb 'duzen', the addressing-relation is relativized to the use of the word 'du' and its special social rules of use. Interestingly, in this case we have three different operative processes that constitute this derived use. Firstly, the addressing-relation that constitutes the nature of second-person pronouns and that is also used to determine the reference of the indexical expressions 'du' and 'Sie' is transferred from the level of character to the level of truth-conditional meaning and constitutes the core meaning of the verbs 'siezen' and 'duzen'. Secondly, the relation of addressing is relativized to a specific linguistic tool suitable for this purpose and from which the new meaning of the new related expression is derived. Thirdly, this expression-relativized way of addressing is grounded in the social rules of use associated with 'Sie' and 'du'. Therefore, we have an additional interesting example of non-truth-conditional meaning transfer that also involves a metalinguistic element, relative to which the device is implicitly mentioned from whom the meaning is derived. Additionally, the derived meaning is both related to the character and the use-conditional meaning of the original expression. These special features make this case an especially interesting case of comparison with our original examples of derived uses of names.

Based on these four different related examples with interesting similarities and differences that, in my opinion, clearly show that there is a different kind of meaning transfer than the one investigated and described by Nunberg, I will now try to show why our original examples of derived uses of names are a fifth example that fall into this new class of cases.

The general idea behind a semantic transfer from a non-truth-conditional level an expression to the truth-conditional level can be applied to the case of names and their original derived uses by making use of the following recipe that is construed in analogy to the mentioned paradigm examples for such a kind of meaning transfer:

(GR)  If a noun 'N' is used as a name that has the condition expressed by 'bearer of the name "N"' as a referential constraining condition as part of its non-truth-conditional meaning, then "N" can also be used as a predicate that is truth-conditionally equivalent to 'bearer of the name "N"'.

This general recipe can be used by a number of different semantic approaches to names, especially by those that assimilate the semantics of names either (a) to indexicals like 'you' or (b) to third person personal pronouns like 'she'.[32] But what should interest us most is how this recipe can be applied to *our* two different versions of a use-sensitive semantics of names. According to the first version of this account, names are functional expressions that are relativized to their uses and that function as a filter on the use-referents that are delivered by the uses of a name and are on this basis transformed to semantic referents if this filter condition is satisfied. The filter condition that is implement in this function contains as one important element the metalinguistic condition 'x is a bearer of the name "N"' that is applied to the respective use-referent of the use of a name. Importantly, this condition is not part of the truth-conditional meaning of a name; it cannot explicitly be modified by any kind of operator, whether they are extensional, intensional or hyper-intensional, if these expressions are applied to the name. The licenced use-referent of the use of the proper name is the semantic contribution of a complex of a functional name in application to a use of this name. The metalinguistic constraining condition 'x is a bearer of the name "N"' has conceptually a very similar role as the constraining condition of third-person personal pronouns mentioned above. On this basis, it seems to be the case that (GR) can straightforwardly be applied to our first semantics. The result is a meaning transfer that closely resembles the case of *third person personal pronouns* in different languages, and that has interesting similarities with our fourth mentioned transfer case with respect to German second person personal pronouns.

This recipe can certainly also be applied to our second more radical semantics for proper names. According to this version, the mentioned constraining condition is not part of the pre-semantic meaning of a referring expression that determines or constrains its reference. It is part of the trans- or post-semantic *use-conditional* meaning of a proper name that distinguishes literal or uses of a name from non-literal uses. On this basis, the meaning transfer with respect to names becomes more closely related to the case of expressions with an expressive meaning or social deictic use-conditional meaning. However, it would also become, against this background, another case among other familiar and existing cases: a case where (a part) of the use-conditional meaning of a source expression is transferred to become the truth-conditional meaning of a target expression.

Therefore, the application of the recipe (GR) is, with respect to both distinguished versions of our *use-sensitive* semantics of names, and the original examples of derived uses of names, in no way *ad hoc* and without independent references. This shows that we clearly have the resources to account for the original examples of names by a second alternative mechanism of meaning transfer that operates on different levels of the meaning of ordinary expressions.

6

# Apparent Anaphoric Uses of Proper Names

In this chapter, I will argue against the thesis that there literally are bound anaphoric uses of proper names, which seem to require a semantic treatment of paradigm names as variables or complex expressions that contain variables. I will focus on five different classes of apparently anaphoric bound uses of proper names that have been proposed by linguists and/or philosophers and I will discuss and criticize three standard accounts that were proposed to capture at least some of the mentioned kinds of examples. My critique will point out some fundamental problems and also severe over generalization problems of these standard accounts, and, on the basis of these problems, I will outline and defend my alternative pluralist pragmatic account of such cases. With respect to the one class of cases, I will defend the thesis that these examples are genuine pragmatic but unbound anaphoric uses of names. With respect to the other three classes of examples, I will show why they only involve non-literal uses of proper names that can be captured by a specific well-known pragmatic mechanism.

## Setting the stage: an overview of different apparently anaphoric or bound uses of names

In the 'Prolegomenon' of this book, we have already seen that especially variabilists make use of examples of anaphoric uses of names to justify their views. As we will see in this chapter, there are also defenders of a predicative view on proper names that have used certain examples to justify their specific views.

In this section I will introduce nine different apparent examples of bound or at least anaphoric uses of proper names that fall into five different classes of these kind of uses.

### Apparently anaphoric uses of names as discourse anaphora

Firstly, there is the class of *apparently anaphoric uses of proper names in the position of discourse anaphora*. Initially, the first two kinds of example were introduced in Burge (1973) to demonstrate that Kripke's conception of reference determination and transmission concerning proper names is false or at least incomplete. Burge makes, for this purpose, use of the following two examples:[1]

(1) The shortest spy in the twenty-first century will be Caucasian. Call **him** 'Bertrand'. **Bertrand** will also be bald.
(2) Someone cast the first stone. Whoever **he** was, call him 'Alfred'. **Alfred** was a hypocrite.

These two different examples share the feature that they both seem to contain a third-person personal pronoun and a name that both are used as anaphoric expressions that borrow their referent from some antecedent expression. The antecedent expressions, the pronouns and the names are, in both cases, used in three different sentences. Hence, these apparently anaphoric expressions seem to be discourse anaphora, that borrow their referent from some expression in a different sense that is part of the same discourse structure. Another interesting similarity between them is the following: in the same way as we can substitute the name 'Bertrand' in (1) with the pronoun 'he' or the complex demonstrative 'that Bertrand' without changing the semantic content of the discourse fragment in a significant way, we can make the corresponding substitution in the case of (2). However, there is also one significant difference between (1) and (2). In the case of (1) the antecedent expression is a definite description and, therefore, at least intuitively a singular term, while in the case of (2) the antecedent expression is the quantifier expression 'someone'. This at least suggests at first sight that we cannot meaningfully interpret (2) as a case of the use of a purely pragmatic anaphoric expression.

Burge uses these examples to show that Kripke's claim is wrong, that the reference of the use of a proper name always depends on some causal-historic relation between this use and the introduction of this name into discourse. In (1) and (2) two new names are introduced and used, but the first use of these names does not depend on or exploit any causal-historic relation. I agree with Burge in this respect. Interestingly, this convincing argument is completely overlooked in the relevant literature. Furthermore, Burge also makes use of these examples and the mentioned substitution observations to justify his own favoured view on proper names that identifies the use of the name 'Bertrand' semantically with the use 'that Bertrand' in the very same context.

More recently, in Cumming (2008) a related example is used to justify a slightly different semantic analysis of proper names, namely the following:[2]

(3) There is a gentleman in Hertfordshire by the name of 'Ernest'. **Ernest** is engaged to two women.

This also seems to be an example where the name 'Ernest' is used as a discourse anaphora. However, there are two important differences between (1), (2) and this new example. Firstly, in (3) no new name is explicitly introduced, but it is explicitly assumed that there already exists a certain bearer of the name 'Ernest'. Secondly, the direct antecedent of the name 'Ernest' is not a pronoun, but a complex indefinite expression. Cumming uses this example to justify his own semantic analysis of proper names as variables that can either be bound or contextually interpreted.

### Apparently anaphoric uses of names as donkey anaphora

The second class is *apparently anaphoric uses of proper names in the position of a so-called donkey anaphora*. Such examples were independently introduced in Geurts

(1997) and Elbourne (2005). The first example is of the *conditional variety* of a donkey sentence and can be formulated as follows:[3]

(4)   If a child is christened 'Bambi', then Disney will sue **Bambi**'s parents.

The second example is of the quantificational variety of a donkey sentence:[4]

(5)   Every woman who has a husband called John and a lover called Gerontius takes only **Gerontius** to the Rare Names Convention.

It is the general characteristic feature of a donkey sentence that it contains an anaphoric expression in a special position, namely intuitively outside the scope of any quantifier but nevertheless intuitively bound by some kind of quantifier. This also highlights an important difference between examples (1)–(3) and (4)–(5). In the former case it is debatable whether they contain a name that is bound by some kind of quantifier or whether this is merely a case of pragmatic anaphora. In the latter case it is clear some expression that appears to be a name is bound by some sort of quantifier. The crucial question here is only whether the expression that looks like a name is really semantically a name. We will investigate this question in detail.

## Apparently anaphoric uses of names as accommodated presuppositions

The third class is the class of *apparently anaphoric uses of proper names that seem to bind an antecedent expression in an apparently accommodated presupposition*. A famous example of this kind can be found in Bach (1987):[5]

(6)   If presidents were elected by alphabetical order, **Aaron Aardvark** might have been president.

Bach points out that there is a reading of this sentence according to which 'Aaron Aardvark' does not refer to a specific object and neither the user of (6) nor the audience of this use need to believe that there is in fact a bearer of this name. In Bach's own words: 'His statement is true if there is a possible world in which whoever possesses that name is president (presumably as the result of the hypothetical voting process).'

More recently, defenders of discourse representation theory have used (6) as an example of local or global accommodation.[6] According to their conception of names, names cannot be used to start a 'proper' discourse. For them, a proper introduction of a name into discourse requires some indefinite expression like 'A ... named N'. However, they also must concede that we often use names out of the blue without such a kind of introduction. In fact, such an introduction is the exception and, hence, the proposed conception of names seems to be a plain over-generalization. However, defenders of this view claim that in these non-standard cases we have to accommodate such a use of a name by implicitly presupposing a proper introduction of a name into discourse. In the case of (6), a global and a local accommodation is possible according to the mentioned account. The globally accommodated reading of (6) can be paraphrased as follows:

(6\*)  [There is a man named Aaron Aardvark:] If presidents were elected by alphabetical order, **Aaron Aardvark** might have been president.

This is obviously not the reading that was intended by Bach. To capture his intended reading on the basis of the outlined conception, we have to make use of the following local way to accommodate the introduction of a name in the desired way:

(6')   If presidents were elected by alphabetical order [and there were <u>a man named Aaron Aardvark</u>], **Aaron Aardvark** might have been president.

This sentence intuitively has at least the same truth-conditions as the described reading of (6) intended by Bach. On the basis of this interpretation of (6), this example is only a specific implicit variation of the example (3) proposed by Cumming. However, as we will see in the following, there is also the possibility of an alternative pragmatic interpretation of the intended reading of (6) which is not plausible and available in the case of (3).

## Apparent anaphoric uses of names as bound by nominal quantifiers

The fourth class is the class of *apparently anaphoric uses of proper names, where these names seem to be bound by a nominal quantifier*. The only originial example of this kind that I know from the relevant literature is due to Hans Kamp:[7]

(7)   In every ancient Roman family, **Quintus** was the fifth son.

Kamp has pointed out that there is a reading of (7) according to which the apparent name 'Quintus' has a co-varying reading and therefore seems to be bound by the nominal quantifier 'In every ...' Such a reading seems to be a surprising result and it also has to be noticed that these uses are quite rare. It is very difficult to get a reading where a name is apparently bound by a nominal quantifier. In most cases this is impossible and, hence, it seems to be a characteristic feature of names that they cannot be bound by a nominal quantifier. But it is a genuine challenge to explain why such rare cases as (7) are possible. It is necessary to have certain background information to get the co-varying reading of (7) as only people who know that 'Quintus' means 'the fifth' in Latin can get this kind of reading. If we, for example, substitute 'Quintus' with 'Paulus' it is not any more that easy to get a similar co-varying reading. However, it is not only possible to get such a reading by using a name which is used as a common noun in some language with a specific descriptive meaning, we can also construe other examples which make use of other more contingent background knowledge. For example, there was a very popular television series between the 1950s and the 1970s about a very clever dog named 'Lassie'. Let us assume that this dog was so popular that several families named their family dog 'Lassie'. On the basis of this background information we can construe the following example, where a co-varying reading of 'Lassie' seems to be possible.

(8)   In many US families of the 1960s, **Lassie** was the family dog.

This shows that specific background knowledge may induce in certain relatively rare cases a co-varying reading of an apparent proper name with respect to a nominal quantifier. We will discuss in detail what the best way is to account for these very special uses.

## Apparent anaphoric uses of names as counterparts of fake indexicals

Finally, there is the fifth rather questionable class of *apparently bound uses of names relative to which they are used in a similar way as so-called fake indexicals*. Nevertheless, I have included them in my list because they function as an interesting class for comparison. This topic has been especially discussed in linguistics and was inspired by certain examples of Irene Heim examples of apparent bound uses of first- and second-person personal pronouns like the following two:

(9)   Only I got a question that I understood.
(10)  Only you eat what you cook.

These sentences seem to have different readings. According to their more natural reading they mean the same as the following sentences:

(9*)  I got a question and nobody else than me understood my question.
(10*) You eat what you cook and nobody else than you eats what you cook.

Most remarkably, they also have a (sloppy) reading relative to which the second occurrence of the pronouns in each sentence seems to be bound by the only conceptually present 'nobody'. Therefore they can also mean, or at least convey, the same as:

(9+)  I got a question and nobody else than me understood *his* question.
(10+) You eat what you cook and nobody else than you eats what *they* cook.

These examples seem to unveil a very peculiar possible interaction between 'only' and the mentioned two kinds of quantifiers. It is not clear what is happening here, whether this is a semantic issue or a special case of pragmatic intrusions. Most linguists at least agree that this special use of 'I' and 'you' should not be counted as the core meanings of these expressions. Such a concession would predict lots of in fact impossible uses. Therefore, they have called indexicals with such a use *fake indexicals*.

I have heard from people who think that we could also have such special co-varying uses with respect to 'only' and names.[8] The following is a variation of the initial example with a name instead of a pronoun.

(11)  Only Peter reads Peter's books.

The most natural reading of this sentence interprets it as equivalent to:

(11*) Peter reads Peter's books and nobody else than Peter read Peter's books.

One thing that is interesting about (11) and (11*) is that because of the use of the second occurrences of 'Peter' in a Saxon genitive construction, it is possible to refer by means of 'Peter' twice to the same person. That is not possible if 'Peter' itself would be in the object position of the verb as in the example 'Peter hit Peter'.

With respect to (9) and (10) it is very easy to get a second additional sloppy reading, without explicitly adding any conversational context. The situation is significantly different with respect to (11). Out of the blue, it seems to be impossible to get such a reading in this case, but some people think that it is possible to get a similar sloppy reading in very special contexts, where (11) probably conveys the following:

(11+) Peter reads Peter's books and nobody else than Peter read their books.

Such a conversational context might be given, for example, in the following way. A TV host invites two authors of which it is commonly known that they are famous and widely read. One of them has the forename 'Peter', the other bears the name 'Paul'. The TV host asks both authors whether they read their own books. Paul denies it, Peter admits that he does. The host summarizes his findings by joking and uttering (11). It is still very unnatural to use (11) for this purpose instead of the more adequate 'Only Peter reads his books himself'. I am not completely sure whether it is possible to use this sentence in the described conversational context for the desired purpose. However, what seems to be clear is that from this observation one cannot conclude that there is an interesting similarity between cases like (9) and cases like (11). In the cases of (9) and (10) we have very stable and context-independent additional loose readings with respect to the use of the indexicals 'I' and 'you'. In the case of (11), such a use can at best only be forced by a very specific contextual setting. The literal and natural reading of (11) is incompatible with the common ground. On this basis, and on the basis of the joking nature of the use of (11), one can probably infer from the natural reading the intended reading more literally expressible by (11+). Hence, in the best case we made use of conversational implicature, where the contradiction between the literal meaning of (11) and the common ground is exploited.[9] So far, nobody has used *in print* examples like (11) to argue for a specific indexical or variabilist semantics of proper names. Nevertheless, these examples show two things. Firstly, they show that in such cases pragmatic mechanisms may be operative that only create the illusion of an apparently bound use of a proper name. Secondly, the use of examples like (9) and (10) always comes with the danger that a too literal interpretation of these cases leads to a semantic conception that over-generates. For these reasons, in the linguistic literature most people interpreted the mentioned uses of (9) and (10) as special and additional uses.

The main reason why I have included the last class of apparent bound uses to my list is to clarify on this basis the dialectical situation. The main task of the rest of this chapter will now be to investigate whether a literal semantic interpretation of the presented cases offers the best strategy to account for them or some pragmatic (or mixed) strategy.

## Three approaches of apparent bound or anaphoric uses of proper names

As far as I know there is no paper in print that really takes all the mentioned apparent bound or anaphoric uses of names and that investigates the question of which account can provide the best analysis for *all* of these cases. Most people only discuss those examples that confirm their own favoured semantics of names. Therefore, there only exist accounts in the relevant literature that have used some of the mentioned examples to motivate a specific semantic analysis of proper names.

## Proper names semantically interpreted as complex demonstratives

The first account that used examples (1) and (2) for this purpose is the already briefly mentioned account by Tyler Burge. He defended the following three main theses concerning the semantics of proper names:[10]

(T1) Names are in general predicates that are semantically equivalent to the predicate 'is a bearer of "N"'.

(T2) The expression 'Peter', if it is used as a singular term, is semantically equivalent to 'that Peter'.

(T3) Demonstratives of the grammatical form 'that F' have the logical form: ɪx:[N(x) & x=y].

For our purposes here, (T2) and (T3) are the mainly relevant ones of his theses. Concerning (T3) Burge is not very explicit whether he aims to make use of a Russellian or Fregeian description theory. Both options seem to be possible. According to a Russellian treatment, a formula like 'F[ɪx:[N(x) & x=y]]' is only an abbreviation of the more complex existential generalization '∃x[∀z((N(z) & z=y) ↔ x=y) & Fx]'. According to a Fregeian analysis, the description-operator 'ɪx:[]' can either get a classical or free treatment. In both cases it is a term-forming operator that transforms a predicate into a term. On the basis of a classical treatment, 'ɪx:[Fx]' denotes a single object if the extension of 'F' has a single element. In any other case it denotes a special kind of object that is excluded from every possible extension of predicates. On the basis of a free treatment, the same holds in the positive case if the extension of 'F' has a single element, but in any other case the complex expression 'ɪx:[Fx]' does not get any denotation.

According to Burge, proper names have *referring* and *anaphoric uses*. In the case of a referring use an additional act of a speaker's reference is required to fix the extension of 'ɪx:[N(x) & x=y]'. In this case, this act of a speaker's reference provides a contextual assignment for the open variable 'y'.[11] Relative to an anaphoric use of a proper name, this open variable gets bound by some quantifier expression. On this basis we can also provide the following formal analysis of our examples (1) and (2). Let us explicitly formulate this kind of analysis for the less complex example (2):

(2LB) ∃z[(z cast the first stone & It is stipulated that z is a bearer of the name 'Alfred') & ɪx:[**Alfred(x)** & x=z] is a hypocrite].

Superficially, it seems to be the case that this analysis can very easily be extended to capture anaphoric uses of names not only in the case of similar examples like (3). In this case the type of analysis of (2) is extended to (3):

(3LB) ∃x(((is a gentleman (x) & in Herfordshire (x)) & is named 'Ernest' (x)) & is engaged to two women (ɪy:[**is named 'Ernest'** (y) & y=x])).

It also seems that it can be extended to examples like (4) and (5). Let us demonstrate by providing Burge's analysis of (5):

(5L2) ∀x∀y∀z(((is a woman (x) & (is called John (y) & is called Gerontius (y)) & husband-of (y, x) & lover-of (z, x))) → takes-only-to (x, ɪu:[**is named 'Gerontius' (u)** & u=z], the Rare Names Convention)).

This gives the desired intuitive truth-conditions. Nevertheless, this analysis has a well-known weakness. It makes use of three different universal quantifiers, although intuitively the sentence only contains one universal quantifier. Therefore, this is a clear weakness of this account that stems from using an extension of predicate logic as formal language.

However, it is not immediately clear how this account can be directly extended to capture Bach's example (6). The best thing Burge could do in this respect is the following: he could claim that (6) is a pragmatically elliptic version of (6'). On this basis, it seems to be possible to apply the strategy that we already know from (2) or (5), also to (6). However, as we will see later, there is a better account that is able to interpret (6) more literally.

Furthermore, it seems impossible to apply Burge's account to examples like (7) or (8). In these cases, we cannot meaningfully substitute the names with the corresponding complex demonstratives of the form 'that N'. Furthermore, it also is completely unclear how the open variable in 'ɩx:[N(x) & x=y]' could be bound by a purely nominal quantifier. Finally, Burge cannot account for examples like (11) in literal terms. But as we have already seen, it is very questionable whether that should be expected from any semantic account. In the next section of this chapter we will focus in more detail on the virtues and vices of Burge's account.

## Proper names semantically interpreted as covert definite descriptions

The second account that I want to discuss and that, among other non-anaphoric examples, make use of example (5) to motivate a specific view concerning the semantics of proper names, is Elbourne's variation of Burge's account.[12] He shares with Burge the main thesis (T1), but he also defends significantly modified variations of the other two theses:[13]

(T2*)  The expression 'Peter', if it is used as a singular term, is semantically equivalent to '[the] Peter', where '[the]' is an unpronounced definite article that is only present at the level of logical form.

(T3*)  Definite descriptions of the grammatical form '[the] Peter' have the logical form ɩx:[N(x) & x=y], relative to a *referential* or *anaphoric* use, and the logical form: ɩx:[N(x)], relative to an *attributive* use.

Although Burge and Elbourne make use of a very similar *formal* analysis of proper names if they are used as singular terms, they significantly differ concerning the general status of names.[14] Elbourne is a defender of The-predicativism and aims to extend his favoured semantics concerning definite descriptions to proper names. For this purpose, Elbourne also makes use of Donnellan's famous distinction between *referential* and *attributive* uses of definite descriptions.[15] According to Elbourne, a referential use of a definite description is such that an additional act of a speaker's reference is necessary to determine the semantic referent of this expression. For these uses Elbourne makes use of roughly the same semantic conception as Burge makes for all non-anaphoric *referring* uses. But Elbourne thinks that there is also a class of referring uses of definite descriptions where no additional acts are required and where the referent of definite description is purely determined in neo-Fregean terms; that is, by the satisfaction of the matrix expression by a unique object. Elbourne's way to account for Donnellan's distinction, therefore corresponds with a significantly different semantic representation of referential and anaphoric uses of names, on the one hand, and attributive uses, on the other hand. Such differences are not accepted by Burge, who rejects the view that proper names have *attributive uses* as they are proposed by Elbourne.

Another significant difference is that Elbourne clearly endorses a Fregean treatment of definite descriptions of the free variety and he also makes use of a situation-semantics framework to defend his view in detail. But for our purpose it is completely sufficient to neglect some of these important formal details and mainly focus on those aspects that are relevant for the analysis of apparent anaphoric uses of proper names. Because of the close *formal* relationship between Burge's and Elbourne's accounts it seems to be the case that they are at least apparently able to capture the same number of the outlined anaphoric uses of proper names in a very similar way. Hence, as we are here only concerned with anaphoric uses of proper names, I will treat the Burge–Elbourne analysis as one type of analysis with respect to these uses, although these two views significantly differ with respect to other uses that are not in the focus of this chapter.

## Proper names semantically interpreted as individual variables

The third account that I aim to introduce is the variabilist treatment of proper names according to Cumming.[16] This account shares with Burge the view that proper names have *referring* and *anaphoric* uses. However, this view proposes a different semantic interpretation of proper names and it rejects all of Burge's three theses on this issue and also Elbourne's alternative version of a predicativist view of proper names. According to Cumming, proper names are relative to their referring uses formally represented as *unbound individual variables*. Semantically, these unbound variables are interpreted by means of a context-sensitive assignment function. Relative to *anaphoric uses* proper names are, on the other hand, formally interpreted as bound individual variables.[17] The semantics of bound variables depends on one's favoured theory of quantification and which role bound variables play in such a theory. On the basis of a standard model-theoretic conception of quantification, a context-insensitive assignment function is sufficient to specify the role of variables in the context of generalizations. Cumming assigns, therefore, to a sentence like 'Peter is tired' the logical form 'Fx', where 'x' is an unbound individual variable. Furthermore, he assigns to (3), which he uses to motivate his specific semantics for proper names, the following logical form:

(3LC)  $\exists x(((G(x) \& H(x)) \& E(x)) \& W(\mathbf{x}))$.

The last bold occurrence of 'x' in (3LC) represents the semantic contribution of the name 'Ernest' as it is used in the second sentence of the discourse fragment (3).

This account can easily be extended to capture Burge's original examples. Cumming would, for example, assign to (2) the following, alternative logical form:

(2LC)  $\exists z[(z$ cast the first stone & it is stipulated that $z$ is a bearer of the name 'Alfred') & $\mathbf{z}$ is a hypocrite].

The account has also the resources to provide plausible truth-conditions for our example-sentences (4) and (5). Let us exemplify this on the basis of (5):

(5LC)   ∀x∀y∀z(((is a woman (x) & is called John (y) & is called Gerontius (y)) & husband-of (y, x) & lover-of (z, x))) → takes-only-to (x, z, the Rare Names Convention)).

This seems to give us the desired truth-conditions, but this analysis faces the same compositional problems as the Burge–Elbourne analysis of (5).

However, it is unclear how this account can be extended to capture Bach's example (6). The best it could do is to claim like Burge that (6) is pragmatically elliptical for (6) with respect to the intended reading and to apply the strategy we know from (2) or (5), to (6). However, the account does not have the resources to provide a literal semantic analysis of such example-sentences like (7) and (8). Interestingly, it has better resources to account for our last type of example represented by (11). If names have uses as bound variables, we could also on this basis account in semantic terms for co-varying readings of the name 'Peter' in (11). However, as we have already seen, it is doubtful that this really is a virtue of such a view. We will now focus on the vices and virtues of this account in more detail in the next section.

## Arguments against the three types of proposed accounts

In this section I will present some arguments against the distinguished existing formal semantic account with respect to anaphoric uses of names: (a) the Burge–Elbourne account and (b) the Cumming account.

### The dilemma of a uniform semantic treatment of referential and anaphoric uses

At first sight, it might seem that the formal analysis of sentences like (1)–(5) offered by Burge and Elbourne has big advantages because it can also be extended to the following embedded uses of sentences that are very similar in structure to (3) and (5):

(12)   It is metaphysically possible that there is a man named 'Jim' and **Jim** is not identical with any actual Jim.
(13)   It is metaphysically possible that if there is a man named 'Jim' and a man named 'Tim', **Jim** is not identical with any actual Jim.

Intuitively, both sentences have true readings if the apparent name 'Jim' that seems to be used in (12) and (13) is interpreted as bound by the used covert universal quantifiers. In fact we can only get such a true reading of (12) and (13) if 'Jim' is not a rigid expression, but an expression that is sensitive to the modal expression 'It is metaphysically possible'. Burge and Elbourne can account for these uses on the basis of the following semantic analysis that they have proposed for the name 'Jim': ɩy:[is named 'Jim' (y) & y=x].

However, this advantage also has its price. The mentioned sensitivity comes from the predicate 'is named "Jim" (y)' that this formal representation of a name contains.

This metalinguistic predicate is sensitive to modal expressions. But this advantage in the case of anaphoric uses of names is a clear disadvantage with respect to referential uses. As we have seen in chapter 1, there are very good reasons to assume that proper names are either actualized rigid designators or of at least four possible kinds. The choice depends on certain background assumptions. However, all these notions are stronger than the notion of a merely weakly rigidity designator as we have seen. That is, names refer to their actual bearers even with respect to worlds where these objects do not bear the name. However, this possibility is excluded if we formalize the name 'Jim' as Burge and Elbourne do. According to their formalization, names are only *merely weakly* rigid designators. As we have already seen, that is an incorrect understanding of the rigidity of names. Hence, what is a virtue in the case of anaphoric names becomes a real problem in the case of referential uses.

One could certainly solve the problem with respect to referential uses by *rigidifying* the predicative condition of the formal representations of names in the following way: ιy:[@(is named 'Jim' (y)) & y=x]. On this basis, we get the right kind of rigidity for names, but then we get the wrong results with respect to sentences like (12) and (13). Hence, if we solve the problem on the one side of the referential uses, we get a problem on the side of anaphoric uses and vice versa. That seems to be a genuine *dilemma* for the Burge–Elbourne view that comes to light if we compare apparent anaphoric uses of names in sentences like (12) and (13) with related referential uses of these names.

I think this dilemma shows two things. Firstly, that a uniform semantics interpretation of anaphoric and referential uses of names is an illusion. And all accounts that purport such an account are cheating in one way or the other. Secondly, in the light of the fact that referential uses are the paradigm uses and that anaphoric uses are limited with respect to their possible environments and limited in number, there seem to be good reasons to assume that anaphoric uses are non-literal or derived uses of names in a similar fashion as predicative uses.

However, this problem is not only a problem of the Burge–Elbourne view on proper names, it is also a problem of the variabilist conception of names. In this case the problem is only a bit more subtle. The variabilist account can analyse sentences like (12) and (13) just by prefixing their standard type of analysis for sentences like (3) or (5) applied to (12) and (13) with a usual modal operator for metaphysical necessity. On this basis, we get the desired true reading of (12) and (13). However, if we have such a simple-minded view on the semantics of names like Cumming, for example, who conceives of names as individual variables that are interpreted on the basis of a standard absolute and context-insensitive interpretation function, then we certainly get the *desired* result with respect to all so far considered anaphoric uses of proper names, but we also get incorrect results with respect to the paradigm referential uses of proper names. According to such a semantics, we can assign any kind of object in a *correct* way to any proper name, whether the object is a bearer of this name or not. Such a simple and unrestricted semantics of names produces a lot of semantically incorrect sentences with wrong truth-values that contain such referential uses of names. A natural solution to this problem adds some sort of restriction with respect to the assignment of proper names.

There seem to be two natural ways to provide such a restriction. Firstly, there is a version of this view which accepts an individuation of names that holds that no name can name different objects and, hence, there are different formal representations for an expression that appears to be a name of different possible bearers. Against this background, we semantically interpret name-variables by making use of an absolute but *restricted* assignment function that only then assigns an object as value to such an absolute assignment function *if the assigned object is a bearer of the name that is represented by the variable relative to the actual world*.[18] An alternative solution is based on a treatment of names that conceives of names in a similar way as third-person personal pronouns as context-sensitive devices. Against this background, we interpret name-variables by making use of an absolute but *restricted* assignment function that only then assigns an object as value *if the assigned object is a bearer of the name that is represented by the variable relative to context of use or the world of the context of use*.[19]

Depending on one's choice with respect to the individuation of proper names, both proposals provide a solution to our problem with respect to referential uses. But this solution again has its price. Both solutions have to face the question: how should one, on the basis of this new interpretation of name-variables, with respect to their referential uses now interpret their anaphoric uses? There seem to be two different options: (i) with respect to bound uses of proper names only the very same restricted assignments are possible as in the case of their referential uses; (ii) with respect to bound uses of proper names all possible assignments relative to the respective domain of quantification are allowed.

If one chooses the first option, one thereby guarantees that proper names have the same semantics with respect to referential and anaphoric uses, but this view thereby faces the problem that intuitively true sentences like (12) and (13) come out as false and impossibly true for semantic reasons.[20] If one, on the other hand, chooses the second option, one can account for the intuitive truth-values of (12), (13) and related sentences, but one has to accept that names have different meanings with respect to bound and unbound use, because different possible assignments are allowed in both cases and unrestricted variables can in no reasonable sense be called names at all. There is an interesting parallel of such a view and the standard account to fake indexicals. We have seen that a sentence like 'Only I did my homework' has a second sloppy co-varying reading relative to which it means the same as 'I did my homework but nobody else did his homework'. A quite popular view to account for these special uses of the indexical 'I' interprets 'my' relative to such a use as an unrestricted bound variable at the level of the logical form.[21] The difference between this view on fake indexicals and the variabilist view on names is that this view is aware of the important semantic differences between the bound and unbound uses of the indexical 'I'. This view acknowledges the ambiguity. The mentioned second version of the variabilist view on names treats bound uses of proper names in the same way as the standard account treats fake indexicals. The main difference is that it is *unaware* of this ambiguity or probably aims to conceal it.

Therefore, the situation of the variabilist view is basically the same as with respect to the Burge–Elbourne account: it is confronted with a *genuine semantic dilemma*. A uniform semantics account for referential and anaphoric uses of a name as it is proposed by Burge, Elbourne, Cumming and other people is an illusion. One cannot have the cake and eat it too. This new problem shows that a variabilist account of names is not only badly motivated for the reasons we pointed out in the 'Prolegomenon', it is also for semantic reasons a bluff package if it proposes to cover bound and unbound uses of names in a uniform and similar fashion as the ordinary Tarskian semantics for individual variables. Hence, both discussed accounts do not provide a plausible uniform semantics of proper names. The use of anaphoric uses of names as motivational factors of their view is a false path.

## Two under-determination problems with respect to the Burge–Cumming examples

The next two problems aim to show that both distinguished accounts with respect to anaphoric uses of names have to leave important aspects of a successful use of a proper name as discourse anaphora under-determined if they aim to analysis examples like (1)–(3) in the way they did. According to the Burge–Elbourne analysis, a sentence like (3) has the following formal analysis:

(3LB)   ∃x(((is a gentleman (x) & in Herfordshire (x)) & is named 'Ernest' (x)) & is engaged to two women (ιy:[**is named 'Ernest'** (y) & y=x])).

According to Cumming, it has the following alternative but equivalent analysis:

(3L)   ∃x(((is a gentleman (x) & in Herfordshire (x)) & is named 'Ernest' (x)) & is engaged to two women (x)).

However, something seems to be wrong with this analysis. There are other sentences that are only slight variations of (3) to which one would intuitively assign either (a) the very same logical form as to (3) or (b) to which the assignment of the mentioned two forms seems to be quite reasonable, but these sentences cannot be seen as examples that contain a possible anaphoric use of a name.

The first variation I would like to discuss is the following:

(3.1)   There is **at least one** gentleman in Hertfordshire by the name of 'Ernest'.
**Ernest** is engaged to two women.

Typically, one can reformulate any sentences of the form 'There is an F' by a sentence of the form 'There is at least one F' without changing the meaning or meaningfulness of this sentence significantly. However, there is clear and interesting difference between (3) and (3.1) with respect to the possibility of an anaphoric use of the name 'Ernest'. It is not possible to get an anaphoric reading of 'Ernest' in connection with (3.1). However, this difference can not only be observed with respect to (3.1), but also with respect to other possible variations of the discourse fragment (3); for example, the following:

(3.2)   Some bearers of the name 'Ernest' are gentlemen in Hertfordshire. Ernest is engaged to two women.

In general, sentences of the form 'There is an F that is G' and 'Some Fs are G' have the very same truth-conditions. Therefore, one would expect that we can assign the same particularly quantified truth-conditions that we assigned to (3) also to (3.2). However, there is a clear syntactic difference between (3) and (3.2). Although the generalizations that (3) and (3.2) contain seem to be logically equivalent, there is an important communicative difference between them. The generalization in (3) is formulated in the *singular*, while the one in (3.2) is formulated in the *plural*. Hence, one might conclude that the binding of 'Ernest' does not work, because 'Ernest' has the wrong syntactic format, it is used in the singular. That might appear to be the source of this problem, but what is now interesting to observe is that the transformation of 'Ernest' into its plural 'Ernests' and the adaption of the rest of the second sentence of the fragment to the plural 'are engaged to two women' also does not lead to a bound reading. Such bound readings in the plural are on the other hand possible if one substitutes 'Ernests' by 'they' or 'these Ernests'. If proper names are sorts of pronouns or semantically nothing but complex demonstratives, one would also expect the possibility of plural anaphoric readings of names. However, that is not the case.

I think this absence of syntactic forms is again an indicator for two things. Firstly, it seems to show that the analogy between names and third-person personal pronouns or complex demonstratives has clear and important limitations. Secondly, it gives some additional indication that the anaphoric uses of names are a non-literal pragmatic phenomenon.

Let us now, on the basis of these findings, come back to the differences between (3) and (3.1). Although the involved generalizations seem to have the same truth-conditions, there are important non-truth-conditional differences between these quantifications. These differences become more apparent if one compares (3) and (3.1) to another possible variation of (3):

(3.3) There is **exactly one/one and only one** gentleman in Hertfordshire by the name of 'Ernest'. **Ernest** is engaged to two women.

Standard approaches to truth-conditional semantics hold that there is an important semantic difference between the quantification involved in (3.3) and those involved in (3) and (3.1): only (3.3) excludes the possibility of more than one gentleman in Hertfordshire that bears the name 'Ernest'. What is interesting now is that on this basis we get the desired anaphoric reading of 'Ernest' back. The quantification in (3.3) singles out an individual, and on this basis it seems to be easy to refer to this individual by the name 'Ernest'. That is the significant difference between (3.3) and (3.1). Sentence (3.1) indicates the possibility of other bearers of the name 'Ernest' in Hertfordshire. From a communicative point of view, (3.1.) does not draw our attention to a single object and that seems to be the crucial difference. There is something that only (3) and (3.3) have in common: they make it explicitly or implicitly clear that only a single bearer of the name 'Ernest' is included in the relevant conversational background. That is, in (3) only a single bearer of the name 'Ernest' is *implicitly* marked as relevant, although we are left in the dark as to who this single object exactly is. The difference between (3) and (3.3) is that (3.3) achieves this goal in purely semantic terms and by *explicitly* excluding the possibility of other bearers of the name 'Ernest' in Hertfordshire, while (3) only excludes other possibly bearers from the relevant conversational context. However, this necessary condition for the success of an apparent anaphoric use in the context of a discourse anaphora clearly distinguishes such uses from other genuine anaphoric expressions. This observation also shows that, *just* on the basis of the outlined logical forms by both

## The over-generalization problem with respect to the Geurts-Elbourne examples

With respect to examples like (5) there is an interesting over-generalization problem lurking. The two given accounts predict that we relatively easily can get bound readings of proper names in the position of donkey anaphora. However, such examples are in fact extremely rare and marked. There is a significant difference between proper names and other expressions like complex demonstratives or third-person personal pronouns that undoubtedly have bound anaphoric readings. For example, it seems to be difficult, if not impossible, to get anaphoric readings of names on the basis of more simple standard examples of so-called donkey sentences. Ordinary speakers are not able to get the desired bound readings of the name 'Alfred' in cases like the following:

(14)  ? Every woman who loves an Alfred admires **Alfred**.
(15)  ? If a woman loves an Alfred, she admires **Alfred**.

This is a rather unfortunate result for accounts that think that anaphoric uses are part of a semantic profile of ordinary names. These sentences have the standard grammatical form of donkey sentences, but in their case the name 'Alfred' cannot be interpreted as bound. The outlined two accounts of the semantics of proper names predict that it should be possible to get such bound readings in cases like (14) and (15). Hence, these accounts face an over-generalization problem with respect to the donkey sentences of the original variety. As it was already observed by Elbourne,[22] the contrastive effect that is created by two different uses of an indefinite expression in an example like (5) seems required (possibly as one among other enablers) to trigger such an anaphoric reading of the involved name. The requirement of such *pragmatic triggers* again seems to be to me another indicator that anaphoric uses of proper names are not a genuine semantic, but a specific pragmatic feature of proper names under very specific circumstances and, hence, do not involve literal uses of proper names.

There is a further interesting thing that has to be noticed with respect to more complex donkey sentences than (14) and (15). A contrastive effect by itself, as in example (5), does not seem to be a sufficient additional pragmatic factor to get a bound reading of a name in the position of a donkey anaphora. This can be shown by examples like the following, where such a contrastive effect is given, but a bound reading of the name 'Alfred' is nevertheless impossible:

(16)  ? Different women in our town love different men named 'Alfred' or 'Paul' and each of these women, who love a man named 'Alfred', admires **Alfred**.

Interestingly, the situation is different if we substitute 'Alfred' in (14)–(16) with 'him' or 'that Alfred'. On this basis it is very easy to get the desired bound reading. This observation provides another reason to question the fruitfulness of the analogy between names and third-person personal pronouns or complex demonstratives that is exploited by the accounts provided by Burge and Cumming.

## A general over-generalization problem with respect to anaphoric uses of names

There is an even more substantial and general over-generalization problem that concerns *paradigm bound* uses of genuine anaphoric expressions. Bound uses of third-person personal pronouns or complex demonstratives in the position of a so-called donkey anaphora are *deviant bound uses*. These uses are insofar *deviant* as we have a quantifier expression and an expression that is intuitively bound by this quantifier expression, but the anaphora seems to be outside the scope of any quantifier expression. *Paradigm bound uses* are uses where we have a quantifier expression and an anaphoric expression, which is not only intuitively bound by this expression, but also clearly in the syntactic scope of this quantifier expression. However, on the basis of this distinction it becomes clear that proper names do not have any paradigm bound uses as the following standard examples for such uses show:

(17)   No Alfred is such that **Alfred** loves everybody.
(18)   Every man named 'Alfred' in our town has a friend that **Alfred** often meets.
(19)   There is at least one Alfred in our town that is such that **Alfred** is admired by everyone.

In all these cases, the proper name 'Alfred' is used in the scope of a quantifier expression that contains a corresponding naming-predicate as nominal restrictor, but in none of these cases is it possible to get a bound reading of 'Alfred'. The situation clearly changes if we substitute again 'Alfred' with 'him' or 'that Alfred'. In the case of these modified versions of (17)–(19), it is quite easy to get bound readings of these substituted expressions. This is again a big challenge for views that assimilate proper names semantically with complex demonstratives or third-person personal pronouns like Burge or Cumming. Furthermore, I think it is again a very important indicator that the apparent anaphoric uses of names are non-literal uses of names and a purely pragmatic phenomenon.

The situation changes only slightly if we move the proper name from the subject into the object position and modify, on this basis, our examples (17)–(19) in the following way:

(20)   No Alfred is such that everybody loves **Alfred**.
(21)   Every man named 'Alfred' in our town has a friend that deeply admires **Alfred**.
(22)   Every man named 'Alfred' in our town believes that the mayor likes **Alfred**.

With respect to these new examples, some people who sympathize with a variabilist or Burge-style account may get, with some forcing, an anaphoric reading with respect to (20) and (21). I am unable to get such a reading and I know that I am not alone in this respect. However, it again seems to be impossible in a case like (22). These examples provide, in my opinion, further evidence that these apparent bound readings of proper names are marked and they seem to depend on certain very specific pragmatic factors.

## An argument against the extended treatment of Bach's example

Let us now focus in more detail on Bach's account and the proposed treatment of this example by Maier and the options for Burge, Elbourne and Cumming to take over this strategy.

It seems to be the case that if Burge, Elbourne and Cumming aim to capture this example and treat it as an example of a bound use of a name, the only way of doing this is by making use of the accommodation strategy proposed by Maier. According to this strategy, the following sentence has a bound use because the name binds some accommodated presupposition:

(6)  If presidents were elected by alphabetical order, **Aaron Aardvark** might have been president.

This accommodated presupposition can be made more explicit by the following paraphrase of (6):

(6')  If presidents were elected by alphabetical order [and there were a man named Aaron Aardvark], **Aaron Aardvark** might have been president.

According to Maier, on this basis it seems to be possible to interpret 'Aaron Aardvark' as a name that binds the accommodated indefinite antecedent. In principle, this strategy can also be used by Burge, Elbourne and Cumming. I will now show that something is completely wrong with this account to capture example (6).

The main reason why (6) can be seen as in interesting example of a use of a name is a reading of 'Aaron Aardvark' that is exclusively triggered by the information that is contained in the conditional and which concerns the choice of the president *by alphabetical order*. If we substitute this condition by any other condition, for example by the condition 'by wealth', we cannot trigger anymore a reading that is at least similar to the reading in (6). However, according to Maier's strategy, such a modification should not make a big difference. We again have used the name 'Aaron Aardvark' out of the blue. Hence, again an accommodation of this use seems to be necessary. We should be able to apply the same strategy that we have used to explain the use of 'Aaron Aardvark' in (6) to this variation. The result would again be a bound use of the name. But Maier seems to get the example completely wrong. Example (6) is not another of many possible uses of a name out of the blue, it is a very special sort of use of a name. In my opinion, this use has nothing to do with anaphoric uses of names at all. It is a metalinguistic use of a name that is triggered by the conversational context that is given by the antecedent of (6). Certainly, we do not use 'Aaron Aardvark' to refer to any man, but we also do not use it to refer back to a presupposed possible situation. The best choice, in my opinion, is to interpret this use of 'Aaron Aardvark' as the metalinguistic use that can be paraphrased as follows:

(6+)  If presidents were elected by alphabetical order, **a bearer of the name 'Aaron Aardvark'** might have been president.

Hence, the easiest way to account for the specific use of 'Aaron Aardvark' in (6) makes use of a common and wide spread non-*ad hoc local* strategy that is in general triggered by very specific contextual settings. This example is one such special case, hence it seems to be inadequate to deal with it like Maier does by employing a more general and, with respect to names, more controversial strategy that does not depend on the very specific contextual setting of (6). Hence, Burge, Elbourne and Cumming are well-advised in not taking over Maier's strategy. But we also learned something from this case, namely, to be aware of the fact that there are special non-literal uses of names, for example metalinguistic uses, which are triggered by a very special and specific conversational setting.

Another example that is very much like (6) that also does not contain a bound, but rather a metalinguistic use of a name is the following non-conditional example:

(23)   Hilary/Andrea might be a man or a woman.

This sentence has one reading, where 'Hilary' is used as a referring name, but it also has a reading where it is used in a non-referring way. The background knowledge that is required to trigger this information concerns the specifical status of the names 'Hilary' and 'Andrea'. Most first names for human people are either only used for female or for male bearers. The names 'Hilary' and 'Andrea' are an interesting exception to this rule. They can be used for people of both sexes. This background information seems to be the main trigger for this alternative reading, which again seems to force a metalinguistic re-interpretation of the two names in (23) in exactly the same way as in the case of (6).

In the light of our observation that anaphoric uses of proper names are very rare, non-paradigmatic and dependent on a very specific conversational and contextual setting, I think we also have good reasons to try to apply this metalinguistic strategy to more genuine cases of apparently bound uses of proper names.

## An alternative metalinguistic pragmatic explanation

In this section, I will defend an account that interprets all the remaining apparent anaphoric uses of names as non-literal uses of names that are created by the general pragmatic mechanism of metalinguistic re-interpretation based on a specific conversational context or relevant background assumptions.

### The application to apparent anaphoric uses of names bound by nominal quantifiers

I will start the argumentation for my strategy by applying it to cases of bound uses of names that cannot be captured on the basis of any so far considered strategy, namely uses of names that are apparently bound by nominal quantifiers as in the following standard example:

(7)   In every ancient Roman family, **Quintus** was the fifth son.

The first thing I will show is that these cases are (a) not only relatively rare, but that they are also (b) highly dependent on specific factors of the conversational context or common ground. In most cases, we do not get a bound reading if we use a name in connection with a nominal quantifier like 'In every F' out of the blue.[23] For example, it seems to be impossible to get such a reading in the following case:

(24)   In every class, **Peter** was the most popular pupil.

An example like this does not *provide* by itself like (6) or *trigger* by itself like (7) any background information that allows us to interpret 'Peter' as a bound expression. This comparison provides another indication that a pragmatic mechanism is operative that is triggered by the contextual background, the common ground, or background knowledge.

What is going on in (7) in opposition to (24) is, in my opinion, the following: the example only works if people have certain background knowledge. The first information that is required is the information:

(B1)   'Quintus' means the fifth in Latin.

Another relevant conventional or metaphysical background information to get the argument going is:

(B2)   One and the same person cannot be the fifth son of different families.

The first assumption (B1) only gets triggered if one knows Latin well enough. The second assumption (B2) is produced by the semantic competence of the relevant user and his application of the cooperation principle to (7).

The main clue for the correct interpretation of the intended reading of (7), however is the following interpretative hypothesis:

(B3)   In Roman families there probably was a habit of calling the fifth son 'Quintus' on the basis of (B1).[24]

The result of the application of these three assumptions based on the semantic and non-semantic competence of a speaker and the use of the general conversation cooperation principle forces a metalinguistic re-interpretation of (7) that assigns to (7) roughly the same meaning as:

(7*)   In every ancient Roman family, **the bearer of the name 'Quintus'** was the fifth son.

On this basis we get the desired result. We have applied a general linguistic mechanism that is triggered by certain background assumptions. Hence, there is no need to extend or alter the semantic of names to capture such purely pragmatic and contextual cases.

I will now show how this strategy can also be applied to the following second example given in the first section of this chapter:

(8)   In many US families of the 1960s, **Lassie** was the family dog.

The first background assumption that is triggered by a natural interpretation of (8) based on one's semantic competence and the application of the cooperation principle is the following:

(B4)   One and the same dog cannot be the family dog of a large number of families.

The desire to find an alternative true interpretation may directly activate the following assumption triggered by the explicit content of (8):

(B5)    Maybe there was a habit of calling family dogs in the same way by a favourite name or a name that was made popular by some iconic bearer of this name.

Those people that additionally know the following and whose knowledge is triggered by the use of 'Lassie' in (8) might hold (B5) with more certainty than other people:

(B6)    'Lassie' is the name of a dog featuring in a famous (US) TV series (of the 1960s).

These assumptions, used in connection with the cooperation principle, again seem to force in a quite natural way a metalinguistic re-interpretation of (8) that assigns to (8) the same content that (8*) literally has:

(8*)    In many US families of the 1960s, **the bearer of the name 'Lassie'** was the family dog.

I think our careful reconstruction of the background assumptions that force alternative readings in cases like (7) and (8) has not only assured our main hypothesis that apparent anaphoric uses are non-literal uses that have to be explained by some pragmatic mechanism, but also shows how natural the common mechanism of metalinguistic re-interpretation can be applied to these cases and which factors distinguish such specifical examples from an out-of-the-blue-example like (23).

On the basis of our new account, we do not only get a plausible and relatively simple analysis of examples like (7) and (8), but we can now also use these examples to generate a recipe for other examples of this kind.

I leave it to the reader to capture and explain on the basis of our proposed account other examples like the following:

(25)    In many British detective stories of the 1950s, **Chummy** is the culprit.
(26)    In many families, **Pooch** is a dog.

This strategy could certainly also be used by Burge or Cumming whose accounts were not able to capture apparent anaphoric uses of names in connection with anaphoric quantifiers. I will now show how our strategy can also be applied to cases that function as important motivations for different semantic accounts of names.[25]

## The application to apparent anaphoric uses of names as discourse anaphora

Let us now show how our pragmatic strategy can also be applied to our first class of cases of apparent anaphoric uses of names exemplified by (1)–(3).

We have already learned one important thing about the conversational and pragmatic background assumptions of examples of this class: an anaphoric use of a name as discourse anaphora is only possible if there is a descriptive expression that introduces an indefinite single object into the conversational context that is marked as a bearer of this very name in the same or a preceding sentence in the right position. In such cases it also seems to be the case that the contextual background information that an indefinite object is marked as bearer of a specific name is sufficient to trigger a specific discourse anaphoric metalinguistic use of a name. We can paraphrase such a metalinguistic use of 'Ernest' in (3), for example, as follows:

(3!) There is <u>a gentleman in Hertfordshire by the name of 'Ernest'</u>. **That bearer of the name 'Ernest'** is engaged to two women.

The metalinguistic complex demonstrative that is the result of such a metalinguistic re-interpretation refers back to the discursive referent that is introduced by the quantifier and the additional pragmatic information that only one object satisfies this condition and, hence, functions as the discourse referent specified by the first part of (3). In this respect such a use of a metalinguistic complex demonstrative is significantly different from a pronoun that would be used in such a context. For example, a sentence like the following has a clear anaphoric reading, although this exclusion condition is not satisfied.

(27) At least one man broke into the shop yesterday. He has stolen every expensive watch.

In such a more genuine case of discourse anaphora the possibility is left open that more than one man broke into the shop and stole the watches. However, this less exclusive discursive setting does not undermine the anaphoric use of the pronoun 'he'. But as we have seen, the situation is different if names are used for such purpose and that speaks for the view that (a) the anaphoric use is not a genuine case of binding, and (b) that the appearance of an anaphoric use is created by the outlined specific demonstrative metalinguistic use of the name. The outlined explanation does not only show why a metalinguistic interpretation of the name is a good and plausible choice, I think the comparison with (27) shows that it is the only plausible choice.

This analysis can easily be extended to capture the other two examples of apparent anaphoric uses of names represented by examples (1) and (2).

## The application to apparent anaphoric uses of names as donkey anaphora

Let us now also finally apply our account to the last remaining class of cases exemplified by such examples as (4) and (5):

(4) If <u>a child</u> is christened 'Bambi', then Disney will sue **Bambi**'s parents.
(5) Every woman who has a husband called John and <u>a lover called Gerontius</u> takes only **Gerontius** to the Rare Names Convention.

These are most interesting cases whose explanation is probably the most difficult task. They are closely related to examples like (1)–(3) but are in a sense more complex than those cases. They have a similar, but more complex pragmatic background assumption with respect to discourse referents. In their case, there must be a one-to-one correspondence between the instances of the universal quantifier and the instances of the quantifications expressed by the involved indefinite expression. Applied to example (4), that means that the conversational background of the quantification is in that way restricted for every single family that has a child that is christened 'Bambi'. In this family, this child is the only child that bears this name. With respect to (5) it means that every woman that has a husband and a lover named 'Gerontius', has only one husband and only one lover with the name 'Gerontius'. As in the case of (3) it can easily be shown why these similar background assumptions are required to enable an apparently bound use of the involved names. If we substitute 'a child' in (4) by 'at least one child' and 'a lover called Gerontius' by 'at least one lover called Gerontius' the possibility of an apparently bound use of the involved name is thereby excluded. Hence, such a contextual restriction of the desired instances of the universal quantifier and the co-varying instances of the indefinite quantifier is one of at least two necessary requirements to enable the possibility of an apparently bound use of a name.

However, what distinguishes examples like (4) and (5) from examples like (3) are two things. Firstly, these cases are more complex, because in these cases the quantified expression does not only contextually single out an individual object, it singles out a whole class of objects that is such that each member of this class has a corresponding single object that functions as a possible value of an apparently bound name. Secondly, while in the case of examples like (3) a contextual restriction to a single contextual satisfier of the predicative part of the quantifier phrase is sufficient to enable the non-literal anaphoric use of a name, in more complex cases like (4) and (5) additional syntactic/pragmatic enablers are necessary.

With respect to example (4), the use of the Saxon genitive seems to be an essential additional condition to enable the non-literal anaphoric use of a name. This can be shown on the basis of the following alternative formulation of (4) that instead of the Saxon genitive uses an alternative possessive construction:

(4*)   If a child is christened 'Bambi', then Disney will sue the parents of **Bambi**.

Relative to this slight and synonymous reformulation of (4) it does not seem to be possible to get a non-literal bound reading of 'Bambi' as part of the possessive construction.

The Saxon genitive seems be a special sort of enabler of non-literal bound uses of names. By using such a Saxon genitive, we can also create an example of a donkey-sentence that is structurally more similar to (5):

(28)   Every married woman who has a lover called Gerontius will not have a deep desire to meet **Gerontius**' parents.

At first sight, it seems to be puzzling why the use of the Saxon genitive makes such an important difference with respect to the possibility of a non-literal anaphoric interpretation of a name. Closer inspection reveals a more general pattern. In chapter 4, we have seen that *stress* and *intonation* might give rise to different non-literal referential uses of names relative to specific conversational situations. Stress and intonation are focus markers that highlight certain parts of a more complex information-structure. The Saxon genitive also seems to shift the focus from the possession to the possessor. And it is a name that is used to indicate the possessor. Hence, we seem to have here a focus phenomenon that highlights the name in a

*Apparent Anaphoric Uses of Proper Names* 195

complex information-structure and thereby functions as an enabler of the non-literal metalinguistic anaphoric use of a name.

Elbourne, who is the inventor of example (5), had the hypothesis that it is the contrast between the *two* used indefinite quantifiers that contain name-predicates in (5) that enables the anaphoric use of the name 'Gerontius'. I think Elbourne is partially right. The contrast that is produced by two different name-predicates is not the essential enabler in the case of (5), it is the contrastive function of the focus particle 'only' that does the trick. We get the same focus-marking by 'only' in a case like the following, where we do not have a preceding contrastive use of two name-predicates:

(29)  Every woman who is in love with a man called Gerontius hopes that only **Gerontius** will love her like she does.

In this case, we again get a bound reading of the name 'Gerontius'. The focus particle 'only' in this example highlights the name 'Gerontius' in a slightly different way than in (5). But it is this expression that enables, in both cases, the non-literal metalinguistic anaphoric use of the name in (29).

A similar result is achieved if we use other focus particles than 'only' as the following example shows:[26]

(30)  Everyone who is married with a man named 'Paul', hopes that **at least** Paul will always stand by her.

In this case, the focus particle 'at least' does a very similar job as 'only' in (5) or (29). There are also other ways to highlight the use of a name by specific markers that are not focus particles. In English, we can use certain *expressive* adjectives to modify proper names. These expressive adjectives can also function as focus markers as the following two examples show:[27]

(31)  Everyone who killed a man called 'Brad' hopes that the corpse of **poor** Brad will never be found.
(32)  Everyone who lost the presidential election against a man he called 'sleepy Joe', will hope that **sleepy** Joe will show mercy after his inauguration.

In both cases, we get non-literal metalinguistic bound readings of proper names; in both cases adjectives with an expressive use, namely 'poor' and 'sleepy', function as enablers of this non-literal use. I think all our observations point in a clear direction. Two essential things are required to force a non-literal metalinguistic anaphoric use of a proper name in the position of a donkey anaphora: (a) specific restrictive pragmatic assumptions that force the above-mentioned one-to-one correspondences, and (b) the use of a focus-marker to highlight the name in such a position. These findings also shine new light on cases of discourse anaphora like (1)–(3). In these cases, the use of the name in the subject position after the initial sentences that contains the indefinite with the name-verbs also seems to clearly lay the focus of the information given by the following sentence on the name. To test this assumption, let us on this basis alter the informational structure in (3) in the following way:

(3#)  There is a gentleman in Hertfordshire by the name of 'Ernest'. Two women are the fiancées of **Ernest**.

I think it is evident that it is much more difficult to get in such a case, an anaphoric reading of 'Ernest' as in the case of (3). It might still be possible because of the other mentioned contextual enabler. But the example is not as smooth as (3) and it again shows how important focus-marking is to get clear cases of apparently anaphoric readings of names.

In my opinion all these observations provide good evidence for the view: apparently anaphoric uses of names in the position of a donkey or discourse anaphora are non-literal metalinguistic uses of names relative to which the involved name 'N' is re-interpreted as a metalinguistic complex demonstrative of the form 'that bearer of "N"'. This re-interpretation is forced by specific pragmatic and syntactic enablers.

## Summary

I hope I was able to show at least two things in this chapter. Firstly, that advocates of a semantics that assimilates names too closely to complex demonstratives, definite descriptions and personal pronouns to be able to capture apparently bound uses of proper names are not able to assign a coherent and uniform semantics to names that capture those and only those apparent bound uses that names in fact have. Therefore, I hope I have clearly shown that Elbourne, among other people like Burge, Cumming and Schoubye, is deeply wrong if he claims the following:

> The existence of grammatical D-type proper names is a very strong argument against the direct reference view of proper names and in favor of the theory currently being advocated.[28]

Secondly, I hope, I have also shown on how many different very specific contextual factors the possibility of apparently anaphoric uses of names depends and that, hence, a pragmatic account that interprets these uses as non-literal is able to provide the best account for these uses.

# 7

# Proper Names in Hyperintensional Contexts

In this chapter, I will defend the view that attitude verbs and epistemic modals can shift the semantic values of proper names. This view concerning the interaction between names, attitude verbs and epistemic modals does not necessarily presuppose a context-sensitive semantics of proper names, but it can certainly be combined with such a semantics. For the sake of simplicity, and to be able to show how the account with respect to only relevant details works, in this chapter I have chosen the simplest semantic representation of proper names that is compatible with our results about the rigidity of proper names. Hence, I have formally represented proper names as individual constants. The account presented in this chapter modifies and extends the formal semantic proposal put forward in Priest (2005, 2016). Like Priest, I will make use of the formal resources provided by so-called non-normal worlds to account for the hyperintensional properties of attitude verbs and epistemic modals. However, unlike him, I will propose that proper names are only rigid with respect to normal, possible worlds, but non-rigid with respect to non-normal worlds. Furthermore, I will also extend the account to epistemic modals. On this basis, I will propose a new solution to the classical substitution puzzle with respect to *de dicto* readings of attitude ascriptions. This solution makes use of attitude-counterparts. These objects can only be part of non-normal worlds and they allow us the formally model erroneous assumptions about the identity of real objects. Additionally, I will also solve the incompatibility puzzle that the standard possible-world semantics for epistemic modals seems to provide for a global rigid interpretation of names.

## Three semantic properties of names in the scope of attitude verbs

Attitude verbs like 'hope', 'fear' or 'believe' have very specific semantic features. Some of them correlate with the special behaviour of proper names in the complement-clause of such an attitude verb.

Firstly, there is the feature of *the lack of substitutability of co-referential proper names*. We have argued for the rigidity of proper names in chapter 1. As a consequence of their rigidity, co-referential names are intentionally equivalent.

A sentence like the following can be used to express a *true* report of a certain mental state of Peter:

(1) Peter assumes that Mark Twain is an author.

Interestingly, the substitution of the name 'Mark Twain' with the co-referential proper name 'Samuel Clemens' may lead us from a true to a false sentence. Hence, we have a *substitutional failure* of co-referential names in the scope of attitude verbs.[1]

Secondly, another remarkable feature is that the truth-value of an attitude ascription like (1) seems to be independent from the actual extension of the embedded sentence and the extensions of *each* constituent term. This seems to allow for the possibility to use a name that lacks a semantic referent in the scope of an attitude verb and nevertheless make a true statement. The name 'Sandy Island' is a name for a phantom island. We have argued in chapter 4 that there are good reasons to assume that this name is at least initially used as an empty name. Nevertheless, the following sentence seems to have a true reading:

(2) Peter believes that Sandy Island does exist.

Hence, the apparent *extensional independence* of expressions in the scope of attitude verbs is another specific feature of these constructions. The truth-value of a sentence like (2) intuitively does not depend on the actual semantic values of the embedded expressions, especially not on the actual semantic value of 'Sandy Island'.[2]

Thirdly, it is an important semantic property of attitude ascriptions like (1) or (2) that they seem to have a reading relative to which they do not entail singular existential sentences that contain the embedded name. Hence, for example, (1) does not intuitively entail the following claim according to such a reading:

(3) Mark Twain exists.

This *existential inferential failure* is a third specific feature of the use of names in the scope of attitude verbs.[3]

Currently, the majority of scholars agree that every reasonable semantics of attitude verbs should be in the position to account for the outlined three specific semantic properties that make them hyperintensional expressions.

## The *de re*/*de dicto* distinction

The three properties mentioned above do not yet provide an exhaustive picture about what is so special about attitude contexts. There is an additional complication that is due to the fact that attitude ascriptions that contain proper names in the scope of the complement-clause can have at least two different readings.

Relative to the so-called *de dicto* reading of a sentence like (1), the proper name has all the three features we have mentioned. Relative to the so-called *de re* reading of a sentence like (1), the proper name 'Mark Twain' has none of these properties. That is, firstly, the substitution of the name 'Mark Twain' with any co-referential name produces only sentences with the same truth-value as (1); secondly, the truth-value of (1) essentially depends on the actual extension of 'Mark Twain'; and thirdly, relative to its *de re* reading, (1) entails (3).

Most current researchers in linguistics and philosophy agree that this kind of ambiguity is an important semantic feature of attitude verbs.

## The nature of the *de re/de dicto* ambiguity

A more controversial issue in this respect is the question of what exactly the source of the *de re/de dicto* ambiguity is.[4] Different attempts have been made so far, but none of them have been overly convincing so I will make use of a classical idea, based on the work of Russel, to draw this distinction.[5] However, my own new contribution in this connection will be a modified version of this account that is also compatible with the rigidity of names. Russell's classical way of drawing this distinction interprets it as a *structural* ambiguity that can be captured on the basis of his famous description theory. We can briefly recapitulate how this strategy works by focusing on the following example:

(4)  It is metaphysically possible that the inventor of the computer is German.

This claim is structurally ambiguous because it has two different readings relative to which (a) the definite description scopes outside the modal operator or (b) the definite description has narrow scope with respect to the modal operator. On the basis of a Russellian interpretation of definite descriptions, the structural ambiguity of (4) boils down to a scope distinction with respect to the logically involved quantifiers. Semi-formally we can represent the two different readings of (4) as follows:

(4.1R)  $\exists x((\text{Inventor of the computer }(x) \ \& \ \forall y(\text{Inventor of the computer }(y) \to x=y)$
&  it is metaphysically possible that German(x)).
(4.2R)  It is metaphysically possible that $\exists x((\text{Inventor of the computer }(x) \ \&$
$\forall y(\text{Inventor of the computer }(y) \to x=y) \ \& \ \text{German}(x))$.

The Russellian version of the structural analysis can only be directly applied to attitude ascriptions that contain proper names if we interpret (referential uses of) proper names as denuded descriptions.

However, we can make use of tools that are proposed by free logicians to provide a similar scope distinction on the basis of a formal representation of names by rigid individual constants.[6] Firstly, we will make use of a new notation for atomic sentences. For example, instead of 'Fa', we will now write '[a] F(a)', and instead of 'Rab', we will write '[a][b]R(a,b)'. This new notation comes with two different ways operators might interact atomic sentences that contain individual constants. Let us exemplify this distinction on the basis of the example of the truth-conditions of negated simple atomic sentences like '[a] F(a)'. There are now two different ways to negate such a sentence, '¬[a] F(a)' and '[a]¬F(a)'. These two negations have structurally different truth-conditions:

V¬[a] F(a)) = W    iff    it is not the case that I(a) ∈ I(F).
V([a] ¬F(a)) = W    iff    I(a) ∉ I(F).

These two negations are equivalent as long as we assume that individual constants refer. However, they become non-equivalent if we allow, as single-domain free logic does, that there are some individual constants without a semantic referent.

Furthermore, this new notation corresponds with a familiar classical formal representation and '[a] F(a)' is semantically equivalent to the following one:

(5)    ∃x(x=a & F(x)).

Hence, the mentioned two negations of '[a] F(a)' correspond with the following two negations of (5): (i) ¬∃x(x=a & F(x)); (ii) ∃x(x=a & ¬F(x)).

We can now make use of this new syntax of atomic sentences to formally represent the *de re reading* of (1) in the following way, if we assume that 'Ass [x, p]' provides a general formal representation of the attitude verb 'x assumes that p':

(1.R)    [Mark Twain] ASS (Peter, [Author (Mark Twain)]).

This formula is in principle only a more compact alternative of the following more classical formal semantic representation:

(1.R*)    ∃x(x = Mark Twain & ASS (Peter, [Author (x)]).

Furthermore, we can assign the following logical form to a *de dicto reading* of (1):

(1.D)    ASS (Peter, [[Mark Twain] Author (Mark Twain)]).

Such an interpretation of (1) uses the name 'Mark Twain' with a *narrow scope* negation and it structurally equivalent to the more classical formalization:

(1.D*)    ASS (Peter, [∃x(x = Mark Twain & Author (x))]).

However, these possible notational differences between (1.R) and (1.D) are only insofar a helpful interest for our purposes if they also lead to significant truth-conditional differences. These differences mainly depend on what kind of semantics we assign to attitude verbs that are formally represented in the outlined way: e.g.: 'Ass [x, p]'.

Therefore, we can only transfer the Russellian strategy of a semantic treatment of names in attitude ascription to our case if we can deliver an adequate semantics of attitude verbs for this purpose. The search for a framework that can be used for this purpose is our next task.

# A comparison of three different formal approaches to attitude verbs

### Attitude verbs as hybrid modal operators

The first and most radical proposal to achieve our goal to draw a clear and desired semantic distinction between (1.R) and (1.D) sacrifices the rigidity of proper names in an interesting way. One can easily get rid of the general rigidity of names represented by individual constants by using a world-relative interpretation function for this purpose that allows us to assign different referents to an individual constant relative to different possible worlds. Against this background, it is possible to interpret attitude verbs as modal operators or predicates and to assimilate the *de re/de dicto* distinction in the case of attitude verbs to the corresponding distinction in the modal case.

However, this strategy has some unwelcome drawbacks. Firstly, the intuitively possible difference in truth-value, between claims of the following two logical forms gets lost:

(6) ∃x(x=a & ◊x≠a).
(7) ∃x(x=a & BEL(p, [x≠a])).

According to the proposed modifications, (6) and (7) can *both* have a true reading. However, if we interpret '◊' as an expression of logical or metaphysical possibility, a true reading of (6) is intuitively impossible, while a true reading of (7) should be possible relative to a *de dicto* reading of the embedded use of the individual constant 'a'. Hence, further modifications are required to capture the desired intuitive difference between a sentence like (6) and a sentence like (7).

The best way to react to this problem, if one aims to stick with the non-rigidity of names, makes use of a non-standard semantics for modal operators. According to this view, modal operators that represent logical or metaphysical modality either shift or fix[7] the semantic value of embedded individual constants to their actual denotation.[8] For this purpose, we have to make use of two different kinds of truth-conditions for embedded and unembedded sentences. There are different ways to achieve this goal. I will make use of two different valuation functions for this purpose that are relativized to the same model: (i) the ordinary interpretation function V(p,w) and (ii) a partially relativized valuation function $V_@(p,w)$. I will now provide all new truth-value conditions that are required to interpret (6):

| | | |
|---|---|---|
| V(s=t, w) = T | iff | I(s,w) = I(t,w); |
| V(s=t, w) = F | | otherwise. |
| $V_@$(s≠t, w) = T | iff | I(s,@) ≠ I(t,@); |
| $V_@$(s≠t, w) = F | | otherwise. |
| V(◊φ, w) = T | iff | for at least one w*, such that w* ∈ W: $V_@$(φ, w*); |
| V(◊φ, w) = F | | otherwise. |
| $V_δ$(∃xA, w) = T | iff | for at least one object d ∈ D it is such that $V_{δ*}$(A, w) = T, where δ* is the same as δ except that it assigns d to x; |
| $V_δ$(∃xA, w) = F | | otherwise. |

On this basis, a sentence like (6) cannot have a true reading if it is evaluated relative to the actual world. However, there still remains the possibility that (6) is false if it is evaluated relative to some non-actual world.

In my opinion, this is a problematic consequence of the proposed strategy for the following reasons. Firstly, I share with Kripke the intuition that names are not only inflexible expressions; that is, they inflexibly refer to their actual referent if they are embedded under non-epistemic modal operators. I also share with him the intuition that they are rigid in the sense that only the actual referent of a name is relevant for the semantic evaluation of an atomic sentence that contains this name with respect to different possible worlds.[9] Secondly, there seems to be no good evidence why we should allow the semantic possibility that names can refer to different objects with respect to different possible worlds if they are not embedded under a reference shifting operator. Thirdly, the proposed view leads to a mismatch between the world-relative truth-conditions of a sentence like (6) in the metalanguage and the intuitively corresponding truth-conditions of the following sentence in the object-language:

(8)     $\Diamond \exists x(x=a \ \& \ \Diamond x \neq a)$.

According to the proposed view, a sentence like (8) is false, although there is a possible world relative to which (6) is true. This mismatch shows that we at least have the *choice* between two different sorts of modal operators with respect to our proposed alternative semantics of names: (a) a set of hybrid modal operators which shifts the world parameter in general, but can only access the actual referent of a name; and (b) a set of non-hybrid modal operators which shifts the world parameter of most embedded expressions and also has access to all semantic referents of a name with respect to all possible worlds. Intuitively, a corresponding distinction between modal notions that express logical or metaphysical modality does not exist. Therefore, the proposed modification of our strategy leads to unwelcome and counter-intuitive results. Because of these counter-intuitive implications, I reject this version of the first strategy as a viable option. In general, I will stick with the more orthodox semantic claim that proper names have the same referent with respect to all possible worlds and, hence, I favour an alternative strategy to solve our problem that does not sacrifice rigidity.

**Attitude verbs as monstrous operators**

A second option interprets attitude verbs as *monstrous* operators (or predicates). According to this view, attitude verbs are meta-semantic operators that *also* can shift the interpretation or denotation function with respect to a name that assigns a referent to a name in the metalanguage.[10] To get this approach going, we must distinguish an *interpretation function* that interprets the extensions of *predicates* relative to possible worlds, from a denotation function that interprets the extensions of singular terms, or in our case more specifically, *individual constants* either *simpliciter* or relative to possible worlds. This distinction seems to be necessary to be able to distinguish meta-semantic operators that modify the interpretations of predicates and those that modify the denotations of individual constants. Attitude verbs can, on this basis, be semantically interpreted as operators that *shift* the world parameter *and* the denotation (or interpretation) parameter. However, there are different options as to how this simultaneous shifting is formally rendered.

If we conceive of attitude verbs as modal operators, we have to make use of a specific accessibility relation: these operators should only have access to those worlds that represent the mental states of specific cognitive agents. Furthermore, the possibility of shifting denotation functions concerning names by means of modal operators should also be *restricted* in some way, because otherwise we would only model the meta-semantic possibility that any name might refer to any *arbitrary* object. For this purpose, we modify the accessibility relation in such a way that it becomes relativized to an agent and a relation between pairs of worlds and denotation functions and pairs of worlds and denotation functions.[11] Additionally, we add specific restrictions to our accessibility relation R by means of an absolute interpretation function that assigns to R extensions. Against this background, we get the following truth-conditions for belief-sentences:

$V(BEL(x, \phi), w) = T$ iff for every worlds $w^*, w \in W$, and every interpretation function $DEN^*$:
$I(R)(<x>,(<w, DEN>, <w^*,DEN^*>)), V_{DEN^*}(\phi, w^*)$;
$V(BEL(x, \phi), W) = F$ otherwise.

However, this second solution to our problem seems to face three further problems. Firstly, shifting the denotation parameter of singular terms or the interpretation parameter seems to be the last resort to provide a plausible semantics of *de dicto* readings of attitude ascriptions and a solution to the substitution problem. By shifting the mentioned parameters, we in fact change the meanings of the so interpreted expressions. If we change the meaning of an expression that is embedded in an attitude context, we certainly can assign different truth-values to any two different sentences that actually have the same meaning if they are embedded in such a context. The question is whether we really have to go that far and change the meaning of an expression to provide the desired interpretation of *de dicto* readings of attitude ascriptions.

Secondly, although the account delivers from the point of view of the distribution of truth-values at least with respect to sentences that contain epistemic modals like 'might' the correct result. But, from an intuitive point of view it seems to be unclear what the informal counter part of the mentioned extended accessibility relation in fact is. In the case of the standard accessibility relation, in a Kripke-style semantics this relation formally models the property of a relative modality. A state of affairs is relative to a given world w possible iff there is some world that is accessible from w and this state of affairs obtains in this world. In this case, there is a clear and straightforward story, what exactly is formally modelled on the basis of such a Kripke-style possible world semantics. However, on the basis of our newly introduced accessibility relation this is not so clear anymore. The world and the denotation parameter are very different in their kind. It is not clear what pairs of worlds and denotation functions in fact formally represent; and, hence, it is also unclear how we should understand an accessibility relation that can obtain between such pairs. It is true that on this basis we get more-fine-grained distinctions as on the basis of a classical accessibility relation, and, hence, we can thereby formally model the desired distributions of truth-values. However, it seems to be more like a technical trick than a plausible formalization of some intuitively meaningful notion of content.

Thirdly, the proposed account seems be able to provide the desired results concerning the correct distribution of truth-values in the case of sentences that contain epistemic modals like 'might'.[12] However, there are reasons to doubt that it can be extended in a straightforward way to attitude ascriptions with their specific semantic problems. There are purely epistemic identity puzzles that concern the identity of a person that might be only known by a pseudonym or a descriptive name. So, for example, if we assume that the name 'Banksy' or the descriptive name 'Jack the Ripper' refers to a single person, it might be true from a certain incomplete epistemic point of view that two completely different people are identical with Banksy or Jack the Ripper from this point of view. Therefore, the following two claims *can* both be true relative to an epistemic reading of 'might' even if A in fact is not identical with B:

(9)   Banksy/Jack the Ripper might be A.
(10)  Banksy/Jack the Ripper might be B.

According to the proposed monstrous account, both sentences (9) and (10) can be true (although 'a' and 'b' actually refer to different things) because there is at least one pair consisting of a world and a denotation function that is accessible from the pair consisting of the actual world and the constant or actual denotation function, and relative to these accessible pairs the following sentences are evaluated as true: 'Banksy/Jack the Ripper is identical to A/B'. The main reason why a sentence like 'Banksy is identical to A', which is in fact necessarily false, can come out as true relative to such a world- and denotation-pair is that we have an accessible world, where the names 'Banksy' and 'A' denote the very same thing. The shifted denotation parameter makes it possible that such a true evaluation is possible and that 'Banksy' and 'A' refer to the same object relative to such a world. However, in such a case the epistemic situation might be so that the information that we have does not rule out all alternative possibilities to the, in fact, obtaining state of affairs. If we have acquired false information, it might even rule out the obtaining state of affairs, but not some false alternatives. Such cases of epistemic possibilities concern real objects and our ability to identify these real objects in a correct or incorrect way. That is, in our toy example all terms involved ('Bansky', 'Jack the Ripper', 'A' and 'B') refer to real objects. The central question in this respect is only whether the information we have about the world allows us to identify certain real objects in a correct or incorrect way. However, the situation is different relative to a *de dicto* reading of an attitude ascription. In the interesting cases, cognitive subjects misidentify real people in a more substantial way. Firstly, they might think that two different names that refer in fact to the same object refer to two different things. Secondly, they might think that two different names that in fact refer to two different things refer to one and the same thing. Furthermore, there are also interesting related *de re* cases: (i) where people have thoughts about one object as if it were two different objects, and (ii) where people have thoughts about two objects as if they were one object. In the cases captured by epistemic modals, we might use a purely epistemic notion of a counterpart of an ordinary object to characterize these cases: x is the epistemic counterpart of a real object y for the subject s iff the information that s has about y does not rule out the possibility that x is identical with y. In our four distinguished cases the situation is different: we do not only have an epistemic problem of identification, we also have the metaphysical problem to provide the right kind of objects to describe these cases. Hence, for example, if one real object is considered as two objects, then we need to assume two different counterparts of this one real object that neither exist nor that could exist in a metaphysical sense. We might call counterparts in this new and alternative sense *attitude-counterparts*. Both real and not-real objects can have such attitude-counterparts. These attitude-counterparts cannot possibly exist in a metaphysical sense, they are only assumed relative to certain attitudes that represent the world in an incorrect way. If someone thinks that Mark Twain and Samuel Clemens are two different objects, then they assume that there are two different objects where in fact there is only one. These two assumed objects are relative to such a case of misidentification of the two attitude-counterparts of the real object Mark Twain. That is, if we aim to formally model such cases by means of a certain Kripke-style intensional semantic framework, we need to extend this framework in such a way that we can also have such very peculiar objects on board. The only plausible and meaningful way to provide these additional objects assumes non-normal or impossible worlds that could also contain such impossible objects. A non-normal world is a world that can either be incomplete, inconsistent or both. Relative to impossible worlds there can also be impossible objects that have certain properties. We might now use such impossible worlds to formally represent the attitude-states that people have if they misrepresent objects in the mentioned four different ways.

However, if the mentioned attitude cases require such an alternative and different extension of the classical Kripke-style framework and if we must assume impossible and non-normal worlds in any case for this purpose, then there is a much simpler and straightforward approach to account for the special and required semantics of attitude ascriptions. On the basis of these resources, we can formally model additional more-fine-grained contents without (a) assuming that the attitude verbs directly manipulate that denotation parameter or (b) assuming the required problematic extension and modification of the accessibility relation. Hence, this third mentioned problem leads us immediately to a third alternative account that I aim to propose as a solution to our outlined problem.

## Attitude verbs as non-normal modal operators

The last and third option that I aim to propose extends the domain of possible referents of a proper name in such a way that they can refer to impossible objects that only can be part of impossible or non-normal worlds. This view is conservative with respect to the behaviour of proper names relative to all *possible* worlds. If a name refers to some object with respect to the actual world, it refers to the very same object with respect to any other *possible* world. If a proper name does not refer with respect to the actual world to any object, it does also not refer to any object with respect to all *possible* worlds. However, this new framework is less conservative with respect to the semantic behaviour of proper names relative to non-normal worlds. In principle, the reference of a proper name is completely unrestricted with respect to non-normal worlds. That is, every proper name could refer in principle to very different objects with respect to different non-normal worlds. However, there are also important exceptions. With respect to those impossible worlds that represent incorrect mental representation of the actual world, names that refer with respect to the actual world to a certain object o can only refer to attitude-counterparts of o relative to those non-normal worlds. x is an attitude-counterpart of y for a cognitive subject S iff either S has two different and independent mental representations of y and x is the object that would exist instead of y if one of the two mental representations of y by S were correct or S has a single mental representation of y and some other object z and x is the object that would exist instead of y and z if the mentioned mental representation of y and z would be a correct individual representation. A real object that is incorrectly mentally represented by two different individual representations has two different attitude-counterparts with respect to a non-normal world that formally represents the content of these representations if they were correct. Two real objects that are mentally represented by a single mental representation have one attitude-counterpart with respect to a non-normal world that formally represents the content of this representation.

We can now intuitively sketch the semantic behaviour of attitude verbs relative to our briefly outlined new semantic framework. Attitude verbs are conceived of as non-normal modal operators (or predicates). We make use for this purpose of an accessibility relation that is relativized to cognitive agents and to kinds of attitudes. The restrictions provided by these more specific accessibility relations are fixed by the interpretation function. It is now possible to assign on this basis different truth-values to our following two example sentences:

(1.R) [Mark Twain] ASS (Peter, [Author (Mark Twain)]).
(1.D) ASS (Peter, [[Mark Twain] Author (Mark Twain)]).

Sentence (1.R) is actually true if relative to all worlds w that are accessible from the actual world that represents Peter's assumptions, the actual referent of 'Mark Twain' is an element of the extension of 'is an author' relative to w.

Sentence (1.D), on the other hand, is actually true if relative to all worlds w that are accessible from the actual world and that represents Peter's assumptions, the referent of 'Mark Twain' relative to w is an element of the extension of 'is an author' relative to w. If the set of accessible worlds that represent Peter's assumptions contains only possible worlds, then (1.R) and (1.D) will always have the very same truth-value. However, the situation changes if this set contains non-normal worlds, with respect to these worlds 'Mark Twain' might refer to an attitude-counterpart of the actual object Mark Twain that literally is not identical with the actual Mark Twain. Against this background, it is possible that (1.R) and (1.D) receive different truth-values.

In a certain sense, we can also say that the referent of 'Mark Twain' is *shifted* relative to an attitude context if the represented content requires a formal representation by my means of non-normal worlds. But this kind of shift is not induced by an attitude operator that shifts the denotation parameter concerning the name 'Mark Twain', it is the result of a more classical semantic mechanism, namely the fact that our modal operator has access to non-normal worlds that contain attitude-counterparts of the actual referent of a specific name. Hence, in spirit our account also makes use of the *Fregean idea* that attitude contexts may induce a certain shift of reference with respect to the expression's use in such a context, but the semantic mechanisms behind this kind of shift are very different from all other so far presented versions of shifting-approaches with respect to *de dicto* readings of attitude ascriptions.

## Attitude verbs as non-normal modal operators: the formal analysis

The proposed formal analysis of attitude verbs is not the first analysis that interprets attitude verbs as non-normal modal operators. Important predecessors of such a kind of approach can be found in Priest (2005, 2016) and Ripley (2012). However, the formal systems in these works do not exclusively focus on the problems that we are mainly interested in; namely, *to solve the classical substitution problem based on a semantic distinction between de re and de dicto readings of attitude ascriptions*. The second chapter of Priest (2005, 2016) is concerned with this problem, but, in my opinion, neither in sufficient detail nor by providing the right analysis of the semantic behaviour of names relative to *de dicto* readings of attitude ascriptions. In Ripley (2012), the substitution problem is only one among several issues and the main focus of the paper is on a comparison between different more-fine-grained modifications of classical possible world semantics.

A treatment of attitude verbs like 'believe' or 'know' as modal operators in analogy to the possibility and the necessity operator has already a longer tradition and was proposed by different authors before Priest.[13] But a standard treatment of this kind of operator on the basis of *normal* possible worlds and standard possible world semantics faces well-known problems that this new framework aims to overcome; especially, it delivers the desired fine-grained semantics for hyperintensional contexts.[14]

Before we address in more detail the relevant technical details for the implementation of non-normal worlds that are conceived of as inconsistent and open in the truth-conditional framework of world semantics, let us address a general philosophical worry concerning such an extension.

People who are happy to admit normal possible worlds might have reservations concerning the acceptance of incomplete or open worlds because according to them a (possible) *world* is essentially considered to be a totality of realizable possibilities, something for which actuality should at least be a logical possibility. But impossible worlds cannot be realized by definition, and open worlds cannot be considered to be genuine (complete) alternatives of the actual world. However, I think such an objection is based on an incorrect understanding of the status and role of worlds relative to truth-conditional world semantics. In my opinion, worlds (or points of evaluation) should be seen as purely technical constructions that allow us to capture the contribution of certain expressions to truth-conditions in a precise and clear way. In this sense, worlds are tools to represent contents, but they are not themselves totalities of realizable possibilities. We can rationally believe or assume inconsistent things because our belief-systems are only incomplete representations of any sort of reality. Non-normal worlds are useful tools that help us to formally model some special semantic features of the contents that are believed or assumed. They help us to model the truth-conditions of attitude ascriptions in a precise and intuitively acceptable way, nothing more and nothing less.

Priest's own semantics is based on a one-dimensional non-normal modal predicate logic based on the relational semantics of first degree entailment (FDE).[15] In the next section, I will introduce a modified version of Priest's formal system that allows us to make some further adjustments to this system that fits our solution to the substitution problem that has been proposed above.

## Our general formal semantic framework

Our formal semantic framework, which is a modified version of the framework defended in Priest (2005, chs. 1, 2), makes use of the following structure: <P, N, A, D, D*,

I, @>.[16] P is the set of all (normal) possible worlds, N is the set of all (non-normal) impossible or incomplete worlds, A is the set of all possible cognitive agents. This set might contain individuals and groups of individual agents as elements. D is a function from worlds into domains of discourse and D* is the union of all domains of all worlds (hence, D is more fundamental than D*). I is our interpretation function and @ is the actual world. Additionally, we will make use of the following derived set: W is the set of all worlds, whether possible, impossible or incomplete.

I will introduce two different semantics for quantifiers, one based on a constant domain framework, the other on a variable domain framework. In opposition to Priest, who uses an absolute total denotation function to interpret singular terms, I will make use of a world-relative partial denotation function. Priest conceives of individual constants as *obstinately rigid designators* that refer to the same object in the single constant domain of discourse relative to every possible world. We interpret individual constants as *actually restricted* rigid designators on the basis of our variable domain framework. That is, any individual constant that refers to an object relative to the actual world refers to the very same object in the domain of the actual world relative to every possible world. This property of individual constants is guaranteed if we add the following additional constraining condition concerning the application of the interpretation function to individual constants:

(C1)   For every possible world w and every individual constant α: I(α,@) is defined iff I(α,w) = I(α,@).

Additionally, we conceive of individual constants without an actual denotation as *obstinately rigid non-designators*. We have to add a second constraining condition concerning the interpretation function when applied to individual constants to guarantee this second feature:

(C2)   For every possible world w and every individual constant α: I(α,@) is undefined iff I(α,w) is undefined.

Relative to *epistemic worlds* the interpretation function can assign arbitrarily either a single object or no object to an individual constant. Hence, a single individual constant can have different denotations with respect to different epistemic worlds.

With respect to predicates, I conceive of the interpretation function in the same way as Priest. Relative to the relational semantic setting of FDE, it is necessary to assign not only extensions to predicates, but also anti-extensions. I(P, +, w) is the extension of the predicate 'P' relative to the world w, while I(P, –, w) is the anti-extension of the predicate 'P' relative to the world w. Hence, we will assign to each predicate two different sets relative to each world that can only contain elements or n-tuples of the domain of the respective world as extensions and anti-extensions of this predicate.

Apart from these two orthodox functions of interpreting individual constants and predicates the interpretation function has two additional unorthodox functions. Firstly, it assigns to each formal expression of an attitude verb like '…BEL[…]' or '…ASS[…]' relative to the actual world a fixed accessibility relation between possible worlds, which is relativized to possible cognitive agents from the set A, that represents the actual meaning of the specific attitude verb. This relation provides the relevant restrictions concerning the accessibility of worlds depending on the specific expressed attitudes and their subjects. If we conceive of 'Ω' as a schematic letter for names of attitude expressions and 'α' as a schematic letter for cognitive agents, we can use the following expressions to specify this non-standard accessibility relation: I(Ω,@)(<w, w'>, α), where I() is our interpretation relation, and w and w can only range over members of W. Intuitively, this complex sign in our metalanguage can be read as follows: The world 'w' that represents the cognitive attitude expressed by 'Ω' with respect to the actual world relativize to the agent α is accessible form w.

Secondly, the interpretation function assigns to every formula of the general form '□A', '◊A' and 'A → B' one of the two classical truth-values relative to each impossible world. Furthermore, we will make use of a total assignment function δ() that assigns to every individual variable an object of D*, which is the union of all world-relative domains. On this basis, we can define a world-relative denotation function d() for *singular terms* as follows:

If x is an individual constant, then d(x,w) = I(x,w).
If x is an individual variable, then d(x,w) = δ(x).

Our FDE framework contains an *evaluation relation* $V_\delta()$ instead of a more usual evaluation *function*. This evaluation relation can relate formulas either to no truth-value at all, to one of the two classical truth-values, or to both classical truth-values. If we use 'A' as a schematic letter for closed formulas, we can specify the evaluation relation in the following canonical way: $V_\delta(<A,w>, T)$. This reads as 'V relates the closed formula A relative to the world w and the assignment δ to the truth-value T'.

We can now formulate truth- and falsity-conditions for *ordinary* atomic sentences, which contain singular terms that are used in a way that is *insensitive* to the above outlined scope-distinction that we introduced on the basis of our toy example '[a]Fa':

$V_\delta(<Pt_1 \ldots t_n, w>, T)$   iff   $<d(t_1,w), \ldots, d(t_n,w)> \in I(P,+,w)$.
$V_\delta(<Pt_1 \ldots t_n, w>, F)$   iff   $<d(t_1,w), \ldots, d(t_n,w)> \in I(P,-,w)$.

But, on the other hand, we can now also formally represent uses of singular terms in *extraordinary* atomic sentences that are *sensitive* to the above-mentioned scope-distinction in the following alternative way:

$V_\delta(<[t_1, \ldots t_n]Pt_1 \ldots t_n, w>, T)$   iff   ($d(t_1,w)$ is defined in w, ..., $d(t_n,w)$ is defined in w) & $<d(t_1,w), \ldots, d(t_n,w)> \in I(P,+,w)$.

$V_\delta(<[t_1, \ldots t_n]Pt_1 \ldots t_n, w>, F)$   iff   It is not the case that ($d(t_1,w)$ is defined in w, ..., $d(t_n,w)$ is defined in w) or $<d(t_1,w), \ldots, d(t_n,w)> \in I(P,-, w)$.

The difference between these two semantics for atomic sentences is crucial for our intended way to distinguish between a *de re* and a *de dicto* reading of attitude ascriptions. We only get the relevant choice between two readings of attitude ascriptions that contain embedded atomic sentences on the basis of our second proposed semantics for extraordinary atomic sentences. Furthermore, our logical framework contains an *identity predicate* that is interpreted as a logical predicate with the following fixed contribution to truth- and falsity-conditions of *atomic identity sentences*:[17]

$V_\delta(<[s,t]\ s=t, w>, T)$  iff  $d(s,w)$ and $d(t,w)$ are both defined in w and $d(s,w) = d(t,w)$.
$V_\delta(<[s,t]\ s=t, w>, F)$  iff  $d(s,w)$ or $d(t,w)$ are undefined in w or $d(s,w) \neq d(t,w)$.

In opposition to Priest, I also make use of a *logical* existence predicate with the following fixed contribution to the truth- and falsity-conditions of *atomic existential sentences*:

$V_\delta(<E!t, w>, T)$  iff  $d(t,w)$ is defined and $d(t,w) \in D_w$.
$V_\delta(<E!t, w>, F)$  iff  $d(t,w)$ is undefined or $d(t,w) \notin D_w$.

The special status of impossible and open worlds concerning the distribution of truth-values makes it necessary to formulate our general truth- and falsity-conditions for closed formulas relative to arbitrary worlds in a *disjunctive* way. This allows us to capture the peculiar status of the assignments of truth-values in the case of certain closed formulas relative to impossible worlds and all closed formulas apart from atomic formulas relative to open worlds.

Our first task is to formulate the truth- and falsity-conditions of *connective sentences with truth-functional connectives*. For our purposes that mainly concern the desired semantic differences between (1.R) and (1.D), we can only make use of a fairly standard semantics of connective sentences.[18] I will only list the truth- and falsity-conditions of *negations* and *conjunctions* as explicit examples here:

$V_\delta(<\neg A, w>, T)$  iff  $V_\delta(<A, w>, F)$.
$V_\delta(<\neg A, w>, F)$  iff  $V_\delta(<A, w>, T)$.

$V_\delta(<(A\&B), w>, T)$  iff  $V_\delta(<A, w>, T)$ and $V_\delta(<B, w>, T)$.
$V_\delta(<(A\&B), w>, F)$  iff  $V_\delta(<A, w>, F)$ or $V_\delta(<B, w>, F)$.

The truth-conditions of modal sentences that express metaphysical modalities are slightly different. These formulas do not only have different truth- and falsity-conditions in non-normal worlds than in possible worlds, they also require a special treatment in the case of impossible worlds to solve the problem of logical omniscience in the desired way.[19]

I will again just specify the truth-conditions for sentences headed by the possibility-operator. It is a quite easy task to formulate the analogous truth-conditions more modal claims headed by a necessity-operator. The former modal sentences have the following truth- and falsity-conditions:

$V_\delta(<\Diamond A, w>, T)$  iff  if $w \in P$, then for some $w^* \in W, V(<A, w^*>, T)$ or
    if $w \in N$, then $I(<\Diamond A, w>, T)$.
$V_\delta(<\Diamond A, w>, F)$  iff  if $w \in P$, then for every $w^* \in W, V(<A, w^*>, F)$ or
    if $w \in N$, then $I(<\Diamond A, w>, F)$.

These truth- and falsity-conditions for modal sentences need some further adaptions, because as they stand they lead to counter-intuitive consequences with respect to the assignment of truth-values to modal sentences relative to impossible worlds. These problems concern the truth-values of modalized atomic sentences relative to impossible worlds that contain different but co-referential names. On the basis of the outlined framework, it is possible to assign, for example, the formula '$\Box Fa$' a different truth-value relative to an impossible world than the formula '$\Box Fb$' even if 'a' and 'b' refer to the same individual with respect to this world. That is a counter-intuitive consequence.[20]

We can add additional conditions to constrain the application of the interpretation function to modal sentences relative to impossible worlds in a similar way as we already did in the case of its application to individual constants. The conditions that block the mentioned unwelcome consequences can be formulated as follows:

(C3)  For every impossible world $w^*$ and every formula A: If $I(\Box/\lozenge A, w^*) = T/F$, then for every formula $A^*$ that is the result of the substitution of an individual constant in A with a different, co-referential individual constant: $I(\Box/\lozenge A^*, w) = T/F$.

In a similar way, we can now formulate the truth- and falsity-conditions for our conditional represented by strict implication:[21]

$V(<(A \rightarrow B), w>, T)$  iff  if $w \in P$, then for every $w^* \in W$: if $V(<A, w^*>, T)$, then $V(<A, w^*>, T)$
  if $w \in U$, then $I(<(A \rightarrow B), w>, T)$.

$V(<(A \rightarrow B), w>, F)$  iff  if $w \in P$, then for some $w^* \in W$: $V(<A, w^*>, T)$ and $V(<A, w^*>, F)$
  if $w \in U$, then $I(<(A \rightarrow B), w>, F)$.

As in the case of modal sentences, these truth- and falsity-conditions have to be supplemented with specific conditions that constrain the assignment of truth-values to strict implications that contain co-referential terms relative to impossible worlds by means of the interpretation function:

(C4)  For every impossible world $w^*$ and every formula A and B: If $I((A \rightarrow B), w^*) = T/F$, then for every formula $A^*$ that is the result of the substitution of individual constants in A with different co-referential individual constants and every formula $B^*$ that is the result of the substitution of individual constants in B with different co-referential individual constants: $I((A^* \rightarrow B^*), w) = T/F$.

Before we focus on the modal semantics of modal attitude operators, let us also specify the truth- and falsity-conditions of quantified formulas. Priest interprets the quantifiers as *world-unbound quantifiers* that range over the objects of the constant domain of discourse. We will give two possible variations of interpretation, *world-bound* and *world-unbound*. For our purposes, I will again in opposition to Priest make use of fairly standard truth-conditions for quantified sentences. I will again only explicitly formulate the following truth- and falsity-conditions for one of the two standard types of quantified formulas:

$V_\delta(<\exists xA, w>, T)$ iff some object $d \in D(w)/D^*$ and every assignment $\delta^*$ that is the same as $\delta$ except that it assigns d to x: $V_{\delta^*}(<A, w>, T)$.

$V_\delta(<\exists xA, w>, F)$ iff every object $d \in D(w)/D^*$ and every assignment $\delta^*$ that is the same as $\delta$ except that it assigns d to x: $V_{\delta^*}(<A, w>, F)$.

This completes my brief overview of the truth- and falsity-conditions of the typical types of sentences bases on a quantified modal logic.

## Our formal semantics for attitude ascriptions

Now we can finally introduce our attitude expressions into our formal semantic framework. I will begin my outline of the semantics for these expressions by the specification of the truth-conditional contributions of the formal counterpart of the verb 'assume', namely the expression '... ASS[...]' that is basically conceived of as a specific relativized non-normal modal operator. Our slight variation of Priest's account makes use of the following truth- and falsitiy-conditions for the paradigm sentences that contain such an expression:

$V_\delta(<\alpha ASS[\varphi], w>, T)$ iff for every world w* that is such that w* $\in$ W and $I(ASS,@)(<w,w^*>, \alpha), V_\delta(<\varphi, w^*>,T)$.

$V_\delta(<\alpha ASS[\varphi], w>, F)$ iff for some world w* that is such that w* $\in$ W and $I(ASS,@)(<w,w^*>, \alpha), V_\delta(<\varphi, w^*>,F)$.

In opposition to Priest, who makes use of a more general and standard accessibility relation that is independent from the interpretation function but relativized to the kind of attitude,[22] we make it a semantic issue, which kind of accessibility relation is operative relative to a given model with respect to a specific attitude verb. In my opinion, it is reasonable to assume that the meaning of our attitude verbs is in a similar way as the meaning of names fixed on the basis of their use in the actual world. It does not make sense to fix the meaning of attitude verbs in the metalanguage, because they are in my opinion not distinctly logical vocabulary.

The most significant feature of these modal operators is the very specific accessibility relation mentioned above that is relativized to attitude-states and attitude-subjects. In more intuitive terms, we could also formulate the given truth-conditions as follows:

$V(<\alpha ASS[\varphi], w>,T)$ iff for every world w* that is such that w* $\in$ W and w* represents the ASSUMPTION-states of α with respect to w, $V_\delta(<\varphi,w^*>, T)$.

Different attitude verbs relate subjects to different sets of worlds that represent the contents of the attitudes of these subjects. Hence, we can easily generalize the proposed semantics for the verbs 'assume' or 'believe' to receive a general semantics of (non-factive) attitude verbs, if we conceive of '$\Omega$' as a schematic letter for attitude expressions, in the following way:

$V_\delta(<a\Omega[\varphi], w>, T)$ iff for every world w* that is such that w* ∈ W and $I(\Omega,@)$
(<w,w*>, a), $V_\delta(<\varphi, w*>,T)$.

$V_\delta(<a\Omega[\varphi], w>, F)$ iff for some world w* that is such that w* ∈ W and $I(\Omega,@)$
(<w,w*>, a), $V_\delta(<\varphi, w*>, F)$.

Let us now also show how this account could be modified and extended to provide a semantics of epistemic modals that neither forces us to change the rigid status of names relative to possible worlds nor to interpret epistemic modals as operators that *shift* the assignment or denotation parameter.

## Our formal semantics for epistemic modals

It is now relatively easy to extend our account to epistemic modals. For our purposes, namely, to solve the puzzle about identity sentences modified by the epistemic modal 'might', it suffices to provide a structural semantics for 'might'. We will interpret this expression as a non-normal modal operator that is represented by '•'. This expression will get a special judge-dependent accessibility relation that again may have access to non-normal worlds. As judges we consider cognitive agents of our set of possible agents A. Hence, the judge-parameter is in any case restricted to the set A. On this basis, there are *two* alternative ways to interpret this additional and syntactically hidden judge-parameter.

According to a relativist interpretation, this parameter becomes an additional evaluation parameter. However, this parameter is only relevant for the interpretation of epistemic modals and it becomes irrelevant in the case of all other formulas. It is an advantage of this approach that it can properly account for the intuitive data that the judge-parameter is insensitive to embeddings. Another very important difference between attitude verbs and epistemic modals relative to our framework is that the requirements for the truth of a sentence of the form 'a might be b' are weaker. For this purpose, it is only necessary that relative to *some* accessible world 'a=b' is true.[23] Against this background, the relativist version of our semantics can be formulated as follows:

$V_{\delta,j}(<\bullet[\varphi], w>, T)$ iff for some world w* that is such that w* ∈ W and $I(\bullet,@)$
(<w,w*>, j), $V(<\varphi, w*>,T)$.

$V_{\delta,j}(<\bullet\bullet[\varphi], w>, F)$ iff for every world w* that is such that w* ∈ W: If $I(\bullet,@)$
(<w,w*>, j), $V(<\varphi, w*>, F)$.

On this basis, it is guaranteed that the following two sentences can both come out as true relative to a specific judge:

(11) Jack the Ripper might be Aaron Kosminski.
(12) Jack the Ripper might be Montague John Druitt.

The reasons for this are the following. Firstly, according to our formal framework it is possible that 'Jack the Ripper' refers to different objects relative to different non-normal worlds. Secondly, there can be two different accessible non-normal worlds where 'Jack the Ripper' refers to two different things and, hence 'Jack the Ripper = A' might be true relative to one such accessible world and 'Jack the Ripper = B' might be true to another world, although 'A' and 'B' are not co-referential with respect to every possible world. Which worlds are accessible from a specific world depends (a) on the choice of the judge and (b) on the specific denotation that the interpretation function assigns to the epistemic modal 'might'. In my opinion, this provides a nice solution to the puzzling situation that names behave quite differently in the scope of metaphysical and epistemic modal expressions. It especially solves this problem, without the need to assume a dual-modal logic or any sort of monstrous operators.

For people that have doubts about the general appropriateness of a *relativist* semantics, I can also offer a second context-sensitive semantics for epistemic modals. According to this version, the judge-parameter is determined by the overall discursive conversational context. For this purpose, we have reserved a specific constant 'j' in our language that is interpreted by the denotation function and only used for this purpose. The interpretation of 'j' is restricted to elements of A. On this basis, we get the following alternative semantics:

$V_\delta(<\bullet[\varphi], w>, T)$ iff for some world $w^*$ that is such that $w^* \in W$ and $I(\bullet,@)$ $<w,w^*>, d(j)), V(<\varphi, w^*>, T)$.

$V_\delta(<\bullet[\varphi], w>, F)$ iff for every world $w^*$ that is such that $w^* \in W$: If $I(\bullet,@)$ $<w,w^*>, d(j)), V(<\varphi, w^*>, F)$.

This completes my general formal outline of our new world semantics for attitude ascriptions and epistemic modals.

## Our two notions of validity

Our semantics, certainly, comes with a specific logic. Hence, we can define validity for our non-relativist relational FDE system in terms of truth preservation relative to the actual world @. That is, $\Delta \models \varphi$ iff for every evaluation V and every assignment $\delta$: If for every member A of $\Delta$: $V_\delta(<A,@>, T)$, then $V_\delta(<\varphi,@>, T)$. For our relativist semantics, the following alternative is possible: $\Delta \models \varphi$ iff for every evaluation V, every assignment $\delta$ and every judge j: If for every member A of $\Delta$: $V_{\delta,j}(<A,@>, T)$, then $V_{\delta,j}(<\varphi,@>, T)$.

## Attitude-counterparts are formally represented by proxy-individuals

We have outlined our semantic framework, but there are still important details that concern our treatment of names relative to non-normal worlds that require more attention. According to our proposed view on the semantic behaviour of names inside the scope of attitude verbs, (a) every name that is a non-empty relative to all normal worlds might be empty or refer to some other object relative to non-normal worlds, and (b) every name that is an empty name relative to all normal worlds might refer some object relative to non-normal worlds or be without a referent with respect to such worlds. Such a conception raises the following question: To which specific objects do actual empty and non-empty names refer relative to non-normal possible worlds? Are they free to refer to anything? One central purpose of the introduction of non-normal worlds is the formal representation of attitudes of cognitive subjects that are based on a misidentification of objects or misassumption concerning the existence of objects. However, it was also our intention to use non-normal worlds to also handle cases of misconception and incomplete information states.

As we have already seen, there are basically two different cases of misidentification: firstly, a cognitive subject can think of a single object that it is two or more objects; and secondly, a cognitive subject can think of two or more objects that they are a single object. A case of *misassumption* is a case where a cognitive subject erroneously thinks that a specific object exists that in fact does not exist. Cases of *misconception* are cases where a cognitive subject erroneously thinks of a certain object that it is a bearer of a specific name, although in fact the object is not a bearer of this name.

Cases of misconception are very easy to handle on the basis of our formal framework. If a cognitive subject erroneously assumes that a certain object bears a name, we assign this name to this object relative to those non-normal worlds that represent the attitude-states of this cognitive subject. It is more difficult to handle the other two cases as in these cases, a cognitive subject postulates entities that do not actually exist, and that might even not exist relative to any possible world. I propose to make use of *proxy-individuals* in our formal framework to fill this gap, which are the formal equivalents of our *attitude-counterparts* introduced above. These proxy-individuals are only used to represent objects whose existence is erroneously assumed by cognitive subjects relative to those non-normal worlds that represent certain attitude-states. We construct these proxy-individuals formally in such a way that, from a meta-theoretic point of view, they do not bring with them any commitments to new or exotic objects of some controversial kind. That is, we make use of the ordinary objects contained in the domain of the actual world and from these objects we construe new proxy-objects by means of set-theoretic constructions that play the desired role of erroneously postulated objects as the representations of these objects in non-normal worlds. In more concrete terms, this means the following for misidentification cases. If someone erroneously conceives of an actual object o as two distinct objects to which he assigns the distinct names 'a' and 'b', we represent this error by an assignment of the set {o,1} to 'a' and the set {o,2} to 'b' relative to a non-normal world that represents such a case of misidentification. If someone erroneously conceives of two actual objects m and n as a single object to which he assigns the distinct names 'a' and 'b', we represent this error by an assignment of the set {m,n} to 'a' and 'b' relative to a non-normal world that represents such a case of misidentification.

With respect to misassumption cases, we assign arbitrarily construed set-theoretic objects that are not required relative to such a world for other purposes to names that are actually empty. So, for example, we may assign the empty set {} as the denotation of 'Vulcan' relative to a non-normal world that represents a specific case of misassumption and we may assign the set {{}} to the name 'Zeus' relative to a non-normal world that represents a different case of misassumption. Alternatively, we may also assign, for example, the individual constant 'a' that represents a specific empty name in a non-normal world to itself relative to this world. It is necessary to add these *proxy-individuals* to the respective domain of discourse of the relevant non-normal worlds, and according to our conception of the existence predicate these objects exist relative to non-normal worlds. By making use of such formal proxy-individuals, we are able to satisfy the formal requirements of our shifting-account with respect to the behaviour of names in the context of attitude operators.

For the solution of our identity puzzles that concern epistemic modals, it is not required to assign any new or construed objects to ordinary names. In most cases, the relevant set of actual referents is sufficient for this purpose. The only thing that changes in this respect relative to different non-normal worlds is that ordinary names undergo a shift in reference from some actual object to some other actual object. Therefore, we only need to export specific actual objects to non-normal worlds for this task. Additionally, there certainly might be similar epistemic identity puzzles that concern names that are non-referential with respect to the actual world. In this case, the same strategy is required to account for possible referents relative to non-normal worlds as in the cases of misassumption described above.

Let us now compare this account to Priest's own account with respect to the classical substitution puzzle.

## A Comparison with Priest's original version of the proposed semantics

As we have already pointed out, there are two important differences between our world semantics for attitude ascriptions and the related account that is given in Priest (2005, 2016). Firstly, Priest *only* makes use of a single total domain of quantification that contains all existent and non-existent objects. Secondly, he defines the interpretation/denotation function as a total function with respect to individual constants. That is, the interpretation function assigns a single object of the single constant domain of quantification to *every* individual constant in a non-world-relative way.

Such a theoretical setting leads to unwelcome consequences with respect to a proper analysis of attitude ascriptions. Firstly, it cannot account for truth-conditional differences between a sentence like (1) according to its *de dicto* reading (1.D) and its *de re* reading (1.R). Hence, there is consequently also no truth-conditional difference between a sentence like (1) and (1*). Both consequences are unwelcome. Secondly, arguments of the following form [ARG1] are *invalid* according to a *de dicto and* a *de re* reading of the single premise of such an argument.

[ARG1]

S believes/fears/hopes/ ... that ... a ...

---

a exists

Intuitively, such an argument is only invalid with respect to a *de dicto* reading of the premise. Thirdly, arguments of the following form [ARG2] are *valid* according to a uniform *de dicto and* a uniform *de re* reading.

[ARG2]

S believes/fears/hopes/ ... that ... a ...
a=b
_____
S believes/fears/hopes/ ... that ... b ...

Intuitively, arguments of this form are only valid relative to a *de re* reading of the premise and conclusion.

Priest is explicitly aware of at least the last of these problems. The second undesirable consequence given above is not so problematic for Priest himself. Since, according to his Meinongian conception of existence, this consequence is acceptable. The first consequence is also an unwelcome consequence for him.

In principle, Priest could import our shifting-strategy concerning the denotation of individual constants with respect to non-normal worlds into his framework. To do this, he has to make use of a world-relative interpretation function with respect to individual constants that always assigns to a single individual constant the very same object of the constant domain relative to normal worlds, but it may assign different objects of the constant domain to this constant relative to open worlds. Priest's own solution, however, is in significant respects different from our solution.

Let us, therefore, now focus on Priest's sophisticated re-interpretation of his favoured constant domain framework to get rid of the first and third unwelcome consequences.[24] The main idea behind his solution is to introduce a new kind of distinction between the denotations of individual constants and the values assigned to individual variables, on the one hand, and, on the other hand, the semantic contributions of these expressions to truth-conditions of sentences. Standardly, the denotations and assigned values are conceived of as truth-conditional contributions. To be able to draw such a distinction, Priest makes a significant change concerning the elements of the constant domain of discourse, and these elements are now uniformly conceived of as (total) *functions from worlds into objects*. This is the technical part of the re-interpretation. From a philosophical point of view, Priest claims that we should interpret these new functional elements in the constant domain of discourse as the formal counterparts of *ordinary objects* and those objects that are the outputs of these functions relative to worlds as the *identities* of these ordinary objects. We will see in due course whether such a philosophical interpretation of Priest's proposal really makes sense.

But before we can do that, let us focus on the technical side of his solution, and let us see which additional technical adaptations are required. This re-interpretation now captures the rigidity of names represented by individual constants in two senses. Firstly, individual constants denote functions from worlds to objects/identities absolutely, and therefore are constantly relative to all worlds. However, this is not the desired sense of rigidity. The desired sense concerns the contributions to truth-conditions. To capture this sense of rigidity, Priest makes the following stipulation concerning the functions from worlds to identities denoted by individual constants: each function of this kind has the very same output relative to normal worlds, but possibly different outputs relative to a subset of non-normal worlds that he calls open worlds. (This way of capturing the rigidity of names has obvious similarities with our way.)

On the basis of the outlined adaptations, Priest's logical framework has, in opposition to our proposed framework, the following different structure: <P, N, O, D*, H, I, @>.[25] P, N and @ have the very same function and nature as they have relative to our variable domain framework; O contains all non-normal worlds that are incomplete that Priest calls *open worlds*; the constant domain D* now contains functions from possible worlds into objects/identities as elements, instead of simple individual objects; the new component H is a set of contributions of singular terms to truth-conditions, and hence contains the outputs of the functions that D* contains. Additionally, Priest assumes a set C, the set of closed worlds that is identical with the union of P and N. The interpretation function assigns, in absolute terms, elements of D* to individual constants. Priest also re-interprets the role of the interpretation function with respect to predicates. The interpretation function assigns world-relative extensions and anti-extension to predicates that are not subsets of D*, but subsets of H. Furthermore, the assignment function assigns to each individual variable an element of the domain D*. This leads to the following conception of the denotation function d():

If x is an individual constant, then d(x) = I(x).
If x is an individual variable, then d(x) = δ(x).

The changes with respect to I() also require the following adaptions of the truth- and falsity-conditions of non-logical and atomic sentences, where we conceive of $d(t_n(w))$ as the value of the function that is the denotation of $t_n$ relative to the world w:

V(<P$t_1$...$t_n$, w>,T)   iff   <d($t_1$(w)),..., d($t_n$(w))> ∈ I(P,+,w).

V(<P$t_1$...$t_n$, w>,F)   iff   <d($t_1$(w)),..., d($t_n$(w))> ∈ I(P,−, w).

V(<s=t, w>,T)   iff   d(s(w))=d(t(w)).
V(<s=t, w>,F)   iff   d(s(w))≠d(t(w)).

These adaptions are sufficient to *validate* arguments of the form [ARG2] relative to a uniform *de dicto* reading and *invalidate* arguments of this form relative to a uniform *de re* reading. However, as we will see, doubts arise whether we can draw the necessary truth-conditional difference between the logical forms 'cBEL[Aa]' and '∃x(x=a ∧ cBEL[Ax])' in an acceptable way.

Firstly, let us see how Priest now deals with the third problem we have pointed out. The following argument is now *invalid* according to Priest's adapted framework.

[ARG2.2]

cBEL[Aa]
a=b
_____
cBEL[Ab]

This is the case because there can be an interpretation relative to which 'a' and 'b' denote different functions from worlds to identities that happen to have the very same output relative to the actual world (and other possible worlds), but relative to at least some open world $o_1$, a different output. Let us now assume that this open world is a world that represents relative to the actual world, the belief-states of c; and this world is also the only world that represents belief-states of c. Furthermore, assume that according to this world 'Aa' is true, while 'Ab' is false. On the basis of this interpretation, the premises of [ARG2.2] can be true relative to the actual world, while the conclusion of [ARG2.2] is false.

Let us now show why, on the other hand, the following *de re* variant of [ARG2] is *valid* according to Priest's adapted formal framework:

[ARG2.1]

∃x(x=a ∧ cBEL[Ax])
a=b
―――――――――――――――――
∃x(x=b ∧ cBEL[Ax])

According to Priest's solution, there are now two different possibilities to account for the truth of the sentence 'a=b' relative to the actual world. Firstly, 'a' and 'b' denote the very same function from worlds to identities that is an element of D*. Secondly, 'a' and 'b' denote *different* functions that are both elements of D*, but that have the same outputs relative to all closed worlds. Relative to the first option, it is a trivial matter why it is impossible that the two premises of [ARG2.1] are true relative to the actual world and the conclusion false. However, the same is also true relative to the second distinguished case because if the function that 'a' denotes is such that it makes the open sentence 'cBEL[Ax]' true on the basis of an assignment of this function to 'x' relative to the actual world, then the very same function would also guarantee the truth of the conclusion of [ARG2.1] relative to the actual world. For example, if the outputs of the function denoted by 'a' are such that they deliver an identity that is in the extension of 'A' relative to each open world that represents the belief-states of c according to the actual world, then this would be sufficient to make the first premise and the conclusion of [ARG2.1] true relative to the second possible scenario.

This shows that Priest's adapted formal framework at least has the resources to solve our third problem. Does Priest's adapted account also solve our first problem?

## A surprising consequence of Priest's adapted account

Priest at least has the resources to capture that formulas like 'cBEL[Aa]' and '∃x(x=a ∧ cBEL[Ax])' that represent the *de dicto* and the *de re* readings of a sentence like 'Peter believes that Mark Twain is an author', have different truth-conditions. An important indication for this fact is the *invalidity* of the following argument according to Priest's adapted logical framework:

[ARG3]

∃x(x=a ∧ cBEL[Ax])
―――――――――――――――――
cBEL[Aa]

This argument is invalid because there is an interpretation that makes the premise true according to the actual world and the conclusion false. There can be a function from worlds to identities that is not the denotation of 'a', but that has the same outputs as the denotation of 'a' relative to all closed worlds. The function that 'a' denotes might have identities as outputs relative to all open worlds that make 'Aa' false relative to these worlds. With respect to such a scenario the conclusion of [ARG3] would be false relative to the actual world if these open worlds represent the belief-states of c relative to the actual world.

However, relative to an assignment that assigns this function to 'x', the mentioned function that is partially congruent with the denotation of 'a' may have outputs that make 'Ax' true relative to all open worlds that represent the belief-states of c relative to the actual world. Hence, we have an interpretation that makes the premise of [ARG3] true and its conclusion false relative to the actual world.

This shows that there is a truth-conditional difference between a *de dicto* and a *de re* reading of a sentence like 'Peter believes that Mark Twain is an author' according to Priest's adapted logical framework. Nevertheless, the question arises whether the invalidity of [ARG3] is really *sufficient* to draw an acceptable truth-conditional difference between a *de dicto* and a *de re* reading of a sentence like 'Peter believes that Mark Twain is an author'. One may argue that from an intuitive standpoint there is an additional significant difference between a sentence like (1*) and a sentence like (1) in its *de dicto* reading. And this difference is not only reflected by the invalidity of [ARG3], but also by the additional invalidity of the following argument:

[ARG4]

cBEL[Aa]

---

$\exists x(x=a \land cBEL[Ax])$

This argument reflects a so-called exportation rule. An exportation rule of this kind, for example, is invalid in the case of the interaction of definite descriptions and modal operators. The sentence (13) does not imply (14) relative to its *de dicto* reading:

(13) It is possible that the winner of the French Open 2014 is German.
(14) The winner of the French Open 2014 is such that it is possible that he is German.

One might have the intuition that the same is the case for (1) and (1*). Sentence (1) does not logically imply (1*) because (1) may report a case relative to its *de dicto* reading, where someone is in error about the correct identity of Mark Twain. [ARG4] is also invalid with respect to actually empty names. Priest's account has to reject this intuition because according to Priest's adapted account [ARG4] is valid. This is the case because relative to all situations where the premise of [ARG4] is true, the conclusion is also true. The premise of [ARG4] is only true relative to the actual world if 'a' denotes a function from worlds to identities that delivers outputs that make 'Aa' true relative to all worlds that represent the belief-states of c. However, on this basis it is inevitable that the conclusion of [ARG4] is also true. The expression 'x=a' is trivially true relative to an assignment that assigns the denotation of 'a' to 'x'. Furthermore, 'cBEL[Ax]' is true relative to the very same assignment if the premise of [ARG4] is true relative to the outlined conditions.

According to our proposed account, the arguments [ARG3] and [ARG4] are both invalid. This is an important difference between the two rival accounts. As we will see later, this peculiar feature of Priest's account is also responsible for an important advantage of his account over our proposed account.

## The main problem of Priest's adapted account

The main problem of Priest's modification of his original constant domain framework concerns the *intuitive motivation* of the proposed sophisticated technical changes. Priest must provide a plausible and independent motivation for the proposed distinction between the denotation and truth-conditional contribution of a name and therefore the corresponding distinction between the domains of discourse D* and H. That is, he must show that there either are good semantic or metaphysical reasons for such a modification.

A *semantic justification* would provide reasons why we should conceive of the denotations of ordinary names not as the objects that bear these names, but as functions from worlds into objects that bear these names. One possible variant of this strategy might claim that the mentioned functions from worlds to objects of the domain H are *semantic intensions* or individual concepts, and that the values of these functions are the objects that fall under these concepts. If we identify the semantic value of a proper name with its denotation, then there does not seem to a meaningful possibility to conceive of individual concepts as semantic values. However, if we distinguish the (compositional) semantic value of a name from its referent or denotation, then a view that assigns individual concepts that are formally represented by functions as semantic values to a name seems to be a prima facie much more plausible option. But even if we grant such a kind of distinction, this strategy faces a serious problem: those functions that Priest assigns as semantic values to proper names are not *proper* individual concepts or intensions. With respect to normal or closed worlds these functions behave like proper individual concepts or intensions because they determine the semantic referent of a name with respect to such worlds. This is exactly the function that an intension or individual concept that is semantically expressed by a name should fulfil. However, in the case of non-normal worlds such a function does not capture the semantic referents of a name, but only the object that someone, who has a certain mental representation of an object, believes to be the object of their representation. This is a consequence of the fact that Priest also wants to make use of non-normal worlds to capture cases of *misconception* of attitude holders. These are cases where either one individual is mentally represented as two (or more) objects or two (or more) objects are mentally represented as one object. However, this shows that an apparently uniform function that maps worlds to objects plays in fact two completely different explanatory roles with respect to normal and with respect to non-normal worlds. Hence, we cannot interpret these functions as an intension or individual concept, which would require a single uniform treatment with respect to all worlds. Therefore, a semantic interpretation of those functions that Priest assigns to proper names is not a possible option.

Priest himself aims to provide a metaphysical interpretation of these functions and he gives a *metaphysical justification* for the distinction between D* and H that conceives of the *functions* themselves that are in his view elements of domain D* as formal counterparts of *ordinary objects*. Is this strategy less artificial and less implausible? At first sight, there at least seems to be a relatively popular conception of ordinary objects, a so-called four-dimensional conception that would, in principle, fit such a functional formal representation of ordinary objects. However, a closer examination shows that the specific way in which Priest characterizes these functions is not compatible with four-dimensionalism. Four-dimensionalists think that we should conceive of objects as complex entities that are constituted by different temporal parts. It might also be possible to extend this conception to the modal case and conceive of an object as constituted by different modal parts. But such an extension of this conception has at least two problems.

Firstly, in the temporal case it is at least intuitively clear which kind of relation obtains between different temporal parts of the same object. In the modal case the nature of this relation is less clear. The only plausible option seems to be a *metaphysical counterpart theory*. But on the basis of this conception, every object has different counterparts relative to different possible worlds. That leads to our second problem. Whether we conceive of the proposed modal parts of an individual as counterparts or in some other way, this picture does not fit with the proposed interpretation of Priest according to which each function from worlds into objects in D* has the *same output* relative to all closed worlds. Given this restriction, it makes no sense to interpret the distinction between D* and H on the basis of a four-dimensional conception of objects. Priest is aware of this problem, and therefore he proposes a different conception of the elements of H that distinguishes different identities of one and the same object in the following way:

> A quite different suggestion is to give up the idea that the members of H are parts [.] Objects may have different [or the same colours] at different worlds, different (or the same) locations at different worlds, and so on. Let us suppose that they may also have different (or the same) identities at different worlds. Thus, in the actual world, George Eliot and Mary Anne Evans had the same identity, but as far as my epistemic state before I learned this fact goes, there were worlds where they had quite different identities. We might, then, take the members of H to be identities. Each object may be mapped to its identity at each world; or, as a matter of convenience, we may simply identify the object with the map.[26]

But this justification for the distinction between D* and H is problematic and misleading. The proposed analogy between different colours and different locations of objects with respect to different worlds, on the one hand, and different identities of an object, on the other hand, suggests that Priest aims to draw a *metaphysical distinction*. He wants to claim that a single object *can really* or *literally* have different *identities* with respect to different worlds. But after making this analogy, he applies the distinction again to a case where a subject *incorrectly conceives* of one object as two distinct objects. Here we are now back to our cases of misconception. If I mentally represent a single object in an incorrect way as two different objects, then my mental representations are incorrect in a certain important respect. However, if we pretend that my mental representations were correct, they would require *two different* objects that are represented by these two representations to be correct. We can assume such *required* objects relative to non-normal worlds; however, this does not mean that a specific ordinary object can have two *identities* with respect to a single or different non-normal worlds. There is no meaningful uniform sense of an *identity* of an object that allows us to capture our cases of misidentification and cases of correct identification. Priest seems to conflate or incorrectly assimilate different levels of formal representation. Misrepresentations of a single object do not represent different identities of an object in a metaphysical sense. Additionally, it also does not make sense to say that a person who represents a single object as two objects, explicitly distinguishes two different identities of *a single* object. Especially, it does not make sense if a person represents two objects as one (twins, for example) that he explicitly postulates a single identity of two objects. He simply makes an error. We must be careful in not conflating different levels of representation here. We have the metaphysical level of objects, the mental level of mental representations and the semantic level of linguistic expressions.

On the semantic level, a proper name that refers with respect to the actual world has only a single and constant referent with respect to every normal world, but different possible referents with respect to non-normal worlds. However, this does not mean that we must or should postulate some kind of *object* that is the semantic value *or* denotation of a name that has the same *identity* with respect to every possible world and possibly different *identities* with respect to non-normal worlds. Such a kind of projection from the semantic to the metaphysical level does not make sense. On the mental level, we have correct representations of single objects and incorrect ones. In the first case, we have for each object a corresponding mental representation, in the second case we have some kind of mismatch between objects and mental representations. However, this kind of distinction also does not require or force the assumption of *objects* with possibly different *identities* with respect to different worlds. On the metaphysical level, we have real objects that are mentally represented in a correct way and we have impossible objects that are not literally represented by any kind of real mental representations, but that are required to simulate the case that would exist if these actually incorrect representations would be correct. Priest's distinction between *objects* and *identities* appears against this background as hopelessly obscure,[27] and additional lopsided analogies like the following do not help to make it in any sense clearer:

> Consider an actor, say Anthony Hopkins. In each play in which he plays, he has a role, or identity – Macbeth, Iago, Caesar. It is helpful to think of metaphysical identities as rather like this. (Identities vary only at open worlds, that is, worlds which realize the contents of some intentional state.) When one watches a play, one *thinks of* Hopkins as Macbeth, Iago, etc. This is who he is in a world which realizes how one thinks things to be.[28]

In the case described in this quote, we explicitly pretend that a certain real object has a specific fictional identity with respect to a film. The actor also pretends that he is, for example, Macbeth. If I misidentify one object as two or two objects as one, I do not *pretend* that a certain object (or objects) has (have) a specific fictional or real identity.

Attitude counterparts themselves also do not pretend to be the objects of certain representations. The analogy clearly does not help to solve our problem.

One purpose of non-normal worlds is to represent cases of *misidentification*. These are cases where a cognitive subject represents one object as two or more objects, or where two or more objects are represented as one object. But if we represent such cases by means of non-normal worlds, we are not committed to the view that a single *object* has in any meaningful uniform and metaphysical sense different *identities* with respect to normal and non-normal worlds.

In opposition to Priest's adapted framework, our variable domain framework has the resources to capture cases of misidentification in an adequate and understandable way. Our conception of formal proxy-individuals allows us to formally represent *simulated* realizations of different cases of misidentification relative to non-normal worlds. These attitude-counterparts are products of a simulation that would be the case if actually incorrect representations would be true. But it does not mean that we thereby postulate any *real* alternatives *identities* of any existing or non-existing things in any of the distinguished senses. Furthermore, we are also in the position to account for the possibility that the truth-conditional contribution of a proper name may change from open world to open world in a more conservative and straightforward way than on the basis of Priest's adapted account. Additionally, we can handle attitude verbs and epistemic modals as expressions with a basically similar semantics. If Priest would carry over his account of identities to the case of epistemic modals, he would have to assume that a specific metaphysical object has one ordinary object as its identity in the actual world and another completely different ordinary object as its identity in some open world. In this respect, it even seems to be more difficult to make sense of Priest's distinction between objects and identities.

## Internally represented *de re* readings relative to our semantic framework

So far, we have seen that there is an important theoretical difference between our proposed variable domain framework and Priest's adapted constant domain framework. According to our framework, arguments of the following form are invalid while they are valid according to Priest's account:

[ARG 4]

| cBEL[Aa] | [= cAss[[a]Aa]] |
|---|---|
| $\exists x(x=a$ & cBEL[Ax]) | [= [a]cAss[Aa]] |

This difference has important consequences when it comes to the analysis of certain intuitively plausible *de re* belief ascriptions that concern incorrect *de re* beliefs about identities. An adequate semantic analysis of attitude ascriptions should be able to account for a possibly true reading of sentences like the following:

*Proper Names in Hyperintensional Contexts* 225

(15) Mark Twain and Samuel Clemens (who are identical) are such that Peter believes that the former is not identical with the latter.
(16) Mark Twain and Wolfgang Clement (who are not identical) are such that Peter believes that the former is identical with the latter.

To formulate this challenge a bit more precisely: a proper semantics requires that we should be in the position to account for a true reading of sentences like (15) and (16) relative to a semantic interpretation that assigns the same actual referent to the names 'Mark Twain' and 'Samuel Clemens' and a different actual referent to the name 'Wolfgang Clement'.

If we take (15) and (16) at face value, and apply our standard analysis of *de re* ascriptions to them, we can assign the following candidates as logical forms:

(15L) (a) $\exists x \exists y((x=a \ \& \ y=b) \ \& \ cBEL[x \neq y])$
     (b) $\exists x \exists y(((x=a \ \& \ y=b) \ \& \ x=y) \ \& \ cBEL[x \neq y])$.
(16L) (a) $\exists x \exists y((x=a \ \& \ y=c) \ \& \ cBEL[x=y])$
     (b) $\exists x \exists y(((x=a \ \& \ y=c) \ \& \ x \neq y) \ \& \ cBEL[x=y])$.

The bad news for our analysis is that we cannot account for a *true reading* of (15) or (16) relative to the given assumptions about the referents of the names, and relative to any of the proposed candidates of logical forms. Our treatment of the denotation of individual constants and of assignments with respect to free variables does not allow us to assign other values to the occurrences of the variables 'x' or 'y' outside the scope of the attitude operator than to those occurrences of the variables inside the scope of 'BEL[]'. Hence, true readings of the distinguished formulas are not possible under the given conditions.[29]

Priest's account, however, has the advantage that he is able to interpret these formulas relative to the given conditions as true. He can interpret (15L)(a) and (b) on the basis of his account as true relative to an interpretation that assigns two different functions from worlds to identities to 'a' and 'b' that fulfil the following additional requirements: they have the same outputs relative to all closed worlds, but different outputs relative to some open worlds. The belief-states of c are represented by some of these exceptional open worlds.

Furthermore, Priest's analysis can account for the truth of (16L)(a) and (b) relative to an interpretation that assigns two different functions from worlds to identities to 'a' and 'c' that fulfil the following additional requirements: they have different outputs relative to all closed worlds, but identical outputs relative to some open worlds. The belief-states of c are represented by some of these exceptional open worlds.

This seems to be a clear advantage of Priest's proposal over our alternative proposal.[30] In light of the difficulties pointed out above with respect to the intuitive motivation of Priest's re-interpretation of the denotation of individual constants, this observation seems to be not good news for the viability of a semantic analysis of attitude ascription by a world semantic framework that conceives of attitude verbs as non-normal modal operators. One only seems to have a choice between two accounts with different weaknesses.

However, things are not as bad as they appear to be at first sight. There seems to be a relatively plausible way of modifying our account that also allows us to satisfy the fourth criterion of adequacy. This solution to our problem regarding (15) and (16) requires two significant changes.

Firstly, we have to reject the proposed *face-value* analyses of (15) and (16), and assign the following different logical forms to these sentences:

(15+L)(a) $\exists x \exists y((x=a \ \& \ y=b) \ \& \ cBEL[((x=a \ \& \ y=b) \ \& \ a \neq b)])$.
(16+L)(a) $\exists x \exists y((x=a \ \& \ y=c) \ \& \ cBEL[((x=a \ \& \ y=c) \ \& \ a=c)])$.

These alternative logical representations of (15) and (16), with respect to the embedded content aim to capture the identity relations that, according to our believers, obtain between certain real objects and the internal representations of these objects whose realizations are formally represented by certain non-normal worlds. In fact, these new proposed formal representations of (15) and (16) reveal that we have to distinguish a *third possible* reading of attitude ascriptions; namely a reading of sentences that apparently have a clear *de re* reading like (15) and (16). At face value, (15) seems to have the following *simple de re* reading:

(15.R) [a,b] cBEL[a=b].

However, our alternative analyses of (15) and (16), namely (15+L) and (16+L), show that we have to distinguish two *different* possible *de re* readings: a *pure de re* reading, that captures only the pure Russellian content of a *de re* attitude ascription, or an *internally linked de re* reading, where the ascriptions link the pure *de re* content with the internal mental *de re* representations of a content. Our new semantics of attitude ascriptions allows one not only to distinguish *de re* and *de dicto* readings in general but allows us to distinguish two different kinds of *de re* reading. An *internally linked de re* reading of (15) is formally captured by the logical form (15+L) according to our semantics. We can also add the following additional symbolism to provide a shorter and more transparent formal representation of this second kind of *de re* reading of a sentence like (15) in the following way:

(15R*) [a,b] cBEL[<a,b>a=b].

In this formula the pointed-brackets '<a,b>' are used as an abbreviation for the *linking condition* '(x=a & y=b) &', which is explicitly represented by (15+L).

Against this background, we now have three different comprehensive expressions for one kind of *de dicto* reading and two kinds of *de re* readings of attitude ascriptions in general. On this basis, we can also now distinguish a third and *internally linked de re* reading of our initial example sentence (1):

(1)   Peter assumes that Mark Twain is an author.

According to such a reading, (1) would have the following equivalent logical forms:

(1R+) $\exists x(x=a \ \& \ cBEL[x=a \ \& \ Aa])$.
(1R++) [a]cAss[<a>Aa].

In this case, (1R+) is the more *elaborated* formal representation and (1R++) the *abbreviated* representation of the very same content.[31]

However, our proposed adaptions of the logical forms of (15) and (16) alone are not sufficient to solve our problem with respect to possible true readings of (15) and (16). Relative to the presupposed assumptions concerning the denotations of the used individual constants 'a', 'b' and 'c', both logical forms still cannot be interpreted as true in our logical framework. Further adaptions are required.

Secondly, we have to admit that relative to non-normal worlds, not only logical *operators* can have a different interpretation than in normal worlds, but also logical *predicates* like the identity predicate. This means that attitude operators may also shift the extension of the identity predicate. These shifts under attitude operators should be conceived of in such a way that the extensional changes reflect true and false identifications of objects by a cognitive subject whose intentional states are realized by specific non-normal worlds. Hence, on the one hand, we have to change the truth- and falsity-conditions of atomic identity sentences in the following way:

V(<[s,t] s=t, w>,T)  iff   if w ∈ P, d(s,w) and d(t,w) are both defined in w and d(s,w) = d(t,w) or
if w ∈ N, d(s,w) and d(t,w) are both defined in w and <s,t> ∈ I(=, +,w).

V(<[s,t] s=t, w>,F)  iff   if w ∈ P, (d(s,w) or d(t,w) are undefined in w or d(s,w) ≠ d(t,w)) or
if w ∈ N, d(s,w) or d(t,w) are undefined in w or <s,t> ∈ I(=, −,w).

On the other hand, the interpretation function must now also assign extensions and anti-extensions to the identity predicate relative to open worlds that reflect true and false identifications of objects of those cognitive subjects whose intentional states are represented by these open worlds. So, for example, relative to those open worlds that represent the belief-states of c that are reported by (15), 'a' designates {o,1} and 'b' designates {o,2}. The extension of the identity predicate relative to these worlds contains at least the following elements: (a) <o,{o,1}>, (b) <o,{o,2}>. Furthermore, relative to those non-normal worlds that represent the belief-states of c that are reported by (16), 'a' designates {o,r} and 'c' designates {o,r}. The extension of the identity predicate relative to these worlds contains at least the following elements: (a) <{o,r},{o,r}>, (b) <o, {o,r}>, (c) <r, {o,r}>.

On the basis of these two adaptions of our formal framework we are now also in the position to analyse *internally linked de re* readings of ascriptions like (15) and (16). This completes the present outline of our semantic approach with respect to interaction of names and attitude verbs and epistemic modals.

# Notes

## Prolegomenon: The Diversity of Uses of Names in Natural Languages

1. Cf.: Frege (1892); Russell (1911).
2. Cf.: Frege (1892, 1906, 1918); Russell (1911, 1912, 1918, 1919); Quine (1948, 1960); Strawson (1952, 1959, 1974); Searle (1958, 1979, 1983); Wittgenstein (1953).
3. Cf.: Donnellan (1972); Kripke (1971, 1972, 1980).
4. Sainsbury (2005, 2).
5. Cf.: Burge (1973); Sommers (1980); Dever (1998); Elbourne (2005); Cumming (2008); Schoubye (2020).
6. Sainsbury (2005, 2).
7. Sainsbury (2005, 44).
8. This distinction very roughly corresponds with Kripke's distinction between a description theory that aims to determine the meaning of a name and a theory that only aims to fix the referent of a name. In my opinion, it is the true core of Kripke's distinction.
9. Cf.: Sainsbury (2005, 98).
10. This characterization is quite popular and can, for example, be found in Kripke (1972, 1980) and Cumming (2013).
11. At least relative to a popular interpretation of Searle (1958). This text is notoriously vague and hence can be interpreted in many different ways.
12. Cf.: Russell (1918); Kneale (1962); Bach (1987); Katz (1994, 2001); Geurts (1997).
13. Cf.: Loar (1976); Lewis (1984); Kroon (1987); Jackson (1998).
14. Mill (1843, 34).
15. Mill (1843, 31).
16. Cf.: Frances (1998, 703); Graham (1999, 555); Predelli (2004, 335).
17. Sentences are not true *simpliciter*, but true relative to a given set of parameters. Sentences can nevertheless be true in an absolute sense if the truth of a sentence is relativized to specific individual parameters.
18. Cf.: Salmon (2007, 3); Soames (2002, 204); Braun (2005, 596).
19. I use 'existence' for those people who believe that everthing exists, and 'presence' as substitute for such a general notion for all people who believe in non-existent objects.
20. Cf.: Kaplan (1989a,b).
21. Cf.: Kaplan (1978, 1989a).
22. Cf.: Kaplan (1989a,b); Salmon (1986, 1987, 1989); Soames (1989, 2002); Braun (2005).
23. Cf.: Kaplan (1989a,b).
24. Marti (2008, 47).
25. Cf.: Hawthorne and Manley (2012, 8–10).
26. Cf.: Evans (1982); McDowell (1984).
27. Cf.: Soames (1989, 2002); Salmon (1986, 1989).
28. Cf.: Adams and Stecker (1994).
29. Cf.: Braun (1993, 2005).

30 In Rami (2020) I argue in more detail against the viability of this strategy.
31 Cf.: Sainsbury (2005).
32 In Rami (2020) I develop a new semantics for empty proper names that overcomes some problems of the more standard-type single-domain free logic used in this book.
33 Cf.: Parsons (1980); Zalta (1983, 1988); Priest (2005, 2016); Berto (2013).
34 More on these options and my views on existence can be found in Rami (2014c, 2017a,b, 2018, 2020).
35 Cf.: Adams and Stecker (1994); Taylor (2000).
36 Cf.: Sainsbury (2005); Rami (2014c).
37 In Rami (2020) I offer a new and alternative semantics based on free logic that aims to overcome some problems of the more orthodox version of free logic used in this book. Therefore, there is also room for improvement in this respect.
38 Cf.: Salmon (1986, 1989); Soames (1987, 1989); Braun (1991, 1998); Predelli (2004, 2005).
39 Cf.: Schiffer (1977); Crimmins and Perry (1989); Crimmins (1992).
40 Cf.: Dummett (1973); Salmon (1986); Taschek (1992); Taylor (2003); Fine (2007); Sainsbury and Tye (2012).
41 Cf.: Evans (1982); Perry (2001); Recanati (1993, 2013, 2019).
42 Cf.: Kripke (2013).
43 Cf.: Adams, Fuller and Stecker (1997); Salmon (1998); Sainsbury (2009); Everett (2013); Kripke (2013).
44 Cf.: Kripke (1971, 1972, 1980).
45 Cf.: Burge (1973); Plantinga (1978); Kroon (1987); Jubien (1993); Stanley (1997); Elbourne (2005).
46 Cf.: Cohen (1980); Kaplan (1990); Taylor (2003).
47 Cf.: Zimmermann (2005); Textor (2005).
48 Cf.: Chalmers (2002, 2006).
49 See: Sloat (1969, 27); Burge (1973, 429).
50 For more on the different options and problems of this view see: Elugardo (2002); Rami (2014a, 2015); Gray (2017); Schoubye (2018).
51 Cf.: Burge (1973); Sawyer (2010).
52 Cf.: Sloat (1969); Elbourne (2005); Matushansky (2006, 2008); Fara (2015).
53 See: Geurts (1997, 321); Elbourne (2005, 181); Matushansky (2008, 601); Cumming (2008, 535).
54 One could test the difference between identity and predictive readings by means of modal embeddings. Only expressions with an identity reading, like 'The philosopher Saul Kripke', are merely weakly rigid designators. (See: Chap. 1).
55 Our last two challenges are also in some detail discussed in Soames (2002). However, in my opinion, he messed up these two different challenges and his analysis is by no means convincing. Also, see on this: Rabern (2015, 307–309).
56 That was famously pointed out in Kripke (1980, 26).
57 See on this: Rabern (2015, 300–301).
58 See on this: Rabern (2015, 309, 314–315).
59 Cf.: Moltmann (2020).
60 See on this: Rami (2015); Delgado (2019).
61 For a more detailed critique of the methodology of predicative views on proper names see: Rami (2014a, 2015); Schoubye (2018).
62 As I will show in detail in chapter 6.
63 It also has to be noticed that (especially classical) description theories of names have made the second methodological error. These theories focused too heavily on the

outlined challenges 1–4 and proposed a view on names that mainly allowed one to meet these challenges, but the initial and paradigmatic uses of names on this basis dropped out of their focus.

## 1 Proper Names and Rigidity

1. This chapter is a substantially revised version of Rami (2019). Reprinted by permission from Springer Nature.
2. Kripke (2011a, 9).
3. Kripke (1980, 48).
4. Cf.: Fitting and Mendelsohn (1998, 95–101); Priest (2008, 308–309).
5. Cf.: Fitting and Mendelsohn (1998, 101–105); Priest (2008, 329–331).
6. Cf.: Kripke (2011a, 10).
7. Cf.: Williamson (2002, 233). See also on this: Williamson (2013).
8. Cf.: Priest (2005, 14–15).
9. This distinction was to my knowledge coined in Salmon (1981, 32–36). It is also explained and used in an interesting overview article on this topic in Stanley (1997, 556).
10. Cf.: Hawthorne and Manley (2012, 11).
11. Cf.: Kaplan (1989a, 492–493).
12. Cf.: Kripke (1980, 21 fn. 21).
13. Cf.: Kripke (1980, 78).
14. Cf.: Kaplan (1973, 1989a); Salmon (1981).
15. See for other works that aim to interpret Kripke's notion of rigidity: Kaplan (1973, 1989a); Steinman (1985); Hughes (2004); Noonan (2013).
16. Cf.: Hawthorne and Manley (2012, 11). Hughes (2004, 20) distinguishes this kind of rigidity from the two already mentioned notions inspired by Kripke and calls it *inflexibility*.
17. Cf.: Putnam (1975, 231); Linsky (1977, 51); Lowe (2002, 89).
18. Cf.: Hughes (2004, 21–22).
19. Kripke (1980, 21 fn. 21).
20. Cf.: Recanati (1993, 111–113).
21. In Stanley (1997, 557), the distinction between *de jure* and *de facto* rigidity is drawn in a different way. According to him: 'An expression is a de jure rigid designator of an object just in case the semantical rules of the language unmediatedly link it to an object. All other rigid designators of objects are de facto rigid designators. [...] A de jure designator is supposed to denote what it denotes without the mediation of some concept of description.' This characterization is vaguer than Kripke's own characterization because it makes use of the vague and unclear notion of unmediated denotation. Furthermore, it also seems to lead to a different extension of both notions. According to this distinction, rigidified definite descriptions come out as *de facto*, because their reference is mediated by a predicate with a rigid application. In the following, I will make use of Kripke's original distinction.
22. Cf.: Kripke (2011a, 13; 1980, 48–49); Hughes (2004, 19–20); Noonan (2013, 61).
23. Cf.: Hughes (2004, 19–20).
24. One might claim that the new tests are less intuitive than the original ones. Certainly, the instances of the new schemas are also sentences of natural language and can be evaluated on an intuitive basis. However, the original examples might be from a distrubtional perspective more intuitive and natural.

25 Kripke (1980, 78); Kaplan (1989a, 492–493).
26 A partially overlapping defence strategy is proposed in Murday (2013, 235–237).
27 Cf.: Fine (2005, 329–332).
28 Cf.: Rami (2020, 6.3).
29 Cf.: Kaplan (1968, 201); Salmon (1998, 289).

Kaplan has suggested the example of the name 'Newman-1' that is introduced into use by means of the description 'The future person who will be born first in the twenty-second century'. There are at least two problems why this example is not a plausible example of the desired kind. Firstly, it is not metaphysically impossible that more than one person is born during the first seconds of 1 January 2100. Secondly, there is also the metaphysical possibility that the earth is destroyed in the twenty-first century and hence no persons are born anymore in the twenty-second century.

Salmon has suggested the example of the name 'Noman-0' that is introduced into use by means of the description 'The person that sprang from the union of a specific actual ovum O and a specific actual sperm S in a normal manner'. There are two problems that seem to show why this is not a plausible example of the desired kind. Firstly, even if the ovum and sperm are united in a normal manner, there are different metaphysically possible ways as to how they are exactly combined. Secondly, even after the union, genetic transformations are metaphysically possible that eventually lead to different possible individuals. Therefore, it is not guaranteed that the name 'Noman-0' picks out any single individual.

30 Cf.: Berto (2013, 209–213).
31 In Berto (2013, 211), an *alternative example* is suggested that has some related, but also some new problems. Berto imagines a case where there is a package of all parts that are required to build a certain Ikea bookshelf. Intuitively, one might claim that there is a single possible actually non-existent object that is the result of combining these parts in the correct way. Berto aims to name this possible object 'Georgina'. But there are several problems that concern this example, one of which is the example seems to be too under-determined. Normally, such packages of parts of Ikea bookshelves can be combined in different ways (as we all sadly know) and different combinations may, hence, lead to different possible individual bookshelves. However, even if we exclude this possibility and assume an Ikea bookshelf whose parts can only be assembled in a *single* way, there remain at least three other problems. On the one hand one might, as in our proposed case, claim that a possible *combination* of certain actual parts that eventually may lead to the creation of an actual object is itself not identical with a *genuine object*. On the other hand, the Ikea bookshelf is an artefact that is essentially designed to be assembled and disassembled again. Typical examples of this kind are *tents*. They are built to be assembled and disassembled many times. However, a tent in a disassembled state still seems to be an actually existing tent. Therefore, it also seems possible and plausible to argue that an Ikea bookshelf in a disassembled state is still an actually existing bookshelf. Hence, the example given by Berto leads (as the original examples proposed by Salmon and Kaplan) to more complications than our proposed knife example. Finally, because such a bookshelf has many different parts with the same size (the shelves), we also run into classical problems associated with the ship of Theseus (C.f.: Lowe (2002, ch. 2)). In this case, we have a ship that is constituted of 1000 similar ship-planks. In such more complicated cases, it is not clear how many parts could be changed without destroying the identity of an actually existing object. In our knife case there are only two main parts and it is in this case, I think, clear that any recombination of these main parts leads to the creation of a new object.

32 Kripke (1980, 4) [my emphasis added].
33 Kripke (1980, 14).
34 In Garson (2001, 280), this restriction is named (L) and considered as a local constraint.
35 See on this additional problem: Rami (2020).
36 Complete individual concepts contain information that allow one to determine with respect to all possible properties whether the represented individual has or lacks such a property.
37 That is, this property may only apply to a subset of all objects.
38 If they would have doubts in this respect, there is an interesting version of a conception of actualized accessible rigidity which restricts the class of referentially accessible objects with respect to the actual world relative to a subclass of the actually existing objects. Hence, also we have in principle a fifth interesting option.

## 2 Proper Names and Reference Determination

1 This chapter is a revised version of Rami (2016).
2 Kripke (1980, 96).
3 Kripke (1980, 135).
4 Cf.: Evans (1973); Kaplan (1973, 1990); Devitt (1981); Berger (2002); Perry (2001); Barker (2004); Sainsbury (2005).
5 Sainsbury (2005, 106).
6 Cf.: Kripke (1980, 8, fn. 9).
7 In this respect, Evans has a view similar to Kripke's: 'The practice of using the name *may* originate in a baptism, or in a situation where a speaker manifestly uses an expression which is not x's given name as if it were x's given name, whether knowingly (a nickname) or unknowingly (a mistake), in Evans (1982, 376) [my emphasis].
8 Kripke (1980, 162).
9 Sainsbury (2005, 121).
10 Kripke (1980, 8).
11 Kripke (1980, 8, fn. 9).
12 A sentence like (1) is the metalinguistic counterpart of (1*): There are many different Alfreds. Such a use of 'Alfred' is often called a predicative use of a name. I do not think that these uses provide good reasons for a predicative conception of names in general. I have shown in Rami (2014a) and Rami (2015) in detail how we can account for theses uses on the basis of a context-sensitive conception of names. There I also show why this account is preferable to a predicative view of proper names.
13 That is Kaplan's name for specific names. I follow Sainsbury (2015) and use the other label in the following.
14 Kaplan (1990, 111).
15 Kaplan (1990, 108).
16 That is, if we translate sentences like (1) and (2) into a formal language, we have to represent their different meanings by means of different formal representations with different truth-conditions.
17 Alternatively, one might claim that a quotation name like '"Peter"' can only be used to refer to generic names. But such a restriction seems to be implausible and *ad hoc*. The quoted passage from Kaplan at least suggests that Kaplan himself does not explicitly hold such a radical view, because he uses quotation names there to refer to both kinds of names.

18 I use the relation expressed by 'x is an instance of y' to capture the essential ontological connection between specific and generic names.
19 This view is similar to a view that holds that propositions are primary bearers of truth-values and that sentences that express propositions are only in a derived sense true or false.
20 We do not multiply the readings of (1) and (2) to four readings (three false and one true reading), if we regard the expressions 'name' and 'bearer' as systematically ambiguous. Two logically possible readings are excluded as semantically not well-formed. Therefore, a sentence like (1) now has a true and a false reading.
21 In Jeshion (2015, 380) the view is defended that generic names can be used to function as name-predicates in sentences like 'Every Peter that I know is nice'. That does not seem to be a viable option. According to the Kripke–Kaplan view, I can use 'the name "Peter"' to refer to a generic name, but I cannot use this expression to designate the extension of the predicate 'is a Peter'.
22 Cf.: Hawthorne and Lepore (2011, 453).
23 Cf.: Kaplan (1990, 111).
24 Cf.: Recanati (1993); Pelczar and Rainsbury (1998); Matushansky (2008).
25 Cf.: Gray (2017).
26 Cf.: Textor (2005).
27 Certainly, it is parasitic in the sense that it exploits the storage and its source to determine the referent of a name, but it does not borrow its referent from a preceding use of this name.
28 In a somewhat similar way, it is argued in McKinsey (2011, §2.1) against the thesis that all semantically correct uses of names are deferential (=parasitic).
29 Instead of conventionalized branches of a name-using practice, we could also speak of *conventionalized referential sub-practices* or of *conventionalized referential name-using practices (simpliciter)*.
30 Cf.: Strawson (1950).
31 This problem was independently pointed out to me by Mark Textor and Manuel García-Carpintero.
32 Cf.: García-Carpintero (2018, 1151).
33 In McKinsey (2011, 330–331), Kripke's preference for an exclusively deferential reference determination is explained by his tendency to mainly focus on his famous counter-examples against a description theory of reference determination.
34 Cf.: Searle and Vanderveken (1985, 56–57, 210–211); Vanderveken (1990, 126, 204).
35 Cf.: Bach and Harnish (1979, 110–115).
36 Cf.: Alston (2000, 86–87).
37 Maybe there are some cultures where the bearing of a name has certain additional social consequences and therefore the act of withdrawing a name might have certain important consequences, but in most of our Western cultures this is not the case.
38 By a *name-change* I mean an event or series of events relative to which a certain individual 'loses' a former name and acquires a new name instead.
39 This was pointed out to me by Hans Kamp.
40 Cf.: Marti (2015, §3).
41 This is a slight modification of an example that was proposed by Hans Kamp at a conference on proper names in Göttingen in September 2011. See also on this issue Textor (2010) and Sainsbury (2015).
42 See: Sainsbury (2015).
43 Cf.: Evans (1985, 11).
44 Cf.: McKinsey (1976, 236–237).

45 Cf.: McKinsey (2011, 329–330).
46 In this important respect I completely agree with McKinsey (2011).

## 3 Proper Names as Use-Sensitive Expressions

1 This chapter is a substantially revised version of Rami (2014b). Reprinted by permission from Springer Nature.
2 It is rejected by a group of very important and prominent philosophers of language: Bach, Evans, Fine, Donnellan, Kaplan, Kripke, Perry, Sainsbury, Salmon and Soames.
3 Cf.: Burks (1951); Burge (1973); Cohen (1980); Zimmermann and Lerner (1991); Recanati (1993); Pelczar and Rainsbury (1998); Pelczar (2001); Elbourne (2005); Matushansky (2008); Sawyer (2010); Tiedke (2011) and Voltolini (2016).
4 Examples of this kind are: Burks (1951); Cohen (1980); Sommers (1980) and Sawyer (2010).
5 *Pure indexicals* like 'I' are conceived of as simple individual constants in Kaplan (1978, 1989a).
6 *True demonstratives* like 'that' are represented as complex expressions of the form 'dthat[the ϕ]' in Kaplan (1978, 1989a).
7 Cf.: Kaplan (1978, 86–97; 1989a, 541–553).
8 Cf.: Predelli (2005, 20; 2012, 550).
9 This view is inspired by Predelli (2012, 555).
10 Cf.: Sommers (1980); Dever (1998); Cumming (2008); Schoubye (2017, 2020).
11 Cf.: Kripke (1980, 82–92).
12 In principle there seem to be two different ways to determine the referent of a mental representation in a causal way: either by means of the *original* causal source, or by means of the *dominant* causal source.
13 In a meeting, someone may point to a specific person and say, 'Peter James is our representative in London'. It seems to be plausible to assume that 'Peter James' is used with the mentioned kind of intention.
14 There are people that are talking about the famous philosopher John Perry. Someone overhears the conversation and says: 'Who is John Perry?'
15 *Parasitic acts of identification* are acts where a speaker identifies the referent of his use of a name by means of exploiting some preceding act of reference by himself or other speakers. In general, these are acts of identification where the reference is 'borrowed' from some pre-existing use of a name.
16 A person may enter a stage, a spotlight may shine on him, and he gets announced by someone who utters, 'We are very proud to present you Peter James.' In this case it is very plausible to assume that the name is used accompanied by an object-related referential intention.
17 Cases of this kind that concern the introduction of a name are presented and discussed in Sainsbury (2005, 107–122).
18 See chapter 2, second section, 'Against a too fine-grained individuation of paper names', for a detailed presentation of these two worries.
19 This view is defended in Delgado (2018, 2019).
20 Cf.: Gray (2018).
21 Cf.: Rami (2015) and Schoubye (2017).
22 This objection was brought to my attention by Aidan Gray.

23 This can be shown by examples like: (E1) He *houdinied* his way out of the trouble. (E1) Yesterday, I *googled* my name. (E2) That was a real *Chuck Norris* deed by Paul. (E3) He shot at the goal *in a CR7-style*. Cf.: Delgado (2019, 3.2.5).
24 A similar example is provided in Burge (1973, 435–436), Geurts (1997, 321) and Cumming (2008, 526, 535).
25 Similar examples are provided in Geurts (1997, 321).
26 Cf.: King (2012, 367–369).
27 According to this view, (10) has the logical form: $\exists x \exists y$(Mary (x) & Paul (y) & Joined the Diogenes Club yesterday (x) & Joined the Diogenes Club yesterday (y) & Nice person (x)). Cf.: Cumming (2008, 535–536).
28 A Fregean theory of definite descriptions holds that definite descriptions are complex singular terms that can either refer to a single object or to no object at all. An atomic sentence that contains a definite description that does not refer to a (single) object is, according to this view, neither true nor false. Cf.: Hawthorne and Manley (2012, 181–184).
29 Cf.: Elbourne (2005, 97, 169–173, 180–181).
30 According to this view, (11) has the logical form: $\forall x \forall y$(((Boy (x) & (Girl (y) & Mary (y))) & Love (x,y)) $\rightarrow$ Admire (x, ($\iota z$)(Mary(z) & z=y))). Cf.: Burge (1973, 433); Elbourne (2005, 97, 169–173, 180–181).
31 Cf.: Cumming (2008, 525–526).
32 Cf.: Burge (1973, 432, 435–436).
33 An example of this sort is: *At least one man thinks that he has lost someone.*
34 An example of this sort is: *Every farmer who owns a donkey, beats it.*
35 Cf.: King (2012, 368–369).
36 The view on names proposed by Elbourne faces an analogous problem that is discussed below.
37 There are also sentences that have a similar structure to (11), but intuitively do not have the proposed anaphoric reading: *Every man, who loves a girl named 'Mary', will invite Mary for dinner.* For most people this sentence only has a reading relative to which 'Mary' refers to a single person. Cf.: Elbourne (2005, 180).
38 Cf.: Hawthorne and Manley (2012, 11).
39 In the context of our examples the expression 'is a Mary' and 'is a bearer of the name "Mary"' can be conceived as semantically equivalent.
40 Cf.: Burge (1973); Sawyer (2010).
41 In this context we take into account the 'Bob Dylan' example of chapter 2. We were standing in front of a Dylan-poster that per coincidence bears the name 'Bob Dylan', uttering 'Bob Dylan will soon give a concert in Bochum'. If we substitute 'Bob Dylan' with 'That Bob Dylan' in this sentence, the reading that refers to the imposter would be not only the dominant, but in this context the only available reading.
42 Cf.: Cohen (1980, 149–150); Bach (1987, 140).
43 Cf.: King (2006, 148–149).
44 Cf.: Predelli (2012, 548; 2013, 6–7); Zimmermann (2012, 2361).
45 char(e) = the character of the expression 'e'; char(e)(c) = the content of 'e' with respect to c. Cf.: Predelli (2013, 13).
46 Cf.: Zimmermann and Lerner (1991, 353–355). See also Haas-Spohn (1995).
47 Cf.: Recanati (1993, 138–143).
48 Cf.: Pelczar and Rainsbury (1998, 294–298); Pelczar (2001, 138); Tiedke (2011, 715–718). See also Matushansky (2008, 591–595) for a cross-over of the views given by Recanati (1993) and Pelczar and Rainsbury (1998).

49 Cf.: Kripke (1980, 90–97); Zimmermann and Lerner (1991, 354); Sainsbury (2005, 106–124).
50 Cf.: Textor (2010, 112). A variation of an example suggested by Hans Kamp is the following: *The tyrant utters: I hereby name every male human being that was born in my empire yesterday* Vladimir. See also Sainsbury (2015).
51 An example of a name with two different origins that link this name to one and the same object is the following. By coincidence, two different tribes, which have no contact with each other, name the very same mountain 'Ateb'. The name is used by both tribes independently for a certain while, but then it happens that the two tribes get in contact and a war breaks out. One of the tribes wins and the remaining people merge to one tribe. Against this background, the two existing name-using practices concerning the name 'Ateb' merge to one practice.

An example of a name with two different origins with two different objects is the following. There are twins that live in two different villages. The inhabitants of both villages are not aware of the existence of the other twin. One village introduces and establishes the use of the name 'Goldilocks' for one twin. The other village uses the same name for the other twin. At a certain time one of the villages is destroyed completely in a war and one of the twins dies unnoticed during this war. The remaining inhabitants of the destroyed village become inhabitants of the other village and the two name-using practices concerning the name 'Goldilocks' merge to one practice with one referent.
52 Cf.: Pelczar and Rainsbury (1998, 254).
53 Cf.: Recanati (1993, 138–140); Perry (2001, 102–113).
54 I think Perry is right if he conceives naming-conventions as *permissive* conventions. Cf.: Perry (2001, 103–105, 109) and Korta and Perry (2011, 75). If a certain object x is the bearer of a name 'N', then it is possible to use the name 'N' to refer to the object x in a felicitous way. Naming-conventions are on this basis certain norms that regulate the felicitous use of specific names. But it might be doubted whether instances of such a convention or norm can be *exploited* either on the basis of the ambiguity view or the indexical view to *determine* the referent of a single proper name. This *explanatory use* of these conventions does not make sense to me, because I do not see that there is a reference-determining link that can be provided by such a convention. I think they can at most be used to *constrain* adequate referents of a proper name.
55 This objection was pointed out to me by an anonymous reviewer.
56 '$c_w$' refers to the possible world of the context c; '$c_a$' refers to the agent of the context c; '$c_t$' refers to the time of the context c.
57 On the basis of this new free semantics for KLD, someone might be worried about the fully compositional nature of the truth-conditions of sentences that contain empty names. A possibility to face such a worry is outlined in Rami (2020) and could rather easily be implement into our outlined semantics.
58 This is an example borrowed from Ziff (1977, 321). It was pointed out to me by Mark Textor. However, how essential the use of stress (focus) is in this case was neither mentioned by Ziff nor Textor.
59 There is also a variation of this example, which alternatively makes use of the apposition 'as you call him', which makes it more plausible to interpret the stressed use of 'Peter Sanders' as a metalinguistic use. (This was pointed out to me by Jan Köpping.) However, an anaphoric interpretation of the demonstrative 'this name' relative to (13) is only one of different options. We could also substitute 'this name' with 'the name "Peter Sanders"' in (13) to make a metalinguistic interpretation of the used name 'Peter Sanders' less plausible.

60 Just for the sake of simplicity I use (IC4) instead of (IC5) as a basis.
61 '$c_{ad}$' refers to the addressee of the context c.
62 Cf.: Saul (1997, 103) and Zimmermann (2005, 55–62).
63 Cf.: Zimmermann (2005, 56–59, 61).
64 A similar example is used in Korta and Perry (2011, 75).
65 I am following Predelli (2012, 557–560; 2013, 192–196), where a very similar strategy is used to solve the corresponding problem in the case of bare-boned demonstratives.
66 Cf.: Taylor (2003, 6–8). This default *expectation* concerns a specific range of relative closeness: but the use of multiple occurrences of a single demonstrative expression as arguments of the identity predicate are exceptions. (Thanks to Christian Beyer for reminding me of this point.)
67 Cf.: Dever (1998, §2.3.2.4.2). This default *expectation* depends on a specific closeness constraint: it concerns occurrences that are relatively close to each other, but not too close. If, for example, two occurrences of a single name are arguments of the very same predicate as in 'Robert hates Robert' or (5), then the default expectation is different. (Thanks to Peter Ridley for reminding me of this data.)
68 It seems to be more difficult to apply such an approach to salience-based indexical views, because it might be questioned that it is meaningful to relativize the salience of a certain object to an occurrence of a proper name in a sentence.
69 This conception is also compatible with so-called mid-sentence shifts of the context of use, but it is not committed to such shifts to account for the mentioned data.
70 Possibly, the use of pointing gestures in such an example might invite some people to the reaction that the mentioned uses are not literally uses of proper names, but masked uses of complex demonstratives like '[That] Alfred Merker', where the demonstrative expression 'that' is skipped out of sheer convenience. For those people I have two things to offer: firstly, we could just skip the additions that indicate a demonstrative use of names; secondly, we could add instead modifiers like 'from Germany' and 'from Austria' or appositives like ', who works at the University of Göttingen' and ', who works at the Ruhr-University Bochum'. This shows that there is a possible version of our example-argument that contains different uses of the same name with different referents.
71 Cf.: Reichenbach (1947).
72 This is in the specific and coarse-grained sense that we have outlined in chapter 2. It is important to notice that this version of our semantics is the *simplified* version of the view that we have defended in chapter 2. According to the *sophisticated* version of our view, a semantically and meta-semantically correct use of a name 'N', must not only (a) refer to a bearer of this name, but this use must also (b) be part of a certain branch of a name-using practice. According to the *simplified* version, (a) by itself is sufficient for (meta-) semantic correctness. The development of the sophisticated version would have required the introduction of tree-like formal representations of uses of names. Structure-wise a specific version of temporal modal logic with branching-times might be the right choice for this purpose. I leave the development of this much more complex formal apparatus for future research.
73 Cf.: Kripke (1979).
74 For this purpose, we also have to give the existence predicate a specific meaning. Namely, a sentence of the form 'Exist [n(i)]' comes out as true if 'n(i)' denotes something; otherwise such a sentence is false.
75 This is the representation relative to our Fregean alternative.
76 One could also extend this approach to the phenomenon of *past names* as I did in Rami (2014b). Against this background, unrestricted and restricted names would have

the same truth-conditional meaning, but a different contextual constraint. Hence, 'Leningrad has more than a hundred thousand inhabitants' would literally express a true content that is use-conditionally odd or infelicitous. However, it is very difficult to specify the use-conditional constraint on this basis and relate the uses of names to the times of evaluation of sentences that contain these names.

77 For some time and under the influence of Charles Travis and some of his pupils I preferred the more progressive version. See for an older version of this sort of semantics for names Rami (2014b). I now have a tendency towards the more conservative version.

# 4 The Fictional Uses of Proper Names

1 There are different views on the exact ontological status of fictional objects. Some believe that they are abstract existing objects, cf.: Kripke (1973); van Inwagen (1977); Wolterstorff (1980); Thomasson (1990); Schiffer (1996); Salmon (1998); Voltolini (2006). Others believe that they are non-existent objects, cf.: Routley (1980); Parsons (1980); Zalta (1983, 1988); Priest (2005, 2016); Berto (2013).
2 Cf.: Kripke (2013).
3 Cf.: Braun (1993); Künne (2007a); Adams, Fuller and Stecker (1997).
4 From a logical point of view, non-normal worlds can be incomplete or inconsistent or both. Normal worlds are always complete and consistent and, hence, possible alternatives to the actual world.
5 Cf.: Sainsbury (2005, 91–92).
6 Probably this is even too strong if one also wants to include flare guns and airsoft guns. Against this background, the killing- or wounding-function only seems to be a functional feature of a paradigm sub-class of guns. This problem was pointed out to me by Jan Stühring.
7 There are also significant semantic and pragmatic differences between names and third-person personal pronouns. Firstly, proper names only seem to have pragmatic anaphoric uses, but they do not have bound anaphoric uses. Some people have argued that names also have bound uses, but, I think, these apparent bound uses are much too restricted and context-sensitive to count as genuine examples of bound uses. Secondly, only in the case of third-person personal pronouns does a demonstrative identification of the semantic referent in some sense seem to be required, while a demonstrative identification is only a possible option in the case of names. Thirdly, predicative uses of third-person personal pronouns are much more syntactically restricted than predicative uses of proper names. Fourthly, names and third-person personal pronouns have different pragmatic profiles in the case of pragmatic anaphoric uses. The repeated use of the same name in a single discourse automatically triggers the assumption of co-referential uses, while the repeated use of the same third-person personal pronouns in a single discourse triggers the assumption of non-co-referential uses.
8 We may consider a scenario, for example, where the name 'Neptune' was introduced by means of an act of naming that aimed to pick out the planet that causes the perturbation in the Uranus orbit, whichever planet this might be.
9 Cf.: Sainsbury (2005, 86–90).
10 Cf.: Burge (1973); Sainsbury (2005).
11 Cf.: Lehmann (1994); Rami (2014c).
12 For people that have doubts whether such a semantics can offer a fully compositional semantics even with respect to sentences that contain a singular term that lacks a

referent I have recently developed an alternative version of this semantic framework that is fully compositional in Rami (2020).
13 The exact content of this premise depends on two issues: (a) whether we make use of a fine-grained or coarse-grained individuation of proper names; and (b) whether we conceive of names as (i) semantically ambiguous, (ii) pragmatically ambiguous or (iii) indexical expressions. According to the coarse-grained individuation, every name can literally have more than one bearer. According to the fine-grained individuation, every name has literally at most one bearer. This view has the consequence that there are, for example, different same-spelled names of the form 'Peter Sutton', for each bearer. There only seem to be three prima facie plausible combinations of the views mentioned under (a) and (b). Firstly, there is a view that makes use of the fine-grained individuation of names and interprets names as semantically ambiguous. According to this view, a name like 'Peter' is in a similar way ambiguous as the word 'bank'. (P4) is literally true on this basis. Secondly, there is a view that makes use of the coarse-grained individuation of names and interprets names as pragmatically ambiguous. According to this view, (P4) is not literally true, but the intended content of (P4) can be captured by the more explicit: *It is the function of every proper name to refer to a single object relative to a use of this name.* Secondly, there is a view that makes use of the coarse-grained individuation of names and interprets names as indexical expressions. According to this view, (P4) is also not literally true, but the intended content of (P4) can be captured by the more explicit: *It is the function of every proper name to refer to a single object relative to a context of use of this name.*
14 For a recent attempt that follows this path see Predelli (2017, chap. 8; 2020).
15 Cf.: Searle (1979, 19–20).
16 I distinguish between *external* and *internal* narrators. The external narrator is the author or fiction-maker himself. An internal narrator may be an element of fiction of a specific sub-variety. The external narrators tells the story externally from a gods-eye point of view. The internal narrator represents what is the case according to fiction from an internal fictional point of view. If an external narrator tells the story in an inconsistent way, or tries to fool the reader with respect to certain aspects of the story, he/she should be regarded as an unreliable narrator. Internal fictional narrators may also be construed by the fiction-maker as partially inconsistent or with the purpose to mislead the readers at least relative to certain episodes of a story. Typically, these false paths are corrected in the due course of the development of a story.
17 Cf.: Sainsbury (2014); Voltolini (2019).
18 Cf. for a similar kind of example, Künne (2007b, appendix §3).
19 Cf.: Friend (2012).
20 In the relevant literature these verbs are very often called 'intensional transitive verbs'. See on this, for example Zimmermann (1993) and Forbes (2006). In my opinion, this is a misnomer; these verbs are hyper-intensional. I prefer to call them 'intentional transitive verbs' because they describe or attribute object-related intentional states to cognitive subjects.

# 5 Apparent Predicative Uses of Proper Names

1 This chapter is a substantially revised and shortened version of Rami (2015). Reprinted by permission from Springer Nature.
2 Cf.: Rami (2014a).

3   Cf.: Sloat (1969, 27); Burge (1973, 429); Elbourne (2005, 170–171).
4   Cf.: Boer (1975, 390). See also: Jeshion (2015, 372).
5   Cf.: Nunberg (1995, 117); Fara (2012, 7); Jeshion (2015, 371).
6   Cf.: Burge (1973, 429); Boer (1975, 399); Fara (2012, 6); Jeshion (2015, 371).
7   Cf.: Nunberg (1979, 1995, 2004); Recanati (2003).
8   This is especially directed against such attempts in Leckie (2013) and Jeshion (2015).
9   Cf.: Nunberg (1995, 109, 113, 116); Recanati (2003, 26–29).
10  Cf.: Nunberg (1995, 112).
11  According to Nunberg, this feature distinguishes metonymys from metaphors. Cf.: Nunberg (1995, 113).
12  Cf.: Nunberg (1995, 112–113).
13  Cf.: Nunberg (2004, 351–354).
14  Cf.: Nunberg (1995, 115).
15  Cf.: Nunberg (1995, 116–119).
16  Cf.: Nunberg (1995, 117).
17  Cf.: Fara (2012, 11–13).
18  Nunberg points out that these rules might have exceptions because they are subject to general conditions of noteworthiness. Cf.: Nunberg (1995, 117).
19  Cf.: Nunberg (1995, 116–119).
20  Cf.: Boer (1975, 391).
21  Such a view seems to be implausible if we individuate names by means of their spelling or pronunciation. Cf.: Boer (1975, 390–391). But the situation changes if we make use of a more plausible approach that individuates names in the historical way that we have proposed.
22  Cf.: Leckie (2013, 5.1); Jeshion (2015, 383–385); García-Carpintero (2018, 1154–1159).
23  Cf.: Jeshion (2015, 381–383).
24  This account is defended in Leckie (2013, 5.2).
25  'Alfred$_1$' can be used in two different ways: as an expression that stands for a specific name or for an instant use of the ordinary name 'Alfred'. The difference can be tracked back to the mentioned two main accounts concerning the individuation of names.
26  The same problem, for example, would affect a proposal that holds that ordinary proper names are ambiguous and tries to capture the meaning of 'is an Alfred' according to its original use on the basis of a disjunction like '$x$ = Alfred$_1$ or $x$ = Alfred$_2$ or … or $x$ = Alfred$_n$'. Such a proposal also has an additional problem, because there can be objects that do not bear the name 'Alfred' in the actual world, but bear this name in some different possible world.
27  Cf.: Predelli (2013, 68).
28  Via google, I have found evidence for both kinds of derived predicative uses of the pronouns 'she' and 'he'.
29  Cf. Recanati (2003, Chs 2 and 9).
30  This example was pointed out to me by an anonymous referee of the journal *Philosophical Studies*.
31  It is difficult to translate this sentence into English, therefore, I will only describe the semantics of the two verbs under discussion.
32  For more details on such applications to other semantics of names see Rami (2015) and Schoubye (2017).

# 6 Apparent Anaphoric Uses of Proper Names

1. Burge (1973, 435–436).
2. Cumming (2008, 535).
3. Geurts (1997, 321).
4. Elbourne (2005, 181).
5. Bach (1987, 146–147); see also: Geurts (1997, 323).
6. Cf.: Maier (2009, 298–300).
7. Cf.: Hawthorne and Manley (2012, 236).
8. Brian Rabern and Jan Köpping suggested this to me.
9. Jan Köpping agrees with me with respect to this diagnosis.
10. Cf.: Burge (1973, 428–434).
11. Cf.: Burge (1973, 433).
12. A related more recent covert description account that also aims to capture certain bound uses of proper names is defended in Fara (2015).
13. Cf.: Elbourne (2005, 167–173).
14. This similarity is a big advantage of Elbourne (2005) over Fara (2015). Fara does not offer a formal semantic version of her view, hence it is unclear how she intends to apply her view to anaphoric uses of names.
15. Cf.: Donnellan (1966).
16. An account that is, with respect to bound uses of names, very similar to Cumming's position is defended in Schoubye (2018, 2020).
17. Cf.: Cumming (2008, 526, 535–543).
18. That is a solution Cumming could use to provide a solution to our problem.
19. Cf.: Schoubye (2018, 2020).
20. It also would not help to transfer these semantic contraining conditions to the use-conditional level. Sentences (12) and (13) are fine as they stand. They do not violate any use-conditional norm.
21. Cf.: Kratzer (1998, 2009).
22. Cf.: Elbourne (2005, 180).
23. Cf.: Horn (2004); Birner (2013, 64–66).
24. The interesting similarity between this case and case (22) is that both cases are driven by habitual background assumptions.
25. Just to mention an interesting side issue. There are other atomic semantic expressions that are neither names nor definite descriptions that clearly have anaphoric uses bound by nominal quantifiers. Expressions like 'Mum' and 'God': (X) In every monotheistic religion, **God** is all-mighty. (Y) For most families, **Mum** is the most beloved person. Our account at least predicts a significant difference between names and such cases. However, there are other people who have other opinions on this issue: Gray (2017).
26. The fact that examples like (29) and (30) contain focus particles was pointed out to me by Sarah Zobel.
27. Maybe in both cases the addition of stress with respect to both adjectives is additionally required.
28. Elbourne (2005, 181).

# 7 Proper Names in Hyperintensional Contexts

1. Cf.: Frege (1892, 33–34); Forbes (2006, 12–13); Sainsbury (2009, 127).

2 Cf.: Sainsbury (2009, 126).
3 Cf.: Sainsbury (2009, 127).
4 Cf.: Kaplan (1968); Salmon (1989); Somes (1989); Crimmins and Perry (1989); Recanati (1993, 2000); Forbes (2006); McKay (2005); Nelson (2019).
5 Cf.: Russell (1905).
6 This scope distinction is proposed in Evans (1982, 345) and Sainsbury (2005, 70-71).
7 Technically, there are different ways to implement this feature. One could assign to each expression two different sorts of intensions or extensions: an actual and a possible intension/extension. On this basis, modal operators shift the intension/extension from the possible to the actual. Alternatively, one could specify the semantics of modal operators in such a way that they fix the intension/extension of embedded individual constants to their actual denotation.
8 Cf.: Gluer and Pagin (2006, 2014).
9 Cf.: Kripke (1980, 10-15).
10 Cf.: Cumming (2008); Santorio (2012). Cumming literally conceives of proper names as *variables*. But the basic idea behind the approach remains the same if we consider names as *individual constants*. For a very interesting critique of the approach of Cumming concerning attitude ascriptions see Pickel (2015).
11 Cf.: Rabern (2018, 13-16).
12 Cf.: Santorio (2012, 377).
13 The *locus classicus* of this kind of analysis is Hintikka (1962). See also: Heim and Kratzer (1998, ch. 12); Zimmermann and Sternefeld (2013, 8.5).
14 Cf.: Priest (2005, 2016); Ripley (2012).
15 Cf.: Priest (2008, ch. 4, 8, 18, 22).
16 I have slightly simplified the semantics for our purposes in this chapter. Priest clearly distinguishes inconsistent and open (incomplete) worlds where everything is possible.
17 With respect to atomic identity sentences we in principle have again the choice between an ordinary and an extraordinary interpretation. For the sake of simplicity, we will only explicitly introduce the ordinary semantics. However, in case of atomic existential sentences the ordinary semantics seems to be the only plausible choice.
18 In Priest (2005, 2016) these truth-conditions are more complex to guarantee that no tautology is trivially believed by anyone. I have simplified the semantics for our purposes here.
19 See: Priest (2005, 12, 20-25).
20 Cf.: Priest (2008, 384-385).
21 An appropriate solution of the paradoxes of strict implication seems to require additional modifications of the truth- and falsity-conditions of strict implications. However, this problem is not the concern of this essay, and therefore I will leave it aside, and use provisionally the standard truth- and falsity-conditions of strict implications.
22 Cf.: Priest (2016, 10).
23 Cf.: Santorio (2012, section 3.3).
24 Cf.: Priest (2005, 42-47; 2008, 367-376).
25 Cf.: Priest (2005, 43-44).
26 Cf.: Priest (2008, 376). See also: Priest (2005, 43-47; 2016, 2.1).
27 Cf.: Hale (2007, 2.2).
28 Priest (2016, 238).

29 One could solve this problem with respect to (15L) by making use of the resources of a non-standard interpretation of the negation operator with respect to non-normal worlds. However, such a solution to our problem seems to be *ad hoc* and not motivated in a plausible and systematic way.

30 Interestingly, the following possibly true *de re* ascription neither provides a problem for Priest's account, nor for our account, although we conceive of existence as a logical property in opposition to Priest:

(X) Mark Twain is such that Peter believes that he does not exist.

According to our account and relative to Priest's account, this sentence receives the following logical from:

(XL) $\exists x(x=a \land cBEL[\neg E!x])$.

Priest can account for the truth of (XL) because he conceives of 'E!' as a discriminating predicate and might therefore exclude the output of the function that is the denotation of 'a' from the extension of 'E!' relative to an open world that represents a belief-state of c. We, on the other hand, can also account for the truth of (XL), although we conceive of 'E!' as a non-discriminating predicate. On the basis of (C1), we are allowed to exclude the actual referent of 'a' from the domain of the non-normal worlds that represent the belief-states of c.

31 There is also a third possible alternative *de re reading* that our account allows us to distinguish and which is represented by the logical form $\exists x(cBEL[x=a \land Aa])$. Such a logical form might be useful to represent belief ascriptions with a stressed use of a proper name, where the stress indicates that the used name is understood by the attitude holder in a non-literal way: Peter assumes that MARK TWAIN is an author.

# Bibliography

Adams, F. and Stecker, R. (1994) 'Vacuous Singular Terms', *Mind and Language* 9, 387–401.
Adams, F., Fuller, G., and Stecker, R. (1997) 'The Semantics of Fictional Names', *Pacific Philosophical Quarterly* 78, 128–148.
Alston, W. P. (2000) *Illocutionary Acts and Sentence Meaning*, Ithaca, NY: Cornell University Press.
Bach, K. (1987 [1993]) *Thought and Reference*, 2nd Edition, Oxford: Clarendon Press.
Bach, K. (2002) 'Giorgione was So-Called Because of his Name', *Philosophical Perspectives* 16, 73–103.
Bach, K. and Harnish, R. (1979) *Linguistic Communication and Speech Acts*, Cambridge, MA: MIT Press.
Barker, S. J. (2004) *Renewing Meaning: A Speech-Act Theoretic Approach*, Oxford: Clarendon Press.
Berger, A. (2002) *Terms and Truth*, Cambridge, MA: MIT Press.
Berto, F. (2013) *Existence as a Real Property*, Dordrecht: Springer.
Birner, B. J. (2013) *Introduction to Pragmatics*, Oxford: Wiley-Blackwell.
Boer, S. E. (1975) 'Proper Names as Predicates', *Philosophical Studies* 27, 389–400.
Borg, E. (2000) 'Complex Demonstratives', *Philosophical Studies* 97, 229–249.
Braun, D. (1991) 'Proper Names, Cognitive Contents, and Beliefs', *Philosophical Studies* 62, 289–305.
Braun, D. (1993) 'Empty Names', *Noûs* 27, 449–469.
Braun, D. (1994) 'Structured Character and Complex Demonstratives', *Philosophical Studies* 74, 193–219.
Braun, D. (1998) 'Understanding Belief Reports', *Philosophical Review* 107, 555–595.
Braun, D. (2005) 'Empty Names, Fictional Names, Mythical Names', *Noûs* 39, 596–631.
Burge, T. (1973) 'Reference and Proper Names', *Journal of Philosophy* 70, 425–439.
Burge, T. (1974) 'Truth and Singular Terms', *Noûs* 8, 309–325.
Burks, A. W. (1951) 'A Theory of Proper Names', *Philosophical Studies* 2, 36–45.
Chalmers, D. (2002) 'On Sense and Intension', *Philosophical Perspectives* 16, 135–182.
Chalmers, D. (2006) 'The Foundations of Two-Dimensional Semantics', in García-Carpintero, M. and Macia, J. (eds), *Two-Dimensional Semantics: Foundations and Applications*, Oxford: Oxford University Press, 55–140.
Cocchiarella, N. (1966) 'A Logic of Actual and Possible Objects', *Journal of Symbolic Logic* 31, 688.
Cohen, J. L. (1980) 'The Individuation of Proper Names', in Van Straaten, Z. (ed.), *Philosophical Subjects*, Oxford: Oxford University Press, 140–163.
Crimmins, M. (1992) *Talk about Beliefs*, Cambridge, MA: MIT Press.
Crimmins, M. and Perry, J. (1989) 'The Prince and the Phone Booth: Reporting Puzzling Beliefs', *Journal of Philosophy* 86: 685–711.
Cumming, S. (2008) 'Variablism', *Philosophical Review* 117, 525–554.
Cumming, S. (2013) 'Names', in Zalta, E. N. (ed.), *The Stanford Encyclopedia of Philosophy*

(Spring 2013 Edition), URL = <http://plato.stanford.edu/archives/spr2013/entries/names/>.
Currie, G. (1990) *The Nature of Fiction*, Cambridge: Cambridge University Press.
Delgado, L. (2018) *David, Some Davids, and All Davids: Reference, Category Change, and Bearerhood*, Doctoral Thesis: University of Barcelona.
Delgado, L. (2019) 'Between Singularity and Generality: The Semantic Life of Proper Names', *Linguistics and Philosophy* 42, 381–417.
Dever, J. (1998) *Variables*, PhD Dissertation, University of California at Berkeley.
Devitt, M. (1981) *Designation*, New York: Columbia University Press.
Donnellan, K. S. (1966) 'Reference and Definite Descriptions', *Philosophical Review* 75(3), 281–304.
Donnellan, K. (1972) 'Proper Names and Identifying Descriptions', in Davidson, D. and Harman, G. (eds), *Semantics of Natural Language*, Dordrecht: D. Reidel, 356–379.
Dummett, M. (1973) *Frege: Philosophy of Language*, Cambridge, MA: Harvard University Press.
Elbourne, P. (2005) *Situations and Individuals*, Cambridge, MA: MIT Press.
Elugardo, R. (2002) 'The Predicate View of Proper Names', in Preyer, G. and Peter, G. (eds), *Logical Form and Language*, Oxford: Oxford University Press, 467–503.
Evans, G. (1985 [1973]) 'The Causal Theory of Names', in Phillips, A. (ed.), *Collected Papers*, Oxford: Oxford University Press, 1985, 1–24.
Evans, G. (1982) *The Varieties of Reference*, Oxford: Clarendon Press.
Everett, A. (2013) *The Nonexistent*, Oxford: Oxford University Press.
Fara, D. G. (2012) '"Literal" Uses of Proper Names', in Bianchi, A. (ed.), *On Reference* (2015), Oxford: Oxford University Press, 251–279.
Fara, D. G. (2015) 'Names Are Predicates', *Philosophical Review* 124, 59–117.
Fine, K. (2005) 'Necessity and Non-existence', in *Modality and Tense. Philosophical Papers*, Oxford: Oxford University Press, 321–354.
Fine, K. (2007) *Semantic Relationism*, Oxford: Blackwell.
Fitting, M. and Mendelsohn, R. L. (1998) *First-order Modal Logic*, Dordrecht: Kluwer.
Forbes, G. (2006) *Attitude Problems*, Oxford: Oxford University Press.
Frances, B. (1998) 'Defending Millian Theories', *Mind* 107, 703–728.
Frege, G. (1892 [1963]) 'Über Sinn und Bedeutung', in Patzig, G. (ed.), *Funktion, Begriff, Bedeutung*, Göttingen: Vandenhoek & Ruprecht, 23–46.
Frege, G. (1906) 'Introduction to Logic', in Hermes, H., Kambartel, F., and Kaulbach, F. (eds), *Posthumous Writings* (1979), Oxford: Blackwell, 185–196.
Frege, G. (1918 [1966]) 'Der Gedanke', in Patzig, G. (ed.), *Logische Untersuchungen*, Göttingen: Vandenhoeck & Ruprecht, 30–53.
Friend, Stacie (2012) 'Fiction as a Genre', *Proceedings of the Aristotelian Society* 112, 179–209.
García-Carpintero, M. (2016) 'Predicativism and the Mill-Frege Theory of Proper Names', in Stalmaszczyk, P. and Fernandez Moreno, L. (eds), *Philosophical Approaches to Proper Names*, Frankfurt am Main, 21–54.
García-Carpintero, M. (2018) 'The Mill-Frege Theory of Proper Names', *Mind*, 127, 1107–1168.
Garson, J. W. (2001) 'Quantification in Modal Logic', in Gabbay, D.M. and Guenthner F. (eds), *Handbook of Philosophical Logic*, vol 3., Dordrecht: Springer, 267–323, doi: 10.1007/978-94-017-0454-0.
Geurts, B. (1997) 'Good News about the Description Theory of Names', *Journal of Semantics* 14, 319–348.

Gluer, K. and Pagin, P. (2006) 'Proper Names and Relational Modality', *Linguistics and Philosophy*, 29, 507–535.
Gluer, K. and Pagin, P. (2014) 'Vulcan Might Have Existed and Neptune Not. On the Semantics of Empty Names', in García-Carpintero, M. and Marti, G. (eds), *Empty Representations: Reference and Non-Existence*, Oxford: Oxford University Press, 117–114.
Graham, P. J. (1999) 'Defending Millianism', *Mind* 108, 555–561.
Gray, A. (2012) *Names and Name-Bearing: An Essay on the Predicative View of Names* PhD Thesis, University of Chicago, Chicago.
Gray, A. (2017) 'Lexical Individuation and Predicativism about Names', *Thought: A Journal of Philosophy* 4, 113–123, doi:10.1002/tht3.164.
Gray, A. (2018) 'Lexical-Rule Predicativism about Names', *Synthese* 195, 5549–5569, https://doi.org/10.1007/s11229-017-1462-4.
Haas-Spohn, U. (1995) *Versteckte Indexikalität und subjektive Bedeutung*, Berlin: Akademie Verlag.
Hale, B. (2007) 'Into the Abyss: A Critical Study of Towards Non-Being', *Philosophia Mathematica* 15, 94–134.
Hawthorne, J. and Lepore, E. (2011) 'On Words', *Journal of Philosophy* 108, 447–485.
Hawthorne, J. and Manley, D. (2012) *The Reference Book*, Oxford: Oxford University Press.
Heim, I. and Kratzer, A. (1998) *Semantics in Generative Grammar*, Oxford: Blackwell.
Hintikka, J. (1962) *Knowledge and Belief: An Introduction to the Logic of the Two Notions*, New York: Cornell University Press.
Horn, L. R. (2004) 'Implicature', in Horn, L. R. and Ward, G. (eds), *The Handbook of Pragmatics*, Oxford: Blackwell, 3–28.
Hornsby, J. (1976) 'Proper Names: A Defense of Burge', *Philosophical Studies* 30, 227–234.
Hughes, C. (2004) *Kripke. Names, Necessity, and Identity*, Oxford: Clarendon Press.
Jackson, F. (1998) 'Reference and Descriptions Revisited', *Philosophical Perspectives* 12, 201–218.
Jeshion, R. (2015) 'Referentialism and Predicativism About Proper Names', *Erkenntnis* 80, 363–404.
Jubien, M. (1993) 'Proper Names', *Philosophical Perspectives* 7, 487–504.
Kaplan, D. (1968) 'Quantifying In', *Synthese*, 19(1/2), 178–214.
Kaplan, D. (1973) 'Bob and Carol and Ted and Alice', in Hintikka, J., Moravcsik, J. M. E. and Suppes, P. (eds), *Approaches to Natural Languages*, Dordrecht: Reidel, 490–518.
Kaplan, D. (1978) 'On the Logic of Demonstratives,' *Journal of Philosophical Logic* 8, 81–98.
Kaplan, D. (1989a [1977]) 'Demonstratives', in Almog, J., Perry, J. and Wettstein, H. (eds), *Themes from Kaplan*, Oxford: Oxford University Press.
Kaplan, D. (1989b) 'Afterthoughts', in Almog, J., Perry, J. and Wettstein, H. (eds), *Themes from Kaplan*, Oxford: Oxford University Press, 565–614.
Kaplan, D. (1990) 'Words', *Aristotelian Society Supplement* 64, 93–119.
Katz, J. (1994) 'Names without Bearers', *Philosophical Review* 103, 1–39.
Katz, J. (2001) 'The End of Millianism: Multiple Bearers, Improper Names, and Compositional Meaning', *Journal of Philosophy* 98, 137–166.
King, J. (2012) 'Anaphora', in Russell, G. and Fara, D. G. (eds), *The Routledge Companion to the Philosophy of Language*, London: Routledge, 367–379.
King, J. C. (2006) 'Singular Terms, Reference, and Methodology in Semantics', *Philosophical Issues* 16, 141–161.
Kneale, W. (1962) 'Modality De Dicto and De Re', in Nagel, E., Suppes, P. and Tarski, A. (eds), *Logic, Methodology and Philosophy of Science, Proceedings of the 1960 International Congress*, Stanford: Stanford University Press, 622–633.

Korta, K. and Perry, J. (2011) *Critical Pragmatics*, Cambridge: Cambridge University Press.

Kratzer, A. (1998), 'More Structural Analogies Between Pronouns and Tenses', in Strolovich. D. and Lawson, A. (eds), *Proceedings of SALT VIII*, Cornell: CLC Publications, 36–54.

Kratzer, A. (2009), 'Making a Pronoun: Fake Indexicals as Windows into the Properties of Pronouns', *Linguistic Inquiry* 40, 187–237.

Kripke, S. A. (1971) 'Identity and Necessity', in Munitz, K. M. (ed.), *Identity and Individuation*, New York: New York University Press, 135–164; reprinted 2011 in *Philosophical Troubles*, Oxford: Oxford University Press, 1–26.

Kripke, S. A. (1972) 'Naming and Necessity', in Davidson, D. and Harman, G. (eds), *Semantics of Natural Language*, Dordrecht: D. Reidel, 253–355, 763–769.

Kripke, S. A. (1977) 'Speaker's Reference and Semantic Reference', *Midwest Studies in Philosophy* 2, 255–276; reprinted 2011 in *Philosophical Troubles*, Oxford: Oxford University Press, 99–124.

Kripke, S. A. (1979) 'A Puzzle About Belief', in Margalit, A. (ed.), *Meaning and Use*, Dordrecht: Reidel, 239–383.

Kripke, S. A. (1980) *Naming and Necessity*, Cambridge, MA: Harvard University Press.

Kripk, S. A. (2011a [1971]) 'Identity and Necessity', in *Philosophical Troubles*, Oxford: Oxford University Press, 1–26.

Kripke, S. A. (2011b [1973]) 'Vacuous Names and Fictional Entities', in *Philosophical Troubles* Oxford: Oxford University Press, 52–74.

Kripke, S. A. (2013 [1975]) *Reference and Existence: The John Locke Lectures*, Oxford: Oxford University Press.

Kroon, F. (1987) 'Causal Descriptivism', *Australasian Journal of Philosophy* 65, 1–17.

Künne, W. (2007a [1995]) 'Fiktion ohne fiktive Gegenstände: Prolegomenon zu einer Fregeanischen Theorie der Fiktion', in Reicher, M. E. (ed.), *Fiktion, Wahrheit, Wirklichkeit. Philosophische Grundlagen der Literaturtheorie*, Paderborn: Mentis, 54–72.

Künne, W. (2007b) *Abstrakte Gegenstände*, 2nd Edition, Frankfurt am Main: Klostermann.

Leckie, G. (2013) 'The Double Life of Names', *Philosophical Studies* 165, 1139–1160.

Lehmann, S. (1994) 'Strict Fregean Free Logic', *Journal of Philosophical Logic* 23, 307–336.

Lehmann, S. (2002) 'More Free Logic', in Gabbay, D. M. and Guenthner, F. (eds), *Handbook of Philosophical Logic*, 2nd Edition, Volume 5, Dordrecht: Kluwer, 197–259.

Lepore, E. and Ludwig, K. (2000) 'The Semantics and Pragmatics of Complex Demonstratives', *Mind* 109, 199–240.

Lewis, D. (1978) 'Truth in Fiction', *American Philosophical Quarterly* 15, 37–46.

Lewis, D. (1984) 'Putnam's Paradox', *Australasian Journal of Philosophy* 62, 221–236.

Linsky, L. (1977) *Names and Descriptions*, Chicago: University Press of Chicago.

Loar, B. (1976) 'The Semantics of Singular Terms', *Philosophical Studies* 30, 353–377.

Lowe, E. J. (2002) *A Survey of Metaphysics*, Oxford: Oxford University Press.

Maier, E. (2009) 'Proper Names and Indexicals Trigger Rigid Presuppositions', *Journal of Semantics* 26, 253–315.

Marti, G. (2008) 'Direct Reference and Definite Descriptions', *Dialectica* 62, 43–57.

Marti, G. (2015) 'Reference without Cognition', in Bianchi, A. (ed.), *On Reference*, Oxford: Oxford University Press, 77–92.

Martinich, A. P. and Stroll, A. (2007) *Much Ado About Nonexistence*, Plymouth: Rowmans Littlefield publishers.

Matushansky, O. (2006) 'Why Rose is the Rose: On the Use of Definite Articles in Proper Names', in Bonami, O. and Hofherr, P. C. (eds), *Empirical Issues in Formal Syntax and Semantics*, Paris: CSSP, 285–307.

Matushansky, O. (2008) 'On the Linguistic Complexity of Proper Names', *Linguistics and Philosophy* 21, 573–627.
McDowell, J. (1984) 'De Re Senses', *Philosophical Quarterly* 34, 283–294.
McKay, T. (2005) 'Propositional Attitude Reports', *Stanford Encyclopedia of Philosophy* (Fall Edition), Edward N. Zalta (ed.), URL = <http://plato.stanford.edu/archives/fall2005/entries/prop-attitude-reports/>.
McKay, T. and Nelson, M. (2010) 'Propositional Attitude reports', in Zalta, E. N. (ed.), *The Stanford Encyclopedia of Philosophy* (Spring 2014 Edition), URL = <http://plato.stanford.edu/archives/spr2014/entries/prop-attitude-reports/>.
McKinsey, M. (1976) 'Divided Reference in Causal Theories of Names', *Philosophical Studies* 30, 235–242.
McKinsey, M. (2011) 'Understanding Names', *Linguistics and Philosophy* 33, 325–354.
Mill, J. S. (1843) *System of Logic*, London: Parker.
Moltmann, F. (2020) 'Names, Light Nouns, and Countability', unpublished manuscript, https://www.researchgate.net/publication/343700185; downloaded 7 January 2021.
Murday, B. (2013) 'Names and Obstinate Rigidity', *Southern Journal of Philosophy* 51, 224–242.
Neale, S. (1990) *Descriptions*, Cambridge, MA: MIT Press.
Nelson, M. (2012) 'Intensional Contexts' in García-Carpintero, M. and Kölbel, M. (eds), *The Continuum Companion to the Philosophy of Language*, London: Continuum, 125–152.
Nelson, M. (2019) 'Propositional Attitude Reports', *The Stanford Encyclopedia of Philosophy* (Spring Edition), Edward N. Zalta (ed.), URL = <https://plato.stanford.edu/archives/spr2019/entries/prop-attitude-reports/>.
Noonan, H. (2013) *Kripke and Naming and Necessity*, London: Routledge.
Nunberg, G. (1979) 'The Non-Uniqueness of Semantic Solutions: Polysemy', *Linguistics and Philosophy* 3, 143–184.
Nunberg, G. (1995) 'Transfer of Meaning', *Journal of Semantics* 12, 109–132.
Nunberg, G. (2004) 'The Pragmatic of Deferred Interpretation', in Horn, L. R. and Ward, G. (eds), *The Handbook of Pragmatics*, Oxford: Blackwell, 344–364.
Parsons, T. (1980) *Nonexistent Objects*, New Haven: Yale University Press.
Pelczar, M. (2001) 'Names as Tokens and Names as Tools', *Synthese* 128, 133–155.
Pelczar, M. and Rainsbury, J. (1998) 'The Indexical Character of Names', *Synthese* 114, 293–317.
Perry, J. (2001) *Reference & Reflexivity*, Stanford, CA: CSLI Publications.
Pickel, B. (2015) 'Variables and attitudes', *Noûs* 49, 333–356.
Plantinga, A. (1978) 'The Boethian Compromise', *American Philosophical Quarterly* 15(2), 129–138.
Potts, C. (2005) *The Logic of Conventional Implicatures*, Oxford: Oxford University Press.
Predelli, S. (2004) 'The Price of Innocent Millianism', *Erkenntnis* 60, 335–356.
Predelli, S. (2005) *Contexts*, Oxford: Clarendon Press.
Predelli, S. (2008) 'Modal Monsters and Talk About Fiction', *Journal of Philosophical Logic* 37, 277–297.
Predelli, S. (2012) 'Bare-Boned Demonstratives', *Journal of Philosophical Logic* 41, 547–562.
Predelli, S. (2013) *Meaning without Truth*, Oxford: Oxford University Press.
Predelli, S. (2017) *Proper Names: A Millian Account*, Oxford: Oxford University Press.
Predelli, S. (2020) *Fictional Discourse: A Radical Fictionalist Semantics*, Oxford: Oxford University Press.

Priest, G. (2005) *Towards Non-Being. The Logic and Metaphysics of Intentionality*, Oxford: Clarendon Press.
Priest, G. (2008) *An Introduction to Non-Classical Logic*, 2nd Edition, Cambridge: Cambridge University Press.
Priest, G. (2016) *Towards Non-Being. The Logic and Metaphysics of Intentionality*, 2nd Edition, Oxford: Clarendon Press.
Prior, A. N. (1971) *Objects of Thought*, Oxford: Clarendon Press.
Putnam, H. (1975) 'The meaning of "meaning"', *Minnesota Studies in the Philosophy of Science* 7, 215–271.
Quine, W. V. O. (1948) 'On What There Is', *Review of Metaphysics* 2, 21–36.
Quine, W. V. O. (1960) *Word and Object*, Cambridge, MA: MIT Press.
Rabern, B. (2015) 'Descriptions Which Have Grown Capital Letters', *Mind and Language* 30, 292–319.
Rabern, B. (2018) 'Binding Bound Variables in Epistemic Contexts', *Inquiry*, doi: 10.1080/0020174X.2018.1470568.
Rami, D. (2014a) 'On the Unification Argument for the Predicate View on Proper Names', *Synthese* 191, 841–862.
Rami, D. (2014b) 'The Use-Conditional Indexical Conception of Proper Names', *Philosophical Studies* 168, 119–150.
Rami, D. (2014c) 'Existence as a Property of Individuals', *Erkenntnis* 79, 503–523.
Rami, D. (2015) 'The Multiple Uses of Proper Nouns', *Erkenntnis* 80, 405–432.
Rami, D. (2016) 'Names, Namings and Name-Using Practices', in Stalmaszczyk, P. and Fernandez Moreno, L. (eds), *Philosophical Approaches to Proper Names*, Frankfurt am Main: Peter Lang, 55–93.
Rami, D. (2017a) 'Drei Varianten des Paradoxons der Nicht-Existenz', *Deutsche Zeitschrift für Philosophie* 65:4, 657–689.
Rami, D. (2017b) 'Existenz', in Schrenk, M. (ed.) *Handbuch für Metaphysik*, Stuttgart: Metzler, 216–223.
Rami, D. (2018) *Existenz und Anzahl*, Paderborn: mentis.
Rami, D. (2019) 'Names and Their Kind of Rigidity', *Erkenntnis* 84, 257–282.
Rami, D. (2020) 'Single-Domain Free Logic and the Problem of Compositionality', *Synthese* (online first) https://link.springer.com/article/10.1007/s11229-020-02651-x.
Recanati, F. (1993) *Direct Reference*, Oxford: Basil Blackwell.
Recanati, F. (2000) *Oratio Obliqua, Oratio Recta. An Essay on Metrepresentation*, Cambridge, MA: MIT Press.
Recanati, F. (2003) *Literal Meaning*, Cambridge: Cambridge University Press.
Recanati, F. (2013) *Mental Files*, Oxford: Oxford University Press.
Recanati, F. (2019) *Mental Files in Flux*, Oxford: Oxford University Press.
Reichenbach, H. (1947) *Elements of Symbolic Logic*, New York: Macmillan Co.
Richard, M. (1993) 'Articulated Terms', *Philosophical Perspectives* 7, 207–230.
Rieppel, M. (2020) 'Quinean Predicativism', *Philosophical Studies* (online first), https://doi.org/10.1007/s11098-020-01419-w.
Ripley, D. (2012) 'Structures and Circumstances: Two Ways to Fine-Grain Propositions', *Synthese* 189, 97–118.
Roberts, C. (2012) 'Information Structure in Discourse: Towards an Integrated Formal Theory of Pragmatics', *Semantics and Pragmatics* 5, 1–69.
Routley, Richard (1980) *Exploring Meinong's Jungle and Beyond: An Investigation of Noneism and the Theory of Items*. Research School of Social Sciences, Australian National University, Canberra.

Russell, B. (1905) 'On Denoting', *Mind* 14, 479–493.
Russell, B. (1911) 'Knowledge by Acquaintance and Knowledge by Description', *Proceedings of the Aristotelian Society* 11, 108–128.
Russell, B. (1912 [1959]) *Problems of Philosophy*, Oxford: Oxford University Press.
Russell, B. (1918 [1985]) *The Philosophy of Logical Atomism*, London: Routledge.
Russell, B. (1919) *Introduction to Mathematical Philosophy*, London: George Allen and Unwin.
Sainsbury, R. M. (2005) *Reference without Referents*, Oxford: Oxford University Press.
Sainsbury, R. M. (2009) *Fiction and Fictionalism*, London: Routledge.
Sainsbury, R. M. (2014) 'Fictional Worlds and Fiction Operators', in García-Carpintero, M. and Marti, G. (eds), *Empty Representations*, Oxford, 277–289.
Sainsbury, R. M. (2015) 'The Same Name', *Erkenntnis* 80, 195–214.
Sainsbury, R. M. and Tye, M. (2012) *Seven Puzzles of Thought and How to Solve Them: An Originalist Theory of Concepts*, Oxford: Oxford University Press.
Salmon, N. (1981) *Reference and Essence*, Princeton: Princeton University Press.
Salmon, N. (1986) *Frege's Puzzle*, Cambridge, MA: MIT Press.
Salmon, N. (1987) 'Existence', *Philosophical Perspectives* 1, 49–108.
Salmon, N. (1988) 'Nonexistence', *Noûs* 32(3), 277–319.
Salmon, N. (1989) 'Illogical Belief', *Philosophical Perspectives* 3, 243–285.
Salmon, N. (1998) 'Nonexistence', *Noûs* 32, 277–319.
Salmon, N. (2007 [1990]) 'A Millian Heir Rejects the Wages of Sinn', in *Content, Cognition and Communication*, Oxford: Oxford University Press, 3–31.
Santorio, P. (2012) 'Reference and Monstrosity', *Philosophical Review* 121, 359–405.
Saul, J. (1997) 'Substitution and Simple Sentences', *Analysis* 57, 102–108.
Sawyer, S. (2010) 'The Modified Predicate Theory of Proper Names', in Sawyer, S. (ed.), *New Waves in Philosophy of Language*, Palgrave: MacMillan Press, 206–225.
Scales, R. (1969) *Attribution and Existence*. Dissertation, University of California, Irvine.
Schiffer, S. (1977) 'Naming and Knowing', *Midwest Studies in Philosophy* 2, 28–41.
Schiffer, S. (1996) 'Language-Created Language-Independent Entities', *Philosophical Topics* 24(1), 149–167.
Schiffer, S. (2003) *The Things We Mean*, Oxford: Clarendon Press.
Schiffer, S. (2006) 'Propositional Content', in Lepore, E. and Smith, B. C. (eds), *Oxford Handbook of Philosophy of Language*, Oxford: Oxford University Press, 267–294.
Schoubye, A. (2017) 'Type-Ambiguous Names', *Mind* 126, 715–767.
Schoubye, A. (2018) 'The Predicative Predicament', *Philosophy and Phenomenological* 96, 571–595.
Schoubye, A. (2020) 'Names are Variables', *Philosophical Review* 129, 53–94.
Searle, J. (1958) 'Proper Names', *Mind* 67, 166–173.
Searle, J. (1979) *Expression and Meaning*, Cambridge: Cambridge University Press.
Searle, J. (1983) *Intentionality*, Cambridge: Cambridge University Press.
Searle, J. and Vanderveken, D. (1985) *Foundations of Illocutionary Logic*, Cambridge: Cambridge University Press.
Simons, M., Tonhauser, J., Beaver, D. and Roberts, C. (2010) 'What Projects and Why', in *Semantics and Linguistic Theory* (SALT) 21, Ithaca, NY: CLC Publications, 309–327.
Sloat, C. (1969) 'Proper Nouns in English', *Language* 45, 26–30.
Soames, S. (1987) 'Substitutivity', in Thomson, J. (ed.), *On Being and Saying: Essays in Honor of Richard Cartwright*, Cambridge, MA: MIT Press, 99–132.
Soames, S. (1989) 'Direct Reference, Propositional Attitudes and Semantic Content', *Philosophical Topics* 15, 44–87.

Soames, S. (2002) *Beyond Rigidity*, Oxford: Oxford University Press.
Sommers, F. (1980) *The Logic of Natural Language*, Oxford: Oxford University Press.
Stanley, J. (1997) 'Names and Rigid Designation', in Hale, B. and Wright, C. (eds), *A Companion to the Philosophy of Language*, Oxford: Oxford University Press, 555-585.
Steinman, R. (1985) 'Kripke Rigidity versus Kaplan Rigidity', *Mind* 94, 431-442.
Strawson, P. F. (1950) 'On Referring', *Mind* 59, 320-344.
Strawson, P. F. (1952) *Introduction to Logical Theory*, London: Methuen.
Strawson, P. F. (1959) *Individuals: An Essay on Descriptive Metaphysics*, London: Methuen.
Strawson, P. F. (1974) *Subject and Predicate in Logic and Grammar*, London: Methuen.
Taschek, W. W. (1992) 'Frege's Puzzle, Sense, and Information Content', *Mind* 101(404), 767-791.
Taylor, K. A. (2000) 'Emptiness without Compromise', in Everett, A. and Hofweber, T. (eds), *Empty Names, Fiction and the Puzzles of Non-Existence*, Stanford, CA: CSLI Publications.
Taylor, K. A. (2003) 'What's in a Name', in his *Reference and the Rational Mind*, Stanford, CA: CSLI Publications, 1-32.
Textor, M. (2005) *Der Sinn und die Bedeutung von Eigennamen*, Paderborn: mentis.
Textor, M. (2010) 'Proper Names and Practices: On Reference without Referents', *Philosophy and Phenomenological Research* 81, 105-118.
Thomasson, A. L. (1999) *Fiction and Metaphysics*. New York: Cambridge University Press.
Tiedke, H. (2011) 'Proper Names and Their Fictional Uses', *Australasian Journal of Philosophy* 89, 707-726.
Vanderveken, D. (1990) *Meaning and Speech Acts, Vols I and II*, Cambridge: Cambridge University Press.
van Inwagen, P. (1977) 'Creatures of Fiction', *American Philosophical Quarterly* 14(4), 299-308.
Voltolini, A. (2006) *How Ficta Follow Fiction. A Syncretistic Account of Fictional Entities*, Dordrecht: Springer.
Voltolini, A. (2016) 'A Syncretistic Theory of Proper Names', in Bianchi, A., Morato, V. and Spolaore, G. (eds), *The Importance of Being Ernesto. Reference, Truth and Logical Form*, Padova: Padova University Press, 141-164.
Voltolini, A. (2019) 'Varieties of Fiction Operators', in Capone, A. et al. (eds), *Further Advances in Pragmatics and Philosophy: Part 2 Theories and Applications*, Dordrecht: Springer, 199-210.
Walton, K. (1990) *Mimesis as Make-Believe*, Cambridge, MA: Harvard University Press.
Williamson, T. (2002) 'Necessary Existents', *Philosophy* 51 (Supp), 233-251.
Williamson, T. (2013) *Modal Logic as Metaphysics*, Oxford: Oxford University Press.
Wittgenstein, L. (1953) *Philosophical Investigations*, Oxford: Blackwell.
Wolterstorff, N. (1980) *Works and Worlds of Art*, Oxford: Clarendon Press.
Zalta, E. N. (1983) *Abstract Objects: An Introduction to Axiomatic Metaphysics*, Dordrecht: Reidel.
Zalta, E. N. (1988) *Intensional logic and the Metaphysics of Intentionality*, Cambridge, MA: MIT Press.
Ziff, P. (1977) 'About Proper Names', *Mind* 86, 319-332.
Zimmermann, T. E. (1993) 'On the Proper Treatment of Opacity in Certain Verbs', *Natural Language Semantics* 1, 149-179.
Zimmermann, T. E. (2005) 'What's in Two Names?', *Journal of Semantics* 22, 53-96.

Zimmermann, T. E. (2012) 'Context Dependence', in Maienborn, C., von Heusinger, K. and Portner, P. (eds), *Handbook of Semantics*, Volume 3, Berlin: de Gruyter, 2360–2407.
Zimmermann, T. E. and Lerner, J.-Y. (1991) 'Eigennamen', in Stechow, A. v. and Wunderlich, D. (eds), *Semantik. Ein internationales Handbuch*, Berlin: de Gruyter, 349–370.
Zimmermann, T. E. and Sternefeld, W. (2013) *Introduction to Semantics*, Berlin: de Gruyter.

# Index

absolute assignment functions 184
absolute denotation functions 56–7
absolute interpretation functions 56–7
absolute occurrences 119
accessibility relations 147, 149
accessible rigidity 43
accidental designators 43
accommodated presuppositions 175–6, 189
acts of naming 66–7, 81 *see also* name-using practices
  authority in 83, 84
  baptisms 65–8, 81, 86
  bringing-about expressions 82
  broad conceptions 81–6
  connecting intention 88
  declarations 82–4
  descriptive 81–2
  effect expressions 82
  effectives 82
  exercitives 82
  explicit 81, 82, 84, 86
  implicit introductions of names 85–6
  in the narrow sense 81–5
  introductory intention 87
  introductory referential use 87
  invitations 83–4
  legal acts of 84, 87–8, 89
  mass baptisms 86, 87, 88
  neo-Strawsonian picture 87–8
  nicknames 83, 84
  on the fly 85, 87
  ostensive 81
  parasitic referential use 87–8, 92
  plural legal acts of naming 86, 87–8
  privilege in 83
  re-naming 83
  referential use 87
  single originating events 86
  sufficient conditions 83
actual dependence rigidity 57

actualized accessible rigid designators 62
actualized accessible rigidity 60–1
actualized obstinately rigid designators 62
actualized persistently rigid designators 63
actualized restricted rigid designators 62
actualized restricted rigidity 58–60
actually rigid designators 208
analytic truths 125–6
anaphoric readings 28
apparent anaphoric uses 26–7, 34, 35, 41, 105–8, 173
  alternative metalinguistic pragmatic explanation 190–6
  as accommodated presuppositions 175–6, 189
  Bach, K. 175–6, 189–90
  as bound by nominal quantifiers 176, 190–2
  Burge-Cumming example problem 185–7
  Burge, T. 173–4, 179–80, 181, 182–3
  as counterparts of fake indexicals 177–8
  Cumming, S. 174, 181–2, 185–7
  as discourse anaphora 173–4, 192–3, 196–7
  deviant bound 188
  dilemma of uniform semantic treatment of referential and anaphoric uses 182–5
  as donkey anaphora 174–5, 193–7
  Elbourne, P. 180, 181, 182–3, 185, 187, 195, 196
  Guerts-Elbourne example problems 187
  Kamp, H. 176
  Maier, E. 189–90
  non-literal 190, 192, 194, 195
  over-generalization problems 187–8
  paradigm bound 188
  proper names semantically interpreted as complex demonstratives 179–80

proper names semantically interpreted
    as covert definite descriptions
    180–1
proper names semantically interpreted
    as individual variables 181–2
under-determination problems 185–7
appositive readings 27, 29
artefacts 137
assertoric sentences 129, 150–4, 156
assignment functions 184
atomic existential sentences 210
atomic sentences 123–4, 135, 147–8,
    199–200
    atomic existential sentences 210
    atomic identity sentences 210
    extraordinary 209
    ordinary 209
attitude ascriptions 14–15, 197–8, 205, 226
    *de dicto* readings 203, 204, 207, 209,
        216
    *de re* readings 207, 209, 226–7, 216,
        224
    formal semantics 212–13
attitude-counterparts 204–5, 206, 214–16
attitude operators 211, 227
attitude verbs 14–15, 41–2, 197–8
    attitude-counterparts formally
        represented by proxy-individuals
        213–16
    existential inferential failure 198
    extensional independence of
        expressions 198
    formal semantics for attitude
        ascriptions 212–13
    formal semantics for epistemic modals
        213–14
    formal semantics, comparison with
        Priest 216–24
    general formal semantic framework
        107–12
    as hybrid modal operators 200–2
    as monstrous operators 202–5
    as non-normal modal operators 205–6
    as non-normal modal operators,
        formal analysis 206–16
    substitutional failure of co-referential
        names 197–8
    validity, two notions of 214
attributive uses 180, 181

Bach, K. 175–6, 189–90
baptisms 65–8 *see also* acts of naming
    empty 81
    mass 86, 87, 88
    unwitting 81
bare rigidity 47
belief about existence 134
Berto, F. 232 n. 30
biological uses of family names 164
bound individual variables 34–5, 97, 181
bound uses 107, 184, 239 n. 7
    anaphoric. *See* apparent anaphoric uses
    nominal quantifiers 191–2
    non-literal 194
bringing-about expressions 82
Buber, M. 170
Burge, T. 25, 173–4, 179–80, 181, 182–3,
    185–7

causal description theories of names 5
character of an expression 96, 108
character of indexical expression 168
circumstances of evaluation 96, 108
classical substitution problem 207
cluster theory of names 4–5
clusters of expressions 73
clusters of linguistic forms 73
co-referential proper names, lack of
    substitutability 197–8
coarse-grained individuation of proper
    names 71–3, 77–8, 97, 102, 109,
    240 n. 13
coarse-grained individuation of use-
    sensitive expressions 121
coarse-grained semantics for name-
    functions and name-uses 122, 124,
    127
cognitive determinations of referential
    uses 75, 99, 100
commitments 142
common currency names 69
communication chain view of reference
    determination 98
complex demonstratives 8, 38, 106–7, 108,
    132
    metalinguistic 193
complex non-logical constants 96
compositional truth-conditional
    semantics 168

Conan Doyle, A. 148
  Hound of the Baskervilles 143–5, 148, 149
  Scandal in Bohemia, A 145–6
Conditional Weak Millianism 12
conjunctions 210
connecting intentions 79, 88, 91–2
connective sentences with truth-functional connectives 210
constant domains 44–5, 56–7, 61, 208, 217, 221
  contingency variant 45
  necessity variant 45
constant mental representations 99
constraining conditions of pronouns 168
constraint 96
content (of an expression) 96, 108
context-sensitive semantics of names 21–2, 95–8
  alternative context-sensitive semantics 119–28
  formal versions of 106–12
  motivations for 98–106
  new context-sensitive semantics 112–19
  occasion-sensitive expressions 120
  use-sensitive expressions 120
contexts of use 96, 108 *see also* context-sensitive expressions
  new semantics 125
  salience 111
(contextual) constraint 96
contextually salient transfer relation 161
contrastive readings 29
Cumming, S. 25–6, 174, 181–2, 185–7

*de dicto* readings 15, 198–9, 200, 203, 204, 207, 209
  Priest, G. 218–20
de facto rigidity 47–8
de jure rigidity 47–8, 63
*de re/de dicto* ambiguity 198–9
*de re* readings 15, 198–9, 200, 204, 207, 209, 224
  internally linked 226–7
  internally represented relative to semantic framework 224–7
  Priest, G. 218–20
*de re* senses 9–7

declarations 82–4
defective empty names 10–13, 39, 133–5, 136–7
defective name using practices 113
defective uses 112, 134
deferential reference determination 100
definite descriptions 5, 236 n. 28
  attributive 180
  defective empty names 11–12
  Elbourne, P. 181
  incomplete 21
  referential 180–1
  rigidified 20, 21, 31–1
  syntactic form 30–3
demonstrative determinations of referential uses 74, 99, 100
demonstrative uses 124–5
demonstratives 118, 131
denotation functions 44, 46, 56–7, 202, 203, 204, 208–9
description-names 31–3, 203–4
  intuitive tests 52
description theories of names 1–5
  attitude ascriptions 15
  causal 5
  cognitive version 3–5
  defective empty names 12
  Frege's puzzle 16
  Fregeian 179
  nominal 5
  rigidified versions 5
  Russellian 179, 199
  semantic version 3, 4
  structural ambiguity 199
descriptive acts of naming 81–2
descriptive determinations of referential uses 74–5, 98, 99–100
descriptive modifiers 27–9
descriptivism 98
deviant bound anaphoric uses 188
diachronic individuation of proper names 73
different referents 117–19
direct reference theory of names 1 *see also* Millianism
direct reference 8–10
directly referential terms 8–9
discourse anaphora 173–4, 192–3, 196–7

discourse representation theory 175
disjunctive view 210
domain functions 44, 216
domain of discourse 44, 45
domain of quantification 61, 216
domains
    constant domain framework. *See* constant domains
    variable domain framework 44–6, 57, 61, 208, 224
donkey anaphora 174–5, 193–7
donkey pronouns 26
Donnellan, K. 1, 180–1
dualist variabilism 97
dubbing in force 109, 110

effect expressions 82
effectives 82
Elbourne, P. 26–7, 107–8, 180, 181, 182–3, 185, 195, 196
    Guerts-Elbourne example problems 187
empty baptisms 81
empty names 10–13, 94, 113, 133–5, 136–7, 214
epistemic contexts 23–5, 41–2
epistemic modals 197, 216
    formal semantics 213–14
epistemic worlds 208
erroneous determinations of referential uses 75–6
etymological name-clusters 72, 73
evaluation relation 209
Evans, G. 75, 88–90
exercitives 82
existence belief 134
existence predicate 45–6
existential inferential failure 198
explicit acts of naming 81, 82, 84, 86
explicit assertions 155, 156
explicit content 142, 146, 147
exportation rule 220
expression-relative indices 119
expressions
    character of 96, 108
    character of indexical 168
    circumstances of evaluation 96, 108
    constraining conditions of pronouns 168

    contexts of use 96, 108 *see also* context-sensitive expressions
    (contextual) constraint 96
    default expectations 118
    expressive meanings 168–9, 170
    extensional independence 198
    functional 121–4
    indexical views 95–7, 108–12, 168
    meaning transfer 159, 160–8
    meanings 159
    name-function 122–6
    non-truth conditional meanings 96, 159, 169–70, 171
    polysemous 130
    pre-semantic meanings 168
    rigid 124
    same use sensitive 117–19
    semantic content of 96, 108
    social deixis 169
    trans-semantic meanings 168–9, 172
    truth-conditional meanings 96, 103, 127, 159, 168, 170, 171
    use-conditional meanings 127–8, 169, 172
    use-sensitive 120–8, 171–2
expressive adjectives 195
expressive meanings 168–9, 170
extended name-function-index combinations 123
extensional indepedence 198
extensional predicates 129, 150–2
external narrators 240 n. 16
externalist conception 2, 3
extraordinary atomic sentences 209

face-value analyses 226
fake indexicals 177–8, 184
false sentences 135
family examples 164–5
famous deeds descriptivism 4
felicitous uses 113–16
fictional identities 223–4
fictional names 18–19, 40–1, 129
    acts of re-telling a story 155–6
    assertions 141–3
    assertoric sentences 150–4, 156
    commitments 142
    defective names 136

different uses in sentential contexts
  137–54
essentially deferential 135
explicit assertions 155, 156
explicit content 142, 143
fictional reports 155–6
gun analogy 138
implicit content 142, 143
in use 129–30
introductory uses 154, 155
irrealist views 135–6, 137, 154, 157
key features 129–31
Kripkeanism 130
meaningfulness of names without semantic referent 131–5
Millianism 130
naïve realism 130
parasitic uses 154
pluralistic view 130
prepositions 143–5
referential status 129
reports about the content of fictional stories 141–50
semantic and pragmatic functions 154–7
semantic status 135–7
sentential modifers 144–5
specific modifiers 143
stipulation 154–5
story-telling 138–41
subsequent uses 155
synthetic views 140–1, 154, 157
fictional stories 141–50, 153 *see also* story-telling
fine-grained individuation of proper names 68–71, 77, 97, 101–2, 240 n. 13
fine-grained individuation of use-sensitive expressions 121
fine-grained semantics for name-functions and name-uses 122, 123–6
focus-marking 195–6
folk-conception of names 102
formal variant of indexical views 95–6
former names 114, 116
four-dimensionalism 222
Frege, G. 1, 35, 206
Fregeian description theory 179
Frege's puzzle 15–18

functional expressions 121–4, 171–2
functionalism 130, 131–3, 137
functions
  absolute assignment 184
  absolute denotation 56–7
  absolute interpretation 56–7
  assignment 184
  denotation 44, 46, 56–7, 202, 203, 204, 208–9
  domain 44, 216
  from worlds into objects 217
  indexed 123
  interpretation functions. *See* interpretation functions
  partial world-relative denotation 57
  restricted assignment 184
  semantic and pragmatic 154–7
  world 202, 203, 204
  world-relative denotation 44, 56–7, 209
  world-relative interpretation 44, 56–7
functions from worlds into objects 217

gappy propositions 11, 12
general higher-order lexical rule 162
generic names 69–71, 101
genuine semantic dilemmas 184–5
German 169–71
Guerts-Elbourne example problems 187

hidden indexical theory of attitude ascriptions 14–14
historic individuation of proper names 102–3
*Hound of the Baskervilles* (Conan Doyle, A.) 143–5, 148, 149
hybrid modal operators 200–2
hyper-intensional predicates 129, 150, 152–3
hyperintensional contexts
  attitude verbs 197–8, 200–16
  comparison with Priest's original version of the proposed semantics 216–24
  *de re*/*de dicto* ambiguity 198–9
  internally represented *de re* readings relative to semantic framework 224–7
hypothetical objects 133, 134

identity predicate 209
identity readings 27, 28
identity sentences 53–4, 210 *see also* Frege's puzzle
identities 217, 221–4, 226,
   fictional 223–4
   identity predicates 227
implicit content 142, 143, 145, 146, 147, 150
impossible worlds 205, 207, 210–11
incomplete definite descriptions 21
incomplete worlds 207
incorrect uses 112–13
indexed functions 123
indexical views 95–7, 108–12, 168
indices 118–19
individual constants 56–7, 216–17
individual mental representations 75
individual variables 181–2
individuation of proper names 67, 68–73
   coarse-grained 71–3, 77–8, 97, 102, 109, 240 n. 13
   diachronic 73
   fine-grained 68–71, 77, 97, 101–2, 240 n. 13
   historic 102–3
   synchronic 72, 73
infelicitous uses 113–14
inferences 118–19
inferential potential 17
inflexibility 50
informal variant of indexical views 95
informative sentences. *See* Frege's puzzle
institutional uses of family names 164
intensional predicates 129, 150, 152
intensions 96
intentional transitive verbs 153
internal narrators 240 n. 16
internalist conceptions 2–3
internally linked *de re* readings 226–7
interpretation 145–6
interpretation functions 44, 56–7, 147, 202–3, 208–9, 216–18
   identity predicates 227
intonation 194
intuitive motivation 221

judge-parameter 213–14

Kamp, H. 176
Kaplan, D. 6–7, 8
   Kaplan-Sainsbury accounts 73
   merely possible objects 232 n. 28
   negative existentials 52–3
   truth-conditional meanings 96
KLD (Kaplan's logic of demonstratives) 96–7, 108, 112–13, 120, 125–6
Kripke, S. A. 39
   acts of naming 81–2
   actualized accounts of rigidity 56
   fictional names 130
   individuation of proper names 68–9
   modal contexts 19, 20
   modal operators 202
   name-using practices 78, 81
   negative existentials 52–3
   reference determination 65–8, 74, 76–7, 173–4
   rigid designators 43–4, 45–6, 47–51, 63

language forms 71–2
Le Verrier, U. 133
lexical meaning transfer 159, 161, 162,
   family examples 164, 165
   production examples 163,
lexical rules
   family examples 164
   production examples 163

Madagascar-example 75, 89–90
Maier, E. 189–90
Marti, G. 8
Matushansky, O. 26–7
mass baptisms 86, 87, 88
meaning transfer 159, 160–8
   family examples 164–5
   metalinguistic 165–7
   non-metalinguistic 167–8
   non-truth-conditional 159, 169–70, 171
   original examples 165–72
   polysemy view 167, 168
   production examples 163–4, 167
   resemblance examples 162–3
   truth-conditional 159, 168, 170, 171
mental files 75
merely bare rigidity 49
merely possible objects 54–5

merely weak rigidity 47
meta-representation errors 91
metalinguistic complex demonstratives 193
metalinguistic meaning transfer 165–7
metalinguistic uses 189, 190–6
metaphysical modal contexts 19–21
methodologies 33–8
might 213–14
Mill, J. S. 5
Millianism 1–2, 3, 5–10
    attitude ascriptions 14
    Conditional Weak Millianism 12
    defective empty names 11–12
    direct reference 8–10
    fictional names 130
    Frege's puzzle 16
    Minimal Millianism 9–10
    semantic referents 9
    singular negative existential sentences 13
    Strong Millianism. *See* Strong Millianism
    Weak Millianism 6, 7, 131
Minimal Millianism 9–10
misassumption-cases 215
misconception-cases 215, 221, 222–3
misidentification-cases 204–5, 215, 224
misrepresentation-cases 205, 223
modal contexts 19–21
modal operators 146–50, 153
    attitude operators 211, 227
    epistemic 197, 213–14
    hybrid 200–2
    monstrous 202–5
    non-normal 146–7, 153, 205–16
modal sentences 210–11
moderate rigidity 46
monist variabilism 97
monstrous operators 202–5
Morning Star 30, 32

naïve realism 130
name-bearer relation 21–2, 65, 68, 70, 87, 90, 93
name-clusters 72, 73
name-conventions 32
name-function expressions 122–4
    coarse-grained semantics 122, 124, 127

fine-grained semantics 122, 123–6
name-predicates 121–2
name-using practices 66, 67, 77–8, 109–10
    *see also* acts of naming
    coarse-grained semantics 122, 127
    connecting intentions 79, 88, 91–2
    conventionalized branches 78, 79–80, 87–92
    defective 113
    errors 90–1
    fictional names 131, 135
    fine-grained semantics 122, 123–6
    fission cases 109
    fusion cases 109–10
    implicit determination of conventionalized branches 90–2
    implicit reference change 88–90
    individual branches 78
    meta-representation errors 91
    non-literal 113–16
    non-parasitic 91
    originating acts of 81
    partially parasitic 80
    purely parasitic 80
    rigid expressions 124
    transmission errors 91, 92
    unintentional constitution of a new (conventionalized branch of a) 90
naming 65–8
naming-convention 109, 110
narrow dubbing in force 110
narrow scope readings 49, 199, 200
natural languages 10, 34
    anaphoric uses of names 26–7
    descriptive modifiers of proper names 27–9
    empty names 10–13
    fictional names 18–19
    Frege's puzzle 15–18
    names in attitude contexts 14–15
    names in modal contexts 19–21
    names used in epistemic contexts 23–5
    past names 22–3
    predicative uses of names 25–6
    shared names 21–2
    singular negative existential sentences 13–14
    syntactic form of definite descriptions 30–3

negative existentials 52–3
negative free logic 53
negative singular existential sentences 13–14, 151–2
neo-Strawsonian picture of reference determination 78–80, 87–8
nicknames 71, 81, 83, 84
nominal description theories of names 5
nominal quantifiers 176, 190–2
non-empty names 214
non-existent objects 11, 13
   intuitive tests 51–2
   rigidity 60–1
non-literal uses 113–16, 127–8, 190, 192, 194, 195
non-logical constants 96
non-metalinguistic meaning transfer 167–8
non-normal modal operators 146–7, 153, 205–16
non-normal worlds 24–5, 146, 205–6, 207, 214–16, 239 n. 4
   Priest, G. 221, 223–4
non-referential uses 36
non-referring names 59
non-referring rigid expressions 60
non-semantic naming-conventions 110
non-truth-conditional meaning transfer 159, 169–70, 171
non-truth-conditional meanings 96
noneist semantics 147, 148, 151–2, 156
nonrigid designators 43
normal worlds 24, 146, 214, 239 n. 4
Nunberg, G. 159, 160–1, 168

objects 214–17, 221
   identity 217, 222–4, 226
obstinate rigidity 43, 44–7, 51, 52–5, 59
obstinately rigid designators 208
obstinately rigid non-designators 208
occasion-sensitive expressions 120
occurrent meaning transfer 159, 161–2, 164, 166
occurrent mental representations 99
occurrent modified use-conditional meanings 128
open worlds 207, 210, 218
ordinary atomic sentences 209
ordinary notion of names 102

ordinary objects 217, 222
   identity 217, 222–4, 226
original examples 165–72
originating acts of a name-using practice 81

Paderewski-cases 124
paradigm bound anaphoric uses 188
paradigm names 19, 20, 30–1
   intuitive tests 51–2
paradigm uses 34
parasitic acts of identification 235 n. 15
parasitic reference determination 66, 76, 77–8, 92, 100
partial world-relative denotation functions 57
past names 22–3, 238 n. 76
   temporal modification 116–17
past tense sentences 116
permissive naming-conventions 237 n. 54
Perry, J. 110
persistent rigidity 43, 44–7, 51–2, 54, 59, 60
persistently individual constants 57, 58
personal pronouns 132
phantom islands 133–4
pluralism
   context-sensitive semantics 112
   fictional names 130
   reference determination 79, 92–4, 98–9, 100–2
polysemous expressions 130
polysemy 37, 162
polysemy view 167, 168
positive existential sentences 151
possible worlds 24–5, 43–4, 205, 207
   individual constants 58–9
postulated objects 133, 134
pragmatic triggers 187
pre-semantic meanings 168
predicate views 34
predicates (names) 68–9, 159–61, 170, 208
   additional examples 160
   dynasty/family examples 160
   extensional 129, 150–2
   hyper-intensional 129, 150, 152–3
   identity 227
   intensional 129, 150, 152

logical 227
original examples 160
production examples 160
pronouns 170
resemblance examples 160
predicative readings 27, 28, 29
predicative uses 25–6, 34, 159–61, 233 n. 12
    secondary 41
prepositions 143–5
Priest, G. 197, 207–8, 216–24, 225
    adapted account consequence 219–21
    adapted account problem 221–4
production examples 163–4, 167
pronouns 103–7, 169–71, 172
    constraining conditions of 168
    social relations 169
pronunciation 71–2
proper names 5, 38, 131 see also fictional
        names
    alternative context-sensitive semantics
        119–28
    apparent anaphoric uses. See apparent
        anaphoric uses
    atomic sentences 123–4
    attributive uses 180
    as bound individual variables 34–5, 97,
        181
    bound uses 107, 184, 239 n. 7
    co-referential 197–8
    as complex demonstratives 179–80
    as context-sensitive expressions 21–2,
        95–7
    context-sensitive views, motivations
        for 98–106
    context-sensitive views, popular formal
        versions 106–12
    as covert definite descriptions 180–1
    defective empty names 10–13, 39,
        133–5, 136–7
    defective uses 112
    demonstrative uses 124–5
    derived uses 160
    empty uses 112–13
    felicitous uses 113–16
    former names 114, 116
    as functional expressions 121–2
    functionalism 131–3, 136–7
    in hyperintensional contexts. See
        hyperintensional contexts

    incorrect uses 112–13
    indexical views 95–7, 108–12
    as individual variables 181–2
    individuation 67, 68–73, 97
    infelicitous uses 113–14
    multiple occurrences of the same name
        with different referents 117–19
    new context-sensitive semantics
        112–19
    non-literal uses 113–16, 127–8, 190,
        192, 194, 195
    non-logical constants 96
    ordinary uses of 122
    past names 22–3, 116–17
    predicate views 34
    predicative uses 103–5, 159–61
    referential uses 34, 35, 105–8, 159–61,
        179, 180–5
    restricted 22, 116–17
    shared names 21–2, 69, 101–3
    stressed demonstrative uses 115
    stressed uses 113–16
    temporal modification 116–17
    as unbound individual variables 34–6,
        97, 181–2
    unrestricted 22, 116–17
    unstressed uses 116
    use-sensitive expressions 120
    variabilist views 34–6, 95, 97, 183–4
    variable indexical views 106–8
proper nouns 159–60
proxy individuals 214–16
pure *de re* readings 226

Rabern, B. 31, 32
Rami, D. 53
re-naming 83
Recanati, F. 110
reference constraining intentions 79, 80
reference determination 65, 74–80, 92–4,
    132
    acts of naming 81–8
    alternative neo-Strawsonian picture
        78–80
    cognitive 75, 99, 100
    communication chain 98
    constant mental representations 99
    deferential 100
    demonstrative 74, 99, 100

descriptivist 74–5, 98, 99–100
determination of reference of names 74–80
erroneous 75–6
implicit and unintentional constitution of name-using practices 88–92
individuation of proper names 68–74, 97
Kripke, S. A. 65–8, 74, 76–7, 173–4
multiple occurrences of the same name with different referents 117–19
object-related 99
occurrent mental representations 99
parasitic 66, 76, 77–8, 92, 100
pluralism 79, 92–4, 98–9, 100–2
reference fixing referential intentions or attitudes 99
Sainsbury, M. 65, 66–8
semantic reference 68
semantically correct 79
temporary mental representations 99
reference determining intentions 79
referential uses 34, 35, 105–8, 159–61, 179, 180–1
  dilemma of uniform semantic treatment of referential and anaphoric uses 182–5
referentially accessible objects 61
referring rigid expressions 60
Reichenbach, H. 120
resemblance examples 162–3
resemblance relation 162
restricted assignment functions 184
restricted names 22, 116–17, 124, 238 n. 76
restricted rigidity 43
Rieppel, M. 29
rigid designators 39, 43–4, 45–6, 47–9
  actualized accessible 62
  actualized obstinately 62
  actualized persistently 63
  actualized restricted 62
rigid expressions 124
rigidified definite descriptions 20, 21, 30–1
rigidity 43, 197, 200–1 *see also* rigid designators
  accessible 43
  actual dependence 57
  actualized accessible 60–1
  actualized accessible rigid designators 62

actualized accounts 55–61
actualized obstinately rigid designators 62
actualized persistently rigid designators 63
actualized restricted 58–60
actualized restricted rigid designators 62
bare 47
conceptions of 61–3
de facto 47–8
de jure 47–8, 63
definite descriptions 20, 21, 30–1
expressions 124
identity sentences, necessary truth of 53–4
individual constants 56–9
intuitive tests 48–52
Kripke, S. A. 43–4, 45–6, 47–52, 56, 63
merely bare 49
merely possible objects 54–5
merely weak 47
negative existentials 52–3
obstinate 43, 44–7, 51, 52–5, 59
obstinately individual constants 56–8
persistent 43, 44–7, 51–2, 54, 59, 60
persistently individual constants 57, 58
possible worlds 43–4
Priest, G. 217
restricted 43
specific 57, 58
weak 47, 50–1
Ripley, D. 207
Russell, B. 1
Russellian description theory 179, 199
Russellian propositions 6–7, 14
  Frege's puzzle 16

Sainsbury, M. 1, 39
  acts of naming 82, 84–5, 86
  baptisms 81
  fictional names 144
  Kaplan-Sainsbury accounts 73
  name-using practices 81
  reference determination 65, 66–8
salience 110–12
Salmon, N. 6, 232 n. 28
Saxon genitive 177, 194
*Scandal in Bohemia, A* (Conan Doyle, A.) 145–6

scope ambiguity 49–50
second person personal pronouns 169–71
secondary predicative uses 41
semantic correctness 126–7
semantic denotation of a name relative to use 122
semantic dilemmas 184–5
semantic indices 119
semantic name-clusters 72, 73
semantic naming-conventions 110
semantic reference relation 22
semantic referents 39–40, 53, 68, 79–80, 93
    fictional names 131–7
semantic value of a name relative to use 122
semantic values 53, 122, 221
semantics 168
    use-sensitive 120, 171
sentences
    absolute truth- and falsity- conditions 7–8
    analytic truths 125–6
    assertions 141–3
    assertoric 129, 150–4, 156
    atomic 123–4, 135, 147–8, 199–200, 209–10
    atomic existential 210
    atomic identity 210
    connective sentences with truth-functional connectives 210
    explicit content 142, 146, 147
    generalized truth- and falsity- conditions 7
    identity 53–4, 210 *see also* Frege's puzzle
    implicit content 142, 143, 145, 146, 147, 150
    informative. *See* Frege's puzzle
    logical truths 126
    modal 210–11
    necessary truths 125–6
    negative existential 52–3
    negative singular existential 13–14, 151–2
    object dependent truth- and falsity- conditions 6
    past tense 116

positive existential 151
singular existential 59
singular negative existential 13–14, 151–2
truth conditions 6–7
sentential modifiers 144–5
shared names 21–2, 69, 101–3
simple non-logical constants 96
single-domain free logic 12–13, 134–5
single name, multiple uses 117–19
singular existential sentences 59
singular negative existential sentences 13–14, 151–2
singular terms 209
Sloat, C. 25
Soames, S. 6
social artefacts 131–2, 137
social deixis 169
sophisticated irrealism 135–6, 137, 154
speaker's reference 76
specific names 69–71, 77, 101
specificity resemblance examples 162
stable transfer relation 162
Stanley, J. 231 n. 21
stipulation 154–5
story-semantics 147–8, 151, 155, 156
story-telling 40, 129, 138–41, 154, 155 *see also* fictional stories
Strawsonian picture of reference determination 78–80, 87–8
stressed demonstrative uses 115
stressed uses 113–16, 194
Strong Millianism 6, 7, 8, 9, 131
    Frege's puzzle 16
substitution problem 207
superlative readings 29
synchronic individuation of proper names 72, 73
syntactic indices 119
syntactic occurrences 118
synthetic views 13, 129, 140–1, 154
systemic ambiguity 163
systemic defects 132

Tarski, A. 35
temporary mental representations 99, 222
third-person personal pronouns 103–7, 169, 172
    constraining conditions 168

trans-semantic meanings 168–9, 172
transfer relation 161–2
transmission errors 91, 92
true readings 225
truth- and falsity-conditions 210–12
truth-conditional meaning transfer 159, 168, 170, 171
truth-conditional meanings 96, 103, 127, 159
truth-conditional semantics 126–8
truth-conditions 59–60 check before
truth values 125, 198, 201–3, 206, 209–10
typicality resemblance examples 162–3

unbound individual variables 34–6, 97, 181
unbound uses 107
uniformity 33–4
universalist views 131
unrestricted names 22, 116–17, 238 n. 76
unstressed uses 116
unwitting baptisms 81
use-conditional meanings 127–8, 169, 172
use-sensitive approaches 38, 40
use-sensitive expressions 120, 171–2
  coarse-grained individuation 121

fine-grained individuation 121
formal semantics 121–6
two-dimensional formal semantics 126–8
use-sensitive type-semantics 120, 171

validity 214
variable domain conception 44–5
variable domain framework 44–6, 57, 61, 208, 224
variable indexical views 106–8
variabilist views 34–6, 95, 97, 183–4
Vulcan example 133

Weak Millianism 6, 7
  truth-conditional variety 7
weak rigidity 47, 50–1
weakly necessarily true 54
wide scope readings 49
wide-scope strategy 20
Wittgensteinian methodology 37–8
Wittgensteinian philosophy 37–8
world-bound quantifiers 211–12
world-unbound quantifiers 211–12

Zeus example 133

Printed in the USA
CPSIA information can be obtained
at www.ICGtesting.com
LVHW011645091223
766046LV00004B/89